THE CHOSEN ONES

The Team That Beat LeBron

TONY MEALE

Copyright © 2012 by Tony Meale

All rights reserved. No part of this publication may be reproduced, stored in a retrieval system, or transmitted, in any form or by any means—electronic, mechanical, photocopying, recording, or otherwise—without the prior written permission of the publisher except in the case of brief quotations in critical articles or reviews.

Certain materials were reprinted with permission of the *Akron Beacon Journal* and Ohio.com and the *Cincinnati Enquirer* and cincinnati.com. Grateful acknowledgment is made to these entities, as well as the Ohio News Network for permission to print game commentary.

Cover design by Dan Phillips

Book design by Susan H. Hartman

Printed in the United States of America.
Published by Press Box Publishing LLC in Cincinnati, Ohio.

FIRST EDITION

Library of Congress Control Number: 2012905217

ISBN 978-0-9851444-0-1

*To my mother, Mary Ann, the strongest person I know.
And to my sister, Gina, for always looking out for me.*

CONTENTS

Preface vii

PROLOGUE • **THE GOOD-BYE** 1

ONE • **THE EARLY YEARS** 45

TWO • **THE GOLDEN BOY** 65

THREE • **THE SPECTACLE** 83

FOUR • **THE SWAGGER** 117

FIVE • **THE CJ GAME** 131

SIX • **THE TRANSFER** 149

SEVEN • **THE SCRAPPERS** 165

EIGHT • **THE COVER** 193

NINE • **THE DOG DAYS** 203

TEN • **THE TRAGEDY** 217

ELEVEN • **THE MOMENT** 235

TWELVE • **THE GUARANTEE** 251

THIRTEEN • **THE REMATCH** 263

FOURTEEN • **THE AFTERMATH** 313

EPILOGUE • **THE HERO'S WELCOME** 335

Acknowledgements 371

PREFACE

Me and LeBron James got a lot in common. We're both from Ohio, we both love basketball and we both graduated high school in 2003 from schools that begin with the word *St.* Those aren't the only similarities, mind you, but those are some that most readily come to mind.

The truth is, I've always been fascinated by LeBron James. Like a lot of Ohio high school boys in the early 2000s, I knew who LeBron was and began following his career when he was still merely a statewide wonder—as opposed to the global icon he has become. He wasn't the only can't-miss prospect I came across in high school (as a Cincinnati native, I began following O.J. Mayo when he was in junior high), but something about LeBron was different. Maybe it was the name itself. *LeBron.* There was something majestic about it, something magical. There still is. But even at the turn of the century, I knew he was special. I knew he was once-in-a-generation.

Technically speaking, LeBron, not even six months my senior, is my peer. But it never felt that way. Cliché as it sounds, LeBron always seemed larger than life to me—and not just because he's a foot taller. When LeBron was a junior in high school, he was well on his way to becoming a national obsession; when I was a junior in high school, I was well on my way to the prom. While I daydreamed of writing for *Sports Illustrated*, LeBron was on the cover. He could dunk seemingly from the free-throw line, whereas I could barely touch net. Things that seemed impossible for me seemed effortless for LeBron.

Maybe that's where the fascination came from.

High school sports are a big deal in Ohio, especially Cincinnati. In Cincinnati, they are a religion. They are something by which people identify themselves—and each other. Where you went to high school is as much a part of you as who you marry and what you do for a living.

Good or bad, for better or for worse, that's the deal. No one questions it. Not locals, anyway.

Thus, most of my Friday nights in high school were spent in a stadium or a gym. Every basketball season, my school played a league rival named Roger Bacon. It didn't matter that my school was Division I and Roger Bacon was Division II; the Spartans always played us tough and, perhaps surprising to some (even me, at first), won with unfailing regularity. Some Division II teams, when facing a team from Division I, get scared; they get flustered. Not Roger Bacon. With Roger Bacon, there was never intimidation; there was never backing down. Win or lose, regardless of talent, the Spartans always played hard. They always played scrappy. They never quit.

By the time I was a junior in 2001–02, I had come to expect this from Bacon. I wasn't surprised when the Spartans beat us that year, nor was I surprised when they kept advancing in the postseason tournament. But all along I knew what awaited them: LeBron James and Akron St. Vincent–St. Mary. And that's exactly what happened. I read a game preview the day of the state final, fully expecting a slaughter. Rooting for Bacon to win never even crossed my mind; I was simply hoping for a close game.

And then I went on with my Saturday.

The next day—March 24, 2002—I opened the Sunday edition of the *Cincinnati Enquirer* (for this was a time when people still learned of news via newspaper) and discovered that Bacon, somehow, had won. I read the coverage, stunned, scores of thoughts meandering my mind.

Colossal misprint? Joke? Hoax?

But the 16-year-old in me realized those explanations were as unlikely as Bacon's victory, and soon I kept thinking the same four words over and over again.

They actually did it.

Once the shock subsided, two thoughts crossed my mind: one, what Bacon had done was special, and two, it would be years before people—even those living in Cincinnati and throughout Ohio—understood just how special the accomplishment truly was. As it turned out, Roger Bacon was the first, last and only Ohio team to beat LeBron James between the lines during his four-year prep career; the fact that it occurred in the state final only made it that much more spectacular, if not improbable. In some circles, that game became known as "the Ohio version of *Hoosiers*," which isn't a bad analogy, but as I discovered, isn't altogether perfect.

Ever since that state final, LeBron seemed more human to me. The fascination was still there, of course, but I became just as fascinated—if not more so—by the team that beat him. LeBron had always seemed otherworldly, untouchable—the exact opposite of Bacon. The Spartans weren't once-in-a-generation players; they were guys from Cincinnati, guys my age, guys who attended a school not far from mine.

They were just like me.

As the years passed, I tucked away the brilliance of Bacon's win. I got a degree, a master's, and set off to make my mark in sports journalism. When it turned out the New York Yankees didn't need a fresh-out-of-J-school beat writer, I ended up back, where else, in Cincinnati, covering, what else, high school sports. It was kind of fitting. High school sports had always been a part of me. After a few months, though, it became painfully obvious that while growing up, my view of prep sports had always been myopic; if the story wasn't about my school, I was in many ways indifferent to it. But now I was covering schools that I had once rooted against or, quite frankly, had never even heard of. I told stories of prep athletes known only in this city who were of interest only to the communities in which they lived. There was no LeBron James among them. But in that time, I realized that every athlete has a story, that every school has pride, that high school sports truly are the heartbeat of this town.

And yet, something kept pulling me back to Bacon. Something kept tugging at me. The same questions I had always asked in passing now demanded answers. *How did Bacon do what it did? What did the accomplishment mean then? What does it mean now?* My curiosity became a thirst I couldn't quench, an itch I couldn't scratch—until finally I gave in. I decided that the story of that team, dormant for a decade, needed to be told.

So I set about telling it.

I sent emails. I made phone calls. One interview became 10. Ten became 50. Hundreds of hours of interviews later, after talking to almost every member of that team and coaching staff, among others, I had it—I had the tale of the only high school basketball team in Ohio history to beat LeBron James.

What follows, as you may have gathered, is not an eye-witness account. I was not among the 18,375 people in attendance at that state final. I was not privy to the practices about which you will read. I knew none of Bacon's players personally. Aside from newspaper stories and box scores, I relied almost exclusively on the memories—dating back five, 10, even 25 years in some cases—of people on, or close to, the 2001–02 Roger Bacon basketball team. In addition to a handful of group interviews, I spoke with almost everyone one-on-one at least once. I listened as former players and coaches told their story and the story of that team and that season. There were times when the same anecdotes were recalled by different people in different settings. Memories, by and large, aligned. Peripheral details weren't always identical, but the basic story remained. Almost every interview request, large or small, was accommodated—the one notable exception being LeBron James, whose representatives respectfully declined on his behalf.

So, no, this is not an eye-witness account. But I wish it had been. I wish I could have been at those practices. I wish I could have been in those locker rooms for those postgame speeches. I wish, maybe most of all, that I could have met Bill Brewer, that I could have known him.

Sure, I learned things about LeBron that I didn't know. I gained insight into who he was in high school and how that has affected who he is in the NBA. But I learned, above all else, that there's a little Roger Bacon in all of us, that the players and coaches on that team were not special in any way, and yet, they were.

Yes, this book is about Roger Bacon. Yes, it is about basketball. But it is first and foremost about the human spirit. It is about any team, any person, any underdog who dares to dream and who, in the face of setback and sorrow and immeasurable odds, chooses to so valiantly and so doggedly chase greatness.

WE'RE ALL UNDERDOGS.

PROLOGUE

THE
GOOD-BYE

If life could ever make sense again, if it could ever offer some semblance of reprieve, if it could ever absolve her of sins she didn't commit, Peggy Brewer would need the question she asks so often in vain answered.

It's a question that goes beyond the *what-ifs*.

What if I had gotten the Tums earlier? What if I had made him go to the hospital that night? Dammit, Bill, what if once, just once in your stubborn existence, you didn't have to be the tough guy?

These are questions Peggy still asks. These are thoughts she still thinks. She knows the answers will never come, but she asks for them anyway. She has to. It's the wife in her; it's the mother in her; hell, it's the widow in her.

But the question she truly needs answered goes beyond all that. It's a question that digs a little deeper and grabs hold of her soul a little tighter. It's a question she asks at the break of day and the twilight of dusk. It's a question she asks when leaves spring daintily to life and dip crisply to their deaths. It's a question she asks when lightning knifes the night to offer a momentary glimpse of what could be but isn't.

Why?

Why did this happen? Why did it happen when it did? Why was Bill taken from me?

Peggy can handle the *what-ifs*. She can reason through scenarios and rationalize what would have happened at every turn. But the *whys*? She can't do anything about those. No one can. Maybe it was Bill's destiny to die that night. Maybe his death could have been prevented. Peggy can't know for certain, and she never will.

When a coach dies, especially at the high school level, students, fans, and players almost always remember the coach as coach before they remember the coach as teacher. They don't remember the math class he taught. They don't remember English or study hall—not initially, at least. No, a fan's first memory is almost always of the coach, images etched in the mind from wins and losses. It's him pacing the sidelines in a packed gym on a Friday night. It's him working the refs almost as hard as he works his players. It's his unbridled joy after beating a rival. It's his unmistakable sorrow at the comeback that came up short.

It's all of that. It's none of that. It's everything.

The point is, most people remember a coach as coach. They don't think of the husband. Bill Brewer was one of those. They don't think of the father. Bill Brewer was one of those, too. They don't think of the brother, the son, the friend. Bill Brewer was all of that. And so, on the day he died—November 2, 2007—it was natural that some of the thousands of people whose emotions swelled and sank in all those fourth quarters were left wondering the same thing:

Who was Bill Brewer?

Bill was shy. When Peggy met him during her freshman year at the University of Dayton in 1983, her first impression of him was not altogether positive. Bill was quiet, unusually quiet; he didn't say much of anything to anyone. He was also a star pitcher on UD's baseball team. Generally, if a guy is quiet and unathletic, he's dismissed as an introvert; if a guy is quiet and athletic, he's dismissed as arrogant. Peggy thought Bill was arrogant. Whenever he missed class for a practice or a game, he'd approach Peggy's best friend, Laura, and ask to borrow her notes. Laura always obliged, but the conversation usually ended there. Bill was all business. He had neither the time nor desire for small talk.

"A lot of us thought, 'The big baseball player is too good to talk to us regular folk,'" Peggy said. "As it turned out, he was a very shy person. Unless you got to know him, he never said much."

So Peggy got to know him. She got to know him well. And by junior year, she and Bill were dating.

Who was Bill Brewer?

Bill had imagination, but there was no make-believe. Case in point: Halloween night, 1985. Bill and Peggy's first date—a "UD date," they called it. They went to Flanagan's Pub with their friends for a costume party. One of Peggy's friends dressed as Ronald Reagan, so she went as a member of the Secret Service. As for Bill? Bill went as a college student hanging out at Flanagan's.

"He wasn't big into dressing up," Peggy said.

After that night, Bill decided to take Peggy on a real date. One-on-one. No friends. Just him and her. He could've played it classic—flowers and candy, dinner and a movie. Nope. He asked her to a Run DMC concert. Peggy wasn't fond of Run DMC.

She said yes anyway.

Who was Bill Brewer?

Bill, for all of his Run DMC shenanigans, still knew how to play it cool. After graduating from UD in the spring of 1987, Peggy moved home to Cincinnati, while Bill got a job as a physical education teacher at All Saints, where Peggy attended grade school. That October, they returned to Dayton for the first time for homecoming and met up with their friends at Flanagan's. Bill and Peggy worked there in the summer of '86—the summer before their senior year. Bill was a bartender. Peggy was a waitress. They took classes during the day, worked together at night and had an absolute blast together. Lots of fond memories from that summer of '86. Lots of fond memories from Flanagan's in general.

Which is why Peggy was perplexed that night when Bill asked her to go for a walk. They hadn't seen their friends in months, and she didn't want to leave their company, even for a few minutes. But eventually, Bill got his way. He walked Peggy to the gazebo next to the campus chapel and asked her to marry him. Peggy thought Bill was joking, but then he got down on one knee and pulled out a ring. Peggy was shocked. She and Bill had talked about getting married, but they were still so young—early 20s, just out of college. And, like a lot of just-out-of-college couples in their early 20s, they were broke. They had agreed to save money and wait at least a year or so before getting engaged, and if all went well, maybe they'd marry in the summer of '89. Bill couldn't wait that long. They married in July 1988.

Once hitched, Bill took Peggy to see Jimmy Buffet every year. Peggy loves Jimmy Buffet; Bill wasn't a fan. But he took her anyway. One year, Bill postponed a family vacation to take her. Another year he drove to Indianapolis to make it happen. Maybe it was all self-imposed penance for Run DMC. Or maybe Bill just loved his wife and wanted to make her happy. But Peggy remembers all of it, especially their first date on that Halloween night in 1985. Because 22 Halloweens later, almost to the day, the man she loved would be dead.

> The Brewer family,
> Our family's best wishes to you as you go through this difficult time. Bill was a great man, a great father and a great basketball coach. Having known Bill since our days at the University of Dayton and through our coaching endeavors, Bill will be truly missed within the basketball fraternity. Our thoughts and prayers are with your family.
> Damon Goodwin
> Capital University

Who was Bill Brewer?

Bill always put his daughters first. After a game, win or lose, he and his staff would almost always go out, even if it was only for a quick beer. But if Katie, Abby and Maddy weren't asleep yet, Bill would stop home, tuck them in and say good night. If they were already asleep, he wouldn't wake them, but if they were still up, he'd stop, no questions asked. Sometimes a daddy needs to kiss his girls.

"That's the thing," said Tom Thompson, who was an assistant coach at Roger Bacon for more than a decade. "I can say I learned this basketball thing from him or that basketball thing from him, but the most important thing I learned was that family came first. Wow, did he love his girls."

Who was Bill Brewer?

Bill only recognized two seasons. He had no use for spring, summer, winter and fall. To him, there was basketball season, and there was grilling season, and there were two models to live life by—work hard, play hard. When you're working, go all out. When you're playing, well, go all out at that, too.

Who was Bill Brewer?

Bill was competitive. Cards, bowling, golf. Everything had a side bet. Even hanging up the phone was a competition. Bill would say what he needed to say, and then the game began. Whoever said, "Gotta go, bye" the fastest, won. Bill didn't lose many of those.

One of Bill's good friends was an avid tennis player, and one day they decided to play each other. Bill wasn't nearly as good, but he was a lefty, and his friend wasn't used to seeing the ball come off the racquet from that angle with that spin. They played one game, which Bill won, and Bill refused to play again. He knew eventually his buddy would adjust and win, so he didn't give him the chance.

Bill once pulled Monty St. Clair, a 6-8 center, out of class in the fall of 2002. *Oh no*, Monty thought. *What did I do?* Nothing. Bill just had one question for his senior big man: "What side of the block do you want to post up on this year? Right or left?" In theory, Bill could have waited a few hours and asked Monty that question at practice. In theory.

"That's how competitive he was," Monty said. "He couldn't go the whole day without knowing that answer."

Who was Bill Brewer?

Bill was superstitious. He could never have dinner before a game. Even though school got out around 3 p.m., even though the game usually didn't start until 7 or 8, even though he'd be at the gym until 10 or later, he wouldn't eat until afterward. A light snack beforehand, maybe. But an all-out meal? Wouldn't do it. A pregame nap, however, was fair game. Bill would drive home, sleep for 45 minutes and head to the gym—almost always in a car driven by one of his assistants—Tom Thompson, Mike Cregan and Dave Bidwell.

"Nine times out of 10, we'd get to his house and he'd just be waking up," Cregan said. "Hair straight up in the air."

Who was Bill Brewer?

Bill never showed his optimism. He'd feel it, but he'd never show it, maybe because he didn't want to look foolish if things didn't turn out the way he envisioned. Every preseason, Peggy would ask Bill for his team forecast, and every preseason, without fail, she heard one of two things: "We're not going to be very good," or, "We'll be all right."

"If you heard, 'We'll be all right,'" Peggy said, "then it should be a pretty good season."

But regardless of his team's talent, the one constant every season was Bill's enthusiasm. He just wanted to get out there and coach—and boy oh boy, he loved working with kids.

Who was Bill Brewer?

Bill had a soft spot in his heart for kids who struggled—and not just players, either. If a student was struggling in class, Bill knew how to connect with him. With a lot of coaches, that gets lost. A lot of coaches are coaches first, teachers second. Not Bill. He was teacher first, coach second; and he wouldn't take excuses—not on the court and certainly not in the classroom. If it were up to him, nobody could fail a class. You couldn't just say, "I don't get it" and give up. You'd have to keep trying until you got it.

Bill knew something that all great coaches and teachers know: the harder you push kids, the more you can get out of them. So that's what he did. He cared about his players not just as athletes, but as people. Bill made a report card that he distributed to teachers, and he'd ask them to fill it out for all his players and return it each week. He wanted to know their grades. He wanted to know how their attitude was. How did he treat his classmates? His family? His girlfriend? For Bill, it wasn't just about basketball.

Who was Bill Brewer?

Bill was the ultimate host. Peggy's parents owned a lake house in Cumberland, Kentucky, and every summer she and Bill would go there for a week with all the assistant coaches and their wives. Bill dedicated as much time and effort into planning those trips as he did to getting his team ready for the basketball season. He'd get up early to make everyone breakfast. He'd make sure everyone was having a good time. Even when he was relaxing, he was working.

Who was Bill Brewer?

Bill was all about the Man Cave. Just like installing the island in his kitchen, Bill had no clue what he was doing when it came to demolition and construction. But he knew what he wanted. He had a vision—not to mention some generous, construction-savvy friends.

"It'd be Saturday afternoon," Tom Thompson said, "and you'd get a call—'Hey, Tommy boy, what are you doing this afternoon?'"

That's how Bill phrased it. He'd never tell you what he wanted right away. If he did, there was a chance you'd make up an excuse as to why you couldn't do something. But if he asked what you were doing, and you said you were available, you couldn't back out.

"I'd be thinking I was getting an invite somewhere," Dave Bidwell explained. "Next thing I know, I'm digging a hole in his backyard."

Bidwell, however, didn't mind. Although married now, he was single for much of the time he worked for Bill at Bacon. It wasn't uncommon for him to spend Christmas Eve with the Brewers and put toys together for the girls.

"Hey, Brew," Bidwell would say, "can you hand me the Phillips screwdriver?"

"Sure," Bill would say, pausing. "Which one's that?"

"Uh, it's the one with four prongs . . ."

If ever a wife should be canonized for entrusting her husband with home projects, Peggy Brewer might be it.

Construction on the Man Cave began in May 2007. Thompson, Cregan, Bidwell and others worked hard on that. Bill never gave them money for their time; instead, he gave them "Brewer currency," also known as Coors Light, his favorite beer.

"Always beer," Cregan said. "Food was an aside."

Three months later, when August arrived and classes resumed, the Man Cave was about 90 percent finished. Bill and Peggy figured it wouldn't be completed until after the upcoming basketball season, but the guys came over whenever they could to help finish. The holy grail of the Man Cave was a big-screen TV that Bill bought years earlier—"for Peggy."

"Bill bought big screens before big screens were big screens," Cregan said. "He didn't go to Best Buy. He bought it from a guy in a truck. No box."

The television hung in the center of the Man Cave, perched on a wall and facing a couch that curled around it. Bill was ecstatic. He couldn't wait for March Madness. To watch the NCAA Tournament with his friends? On a big screen? In his home? With Coors Light? Brother, that's the life.

But sadly, for Bill, it wasn't. He never made it.

> Billy and I were teammates and friends at the University of Dayton. I just got news of his passing from a former teammate. My heart goes out to Peggy and her family. Billy and I, along with four other teammates, drove from Dayton to Daytona, Fla., after our season ended in 1987, and we had a blast. I will cherish those memories, Billy. Please rest in peace.
>
> Mike Devlin

Who was Bill Brewer?

Bill cherished his timeouts. Once, one of Bacon's players, 2001 graduate Dan Huerkamp, was on the court and about to get physically ill during a game.

"Hey," Bill says to a ref, "he's gonna throw up all over the floor."

"Well," the ref says, "if you want to sub for him, you have to call timeout."

Call timeout? Screw that. Bill wanted to get Dan out of the game, sure, but he sure as hell wasn't going to waste a timeout to do it. So Dan puked all over the court. The refs had to stop the game and clean up the mess. And Bill, pleased as a peacock, saved his timeout.

Who was Bill Brewer?

Bill had a way with officials. He rode those guys from the opening tip to the final buzzer, and he knew all their names. It was never, "Excuse me, Mr. Official?" It was, "Come on, Carl! Jesus! Don't do this to me now!" Tom Thompson vividly recalls Bill getting into it with one official in particular, an official Bill respected a great deal and with whom he had played baseball.

"Johnny, you gotta call that!" Bill barked, protesting what he thought should have been a foul.

"I didn't see it, Bill!"

"Then you're out of position!"

"It wasn't a foul, Bill!"

Coach and ref go back and forth, and finally Bill just says, "Fuck you, Johnny." And Johnny, stunned, responds, "Fuck you, Bill."

"If another coach would have found out Johnny and Bill were friends," Thompson said, "they never would've guessed it by the way they acted with each other."

Who was Bill Brewer?

Bill was hard on his players. Many feared him; some hated him. If Bill didn't like something you were doing—whether in practice or a game—he'd call you out. He'd call you names. If he thought you were soft, he'd tell you. He was a coach who players sometimes hated to play for, a coach who could make you hate the sport you loved while you were playing it.

"For me, that's a sign of a great coach," said Tim McCoy, a 2002 Roger Bacon graduate. "You shouldn't be happy all the time when you're playing a sport. It's gonna be work if you wanna be good at it. But it probably took me a year after graduating to realize, 'Wow, he was special.'"

Who was Bill Brewer?

Bill was always upfront with everything. Every preseason, he would meet with each player individually and discuss expectations for the season. Would you start? Would you come off the bench? How many minutes would you get? Everything was always clear. If Bill didn't see you getting much playing time, he'd tell you, and if you were unhappy about it, you couldn't have mommy or daddy call and ask what the deal was. Bill gave parents his cell number at the beginning of the season. If a parent had a question, he or she could call. Any topic, any time. But if a parent called to talk playing time, the conversation was over. As a player, you had to be a man, approach Bill face-to-face and state your case as to why you should start or get more minutes. If you merely approached Bill and complained and asked why you weren't getting more time, he would tell you. *Because you can't shoot. Because you can't play defense. Because you're not tough enough.* Bill always let you know exactly what you were doing wrong. It was on you to fix it.

"It was none of this, 'Well, we're gonna try and get you in here and there,' like most coaches do," Tim McCoy said. "He was straightforward about everything. I was afraid of him, but I loved that about him."

Who was Bill Brewer?

Bill was always honest—sometimes brutally so. One of the players Bill coached during his first year at Roger Bacon in 1993–94 was Mitch Perdrix. Mitch, who graduated in 1995, was the best player on Bacon's team and had serious aspirations to play college basketball. But when he was a senior during the 1994–95 season, he sat in Bill's office and listened as his coach advised him that playing in college, for him, wasn't a good idea.

"You're not going to play college basketball the way you want to play college basketball," Bill said. "You're not going to get a scholarship. Even if you walk on somewhere, you're not going to play. You're going to be a glorified student manager in a uniform."

If anyone else had told Mitch Perdrix that during his senior year of high school, he would have been crushed. If his own father had told him that, he would have been devastated. But when Bill said it, somehow it wasn't as bad. He knew Bill said those things not because he didn't care, but rather, because he did. Bill knew how hard Mitch would work at it, how much he would put into it, but he knew Mitch wouldn't get out of it what he wanted. He didn't want him to be let down.

"That's one of the great things about him," Mitch said. "Everything he did came from a good place."

> As a former athlete at Roger Bacon, I could tell that Bill Brewer worked just as hard in the classroom as he did on the basketball court. Bill taught me geometry my sophomore year at Bacon. He kept class entertaining and interesting. No doubt Coach Brewer's claim to fame is defeating LeBron James in the 2002 state final, but I truly believe that his real claim to fame is how he could teach students about life, things that were not in textbooks. Coach Brewer will be sincerely missed.
> Thomas Raabe

Who was Bill Brewer?

Bill always had a plan, but he wasn't afraid to stray from it. He made a schedule for every practice. Every detail down to the minute was explained, and everything—every drill, every run—was timed. Like a teacher reviewing his lesson plan before class, Bill would go over his schedule time and time again before practice, but depending on any number of factors, he was always willing to scratch it and freelance.

Bill had just one requirement for practice: everything had to involve learning. One day, he was running late going from a Roger Bacon practice to a practice at All Saints, where he coached Katie and Abby in grade school. He hustled into the gym and couldn't believe what he saw. His assistant, Elliot Adams, had the girls playing knockout.

Knockout?

Bill walked straight up to Elliot.

"If I ever see you playing knockout at one of my practices again," he said, "you're not coaching with me anymore."

Bill wasn't completely serious, but he wasn't completely kidding, either.

"He wanted you to have fun," Peggy said. "But he wanted you to learn something."

Who was Bill Brewer?

Bill entered realms most coaches didn't even know existed. Marcus Smith, who graduated from Roger Bacon in 2003, remembers the postgame speech—if you can call it that—after losing to Alter at home during his senior year. All the players were sitting on a U-shaped bench when Bill stormed in.

"I don't remember if he kicked the water cooler over on his way in or his way out," Marcus said. "But he kicked it over."

Bill proceeded to tell his players—some of whom had won a state title one season earlier—that they were lousy, that they were pathetic, that they didn't deserve to wear the jerseys they had on their backs. He pointed at each of them, his finger two inches from their faces.

"I don't remember the exact words," Marcus said. "It was so emotion-driven, the words are useless at that point."

But the message was clear. Each and every one of them was useless. They were nothing. They didn't deserve to be on the planet. They should dig a hole, bury themselves and disappear forever. And then came the ultimatum.

You've got 12 seconds to get out of this locker room, or you're kicked off the team.

Players hopped up as if there were springs on the bench. They frantically worked their locker combinations. Clothes were grabbed. Shoes were snagged. Players bolted out the back door of the locker room, huffing and puffing like it's the fourth quarter. They had sweatpants on one leg, a hat over one ear. The snow was serenely silent in the December night.

"I'll never forget that moment," Marcus said. "That's probably the most scared I've ever been."

The players finished dressing, exhales streaming into the air. They looked around, waiting for Coach Brewer to come outside and tell them something. Anything. But it never happened. Bill was so disgusted that night, he huffed right out of the locker room, fumed through the gym, collapsed into his car and drove straight home. He didn't stop and talk to any coaches. He didn't go over plans for the next day. He didn't mingle with fans or parents. He just walked out.

"That guy, I mean, that guy, I can't even find the words," Marcus said. "Coach Brewer, man, he was unbelievable."

> Peggy,
> I have enclosed a check from the Greater Cincinnati Basketball Officials Association. We raised this for the girls' education fund. I have also enclosed the game fee from my first boys game this year.
> The last game I did for Bill was at Western Brown in the 2006–07 season. The best line I ever used on Bill was the last game I did for Roger Bacon. It was a Friday home game and at halftime he asked: "How do you think your crew did in the first half?" My answer was simple: "Bill, we didn't miss a free throw and we played better defense than your boys." He just gave me that look.
> May God bless you and your family during this time of grief.
> Jeff Ayers

Who was Bill Brewer?

Bill always listened to what his coaches had to say. He didn't want yes-men for assistants. He wanted assistants who would tell him not what he wanted to hear, but what he needed to hear. Tom Thompson remembers one game during the 1997–98 season in particular. Roger Bacon was playing Mariner High School out of Cape Coral, Florida. Mariner had a stud scorer in Teddy Dupay, who was named the state's Mr. Basketball that year and led the University of Florida to the national title game in 2000, where the Gators fell to Mateen Cleaves and Michigan State.

Thompson scouted Dupay extensively and told Bill, "Bill, this kid can flat out shoot. He will score. He crosses halfcourt and the shot's up." So Bill, somewhat skeptical, went over the scouting report with the team and said, "Thompson says this guy can score. Thompson says he'll cross halfcourt and shoot." Almost every sentence began with the disclaimer "Thompson says."

Well, Thompson was right. Dupay drilled three treys to start the game. Bacon was down 9–0 in a hurry. Bill, befuddled, called timeout and looked at Tom.

What the fuck was that?

Bill gathered his players. "All right, Thompson's right," he said. "We're gonna change our defense."

After the game, which Bacon came back to win 93–89—despite 47 points from Dupay—Bill said to Tom, "I think that went pretty well."

Thompson was in disbelief.

"He scored 47, Brew!"

"Yeah," Bill deadpanned. "But it was a quiet 47."

Who was Bill Brewer?

Bill always put the team above individual players. In his first year coaching at Princeton High School during the 2005–06 season, Bill had a player who—as he used to say—wasn't buying what he was selling. Even though Princeton had a good record, it bothered Bill that this kid had the attitude he had. The kid would mouth off. He wouldn't play team-first ball. He'd complain if he thought he wasn't getting enough shots. He was, in Bill's estimation, preventing the team from realizing its potential.

After a road loss late in the regular season, Princeton's players and coaches headed to the locker room, and this same player was jawing yet again. Bill, already angry at the loss, reached his breaking point. He kicked the player off the team, right then and there. Didn't even let him ride back to school on the team bus. It was, "Get your stuff, get out of the locker room, find your mom and make sure you have a ride home."

In short, get out of my sight.

And this wasn't just a role player arguing for more minutes; this was a starter, and this was right before the state tournament. Bill didn't care.

"If you put yourself before the team," Thompson said, "you were done."

Even if you didn't put yourself before the team, even if you were a good teammate who made an honest mistake—no matter how minor—Bill wouldn't let it go unpunished. At the beginning of each season, Bill gave his players guidelines to follow. One of them was, "Be early, not just on time, to all team functions." Monty St. Clair loved that rule.

"I'm never late," he said. "Ever."

On January 22, 2002, Roger Bacon, the top-ranked Division II team in Cincinnati, hosted La Salle, the third-ranked Division I team and a member of the vaunted Greater Catholic League South division. After school that day—it was a Tuesday night game—Monty and Frank

Phillips went to Dave Johnson's house to kill time before tip-off. Monty was the starting center, Frank was the starting small forward and Dave was the starting point guard. They were playing pool and hanging out. Monty, who had lost, was watching Frank and Dave play when suddenly that nervousness, that fear of being late, crept into his body.

Monty told his two fellow starters they should all head to the game. "Oh, we've got plenty of time," Frank and Dave said, still focused on billiards. Minutes later, Monty grew tense, anxious. It was crippling. This time, he urged them to leave. Frank and Dave gave in, and they all piled into Dave's car. Monty felt better. But on the way to campus, they approached the train tracks on Vine Street—which cuts through the heart of St. Bernard, the community in which Roger Bacon is located—and spotted in the distance a locomotive as long as the Great Wall of China. Slowing, slowing, slowing. Stops. This wouldn't be a big deal if not for one thing. As a rule, all varsity players had to be in the gym with butts in the stands in time for tip-off of the JV game, which, on that night, started at 6.

It was past 5:30.

This wasn't the first time a Bacon player had been stuck behind a train. Sometimes the train would stop for mere seconds. Sometimes it was a couple of minutes. Sometimes, even longer. That night, the train just sat. After about 15 minutes of waiting, Dave decided to backtrack and take a different route to Bacon. Monty tried to remain calm, but he couldn't. His pulse quickened. He was sweating. He fidgeted. Dave sped to Bacon and arrived at 6:03 p.m. Three starters, three minutes late. Now, any other night, they would have walked into the gym through the front entrance, but on this night, hoping to avoid Bill, they snuck in through the bottom door.

It didn't matter.

"We walked in, and Brewer saw us," said Monty, ashamed. "He didn't say a word. He just looked at his watch, nodded his head and walked away. We thought, 'Oh, shit, we're gonna have to run tomorrow at practice.'"

Not quite. Frank, Dave and Monty joined the rest of the team and watched the first half of the JV game. After that, as was customary, they headed to the locker room to get ready for their game. In walked Bill.

"So, who wants to start tonight?" he asked jovially.

Monty, Frank, Dave and every other Spartan raised their hand.

"Okay," Bill said. "Who wants to start tonight and was on time?"

The tardy trio sat in stunned disbelief. This was three-fifths of the starting lineup. This was Bacon vs. La Salle. This was the game of the week—on a Tuesday, no less. The gym was packed. College coaches, including ones from the ACC, were there scouting.

Monty, Frank and Dave pleaded their case, but Bill didn't care. He sat all three of them. Bench players Tim McCoy, Jon Newton and Leonard Bush started in their stead.

"I remember looking at my dad during the national anthem; I was so mad," Monty said. "It's not that Brewer didn't believe us. He just had a no-excuses policy."

It wasn't just a slap on the wrist, either. Monty, Frank and Dave didn't enter the game at the first dead ball. Bill sat them the entire first quarter against the best team in the GCL-South. Bill's discipline didn't cost his team a win that night—Bacon hammered La Salle 61–37, further evidence that the 2001–02 team was special—but the benching stuck with the players, even the ones who weren't punished.

"If you weren't there on his ship ready to go at high noon, you were left on the dock," Jon Newton said. "He didn't care who you were, what you were, who your parents were—he didn't care. Honestly, Brewer didn't care. Looking back, that's probably one of the most respectful things I've ever seen."

> Mr. Brewer was my coach from sixth grade to eighth grade. I was the new kid in sixth grade, but right off the bat when I met him I respected him more than you can imagine. As a coach, he had his catch phrases that instantly come to mind when I think of him. "Just give the effort." "Seven lengths, GO!"
>
> His criticism, comments, and his viewpoint on everything was something that I always took into account. I worked as hard as I could to achieve what he wanted. Speaking to Coach was like speaking to someone who many people only dreamed of talking to. He was so knowledgeable. That and the rides in his car are what I remember most fondly and what I am going to miss the most. He'd pick us up, and

> then we'd jam to the music we all liked. He had a good taste in music.
> Mr. Brewer wasn't just my coach or my friend's dad. He was a mentor. That's what I am going to miss so much – seeing someone I cared for and respected so much in everyday life.
> Love,
> Kathryn Reynolds

Who was Bill Brewer?

Bill kept tabs on his players and responded accordingly. If he found out there was a party Friday night, he'd schedule Saturday's practice for 7 a.m. He didn't want to get up that early on a weekend, but he knew if he made his players get up that early, there was a chance they'd leave that party a whole lot earlier than they would have otherwise—or they might not go at all. It's not that Bill didn't trust his players; he just didn't want to take any chances. It's hard to get in trouble, he reasoned, when you're home by 10 on a Friday night—or if you never even left the house.

And Bill almost always found out about the parties. But even when he didn't, that didn't mean his players were safe. Every Monday, he'd barrage students with questions: *What happened this weekend? Did you see Josh out? Did you see Beckham? What about Frank and Monty?*

"Brewer found out stuff you could never imagine," Jon Newton said. "He knew who would talk."

It was the girls, mainly. Of course it was. High school girls always talk.

Who was Bill Brewer?

Bill made everybody feel important, especially student managers. To him, they weren't there to get water for the players. In fact, if you were a player, and you wanted water, go get it. The way Bill saw it, student managers were assistant coaches, and they deserved to be treated as such. One of the best student managers Bill ever had was Thomas "TJ" Coby, who served as varsity assistant from 1993 to 1996.

"He worked harder than any other kid I've seen to make the team better," Tom Thompson said.

So for the final home game of TJ's senior year, Bill, as a reward, arranged for him to not only dress in uniform and go through warmups, but also to get in the game against league rival Purcell Marian. TJ even got a shot up. It didn't go in, but he got in the scorebook. TJ's parents cried tears of happiness in the stands that night.

"People always say how competitive Bill was—and he was; he was the most competitive person I've ever met," Thompson said. "But when it came to treating people right, he treated people right."

Years later, when Bill became the coach at Princeton, TJ would go to games and make a point to let Bill know he was there—because what Bill had done for him a decade earlier was still important. It still resonated.

Who was Bill Brewer?

Bill considered himself the luckiest man alive. The way he saw it, he got to do the one thing that he absolutely loved—coaching—and he got to do it for a living; he was married to the best person in the world; and he had the three most beautiful girls in the world. He never knew what he did to deserve all that, but whatever it was, he was damn glad he did it.

Bill always lived in the moment, but that didn't stop him from preparing for the future. In 2005, three years after he became The Man Who Beat LeBron, Bill, only 40, was already thinking about retirement. That's why he left Bacon for Princeton. Yes, the challenge and limelight of coaching Division I was a bonus, but the main reason for leaving was the better retirement package a public school could offer. Bill figured he and Peggy could retire in their early 60s, buy a house at Norris Lake in Tennessee and spend half the year there, every year for the rest of their lives, grilling and drinking Coors Light. Going to Princeton wasn't about paycheck money. It was about the long-awaited time he and Peggy would one day have, time when they could live in ease and look back at the wonderful life they shared together. But that time never came.

And it never will.

> Bill was a great man, coach, husband and father. I was grateful to work with him from 1993 to 1996 as a student manager at Roger Bacon. He was not only a great coach but also a great teacher (I had him all four years for math and gym). I, as well as many others out there, will miss him a lot. My thoughts go out to Peggy and his girls.
>
> *Thomas (TJ) Coby*

Aside from Peggy and her girls, Dave Bidwell was the last person who saw Bill Brewer alive.

If anybody was going to claim this honor, Bidwell was as good an option as any. He had known Bill since college and went to grade school with Peggy at All Saints in Montgomery, located on the east side of Cincinnati. Like a lot of All Saints boys, Bidwell went to Moeller High School, which boasted one of the nation's premier prep football programs in the 1970s and '80s. He returned to his alma mater to coach freshman basketball in the late '80s, not long after a Moeller baseball player, Ken Griffey Jr., was drafted first overall by the Seattle Mariners. Bill joined Bidwell at Moeller and was on staff for both baseball and basketball. The Crusaders won two state baseball titles during Bill's tenure—one in 1989 and one in his last year, 1993.

Bill loved baseball. He was a baseball guy. Although never drafted, he graduated from Dayton as the winningest pitcher in school history and was second, by one, in complete games. He still ranks among the top five in both categories. After graduation, Bill attended several three-day tryouts with the Cincinnati Reds. He'd always make it to the third day, but he was never offered a contract. At 22, he was too old for the majors. That's what he was told, anyway. He loved coaching baseball, but he loved the intensity of coaching basketball more.

Bill became the head coach at Roger Bacon in 1993, and Bidwell left Moeller the following year to man the clock for him during home games. In the more than 20 years that Dave knew Bill, Bill called him by his first name all of about five times. Sometimes it was "Bidwell," but it was almost always and more affectionately, "Bids."

It is said that a friend in need is a pest. For Bill Brewer, a friend in need was a friend in need. So when Bids wanted to move his boat out of the Ohio River, he went to Bill, an avid boater himself, and asked for help. Bill obliged. They had been trying all week to find a night to meet up, but nothing worked well for either of them. Even that Thursday—November 1, 2007—wasn't particularly great (Bids had parent-teacher conferences, and Bill had practice at Princeton), but that was the best they could come up with. Bids got to the dock that night only to discover it was locked. He wouldn't be able to access his boat, much less move it. Bill arrived late.

"Sorry I'm late, Bids," Bill said. "I would've called, but I left my phone at home."

Bids didn't mind. He just appreciated Bill driving all the way down to the river, especially after having put in a full day at school and practice. The two friends decided they'd try to move the boat again that Sunday. Bids had a case of Coors Light that he intended to give Bill for his assistance that night, and even though they weren't able to move the boat as planned, he gave him 18 of the 24 beers.

"You'll get the other six on Sunday," Bids joked.

The two friends chatted by the dock for a bit, and just as they were about to leave, Bill gave Bids some advice—advice he remembers to this day.

"Keep your boat," Bill said. "You'll always enjoy time with your family and friends on your boat—like we've always done on mine, and like we've always done on yours."

It was a simple comment, really. Honest, sincere. At that moment, Bids didn't think anything of it. But looking back, it was almost out of character. Bids had known Bill for more than 20 years. Boating was a fixture of their friendship. Never before had Bill made a comment like that, a comment that focused so directly on Bids' future happiness and the role a boat had in it. Looking back, there was a certain finality to the advice, a certain foreshadowing.

Bill got into his car. Bids got into his. They drove almost the whole way home together until Bill exited Interstate 71 and got off at Montgomery Road in Kenwood. As Bill headed home, Bids looked over and waved.

"I still remember that spot," Bids said. "It was just a quick little bye, a see-you-later."

It was around 10 p.m. Bill Brewer would be dead in four hours.

> Dear Peggy,
> My deepest sympathies. I heard about Bill and it stopped me in my tracks. Bill was the first person to take me under his wing and teach me how to be a man. I'll never forget Bill's gutty performance when he relieved me in 1987 at the Wright State Tournament to win the championship game after he threw a complete game just a day before. But

what impressed me most was when they named the all-tournament team and left Bill off. He did not cry or complain. He just stepped up and thanked the team. It's little wonder he went on to be a great and accomplished coach and person.

Warm regards,
Thad Stauber

When Bill got home that night, it wasn't long before the chest pains started.

Bill's father developed heart problems at a young age, so once Bill hit 40, Peggy was adamant that he receive a full-blown physical every year just to be safe. Bill always checked out okay, but lately, he felt fatigued. That, of course, was nothing new for this time of year. Bill was teaching, finishing out the girls season at All Saints, running tryouts and getting ready for the boys season at Princeton. He was always on the go, jetting from this to that and that to this. He was putting in a lot of hours. He was tired. Peggy, though, had come to expect this and didn't think anything of it.

The previous night, on Halloween, Bill dismissed the Princeton boys from practice earlier than usual so he could go trick-or-treating with Peggy and his daughters. The girls loved that. Parents would meet up and take dozens of kids around the neighborhood. But even though everyone loved having Bill there, even though he had done this many times before, that night was different. That night, for Bill, was a struggle. He wasn't long into his rounds before he grew winded.

"Man," he told one of the neighborhood dads, "I didn't think I was this out of shape."

The next night, when Bill got home after meeting Bids at the dock, he went downstairs and talked for a bit with Katie, who was watching *Grey's Anatomy*.

When he went upstairs to go to bed, he told Peggy he wasn't feeling well.

"Do we need to go to the hospital?" Peggy asked.

Peggy was extra sensitive to health ailments that week, as Abby had to be rushed to intensive care four days earlier. That Sunday—October 28, 2007—Bill and Peggy had settled into their living room to watch the Cincinnati Bengals play the Pittsburgh Steelers when Abby suddenly came home from a neighbor's house saying she didn't feel well. At first, Peggy thought Abby might have snuck too much candy that Peggy had recently purchased for Halloween, and once Abby vomited, Peggy's suspicions seemed confirmed. Only they weren't. Within minutes, Abby couldn't remember her name, where she was, or even say her ABCs. Bill and Peggy got her into the car and drove to the hospital. On the way there, Abby lost consciousness. Doctors ran countless tests on Abby but couldn't determine exactly what was wrong. They sent the Brewers home without any definitive answers.

Peggy was scared. What was wrong with her daughter? How could she prevent it from happening again? What if it happened at night or if Abby were alone?

Months later, in May 2008, Abby had another attack, and it was determined that she suffers from a rare form of migraine that settles on the brain stem and can cause a person to stop breathing. Abby is now on preventive medicine and has not had any bad episodes since.

But in November 2007, Peggy, still without answers, was on high alert about everything. If not for Abby's original attack, the thought of taking Bill to the hospital when he said he didn't feel well probably wouldn't have even entered her mind—not that quickly, at least. Bill scoffed at the suggestion.

"No, no, I'll be fine," he said. "I'm just tired. I have a little heartburn."

Peggy went to find Bill some Tums, but they were out.

"You want me to run to the store and get some Tums?" she asked.

"No, no," Bill said. "I'll be fine."

"Are you sure?"

Bill, figuring he'd be good as new by morning, said he was sure and went to bed. But around midnight, he woke up with sharp pains in his chest and in desperate need of Tums.

"Are you sure it's just heartburn?" Peggy asked. "We can get to the hospital in two minutes flat if we need to."

"No, no," Bill said again. "I'm going to be fine."

Peggy called her sister, Karen, who lived in the neighborhood, and asked if she could borrow some Tums.

"Sure," Karen said. "Come on over."

Peggy walked to Karen's house, got the Tums and returned home. She was gone all of about two minutes. But when she walked back upstairs, she found her husband lying on their bed with eyes wide open.

He wasn't breathing.

> Dear Brewer family,
>
> I want to start off by saying I'm truly sorry about the loss of Coach Brewer. Coach was a true mentor to me; he taught me a lot about the game of basketball and about life in general. Coach and the Brewer family will always be in my prayers.
>
> Mrs. Brewer, I want to personally thank you. You and Coach helped me get into Roger Bacon without even actually getting to meet me personally. Going to Bacon was one of the best experiences of my life. So again, I thank you for that, and I also thank Coach for believing in me and pushing me so hard.
>
> Coach Brewer may not be here anymore to teach people his wisdom and befriend them, but he has taught many and he will still be remembered and loved by everyone.
>
> I would like to share a quote with you...
>
> With praying hands—"More things are wrought by prayer than this world dreams of."
>
> Truly,
> Josh C. Nolan

It wasn't the creaking of footsteps that stirred Abby Brewer from her bed that night, nor was it the gasping and crying of her mother. In fact, Abby Brewer didn't hear a thing. She just woke up.

Abby, who was a sixth-grader at Sycamore, a nearby public school, walked to her parents' room and saw her daddy lying there.

Peggy called 911. Her sister, Karen, had a night nurse, Tracie, who was at the house caring for a sick child. Tracie, a Roger Bacon grad, knew Bill and hurried to the Brewer's home and performed CPR until the ambulance arrived.

Abby froze. She stood there and watched, not knowing what to do. Katie woke up a few minutes later, staggered to the scene and started crying. Abby started crying, too. And soon the sounds of sirens were upon them.

"I hate ambulances," Abby said.

When Peggy discovered Bill was unconscious, she knew instantly that something was wrong. She knew this wouldn't end well. It didn't matter that a nurse had been administering CPR. It didn't matter that Bill had a heartbeat when the ambulance arrived. It didn't matter that people kept telling her it was going to be fine. She knew it wouldn't be. Something, something deep inside her, just didn't feel right.

Peggy went to the hospital alone with Bill. Karen stayed and watched the girls. Katie went back to her room, but she couldn't sleep. She sat and waited, staring into the November night. So did Abby. Maddy, still in her bed, slept through the whole ordeal—the heart attack, the ambulance, everything. Peggy didn't have the heart to wake her.

Bill didn't make it to dawn. He was pronounced dead at the hospital. The man who coached and worshipped at All Saints lost his life just as November 1 became November 2, just as All Saints Day became All Souls Day.

"We said our prayers that night," said Peggy, a devout Catholic. "Unfortunately, those ones didn't work."

> Dear Brewer Family,
>
> I am extremely sorry about your loss. My greatest sympathy goes to you and your family.
>
> I was so fortunate to have him in my life during my career at Bacon. I've learned so much from him. He was a huge contributor in the molding of the person I have become! Thank you so much for sharing such a wonderful man.
>
> Sincerely,
> Abby's favorite player in 2002 . . .
> Matt Reed #51

Mike Cregan, a marvel scorekeeper always armed with a pencil in each hand, was the first to get the call.

Cregan—known as "Creegs"—had know Bill upwards of 20 years. A native New Yorker, Creegs was born in Westchester County and moved to Springfield, Ohio, in 1986. His brother-in-law was the head wrestling coach at Moeller and always talked about how great Cincinnati was, so two years later, Creegs and his wife, Jeanne, made the move.

Creegs met Bill in the fall of 1988 at Moeller, where he served as scorekeeper until he and Bids left to join Bill at Bacon. They followed him to Princeton, too, even though Bill never officially offered them jobs. But then again, Bill didn't have to. It was just assumed they were going. They were all that close.

That's why the phone call around 2:30 a.m. on Friday, November 2, was so jarring. Creegs staggered out of bed and answered just as the call went to voicemail. The conversation with Peggy was recorded, and Creegs listened as she relayed the events of the last several hours.

"Well, how's he doing?" Creegs asked.

There was a pause.

"He's dead."

Dead?

"I remember that vividly," Creegs said. "She said, 'He's dead.' And I said, 'I can't believe that.'"

Creegs, dismayed, didn't know what to say, except, "I'm sorry. I'm so sorry." He went back upstairs to Jeanne, who was awakened by the commotion.

"Bill's dead," Creegs said.

"What?"

"Yeah, that was Peggy. Bill's dead."

Creegs sat there, powerless, still not entirely awake, but he knew what he had to do. He grabbed his phone and started making calls. He called Bids. He called Brian Neal, Bill's former assistant who succeeded him as head coach at Bacon. He called Joe Corcoran, Bacon's athletic director. He called them all. It was around 3 a.m. Creegs wouldn't fall asleep until the next night. He lay in bed, weeping.

"Imagine, if you will, your best friend in the world, for good or for bad, is gone," Creegs said. "And there's nothing you can do about it."

> Bill was truly a special human being. He could relate to people on any level, including kids of all ages. Our whole family enjoyed knowing Bill through church and school for the past nine years. He actually took our son, Brian, to his basketball camps in the summer, and it had a great impact on his young life. We will always remember the positive attitude, great sense of humor, and his devotion to Peggy and the girls. He will be sorely missed, but his spirit will live on through the many lives he has positively touched, both on and off the court. Our thoughts and prayers go out to the entire Brewer family during this difficult time.
>
> *Greg and Karen Jacobs & Kids*

Joe Corcoran knows he should let go, but he just doesn't want to. So he doesn't.

Sometimes by accident, sometimes on purpose, he'll pull out his cell phone, scroll down the contacts list and peek at the number. Sometimes he'll think about calling. Sometimes he actually does. But mostly, he just stares at the screen, thinks of his friend and misses him.

He thinks of those nights during the season when Bill would call from Dayton after scouting one of Bacon's upcoming opponents. "You wanna get a pizza?" Bill would ask. "Maybe some wings? A beer?" Joe almost always obliged—not because he was an assistant on Bill Brewer's staff, but because Bill Brewer was his friend. And Joe—"Cork," as they call him—wasn't one to turn down pizza and wings with his buddy.

Cork remembers the weekday-morning racquetball, 6 o'clock sharp. He remembers the Reds games. Like Bill, Cork was a baseball guy, and like Bill, he played in college, first at Triton in Chicago and then at Birmingham-Southern in Alabama. He remembers the Super Bowl parties and the weekend hangouts with the coaches and the wives. He remembers Bill calling at all hours of the day—and night—just to blare the song "You Dropped a Bomb on Me." Cork loves that song. Whenever Bill heard it on the radio, he'd call Cork and put the phone by the speaker.

Cork remembers the shit-giving, something that only the best of friends perfect—and only after years and years together. Bill and Cork had it down pretty good. Bill would throw shit at Cork, Cork would throw it right back, and they'd start fresh the next day. Cork remembers the day Bill told him he was thinking about leaving Roger Bacon. Cork understood. He was sad, but he understood. Even when Bill left for Princeton, though, their friendship didn't diminish. Not at all. Not one iota.

But if there's one memory Cork could erase, it'd be the middle-of-the-night phone call from Creegs. Maybe that would mean nothing bad happened, even though it did. Maybe his friend would still be here, even though he isn't. Maybe he wouldn't find himself staring at an old phone number, even though he does. But it's a memory Cork can't forget. He remembers every detail of it, every word, every second. His wife, Linda, handed him the phone. "It's Creegs," she said.

"Cork?"

"Yeah?"

"Brew's dead."

"What?"

"Yeah, Brew's dead. Had a massive heart attack."

Cork was dumbfounded. *Brew's dead? Brew's not dead. I just talked to him not too long ago. He's got a wife and three daughters. Massive heart attack? Brew's not even overweight. There's got to be a mistake.*

"What?" Cork asked again.

"Yeah," Creegs said between sobs. "Brew's dead."

Cork, like a lot of people, didn't bother going back to sleep that night. He just sat there, not believing what he'd been told. Eventually, he got up, took a shower and drove to Roger Bacon. He arrived well before sunrise, went straight to his office and sat alone for hours, waiting, waiting to spread the news.

> To the Brewers:
>
> My dearest sympathy to your family. God must've had a plan and a few reasons for what has happened. I will keep you in my prayers, but God will comfort you the most. Mr. Brewer was a great man in many ways and he will be treasured always and forever. He's in pure happiness now. I'll always be proud that he represented All Saints.
>
> Love,
>
> Liz Bender

Peggy got back from the hospital around 4 a.m. and told the girls that their wonderful, sweet daddy had died. Maddy, only seven at the time, didn't understand.

"Do I have to go to school today?" she asked.

Peggy tried calling Princeton's athletic director, Scott Kaufman, to tell him what happened, but she couldn't reach him. His cell phone was turned off. It was still just five in the morning. But it wasn't long before Peggy's house was filled with family and friends. No one knew what to do—there was nothing they could do—but they all knew they needed to be there. Creegs was there. So was Tom Thompson, still dazed from the phone call he received from Creegs a few hours earlier. Tom and his wife, Jill, who was due to have the couples' fourth child any day, came with him. Someone got the fireplace going. Mourners huddled close on that cold November morning, but the warmth emanating from the cackling logs did little to thaw the numbness, the ache of emptiness, they all felt inside.

Around 6:15 a.m., Peggy got a phone call. It was from a student at Princeton who Bill tutored before school. The boy called to see if Bill was running late. Peggy tried to tell the boy what happened, that Bill wouldn't be there that day or any day, that he was dead. But she couldn't speak. She tried, but no words came out. No noises. All she could do was hand the phone to her brother, turn away and cry.

> Bill Brewer was a gentleman. Bill Brewer was a champion. Bill Brewer was a leader. I was a student in his geometry class at Roger Bacon High School. If you were a student, he didn't want to just be your teacher; he wanted to be your friend. It was his presence that affected you. He brought humor and wisdom and guidance into your life, even if you didn't need it. He was a sportsman and a die-hard Dayton Flyers fan. I wanted to be a coach or a manager, and he worked with me and allowed me to work with him.
>
> Bill Brewer was a doer and a planner. It didn't matter if it was basketball or geometry. He would break it down into terms that you could understand, and he wouldn't go to the next step unless you were ready. He made sure that eventually the goal would get accomplished. I only knew Coach Brewer for five years, but he helped me become the best individual I could be. And that's all he wanted out of everyone.
>
> Jerry Turner

Beckham Wyrick was sitting on his back porch in Germany when he got the email. It was from his father, David, who had a simple request for his only son. Call home.

"I was just shocked," Beckham said.

Spend five minutes with Beckham Wyrick, The Guy Who Guarded LeBron, and you wouldn't think he was capable of hating anyone. But there were times in high school when he hated Bill Brewer. Flat out could not stand him. One year, when it was Beckham's turn to host a team dinner, he refused to have it at his house—not because he didn't want to have the team over, but because he didn't want to have Bill Brewer over.

"He's not coming to our house," Beckham told his father.

"What do you mean he's not coming to our house?" David Wyrick asked.

"He's not coming to our house."

"Beck, everybody else has had a dinner. We need to do this."

"He's not coming to our house."

David didn't understand. Was there something wrong with the house? Was Beckham embarrassed about something? No, it was none of that.

"Then what's the problem?" David asked.

"He's not welcome here."

David gave in. Instead of inviting the players and coaches to his house, he took them to JB's Bar and Grill in Finneytown, not far from the Wyrick household. That's how strong Beckham's feelings were on the matter. At Roger Bacon, he belonged to Bill. At practice and in games, he belonged to Bill. But at home? No dice. That was Beckham's safety net, and Bill Brewer, well, he just wasn't welcome.

Five years after graduating, however, whatever disdain Beckham once had for his former coach was no longer there. It had long since vanished. Now, Beckham was playing professional basketball in Germany, and he knew that without Bill, he wouldn't be.

Without Bill, he might not have made it through college.

The same could be said for Monty St. Clair. At certain points in his high school career, Monty, like Beckham, couldn't stand Bill Brewer. It got so bad that Monty almost quit the sport he loved. But on November 2, 2007, the boy once labeled soft was too tough for his own good.

At first, news of Bill's death, which Monty learned via text from Dave Johnson, didn't affect him. Monty wouldn't let it. Everybody knew him as a tough, emotionless guy, someone who could deal with anything. Besides, he had talked to Bill maybe once in the last year and a half, so in a way, it didn't feel like he had lost anyone. Monty got dressed and went to work. Just another day.

Once there, however, it wasn't long before the pain of life's regrets set in. It wasn't long before the guilt set in. Five months earlier, LeBron James had led the Cleveland Cavaliers to the NBA Finals, prompting the *Cincinnati Enquirer* to do a looking-back piece on Roger Bacon—on The Team That Beat LeBron. The *Enquirer* was quite familiar with Monty, who played college ball for nearby Miami of Ohio from 2003 to 2007. Monty always gave colorful postgame interviews. "Monty, what do you think of your RPI?" reporters would ask. "You know, I don't even know what that is," Monty would reply. Simply put, he was a college kid who said funny stuff. He was the kind of athlete reporters love, the kind who kept the "one game at a time" mantras to a minimum.

The *Enquirer* interviewed Bill for the story, and a photographer came by his office to get some photos. In one of the photos, Bill, sporting blue jeans and a black collared shirt, is leaning back in his office chair with his sneaker-clad feet resting on his desk, right foot over left. His fingers intertwine behind his head. He poses as if sun-bathing by a pool. The June 11, 2007 issue of *Sports Illustrated*—with LeBron gracing the cover with the words "LeBron Arrives" and "Cleveland's in the Finals and a New Era Begins"—is draped across Bill's abdomen. His eyes are closed. He's smiling, appearing to ponder, if only for a few moments, the magnitude of what he accomplished—of what that team accomplished—five years earlier. It's a moment of triumph frozen in time.

And Monty isn't there. He could have been. He wishes he were. But he isn't. The *Enquirer* asked him to swing by for the photo shoot, but Monty declined. Maybe there was a Reds game to go to. Maybe there was a family function to attend. Maybe he just didn't feel like going. But if ever there were a photo that Monty wishes he were in, it's this one. He wishes he had said *yes*. He wishes he had been there to share that moment with Bill, to reminisce with him, to laugh with him. He wishes, more than anything, that he could've seen him one last time.

But he didn't, and soon the sadness and guilt consumed him. The first tear came. Then the next. And the next. By that night, he was a mess.

"I never cry," Monty said. "But I probably cried four days straight."

Josh Hausfeld, a 2002 graduate, got word of the passing early in the morning from his mother. There was shock, of course, and sadness. The life of someone Josh cared deeply about was taken too soon. He reflected on all the great times he had shared with his former coach—

the annual trips to Columbus for the state tournament, the spaghetti dinners Bill and Peggy hosted before games against Moeller, the subtle and not-so-subtle compliments Bill gave when no one else was looking or within earshot. That's when Josh realized he would never get to hear Bill offer another piece of sage advice, that he would never receive another heartfelt email. It was over.

Josh was living in Tampa, Florida. He was one of the few members of his family to ever leave home, to ever leave St. Bernard. But on that morning, with a visitation and funeral upcoming, Josh booked a flight home without the slightest hesitation.

"I just knew I had to be there," he said. "I just knew I had to be there."

One by one, the other state champions found out.

Nate Wyrick was asleep in Casper, Wyoming, when his phone buzzed incessantly with texts and phone calls. Leonard Bush was in Indianapolis. Tim McCoy was driving from Cincinnati to Columbus for a teachers' meeting when he got the call from Cork, who also called Bobby Holt, an assistant coach on that state title squad. Bobby found out around 5 a.m. He went back to his bed, clung to his wife and wept. Jon Newton, meanwhile, was on campus at the University of Cincinnati when he got a call from his father.

"Earlier that year, me and my dad were talking about how we wanted to go to Princeton and see him because I hadn't seen him probably since I graduated," said Newton, who graduated from Roger Bacon in 2003. "I really wanted to see him, too. I really did. We wanted to go to a game, but we never did. I never got a chance to talk to him."

Marcus Smith, who was working as a teller at a credit union, got the call at work. It was from one of his fellow 2003 grads. At first, he ignored it—he didn't want to appear unprofessional by taking a personal call—but the former classmate kept calling. Finally, Marcus stepped away from his teller line. He answered. He listened. He couldn't believe it.

It didn't seem real.

He returned to his post and tried to be chippy and cheery, but it was a lost cause. It wasn't until his lunch break about 45 minutes later that he was able to sit down and decompress. That's when he started thinking. A few months earlier, Marcus wanted to go to Princeton and help Bill with summer camp. Whatever his former coach needed, Marcus was willing to do. Bill hadn't asked him to do that, but Marcus wanted to, maybe to show appreciation for what Bill did for him when he was a junior and senior at Bacon. But Marcus never went. Things happened. Things came up. There just wasn't enough time.

"I remember thinking, 'Man, I should have done that,'" Marcus said. "But I didn't."

Tim McCoy was still on his way to Columbus when he called Matt Reed, who was scheduled to fly to Florida that day. Matt, who lived in Cincinnati, was relocating to Estero in a few weeks and was flying down to move some of his belongings. He went to work that morning and read an online article about Bill's death. Matt thought immediately of Katie, Abby and Maddy—how young they were, how they still had so much growing up to do, how Bill would never get to see it. His eyes welled. He sat and thought of all the memories he had of Coach Brewer. He remembered how they would play H-O-R-S-E before practice and how the loser had to buy the winner a can of Pepsi for lunch the next day. Somehow, Bill always won, and somehow, Matt was never held to his end of the bargain. Matt flew to Florida that day. He did what he had to do and returned to Cincinnati the night before the visitation, grateful for the chance to pay his respects to his former coach.

Frank Phillips, who was playing pro ball in Luxembourg, didn't have that same luxury. He was sitting in his apartment watching an NBA game on his laptop when his mother called. It was the first time in Frank's life that someone close to him had died, and there was no shoulder to turn to. He was alone in a foreign country, not yet fully healed from the racism he had encountered back home. Frank stared at his phone and cried. He sat in his room for hours, thinking of all the good times he and Coach Brewer had together, thinking of all the ways in which Coach Brewer changed his life. Frank tried to make sense of Bill's passing, but nothing came. He wanted to say good-bye in person, but he couldn't. He was overseas, he was in season and he had a job to do. He couldn't make it home for the funeral.

The news spread beyond former players—and fast. In fact, Frank's uncle, Jerome Harris, also a coach, doesn't know how many calls he got that day. Jerome was lucky. About a week before Bill passed, Jerome called him just to say hello and see how he was doing. They hadn't talked in a while, and when two basketball coaches haven't talked for a while, the main—if not sole—topic of conversation is usually basketball. But for that call in particular, little was said about the game both men loved. Jerome asked Bill if he'd heard from Monty, if he'd heard from Beckham, if he knew about Frank and the award he had recently won. Jerome asked about Peggy. He asked about Bill's daughters. He asked how he liked coaching them—and girls in general. Jerome couldn't picture Bill coaching girls; he figured he was too intense.

When the conversation concluded, Jerome promised Bill he'd come to a Princeton game that season and see the team Bill had assembled, the team that was one year away from going on a magical run without him. It's not that Jerome had any kids on that team. But even after Frank graduated from Bacon in 2002, Jerome came to at least half of the Spartans' games the following season. Because he believed in that team. Because he believed in those kids. Because he believed in Bill Brewer and everything he stood for—and not just on the court.

"Most reputations of coaches come from who they are as a coach, but Brewer was a good person," Jerome said. "I really miss him."

> My son played for Coach Brewer for three years and had the great fortune of winning a state championship under Bill. The news of his death brought indescribable sorrow and a flood of great memories of those three years. On the floor, that (2001–02) team was as good as any team to come out of this city. That team could play, and that was a direct reflection of Coach Brewer. Off the floor, the team was a family. They were as close as brothers. This was also a reflection of Coach Brewer and the emphasis he put on family. This combination resulted in a state championship and a lifetime of memories, for which I will forever be thankful.
>
> Tim McCoy, Sr.

Mitch Perdrix was teaching at Aiken High School when he got a call from his best friend.

"Hey, man," the friend said, "I don't know what to tell you, but I just turned on the news . . ."

Mitch sat for the next half hour not believing what he'd been told. Mitch thought of the two years he played for Bill and the effect his former coach had on him. He ignored Bill's advice and went on to play college basketball. His experience was quite similar to what Bill said it would be; he played at Northern Kentucky University and more or less rode the bench all but one year. Bill always wanted Mitch to coach with him at Bacon, but for years Mitch resisted.

"When you're not the player you want to be," Mitch said, "coaching just doesn't sound that appealing."

But when Mitch graduated from NKU in 2000, he gave in. He coached at his alma mater from 2000 to 2003. He did it for Bill and the players, and he enjoyed being part of that experience, being part of that state title. But as hard as he tried, he could never take coaching as seriously as Bill and the rest of the staff did. In some ways, being around the game was painful for Mitch. It reminded him of how much more he wanted to achieve in high school and college. He never regretted his choice to play college basketball—mainly because of the strong friendships he made as a result—but as happy as he was for Bill and the players for their success, something was missing. Mitch stepped down in 2003.

When Bill went to Princeton, he always tried to get Mitch to come to a game. He always tried to convince him to coach with him, to give it another try. He even tried to entice Mitch with a teaching job at Princeton, but Mitch, despite feeling somewhat guilty, never took the bait.

"I always felt like I disappointed him a bit," Mitch said. "I think every coach who's trying to build something wants to find another coach to groom along, and part of him would have really enjoyed having a former player coach with him. I just couldn't live it and breathe it the way he could. Brian Neal went to Bacon, but he didn't play for Brew, so even that was a little different. I think Brew always hoped I would coach, but there's just other stuff I'm into, and I think we grew to understand that."

But Mitch still felt guilty. He always figured he'd have a chance to go to a Princeton game that season, to hang out with Bill afterward and catch up. But he never got that chance. Mitch never went to the week-long getaways in Cumberland, either. Bill always invited him. Even after Mitch stopped coaching, Bill invited him. But Mitch never went. He was single; he was in a different age bracket; he would have felt out of place. When he found out Bill passed, Mitch regretted never taking advantage of some of those opportunities and never telling Bill how much he meant to him. Sure, there were times they would have a beer and take jabs at each other, which Mitch loved, but he wished he had said and done more.

Maybe that's why he called Bill's cell phone while driving home from work that day. He had known of Bill's death for a few hours, but it still hadn't sunk in. Bill wanted to call Peggy and tell her he was sorry, but he didn't have her phone number. He didn't have the house number, either. So he called Bill's cell, figuring Peggy might answer it. She didn't. It went straight to voicemail. Mitch listened to Bill's voice, and then came the beep. Three words later, Mitch started bawling.

He never asked Peggy about that voicemail. He doesn't even know if she got it, but he knows it would have been incomprehensible even if she did. Mitch had no idea what he was trying to say that day, but he knew he had to try to say it. He knew he needed to call.

For a long time, Mitch was mad at Bill for never coming to one of his college games. Mitch didn't understand. He and Bill remained close even after Mitch graduated from high school, and NKU wasn't far from Bacon. Bill had four years to go to a game and watch the first player he ever coached at Bacon, the first player who ever bought into him. But Bill never went. Not once.

At first, Mitch figured it was because he rarely played, which was hard to accept. But eventually he realized that wasn't it. That wasn't it at all. Bill didn't care how much Mitch played or didn't play, how much he scored or didn't score. Who Mitch was as a person was always far more important to Bill than who he was as a player—and he never wanted Mitch to think otherwise.

"For him, basketball wasn't my value," Mitch said. "There were times when he was listening to me, and I could tell he wasn't listening to anyone else."

> I first met Bill when we were freshmen at the University of Dayton. I have too many memories of the good times we had to even start jotting them down. I was deeply saddened last night when I got the call that Bill passed away. The first thought that came to mind was that he was way too young to die. Then it occurred to me that Bill touched so many people and accomplished so much in the 42 years he had on this earth that he had already lived a great life. My thoughts and prayers go out to the whole Brewer family.
>
> Joe Heffernan, college roommate

For Bids, middle-of-the-night phone calls had become routine. His parents were older. Their health was failing. These days, the phone calls were just a part of life, a sign of getting older, like a driver's license at 16 or an engagement ring after college. Dave never got used to the phone calls—does anyone ever?—but they didn't jar him out of bed like they used to. So when his phone rang that night, he assumed something was wrong with his mom or dad. But when he heard Creegs' voice, he knew that wasn't the case.

Heart attack? I just saw that guy. He was just driving down Montgomery Road, going home to see his family.

But as Creegs summarized what happened and when, Bids realized the timing aligned. It was true.

Somehow, Bids went into work that morning. He figured he'd go to Peggy's later that afternoon and be a fresh face for her to see, maybe relieve some people who had been there since before sunrise. But his co-workers knew of his close relationship with Bill, and when they saw him at work that day, they all asked him essentially the same thing.

What the hell are you doing?

But that's the thing. Bids didn't know what he was doing. He didn't know what to do. He had never lost a best friend before.

When Bids left work that afternoon, he called Peggy and asked if he could bring anything. Ice, Peggy said. People brought plenty of drinks, but she was short on ice. Bids took care of it. When he got to the house, he and Peggy ended up on the driveway, arm in arm.

"I can't believe he's gone," Peggy said. "How am I gonna deal with this?"

"There just aren't any answers right now," Bids said. "But that's what we're all here for—to help out in any way we can."

After Dave made the rounds, he noticed the ice he brought was melting. Not that that was a big concern at the time or anything, but he offered to grab some coolers out of the garage. Bids knew exactly where the coolers were and what they looked like. Every summer, Bids had a party—the Bidwell Bash—and every summer, he'd borrow Bill's coolers for it. Bids would come by and pick them up and ask if they were clean.

"Oh, yeah," Bill would say. "Cleaned 'em the other day."

'n Bids would pick up the coolers, they were always—
 nasty as could be. So he'd sigh, smile, shake his head in
 .agrin and clean them. That day at Peggy's, he went into the garage and spotted one of the coolers. It looked pristine, immaculate. And then Bids opened it. A red and yellow Kool-Aid mix had congealed at the bottom. It sludged along like tar.

"Probably four weeks old," Bids said. "Just stunk."

But in that moment, Bids found, however brief or fleeting, a little bit of peace. Peggy's house was packed. Any number of people could have stumbled upon that cooler, but they didn't. He did. Of course he did. He always did. And as he stood there, he couldn't help but imagine Bill's voice.

"I gotcha one last time!" Bill would have said.

And with that, Dave Bidwell bent over and cleaned Bill Brewer's cooler.

> I went to high school with Bill Brewer at Northwest. I remember him as a very kind person—always smiling and a part of everything. He was one of those people you knew would turn out to be a success in life because he had such a positive attitude. What an awesome legacy he has left. To touch the lives of young people in such a positive way—what a powerful tribute to his life! His spirit and influence will live on in the lives of his wife, daughters, loved ones and those he coached and worked with. You will all be in our prayers.
> Bethany (Little) Zink

The visitation for William Roy Brewer was held Tuesday, November 6, 2007, in a high school gym. That was the one place that could accommodate the amount of people who were likely to attend.

Besides, that's where Bill would have wanted it.

Katie Brewer was a freshman at Ursuline Academy, an all-girls school on the east side of Cincinnati in Blue Ash. Ursuline offered to host the visitation, but Peggy couldn't bear the thought of Katie going to school for four years and thinking, *This is where my daddy died.*

Instead, the visitation was held at Princeton's gym four days after Bill's death. His body was wheeled along the baseline under the basket. Lights were dimmed. Flowers unfurled along the casket. A video of photos played in the background. Somehow, despite the nets and banners and floorboards, it didn't feel like a gym. It felt like a visitation.

Princeton's athletic director, Scott Kaufman, arrived early to set up the arrangements. Bids, Creegs and Tom Thompson, among others, also arrived early, even before Peggy.

"How does it look?" Kaufman asked.

None of them had ever been to a visitation in a gym.

"It's beautiful," Tom said.

Peggy and the girls arrived, and it wasn't long before the line of well-wishers stretched out of the gym, into the hallway and outside into the crisp fall air. The line was vast. More than 2,000 people attended the visitation, including most of the 2001–02 Roger Bacon basketball team.

"It was the longest line I've ever seen," Monty said.

Monty felt bad that day. He felt bad for Peggy, of course, and he felt bad for Katie, Abby and Maddy. But he felt just as bad when he saw Princeton's basketball team, when he saw players who got to play for Bill for a season or two but who didn't get the full experience. And then he thought of the hundreds of players over the next 15 or 20 years who would come through Princeton and not have the opportunity to play for Coach Brewer at all. He thought of all the players who wouldn't benefit from that great man the way he did.

It just seemed unfair.

Other Bacon players were there, too. Tim McCoy. Dave Johnson. Jon Newton. Matt Reed. Josh Hausfeld. Josh waited in line for a few hours, saw Bill's body, hugged Peggy and wept. Later that night, Cork took the players to a pub near Princeton. He bought everyone a round of Coors Light. They stayed for hours, catching up, drinking and telling stories about that season, about that team, about Bill.

Marcus Smith also went to the visitation. He wore his state championship jersey under his shirt and tie. Right away, he spotted Brian Neal standing alone. Brian was Bill's varsity assistant at Bacon for almost a decade. When Creegs called to inform him of Bill's death, it took Brian about 15 minutes to comprehend what exactly happened. Creegs wasn't coherent; he was crying. Brian was crying, too.

Brian saw Bill at Bacon about three weeks before his death. There was a meeting for the Southwest Ohio Coaches Association, of which

Bill was president. Brian still talked to Bill several times a week, but he hadn't see him nearly as often since Bill left for Princeton more than two years earlier. Brian wishes he had. Maybe he would have recognized something was wrong in the days and weeks before Bill's death. Maybe Brian could have prevented it in some way. He knows he probably couldn't have—nor could anyone else—but it's a thought he still ponders.

Brian would stop by Bill's practices at Princeton on occasion. They'd talk, ask each other for advice. Brian would get a refresher on the way Bill ran things and then apply it at Bacon. The two teams would even scrimmage in the preseason. That year, they had scheduled a scrimmage for November 10, but Bill never got to coach it. His replacement, Josh Andrews, approached Brian and suggested that Bacon and Princeton should still play the game—both to honor Bill's passing and help each team prepare for the season.

Brian saw the sense in that. He saw the good in it. So he let his team scrimmage—but he asked his assistants to coach it. For Brian, it was just too soon. He figured his absence would be better for his players anyway. He wanted it to be business as usual for them. If he had been there, it wouldn't have been.

"I wouldn't have been a very good coach that day," Brian admitted.

At the visitation, Brian bypassed the line and stood with Peggy and her extended family. Of course he did. Brian practically was family. The trips to Cumberland. Golf outings to Elizabethtown, Kentucky. Bill and Peggy were at Brian's wedding. They threw him and his wife, Amy, a baby shower when they had their first son. When Bill passed, Brian didn't just lose a former boss; he lost a best friend. So he spent his time at that visitation talking to people about what a great man Bill really was.

But when Marcus walked in and saw Brian, Brian was alone. Literally and figuratively alone. Marcus hadn't seen him in four years, but there are certain instances in life where the passage of time is irrelevant, where time cannot diminish the bond of those who were once close. So Marcus, seeking both to comfort and be comforted, walked straight up to Brian, a state championship jersey clinging to his chest, and asked if he was okay.

"No," Brian Neal said. "I'm not okay."

> To the Brewer Family:
>
> For the past several weeks I have struggled with trying to figure out why things are the way they are. Unfortunately, I still don't know. My personal roller coaster of emotions has included shock, sadness, loneliness, anger, disappointment and fear.
>
> Bill was a special teacher, an inspirational coach and a fierce friend. I will always be grateful for our time together—I will miss his ability to see the good in everything and everyone, his ability to light up a room just by walking through the door and the occasional dig just to keep me honest.
>
> Bill had three fundamental expectations for everyone, regardless of ability, position or job title:
> 1. Try your best ALL the time:
>   - He knew people made mistakes—he would forgive mistakes; he wouldn't forgive a lack of effort
>   - If he didn't think you were giving your best, he would let you know and expect more
> 2. Team:
>   - Our team will always be better than our individuals
> 3. Don't Quit
>   - Pain, frustration and disappointment are temporary
>   - Quitting lasts forever!
>
> I know that I am a better person because of Bill—a better AD, a better father, a better husband and a better friend. I will always remember what Bill worked for, stood for and what he tried to teach his players and his students. I will miss him very much!
>
> It is hard to believe that our families met over 16 years ago—the time has moved by so quickly. I will always be grateful that our careers brought our families back together. Your family will always have a special place in my heart.
>
> All my love—Scott Kaufman

The funeral was held at Good Shepherd in Montgomery. Peggy had hoped to have the service at All Saints, but it was undergoing renovations and therefore unavailable. Peggy met with the priest at Good Shepherd and listed which songs she wanted played and when. One of them, the closing song, made the priest do a double take. It was the national anthem.

"Oh, no, you can't do that," the priest explained. "That's not an appropriate song."

"It's in the church book," Peggy countered. "I'm allowed to have it."

Peggy pulled out the hymnal. There it was. Number 891 in the Gather book. The Star Spangled Banner.

"But . . ." the priest stammered, "I've never seen that done before."

And that's when Peggy stated her case. On almost every important day of Bill's life, he heard that song. He heard it when he was a three-sport athlete at Northwest High School in Cincinnati. He heard it when he was setting pitching records at Dayton. He heard it when he coached basketball at Bacon and Princeton and when he won a state title. Whether playing a sport or coaching one, that song was a fixture of his life, a life that was always lived in tip-off mode, the moment when the excitement of game day was at its highest.

That was Bill Brewer. That was his song. And he needed to hear it one last time.

The priest gave in.

"You're not going to tell Peggy no," Tom Thompson said.

The funeral was much like the visitation—packed. The crowd was much like those on a Friday night during Bill's heyday at Bacon—standing-room only. At the end of the funeral, as Creegs helped carry Bill's casket to the hearse, sounds of the national anthem filled the church. One by one, mourners began singing as if at a basketball game, as if tip-off were moments away. It was at least a year before Creegs could hear that song and not immediately think of his dead friend.

Bill was buried at Gate of Heaven Cemetery. A reception followed at All Saints.

After the reception, Josh Hausfeld and Monty St. Clair drove to Dave Johnson's apartment in Hyde Park. They sat in their suits and did the only thing they could think of, the only thing that felt appropriate, the only thing that felt right.

They watched the 2002 state final.

> Bill had a reason for everything.
> No one could limit his dreams. He wouldn't accept no for an answer.
> The man had the biggest heart of anyone. Anyone who spent any time down at the lake could attest to that. "The Brewers down at Cumberland" was an event, and they had that event when anyone was willing to be entertained.
> Peg called the man stubborn, among other things (all well-deserved). But she, along with all of us, loved the man.
> His life ended Friday, ironically when the big heart stopped beating. And yes, Brew, you had the last word when you were ready, saying, "Gotta go, bye" before we were ready, and left us sitting there with the receiver still in hand wishing we would have done something more.
> Tom Thompson

There's a reason grown men tear up just talking about Bill Brewer. There's a reason women weep. Bill won 202 games in his coaching career, an impressive number by almost any prep standard. But one game stands out. One game remains a cut above the rest. In 2002, Bill Brewer became The Man Who Beat LeBron. In many ways, it was a win one decade in the making. To the casual observer, Bill is known solely for that game.

But to those who knew him—and knew him well—his legacy extends beyond it. It has to. If not, there wouldn't be people like Mike Cregan or Joe Corcoran or Tom Thompson or Dave Bidwell who were all stirred from slumber in the middle of a November night in 2007 and never once considered going back to sleep. There wouldn't be people like Brian Neal who still wonder if there were something he could have done, something he might have seen, that in some way could've prevented his best friend from dying. There wouldn't be people like Mitch Perdix or Jon Newton or Marcus Smith or Monty St. Clair who still regret not having gone to see their former coach one last time.

There wouldn't be any of these people.

But there are.

"I never would have sat there and told him how much he meant to me, how much he helped me," Monty said. "But you wish you would have. I wish he knew. Because he doesn't know the extent he helped people. That's the one thing I wish Peggy did know. It was more than what he thought. And unless you played for him, it was more than what you would think."

CHAPTER ONE

THE EARLY YEARS

When Bill Brewer assumed head coaching duties at Roger Bacon High School before the 1993–94 season, the basketball program, 11 seasons removed from its first and only state championship, was in shambles.

And Bill knew it. When he was an assistant coach at Moeller, he attended a Bacon game in the early '90s to scout one of Moeller's upcoming opponents. When Moeller coaches asked Bill what he gleaned from the game, he gave them his full scouting report, saving the most telling observation for last.

"Oh, and one more thing," Bill said. "I'm gonna be the next basketball coach at Roger Bacon—because they're a mess."

Bill's statement was prophetic. The man he replaced, Fred Cooper, went just 9–31 in two regular seasons before being asked to step down. His first year, 1991–92, wasn't all that bad; Bacon went 7–13 and won five league games. That following year, however, the bottom dropped out; Bacon, the only one of six teams in the Greater Catholic League North division without a first-team all-star, finished 2–18 during the regular season and went winless—*winless*—in the GCL, losing all 14 league games. Tom Thompson, who joined Bacon's staff in 1988, maintains that Cooper wasn't a bad coach and that he knew a great deal about basketball; he was simply family first.

"His time commitment was going to be X number of hours per week, and when he signed on, that was going to be okay," Thompson said. "But then it wasn't."

The wins just weren't there. Bill was hired in 1993, one week after his first daughter, Katie, was born. Generally speaking, whenever there's a coaching change, things are either really good or really bad, because someone either retired, got promoted or got fired. Bill knew Bacon's situation was dire. He knew he had a lot of work to do, and immediately he began molding the program in his likeness. He knew it wouldn't be easy, and he knew it would take time, but he was going to do it. And he knew exactly how: by making Fred Cooper—and just about any high school basketball coach—look like a vacation. Tom Thompson still remembers the first speech Bill gave to that 1993–94 squad when he walked into Bacon's gym, the Thomas J. Fogarty Activity Center—called "Fogarty," for short. It went something like this:

"You have to be about the team. Everything that you do, every choice that you make, on the court or off, has to be about the team. I don't care if you're the best player or the worst player; the team is your first priority. If it isn't your first priority, you're not going to play. You have to play defense—not passionless defense, not indifferent defense, but fundamental, sit-your-ass-down-and-guard defense. I don't care how well you can shoot. If you don't play defense, you're not going to play. You have to give 100 percent at all times. If you don't give 100 percent at all times, you're not going to play. What I say goes. If you don't do what I say, you're not going to play. Any questions?"

There really weren't too many. Most high school kids tend not to talk when you scare the crap out of them.

"It was a very clean-house kind of meeting," said Mitch Perdrix, who was a junior on that '93–94 squad. "'If you're not in, get the hell out.' Those were pretty much his exact words. I remember thinking, 'God, you work your ass off for two years, and then this guy comes in and everything you've done means nothing.' Of course, we were terrible, so it should have meant nothing."

If one player bought into Bill from the start that year, it was Mitch—not because he admired Bill (in fact, for most of that first year, Mitch couldn't stand him), but because that's the way he was raised. Mitch grew up on Greenlee Avenue a few blocks from Roger Bacon. His father, Roger Perdrix, taught in the Cincinnati Public School system for 35 years and was a football coach at Western Hills High School. Roger raised his son to be disciplined and respectful—a yes-sir, no-sir kind of kid. If Mitch ever had a problem with a coach, teacher or authority figure in general, it was his fault no matter what, and it was on him to figure out how to make it right.

As for Mitch's teammates, they were all good guys—and some of them were actually solid players—but high school basketball wasn't life or death to them. It was something they did to have fun. They weren't lazy by any means, but they didn't live and breathe the game the way Bill did. Or the way Mitch did. So there were a lot of times, especially that first year, when Mitch and Bill were the only two guys in the gym going all out—really, truly all out. Because of that, Mitch and Bill developed a mutual respect, a common bond.

Bill's biggest problem that first year, however, was that his players didn't fit the system he wanted to implement—at all. When Bill took over at Bacon, he was 28. He was full of innovative ideas. He didn't want to merely blend in and go with the crowd. He wanted to be a trendsetter. The Greater Catholic League, by and large, is a grind-it-out league; it's not a high-scoring, get-up-and-down-the-floor league. It's a league where desire, will, suffocating defense, and execution in the halfcourt win the day. Games aren't played in the 80s and 90s; they're played in the 40s and 50s—sometimes lower.

But that didn't stop Bill from preaching a pressing, run-and-gun style at Bacon. It didn't matter that the gym that first year was full of slow, hulking players, several of whom ranged in size from 6-3 to 6-7. How slow was Bacon? As a sophomore, Mitch was an all-league center. In '93–94, Bill didn't have anybody who could play on the perimeter, so he moved Mitch to a shooting guard/small forward combo. By Mitch's senior year, he was the starting point guard. He'd bring the ball up the court like Magic Johnson, barreling his butt into a defender and taking about nine-and-a-half seconds to back his way across the timeline.

"If I'm your point guard," Mitch said, "you're a slow team."

Mitch says that now, but at the time, he and his teammates thought they could run any system Bill wanted. When you're in high school, you think you're fast. You don't know your limitations. A lot of first-year coaches would have walked into Bacon's gym in the winter of 1993, looked around and thought, *Okay, this team's too slow to press. Actually, this team's too slow to play man-to-man. Match-up zone it is.* And Bill saw that. He recognized it. But he ignored it. He was young, he was stubborn, he had his style—and he was going to stick with it.

But what frustrated Bill the most was not his team's lack of speed, but rather, its lack of basketball IQ. The team lacked any sense of basic man-to-man principles. Bill, Tom Thompson and the other coaches would shout terminology, and the players would look at them like they were speaking a foreign language.

"Not only were we slow," Mitch said. "We were slow and uneducated."

By the end of the '93–94 season, Bill didn't abandon the press completely, but he adapted and went to a 2–3 zone. Bacon got better. The Spartans won five games in Bill's first regular season—more than double what they won the previous season under Fred Cooper.

"It just took a while for Bill to adjust to us as opposed to trying to make us adjust to him," Mitch said. "But that year, he adapted. That's a total tribute to him. That's the sign of a good coach."

But the changes Bill made weren't limited to style of play. He knew what a lot of great coaches know: when you're new, and things are bad, you want to make as many changes as possible—and the more visual the changes, the better. That first year, unbeknownst to Bill, the players desperately wanted new uniforms. The ones they had were old, faded, and worst of all, short. John Stockton short.

Mitch entered high school the same year five freshmen basketball players entered college at the University of Michigan. The Fab Five—Chris Webber, Jalen Rose, Juwan Howard, Ray Jackson and Jimmy King—revolutionized the college game with its hip-hop style, which featured, among other fashion statements, long, baggy shorts. Mitch and his teammates loved the Fab Five. The shorts, especially. One of Bacon's players had a father who owned a business, and the players asked if his dad could find someone to sponsor new jerseys for the team—gold jerseys with baggy shorts, just like the Fab Five.

When Bill found out about this, he wasn't happy—not because his players wanted new uniforms, but because they didn't go through him to get them. Bill took it upon himself to raise the necessary funds.

Because Mitch was captain, Bill asked him what he thought would be a good design. Mitch suggested the design be identical to Michigan's gold jerseys except for one thing—replace the "M" on the shorts with a Spartan head, Bacon's mascot. So that's what Bill did. Mitch doesn't know how Bill raised the money, but he made it happen. During Mitch's senior year before a game against league rival McNicholas, Bill walked into the locker room as usual, seemingly to go over pregame strategy, but instead, he busted out the gold jerseys in the locker room, dumping them in the middle of the floor. The players dived in headfirst.

"You would've thought we were starving and someone threw three pizzas in the room," Mitch said. "We were going apeshit."

One pair of shorts, however, was missing a drawstring, and the players started fighting over who would have to wear that one. Bill couldn't believe it.

"God dammit!" he yelled. "I finally get you guys these fucking uniforms, and you're fighting over the fucking drawstrings!"

The players calmed down. They put things in perspective. The important thing was, they had the jerseys. Bill earned a lot of respect and appreciation from his players that day. They saw it as Bill throwing them a bone. Bacon wore gold for most of its home games, but every now and then, the traditional browns and whites would come out on the road. Mitch didn't know if that was punishment for the guys not playing well or if Bill was just worried about wear and tear due to excessive laundering. Either way, the jerseys became Bill's carrot to dangle in front of his players. They were a reward for hard work, but if the work ethic slipped, they could be taken away at any time.

Of course, there were those who would've been okay with that. Yes, even though Bacon's players cherished the new-generation look inspired by the Fab Five, some of the old-school Roger Bacon diehards could've done without it—especially the jersey color itself. Bacon—along with Purcell, Elder and St. Xavier—was one of the four founding members of the GCL, which was formed in 1931. Since opening in 1928, Roger Bacon's school colors were brown and white. Even when Bacon became co-educational—this after Our Lady of Angels closed in 1984—the colors remained brown and white. For a tradition-rich school like Roger Bacon, which played in a tradition-rich conference like the GCL and was located in a change-averse community like St. Bernard, swapping blend-in brown for stand-out-in-a-crowd gold was too much, especially since the coach responsible for that change really hadn't accomplished anything yet.

Even though he was still relatively new to the job, this wasn't the first time Bill had a run-in with the older Bacon crowd. Bill's first run-in came right after his very first game in 1993. Bacon lost at home that night, and the stands were almost empty. Aside from families of players, aside from a couple of students, aside from some loyal Bacon alums, no one really followed the program. And because the stands were nearly empty that night, everyone in attendance could hear every word Bill said, including his conversations with refs—which wasn't a good thing.

"Bill was known for dropping a couple of bombs," Tom Thompson said diplomatically.

For the next several days, Bacon's principal, Father Roger Bosse, got phone calls from angry alums complaining of Bill's language. Father Roger called Bill into his office.

"Bill, I've got to know," he said. "Some people say you're using language on the sidelines that you probably shouldn't be using."

"Yes, Father . . ." Bill said, treading water.

"Did you really say what they're saying you said?"

"Yes, Father," Bill said. "I did."

Bill was worried. It'd be one thing if he were a coach in his 50s or 60s who had been at it several decades. But he was a rookie, a 28-year-old kid not much older than the highly impressionable kids he was coaching. In that meeting with Father Roger, Bill truly thought that his first game at Bacon might be his last. He could have denied the complaints, but he didn't want to lie, especially not to a priest. Bill sat, waiting for his pink slip.

"All right," Father Roger said. "Well, hey, better luck next time."

Thus began the Bill Brewer era at Roger Bacon.

After that, Bill knew he was going to be okay. The refs didn't have a problem with his language. The principal didn't have a problem with his language. Bill was given free rein to coach the way he wanted to coach, which meant saying whatever he wanted to say. Besides, he was sorry that people heard the words he said, but he wasn't sorry for saying them. The way he saw it, he wouldn't have to yell if the refs did their job right. His players worked hard and deserved better.

If any alums had a problem with that, well, too bad. They were going to have to get used it. Same with the jerseys. For Bill, those weren't just about endearing himself to the players or having a carrot to dangle in front of them. The jerseys were about change. It was a new era, and he wanted everything fresh. A couple of years after Mitch graduated, Bacon footed the bill for a new set of browns and whites—only these had long, baggy shorts. Over time, the gold uniforms were handed down from varsity to JV, JV to freshman. But for Bill, they served their purpose.

As for the language, Bill knew people wouldn't be able to hear him if the stands were full, and he knew the one sure-fire way to fill the stands was to win.

And win often.

● ● ● ●

THE MOST IMPORTANT CHANGE Bill Brewer made at Roger Bacon was a subtle one—subtle to the fans, anyway. It wasn't the jerseys they saw on the court or the language they heard on the sidelines. It was behind the scenes. It was the way, it was the attitude, with which Bill ran the program.

In his first year, Bill decided he was going to bench Mitch Perdrix. Mitch hadn't been playing well, and Bill thought coming off the bench for a few games might do Mitch some good. But before Bill could do this, he wanted to meet Mitch's father and explain the situation. Bill approached Roger Perdrix after a game and introduced himself, but before he could even mention the benching or explain the reasoning behind it, Roger looked him square in the eye and said, "Hey, you're the coach. You don't need to explain anything to me."

That was the coach in Roger Perdrix. He knew how parents could be. So did Mitch. When he played for Fred Cooper, Mitch remembers how a couple of parents tried to run the show and how they made it difficult for Fred to foster a team atmosphere. Fred knew basketball, but compared with Bill, he was much more willing to listen and accommodate. Bill wasn't like that. He learned not to be like that.

"You could sit Bill down with the pope or the President, and there's a big part of Bill who wouldn't give a crap who he was sitting down with," Mitch said. "That was just his personality. Bill always thought he was right—and I loved that about him."

But for Mitch, Bill was an acquired taste. That first year, Mitch didn't think Bill was tough; he thought he was unfair. Mitch was never a proponent of the "You've got to be hardest on your best player to show everyone you mean business" approach. But that's what Bill did. Mitch finally realized, however, that Bill didn't do that to show he meant business; he did it because Mitch was the only one who responded to it.

"If guys are laughing it off, he's not gonna bother with them," Mitch said. "If you're the only guy who cares as much as he does, you're going to catch an amazing brunt of shit."

Bill tried to get the other guys to care. He tried hard. One night during that first season, Bacon was playing at Hamilton Badin, which would become one of Bill's biggest rivals. It was at a point in the season where the players weren't totally demoralized with how bad they were, but they were getting close, and that night, Badin thoroughly outplayed Bacon through two quarters. Bill chewed his players out at halftime.

"God dammit!" he yelled. "You guys can't play like this all fucking night!"

After Bill stormed out, it got quiet. Real quiet. But about 30 seconds later, one of the players broke the silence and said, "We're not playing all night, are we?" The entire team erupted in laughter. Even Mitch couldn't help but smile and shake his head.

"That's the shit Brew had to deal with when he first got to Bacon," Mitch said.

Bill did what he could with what he had. He gave each player a binder. It was Bill's gospel. It told players what to do and how to do it in just about every possible situation. For a time, Bill even tested his players on the material, but it wasn't long before he abandoned the quizzing. It was too much, too soon. He was alienating his players. So, he took the binder and whittled it down to his core principles. What he came up with was this:

PLAYER EXPECTATIONS
1. Be early, not just on time, to all team functions and school.
2. Do not miss school or practice anytime. You will play when you are hurt. You will not practice when you are injured. Consult the trainer anytime you are injured. Your coach will listen to him. Make appointments with teachers when you do not have practice. Consult your coach before any conflict can occur.
3. Be a positive person and not a complainer. If you have a problem, talk to a coach.

4. Support all other levels.
5. Look the coach in the eye when he's talking to you and nod to him when he is finished.
6. Dress appropriately for all team functions. If not sure, overdress. On game nights, wear Mass-day attire.
7. No individual attire, such as earrings, strange haircuts, etc.
8. Keep locker room clean at all times.
9. Shower after every practice and game.
10. Treat your teachers with respect. Stay out of detention.
11. Have your own water bottle at each practice.
12. Keep your shirts tucked in at all times.
13. Keep everything locked in your lockers.
14. Absolutely no cursing or profane language.
15. Maintain a drug/alcohol-free lifestyle.

"Following the rules takes discipline, either yours or ours."

TEAM COVENANT—GET IN OR GET OUT!

It might seem odd that a coach known for dropping a couple of bombs was so insistent that his players refrain from foul language. It might even seem hypocritical.

"You can call it a double standard, but I don't think it was like that," Tom Thompson said. "Bill expected certain things to be done. He wanted the kids to be respected and to come away with values. He wanted them to be someone in the league everyone looked up to. He wanted Bacon to be a special place where kids were always prepared to play and succeed. It didn't always mean winning, but it meant playing harder than the other team."

Another addition Bill instituted was dawn patrol—summer workouts beginning just after sunrise. Bill opened the gym to players who wanted to get better and had them perform basketball and conditioning drills. He asked Mitch to commit to coming to dawn patrol every day; Mitch obliged. Bill thought if one player did it, more players would do it the following year, and even more would do it the year after that. Eventually, Bill figured, his entire team would do it. And that's exactly what happened.

"Dawn patrol was one of the biggest things Bill did," Mitch said.

In Bill's second year, 1994–95, Bacon finished the regular season 5-15 once more but managed to win two tournament games. Mitch, having transformed his body the previous summer, averaged 14 points per game and was a first-team GCL all-star. It was the program's best season in years. Maybe it was because of the gold jerseys. Maybe it was because of Bill's no-nonsense approach to just about everything.

Or maybe it was because Bacon had a supremely talented freshman named Brandon McIntosh.

Anybody who saw Brandon McIntosh play, even as a freshman, knew he was going to be a special player. That was also true for Eugene Land, who enrolled at Bacon with Brandon in the fall of 1994 and joined the varsity team as a sophomore.

The three years that Brandon and Eugene played varsity together were a special time for Bacon. The days of playing in empty gyms were over. Stands overflowed. Fans stood in hallways trying to catch a glimpse of the action. Brandon was 6-5. Eugene was 6-7. Both could play the pressing, run-and-gun, get-up-and-down-the-court style Bill wanted to implement since the day he was hired. In 1995–96, Eugene, only a sophomore, led the GCL-North in scoring with an average of 18.5 points per game. The Spartans finished the regular season 12–8, giving Bill his first winning season at Bacon.

The following season, in 1996–97, Bacon took it a step further. Eugene averaged 20.2 points per game; Brandon averaged 14.1. The Spartans went 16–4 and advanced to the regional finals, where they lost on a last-second shot to league rival Badin. It was a heartbreaking yet encouraging defeat. Four years into his tenure, Bill took a program that had gone winless in the GCL and brought it to within one game of the state semifinals. Even better, Brandon and Eugene were only juniors.

Things were looking up.

• • • •

AFTER THE 1996–97 SEASON, Bill made a key addition to his coaching staff—Brian Neal.

Brian Neal, like his father, is Roger Bacon through and through. Wesley Neal was hired as band director at Bacon fresh out of college and spent his whole career there. Brian, in turn, spent much of his childhood tagging along his father. There was never any doubt where he was going to high school. Bacon was home to him.

Brian played high school basketball in the late '80s, a time when Bacon was still primarily a losing program. He entered high school only 5 feet tall but managed to get a spot on the freshman team. He didn't get many minutes in actual games, but he did get a chance to showcase his skills in the "fifth quarter," a short scrimmage played after each freshman game. The fifth quarter was mainly for guys who didn't get to play much—if at all—in regulation. It gave them a chance to practice against competition their own age from other schools. For much of Brian's freshman year, fifth quarter was the only time he saw the floor.

But by the time he was a sophomore, Brian had shot up eight inches. A couple of his classmates were moved up to varsity, leaving a void on JV. So Brian got a lot of minutes that year. He even started fairly often. Brian was feeling pretty good about himself, but there was one thing he didn't realize—all of his sophomore buddies on varsity were still ahead of him on the pecking order. So were all the juniors. And when Brian became a junior, it happened. He got cut.

Nowadays, it isn't uncommon to see a junior play JV. In the late '80s, however, that practice wasn't really accepted, especially in the GCL. So Jim Rice, Bacon's varsity head coach at the time, cut Brian Neal. It ended up being a good learning experience for Brian, who never really worked on his game a great deal in the offseason—not because he didn't want to, but because he didn't have time. He played soccer. He had a job. He had schoolwork. He was a busy kid. AAU wasn't nearly as popular then. Heck, a lot of guys didn't even play summer ball. Basketball, like a lot of other sports at the time, was still seen by and large as an in-season endeavor.

But as a junior, Brian decided to play for his CYO team, which ended up being a wise decision. Brian was a passive player. As soon as he got the ball, he would try to get rid of it. Before even seeing what was available for himself, he'd look to see what was available for his teammates. There's a fine line between being unselfish and being unselfish to a fault; Brian was unselfish to a fault. That year, though, he learned to be more aggressive. He learned to look for his own shot. If it wasn't there, he'd create one. He wasn't selfish, but he developed selfish tendencies—in a good way. More than anything, he became confident.

Confidence, especially for Brian, was important. Some players can overwhelm you with raw talent. Some players can overwhelm you with size. Some players can overwhelm you with shooting ability. Well, Brian Neal, even to this day, just looks like an underdog. If anyone embodies the scrappy spirit of Roger Bacon, it's him. He's 5-10, 135. He hasn't grown an inch or gained a pound since his senior year of high school. But there's hunger in his eyes. There's a quiet confidence in his gait. There's no quit in him.

"At Roger Bacon, that's kind of the way it is," Brian said. "That's kind of the way the students are. That's kind of the class of families we get. More middle class, hard working. Guys play hard because that's what they do in all the parts of their lives."

As a player, Brian was heady, he could shoot it a bit and he tried as hard as he could on defense. Beyond that, he didn't have a whole lot to fall back on. But confidence, it turns out, is underrated. When juniors get cut from a basketball team, most take the hint and move on with their lives. Brian wasn't ready to do that. He went out for the team as a senior. At tryouts, Jim Rice made everyone run a mile. Brian finished first. That's when Rice took him aside.

"Look, Brian, you're one of the hardest workers in the gym," he said. "But you're just too small. You're not fast enough. But I'm not going to cut you. If you want to be on this team, you can be on this team. Just understand you're not going to play. You're not going to play a minute. If you're okay coming to practice every day and working as hard as you work and sitting on the bench, then you're more than welcome to be on this team."

Most seniors would have walked away right then and there. Why spend your last year of high school practicing a sport just so you can sit on a bench? Brian Neal, however, wasn't most seniors. He fired right back at Jim Rice, the newfound confidence on full display.

"Well, coach, I'd love to be on the team," Brian said. "And I'm gonna prove you wrong—because I'm gonna play."

It was a bold statement, a bold statement that ended up being accurate. Brian Neal started the last six games of the 1989–90 season.

Bacon advanced to the district finals. It was the program's best season in years.

Brian's life came together pretty soon afterward. He asked a freshman to senior prom. That freshman is now his wife. He graduated from Bacon in 1990. The next year, he returned to his alma mater to coach under Fred Cooper. For eight years, all through high school and college, Brian worked at a mom-and-pop pharmacy. He went to Xavier University and studied business. When Brian graduated, he knew everything there was to know about pharmaceuticals, and his boss made him director of human resources for a bigger pharmacy he owned. It was a good job. It's what Brian went to school for. But after about 18 months, he realized it wasn't for him. All the while, he couldn't help but think of the life his father had at Bacon and how special it was. Brian was drawn to it. So he went back to Xavier, got a master's in education and got hired at Bacon as an assistant athletic director. After Fred was let go, Brian became a varsity assistant for the girls team. It's not that he didn't want to coach boys anymore, and it's not that Bill doubted Brian's ability to do that; it's just that Bill didn't know him. New coaches typically don't retain the staff of a coach they're replacing, and this case was no different.

Brian spent four years with Roger Bacon's girls team, and in that time, he grew exponentially as a coach. In his first year, 1993–94—which was also Bill's first year at Bacon—Brian helped coach the girls team to the Division II state final, where the Lady Spartans lost to undefeated Avon Lake on a heartbreaker at the buzzer.

"It was tied," Brian said, appearing in physical anguish as he recalled the details. "They (Avon Lake) had the ball with 40 seconds left. They held it. We let them hold it. We weren't a pressing team. We were a zone team. We got them to take the shot we wanted, but it was such a bad shot, the rebound went crazy. One of their girls grabbed it and threw it up. It went in as the buzzer went off."

Final score: 41–39. Bacon finished the year 26–2. Avon Lake finished 27–0.

Roger Bacon, however, was comprised almost exclusively of juniors. In 1994–95, a virtually all-senior team got back to the state final—and this time, won, 64–48 over previously unbeaten Elida. Bacon finished the season 28–0.

One of the seniors on that team was Katie Gutzwiller. What made that girls team so successful, she said, was that they all played together for so long. When they were freshmen, no one was moved up to JV or varsity. The coaches wanted to keep that class together to develop team chemistry. After four years of playing together, the girls knew everything about each other on the court, and they were best friends off it. There was no way they weren't winning that state title, especially after coming one shot shy the previous year.

The girls' head coach, Tom Singleton, was fiery and intense. He had coached boys all his life—and it showed. Many coaches who have coached both sexes believe you can't yell at girls the same way you yell at boys. You can't cuss. You can't yell as much. You can't yell as loud. You can't yell about certain things, period. Well, Tom Singleton had no use for that garbage.

"He yelled," Brian said. "Just as much."

On days when Tom got too intense, the girls would look to Brian for support. Brian became the good cop on that coaching staff, which was good preparation for working under Bill. Brian stayed with the girls program through the '96–97 season before switching back to boys. By that time, he had developed a good relationship with Bill. Ironically, when Brian coached the girls, he didn't think Bill was all that tough. There were days when Brian would peek into the gym and catch spurts of the boys' practices. He'd see Bill in action and think, *Man, he sure doesn't work 'em that hard.* It wasn't long into that 1997–98 season before Brian realized his assessment was decidedly inaccurate. Bill worked his players—hard.

But there might have been one he could have worked a little harder.

● ● ● ●

BILL ENTERED HIS FIFTH year at Roger Bacon with serious aspirations to win a state title. Five years earlier, that wouldn't have even been a pipe dream; it would have been flat-out crazy. But in that short amount of time, Bill took a program with the faintest of pulses and turned it into a state title contender. He returned all five starters from an Elite Eight team that had two of the best scorers—seniors Brandon McIntosh and Eugene Land—in the entire state. Brandon and Eugene were studs. Either one could net 20 or more on any given night, and sometimes, oftentimes, they both did. Bill surrounded them with dead-eye shooters to spread the floor and give Brandon and Eugene spot-up weapons in transition. The Spartans might not have been Division I, but they were *the* ticket in town that year, and they were going to be mighty hard to beat—and Brandon and Eugene were big reasons why.

But away from the game, life wasn't always easy for Eugene Land. For him, nothing was guaranteed. Tom Thompson was one of the coaches responsible for making sure Eugene was at practice every day, mainly on weekends and during Christmas vacation—times when Eugene wasn't already on campus for school. On those days, Thompson would sometimes get a phone call from Eugene, who was in need of a ride to practice.

"Of course, Gene," Thompson would say. "I'll be right there."

But Tom remembers other days when he would be on his way to Bacon and see Eugene walking to practice in the snow and cold. Tom would pull over and let Eugene into the car. More often than not, it was apparent to Tom that Eugene hadn't gotten enough sleep, hadn't had enough to eat. Tom always gave Bill updates on Eugene, but he didn't have to. Bill knew. Bill knew how hard Eugene had it.

Bill was notorious for being hard on his players. He knew the harder you pushed kids, the more you could get out of them. Whatever a kid thought his limits were, Bill saw it as his job to push the kid beyond them. Bill tried to not treat Eugene any differently, but there were some days Bill couldn't help it, especially the days when Eugene walked to practice underfed in the dead of a Midwest winter. Bill wouldn't go soft on Eugene, but he wouldn't ride him for three hours, either. He just couldn't.

But maybe he didn't have to.

By the end of the 1997–98 regular season, the Spartans were 18–2, had won the first league title of Bill's tenure—and the program's first league title since 1975—and were ranked No. 1 in the state. Brandon and Eugene had both scored exactly 379 points—an average of 19 points per game—and were named GCL-North Co-Players of the Year. The Spartans outscored their first four playoff opponents by an average of 35.5 points and advanced to the Elite Eight for a second straight season, knowing in their hearts that this time would be different. All that stood between them and Columbus, the site of the Final Four, was a regional-finals rematch with Badin, a team Bacon had beaten twice during the regular season.

Badin's coach, Gerry Weisgerber, entered that regional final with an intriguing pick-your-poison game plan. He could either play man-to-man defense and risk having Brandon and Eugene exploit one-on-one coverage, or he could double- and triple-team Brandon and Eugene and leave the Spartans' sharpshooters wide open from distance.

Most coaches would focus on containing an opponent's top two players. If the supporting cast wins the game, then the supporting cast wins the game. Opposing coaches sleep a little easier when that happens. But getting beaten by the studs? Letting the opposition's two best players have their way with you? That can drive a coach mad, especially since Eugene had a combined 48 points and 25 rebounds in two regular-season wins against Badin.

But what made the Spartans a unique matchup that year is that they didn't have just one great three-point shooter or even two great three-point shooters. They had three. Juniors Brian Lakes and Jared Niesen graduated first and third, respectively, on Bacon's all-time three-point shooting list, with 184 and 103 three-pointers made. Senior Brian Schaefer, who averaged 17 points per game that season, graduated second with 144. They are the only players in Bacon's history who made more than 100 threes in their career—and they all played on the same team.

Weisgerber knew that if he gave Lakes, Schaefer and Niesen open looks and allowed them to get in rhythm, Badin was going to lose. Lakes once hit 11 threes in a game. *Eleven* threes. Niesen once hit eight. Schaefer once hit six. Any one of them—or all of them—had the potential to erupt. So Weisgerber decided he wouldn't let them. He decided to play man-to-man defense and see what his bigs, Brian Alexander and Matt Broermann, could do against Brandon and Eugene.

Weisgerber's strategy proved effective. Brandon and Eugene, who averaged close to 40 points per game combined during the regular season, were held to 24, with Eugene scoring 14. Brian Schaefer scored a team-high 20, and Jared Niesen hit a three-pointer with 4.1 seconds left to send the game into overtime, but it wasn't enough. Badin won 59–53.

After the game, Bill hugged Gerry Weisgerber and told him he deserved to be in Columbus.

Eugene, who was named Ohio's Division II Player of the Year, graduated as Bacon's all-time leading scorer with 1,494 points—202 points more than Brandon, who graduated second with 1,292. Brandon and Eugene were the two most prolific scorers to play for Bacon since Dan Doellman, who played varsity from 1973–75, and they just happened to graduate in the same year. And then you pair them with the three most dead-eye perimeter shooters in school history? If ever stars align for a state title run, that was the year. Bacon, without question, had the talent to do it. But in the regional finals against Badin, Brandon and Eugene couldn't carry the team to victory.

As time went on, and as Bill thought more about that season and what could have been, he couldn't help but think he let that team down. He couldn't help but think he let Eugene down.

"Eugene dealt with so many hardships," Tom Thompson said. "But Bill always thought, 'I didn't do that kid a service. If I had pushed Eugene harder, we would have won that regional final game, and Eugene would have wanted that.'"

At the time, Bill thought he was doing what was best for Eugene—and maybe he did do what was best for him. But he always wondered about Eugene and how things might have turned out if he had pushed him—truly pushed him—every day. Would that team have won state? Bill always looked back at that season and asked *What if?* Some coaches might have said, "Oh well, it's just high school basketball," and moved on. Bill couldn't do that.

"Basketball wasn't a game to him," Thompson said. "It was something he took personally."

Bill's handling of Eugene was perhaps his biggest coaching regret. But Bill was still just five years into his tenure. He was 33. He was young. He was still learning. Brandon and Eugene were the first truly great players he had coached. Bill learned what worked. He learned what didn't work. The loss to Badin was a career-changer for Bill, who, at Brian Neal's urging, altered his style of play thereafter.

"We couldn't grind games out with that ('97–98) team; we just couldn't," Brian Neal said. "We were a pressing team, and we ran into a team (Badin) we couldn't press."

The talent level in every state varies by season, but Bill realized if he couldn't win a state title using a fast-paced style with Brandon and Eugene, he wasn't going to win a state title using a fast-paced style with anybody. He knew he had to change philosophies. He knew he had to slow down the tempo and become a team that could win in the halfcourt. Some teams simply won't allow themselves to be run-and-gunned, but scoring in the halfcourt is conducive to any setting. What it lacks in style, it more than makes up for in substance.

But it wasn't just the style of play Bill knew he had to change; it was the way he handled players, especially stars. Bill had good intentions with Eugene, but he was determined to not make the same mistakes with his next truly great player. He was determined to push the next truly great one as hard as he could, no matter what. He was determined to never have to ask *What if?* again.

Bill didn't have to wait long for that next chance.

The next truly great player fell into his hands the very next season.

CHAPTER TWO

THE
GOLDEN BOY

Nestled in the heart of St. Bernard—a blue-collar community that hugs Vine Street, which divides the east and west sides of Cincinnati—there's a family, the Hausfelds. There's a certain aura to this tiny community and the large family that so richly populates it. The city of St. Bernard—population less than 5,000—is a throwback jersey, a fashion statement that turns heads and yet elicits no judgment. In St. Bernard, people look out for each other. They know each other by their first names. They know everybody and everybody's business, which, depending on the business, can be a good thing or a bad thing. But that's the give and take of a small town, a place where nobody locks their doors. People who are born there tend to stay there. They grow up there, they get married there, they raise a family there, they die there—all in a span of less than two square miles.

"You could never find a place to live in St. Bernard unless you had a connection," Mary Beth Hausfeld said. "It's like its own little private German community."

Within this tiny cluster of an enclave are the Hausfelds—the Kennedys of St. Bernard. The Hausfelds are a family of public service. Policemen, firemen. Ron Hausfeld, a Roger Bacon grad, is a cop in St. Bernard. Tall, quiet, buzz cut. His brother, Steve, is chief of police. Ron's father, Jack, was once mayor of St. Bernard, this after spending many years laying brick. Ron's wife, Mary Beth, attended Our Lady of Angels and works in the front office at Roger Bacon. Her father was a milkman in St. Bernard. He got up early every morning, drove his milk truck around town and dropped off little jugs of milk for everyone.

Yes, St. Bernard had a milkman.

Ron and Mary Beth gave birth to four children—two boys, two girls. One of those boys was Josh Hausfeld. Who was Josh Hausfeld?

Josh Hausfeld was the Golden Boy. He was the kid everyone knew and the kid everyone wanted to be. Anything you were good at, Josh was better. Anything you always won at, Josh would beat you. That's the way it seemed, at least.

St. Bernard has a community pool. Right next to it is the Pavilion, a collection of a half dozen or so basketball courts. These courts were a staple of Josh Hausfeld's childhood. Every day during the summer, if the weather cooperated—and even if it didn't—children in St. Bernard would go to the pool and play pickup basketball at the Pavilion. Each court would be full. Anybody who was anybody was there, and Josh always was.

And he was always the best player.

When Josh was a kid, Ron built him a basketball court in the backyard. For Josh, this meant one thing: he could practice as much as wanted, whenever he wanted. Day or night, spring or fall, snow or shine, he could go out back and shoot hoops. Josh played other sports—football, baseball—but basketball was his true love. Giving him his own hoop in the backyard was like giving Forrest Gump a ping pong table and a lifetime supply of Dr. Pepper.

Josh had all he needed.

He and Emily Holt—his cousin and best friend—would play ball together for hours. Emily was a phenomenal athlete. She'd play baseball with the boys and hold her own, but it was on the basketball court where she shined. So did Josh. They'd watch Pistol Pete Maravich videos, study his moves and do drills. They'd dream up late-game scenarios, pretend it was the final shot and play out the sequence. It was in Josh's backyard where they planned their futures: They would both go to Roger Bacon; Emily, who was two years older than Josh, would win state for the girls team, and he would win state for the boys; they would both play college ball at the University of North Carolina; and after graduation, Emily would play in the WNBA and become the next Rebecca Lobo, while Josh would go to the NBA and become the next Michael Jordan.

They had it all figured out.

"When we were happiest," Josh said, "we were either playing basketball or talking about basketball."

Like many children in St. Bernard, Josh went to grade school at St. Clement, located just down the street from Roger Bacon. Josh was a fabled grade school player. Whatever the school record, there's a good chance Josh Hausfeld holds it, which, given his upbringing, shouldn't come as a surprise.

Sports were encouraged in the Hausfeld household. Ron was a standout athlete in his day. Good football player. Played noseguard at Ohio University. Ron loved sports, but even more than that, he loved what they instilled in a young man—teamwork, discipline, a strong work ethic. So Ron set about instilling those qualities in his children, all of whom at least dabbled in athletics. Neither he nor Mary Beth pressured their children to play sports, but when they decided to play, Ron and Mary Beth attended every game. Win or lose, they displayed in the stands a quiet grace that Josh picked up on. But most of what they taught him, they taught away from the basketball court, away from the football field, away from the baseball diamond.

Ron and Mary Beth were avid campers. They would take their children for weekend camping trips, but when it was time to go home—when the tent was taken down and they had loaded all their belongings back into the car—they wouldn't leave right away. Ron would notice the stray trash and unclaimed belongings other campers would leave behind, so he'd gather his family together.

"We're gonna leave this place looking better than it looked before we got here," Ron would say.

At first, Josh thought that sounded unreasonable—impossible, even. But then he watched as his father bent over, got on his hands and knees and set about picking up garbage until the campsite and the surrounding area were immaculate. That always stuck with Josh. It was one of the unspoken lessons of his childhood.

Always go the extra mile.

Do the right thing—even when no one's watching.

Do good things, and good things will happen to you.

Josh thought it was so cool that his dad was a cop. He saw how much his father loved helping people and protecting them. Even when he was off duty, Ron would help neighbors with home projects. He'd cut grass, trim bushes. He never wanted anything in return, either.

He assigned chores to his children. If they did them—and did them well—they were rewarded. If they didn't do them, well, they had best get to it.

That's how Josh was raised.

"I learned so much from my dad—so many lessons," Josh said. "When it came to playing sports, I felt like I was at an advantage."

It showed. Growing up, Josh was always the best player on his team in every sport, especially in basketball.

"I've never seen or coached any other kid who cared as much as he did in grade school," said Bobby Holt, who coached Josh at St. Clement. "Even back then, everybody knew that he was gonna be special. He was always confident. He knew nobody could guard him. But at the same time, he was a very unselfish player. I had to force him to shoot more and get to the basket more."

When Josh wasn't playing basketball, he was watching Roger Bacon play it. Bobby and his wife, Amy, would take Josh—along with friends Jeff Holt and Megan Bien—to Bacon's games, which were almost always on Tuesdays and Fridays. They went to virtually every game, home or away, and called themselves the Tue-Fri Club. When Josh was in seventh and eighth grade, he watched as Brandon McIntosh and Eugene Land led Bacon to back-to-back appearances in the regional finals. Josh was there in March 1998 when Bacon lost to Badin in overtime. He remembered how hurt everyone was—the players, the fans, the entire community.

"After that loss," Bobby recalled, "I turned to Josh and said, 'You're gonna be a part of the next group that has a chance to play in the regional finals and go to state. You've got to do whatever you can to not let your team lose.'"

Josh dreamed of how wonderful it would be to one day deliver a state championship to Roger Bacon, to the people of St. Bernard.

When Josh was in junior high, he'd often play against a team called St. Bart's, which had some pretty good players—Nate Wyrick, Beckham Wyrick, Matt Reed and Tim McCoy, among others. St. Bart's and St. Clement would get after it. They'd battle each other. Games would get intense. But all the while, Josh realized these four rivals were going to Bacon and would one day be his teammates, which made him happy—mainly because he knew they'd be good.

So did Bill.

Indeed, Bill knew exactly what he was getting with Josh Hausfeld—so much so, in fact, that he would attend many of Josh's games in eighth grade. He'd come and study the player who would soon be his. Some days, Josh didn't know how to handle that. Bill was the head coach of a team Josh idolized—the head coach of the top-ranked team in the state—and here he was at St. Clement watching some eighth-grade kid play basketball.

Here he was watching Josh Hausfeld.

"I remember on several occasions when he was there," Josh recalled. "I don't think I ever knew before the game that he would be there, but St. Clement is such a small gym where, if someone is there, you know. I remember he would stand kind of by the door, and when he caught my eye looking at him, I thought, 'Oh, great. I really gotta show him what I can do now.' It was exciting being an eighth-grade player and having a high school coach there, especially Coach Brewer, knowing his reputation and how good Bacon was. It definitely gave me some added pressure to perform. Even though I knew I was going to Bacon, I wanted him to want me on his team."

If Bill's attendance at those grade school games seemed shady, it wasn't. Bill wasn't recruiting by any means. Far from it. It didn't matter who the coach was at Bacon; Josh was going there regardless. Oh, sure, Josh heard the outside whispers. *Hey, you should go to Moeller*, the voices said. *You should check out St. Xavier.* But it was never in doubt. If you're a Hausfeld, going to Bacon is just what you do.

Bill was so impressed with Josh that he let him practice with Bacon's varsity team the summer before his freshman year in 1998. Josh was stunned. Playing varsity as a freshman had been a goal of his since fifth grade. Now, here he was, a kid barely out of grade school—hadn't attended a single day of high school yet—and he was practicing with 16- and 17-year-olds, chiseled varsity veterans.

Josh wasn't intimidated that summer. If anything, he played with a chip on his shoulder. It was around this time that he was cut from his club team—for political reasons, as Mary Beth recalled. Josh had never been cut from anything in his life. He had enjoyed nothing but success in sports, but now, for the first time in his life, he felt a sense of inadequacy. He felt a sadness he had never known.

"It was my 'Michael Jordan moment,'" Josh said, referring to Jordan getting cut from varsity as a sophomore. "A few days after being cut, I made a promise to myself that I never wanted to feel this way again."

Josh retreated to his backyard and immersed himself in the game even more. He worked harder than he ever had. It was a retreat, a journey, a pilgrimage—psychological more than physical. He wanted to prove he belonged on that club team. He wanted to prove his doubters wrong. As Mary Beth recalls, that same club team approached Josh the following year and asked if he wanted to play for them. Ron and Mary Beth said it was entirely up to Josh to decide what he wanted to do.

Josh respectfully declined.

Anyone who saw Josh play, even as a just-graduated-eight-grader, knew that he would be great. It was reminiscent of Brandon McIntosh, albeit with one important distinction. When Brandon was a freshman in 1994, Mitch Perdrix and the rest of the varsity team welcomed him with open arms, mainly because they weren't that talented, and they knew Brandon, even at 14, could help them. But with Josh, a handful of guys on that 1998–99 team weren't quite as accepting—not at first, anyway. They didn't think they needed him. These were upperclassmen who had been on teams that had advanced to back-to-back regional finals. It was their time to shine now, and they didn't want to share the spotlight with a freshman. They didn't even like Bill watching Josh's games the previous season at St. Clement. They didn't understand why an eighth-grader who hadn't played a minute of high school basketball was getting so much attention.

It didn't help matters that Josh was a starting guard midway through that '98–99 season. The jealousy was so thick that a few of the upperclassmen, as a protest, wouldn't pass to Josh, even if he was wide open. Eventually, after some stern lectures from Bill—not to mention a few parents—the freeze-out ended.

But that first year was a struggle. Josh had always been the best player on the court; now he was going against guys who were bigger, faster, stronger and quicker. He watched as his friends played freshman and junior varsity basketball; he saw the success they had; he saw them scoring and playing with their classmates and forging friendships.

Josh, meanwhile, was on his own—and that was a lonely place to be. Even though he grew up as a standout athlete, Josh was always a quiet kid, a sensitive kid. He wasn't cocky—"If anything, Josh could have used a little cockiness that year," Brian Neal said—he wasn't arrogant, and he wasn't outspoken. Any hardships Josh dealt with, he dealt with in silence.

There were times that year when Josh, for the first time in his life, considered giving up the game. It just got to be that hard.

Josh never complained to Mary Beth—and he sure as hell never complained to Bill—but she could see how unhappy her son was. Mothers can always tell.

"I think it was a year he probably couldn't wait to get over," she said.

Bill handled Josh with kid gloves that year, mainly because he knew how hard Josh struggled to fit in and gain acceptance. The Spartans struggled as a team, too. They went 10-10, including 5-9 in the GCL. Graduating Brandon and Eugene was just too much to overcome.

It wasn't all bad, though. Josh grew up fast and wound up earning respect from his teammates, who eventually realized he wasn't there merely to take their spot; he was there to make the team better. More important, Josh discovered what it meant to play varsity basketball in the GCL, and he knew that next year he would be counted on to lead Roger Bacon.

And he did.

* * * *

IF YOU REALLY THINK about it, it's absurd. Unimaginable, even. You look at the stat sheet, you see the proof—and still the question needs to be asked.

Did a sophomore really do that?

The 1999–2000 season at Roger Bacon was by and large forgettable. The last remnants of the Brandon-and-Eugene era were gone. The Spartans, in all-out rebuilding mode, finished the regular season 8–12. It was their first losing season in five years.

But none of that mattered. Why? Because that's the year it happened. It happened against one of Bacon's fiercest rivals, Chaminade-Julienne, a co-ed school an hour away in Dayton. It happened on the road. It happened in CJ's gym.

"Kind of a long drive, kind of a small gym, the locker rooms are really far away from the court," Josh said of CJ. "It was by no means our favorite place to play."

By the end of the game, CJ's players didn't want to play there, either.

Because on that night, Josh had everything working. He was getting to the bucket, his jumper was on, his threes were deadly. Free throws, fallaways, leaners—Josh showcased the full repertoire.

"I remember being real aggressive," Josh said. "Everything was hitting."

Everything—including a three-pointer to send the game into overtime, where Roger Bacon prevailed.

When the smoke cleared and the dust settled, when the clock authored zeroes and the individual onslaught had ended, when Mike Cregan crossed the final *t* and dotted the final *i* in his scorebook, there stood but one mesmerizing number next to the name of a savvy sophomore from St. Bernard.

42.

Forty-two...

It was spellbinding. Scoring 42 in the GCL is rare. In fact, Josh became the first Spartan to break 40 in a quarter of a century; the last to do so was Dan Doellman, who accomplished that feat in the mid-1970s. Josh was already in rarefied air. The fact that he did it as a sophomore? That's unheard of.

"I just tried to will our team to victory," Josh said in his easygoing twang. "And on that night, it took scoring a lot of points to do it."

"...on that night..."

That's the problem. It wasn't just that night. It was every night. That's what Josh had to do that year for the Spartans to be successful. It'd be insulting to his teammates to call Bacon a one-man show, but simply put, if Josh wasn't scoring 20, Bacon wasn't winning. Josh led the GCL-North in scoring with 18.2 points per game that year. Like dropping 42, that's just something you don't see from a sophomore.

It became increasingly obvious to everyone, including Bill, just how good Josh was. Shades of Eugene, no question. And Bill knew what he had to do. He had to get the most out of Josh. He had to squeeze every drop, sap every ounce. The only way to do that was to do what he didn't do with Eugene—hound him, every minute, every practice, every day.

So that's what Bill did. The kid gloves came off, and he didn't hold back. Nothing was off-limits. Nothing Josh did was ever good enough.

"There were film sessions where he would just rip me," Josh said. "That game I had 42, he ripped my defense and said my guy had 52."

Bobby Holt witnessed the punishment firsthand. After Josh graduated from St. Clement, Bill asked Bobby to join his staff and coach Josh and some of the players from St. Bart's in AAU during the summer of 1998. Bill wanted all those guys to get some experience playing together, perhaps because he knew Josh would be playing varsity as a freshman. Bobby loved being on Bill's staff. At the same time, however, the film sessions weren't pretty.

"Every film session, Bill was all over Josh," Bobby said. "It didn't even matter if Josh made a great play. I could tell Bill was pushing him because he knew what Josh was capable of and wanted to get that out of him. But he was hard on him."

And it wasn't just Josh's defense. It was his rebounding. It was his turnovers. After seemingly every miscue, in practice and in games, Bill would call Josh out. Eventually, Bill dubbed him "Turnover Hausfeld" and said that one day a banner would hang in Roger Bacon's gym that read, "Most turnovers in a career: Josh Hausfeld."

If Bill was joking, he certainly wasn't laughing.

"There were times in practice, Bill would just go crazy on Josh," Tom Thompson said. "Probably beat him down worse than anything you can come up with."

For Bill, being hard on Josh wasn't just about making him a better basketball player; it was about making sure his head didn't get too big—and playing football for Bacon, which Josh did, could easily have done that.

It's possible that Josh was better at football than basketball. Great quarterback. Good vision, accurate. And when Josh didn't throw, he'd take off running, eluding tacklers like ball-carriers in those old black-and-white highlight reels. Because of his quickness and elusiveness—not to mention his height (he was 6-3)—Josh played wide receiver a lot, too.

Even as a sophomore, he was the best athlete in school.

Just as Bill knew what he had with Josh on the hardwood, the football coaches knew what they had with him on the gridiron. Their response, however, was a little different. Bill was quick to give Josh a kick in the ass—even if he didn't deserve it. But the football coaches, well, they weren't the kicking bunch—not with Josh, anyway. They wouldn't yell at him. They wouldn't push him. They were so paranoid he might quit that they let him get away with anything he wanted.

As one story goes, a football coach, having mistaken Josh for another receiver, yelled for him to run hard and quit slacking. When Josh turned around, the coach, realizing who it was, bit his lip.

Josh was going to play football no matter what—he loved the game too much not to—but the coaches didn't want to risk it. To Josh's credit, he didn't take advantage of the situation as much as he could have, but it was still something he wasn't entirely comfortable with.

"I definitely got away with more things playing football than I ever would have with basketball," he said. "It was like night and day. With football, I couldn't do any wrong. I didn't try to take advantage of it. I tried to go out there and give my best. But if I'm being honest with myself, there was never a time in football when someone was just gonna be in my face cussing me out or screaming or hollering. That just wasn't gonna happen in football. In basketball, it happened every day."

Although the preferential treatment annoyed Josh a little bit, it annoyed his teammates even more—and dissension among the ranks was not something Bill was going to allow.

"One time at practice, Josh went up for a layup and somebody fouled him," Monty St. Clair said. "And Coach Neal said, 'Don't take it up like a girl!' And Josh yelled, 'I ain't taking it up like a fucking girl!'"

Monty was stunned. Josh rarely talked back—in fact, Monty remembers this story because that was one of the few times Josh ever did—but Bill witnessed the exchange and quickly administered one of his favorite punishments. He ordered Josh to grab a folding chair, hold it above his head and start running.

"And don't stop until I say so!" Bill ordered.

Players hated that punishment. It wasn't long before their arms and shoulders were screaming in pain.

"Brewer let Josh go forever," Monty said. "Like an hour."

The football coaches never would've treated Josh like that. They never would've made him run. If he were upset or frustrated about something, they would've let him vent and do what he needed to do. Bill wouldn't stand for that. He wouldn't stand for backtalk or disrespect or giving anything less than your best. That's just not how he operated.

As his best player began running—chair in hands, hands above head—Bill slung one last arrow into him, uttering four words that reminded everyone in the gym of something that was plain-as-day obvious:

"This ain't football, Josh."

Instances like these weren't necessarily annual early season rituals, but whenever Josh needed to be reminded what sport he was playing, Bill was there to lend a hand.

"He knew," Josh said. "Brewer knew the way it was. At the time, I was mad. I don't know if I was having a bad day or what. I wasn't really one to talk back and show my emotions, but I snapped at Coach Neal. But looking back, Brewer was right. He demanded your best, and if you didn't give it your all every day at practice, he had a way of letting you know you weren't giving your best."

Bill was going to ride Josh either way—and oh, did he ever. He rode Josh relentlessly. He rode him harder than a stationary biker trying to pedal from Boston to Bismarck.

But he also rewarded him. Beginning when Josh was a freshman, Bill would take him to Columbus every March for the state tournament. Some of the other coaches went, too, but there was only one player.

Josh Hausfeld.

It was a good experience for Josh. By staying with Bill and the coaches for an extended weekend, he saw a different side of them. They were still coaches, they were still role models, they were still authority figures; but they seemed more human.

Maybe Bill wanted to show that side to Josh. Maybe he wanted to be nice to his young gun. Or maybe—and perhaps more likely—he wanted to motivate him. Maybe he wanted Josh to see the spectacle of the state tournament, to show him the destination that potentially lay ahead.

"I think it was all part of his plan," Josh said. "The first time I went, I remember getting back and telling the guys, 'It's amazing. We're gonna get there. We're gonna get there.' After that first time, in my mind, it was, 'We're gonna get there next year.' And when that didn't happen, I decided I was gonna go there every year as a fan until we got there as a team."

Bacon, which finished the regular season 8–12, didn't make it to state when Josh was a sophomore. The Spartans didn't have a chance. Josh's junior year, however, was a little different.

In 2000–01, Roger Bacon took a trip to Savannah, Georgia, for a holiday tournament. On that trip, the Spartans played a team from South Carolina—Orangeburg-Wilkinson, one of the most athletic squads Brian Neal had ever seen. With Bacon struggling to score against an active 2–3 zone, Bill called a backdoor lob for Josh, who went up and got it and slammed it home. Just dunked all over his defender. The gym erupted. On Bacon's very next trip down the floor, Bill called the exact same play. Orangeburg-Wilkinson knew it was coming. Only it didn't matter. Josh went up and stuffed it home again.

That's the kind of player Josh Hausfeld was. That's the unflappable, above-the-rim talent he possessed. Unfortunately, Josh's junior year was around the time his ankles started bothering him. He'd twist them, turn them, sprain them. The game against Orangeburg-Wilkinson was actually his first game back after missing time for that very reason—a sprained ankle.

"My legs were fresh," Josh said. "I felt good."

But it didn't last. Josh tweaked his ankles time and again. His explosiveness, once limitless, seemed limited. He still averaged double figures—in fact, he averaged 14.7 points and was named GCL-North Player of the Year—and he still had countless highlight reel-caliber plays, including a three at the buzzer to beat league rival McNicholas in January 2001.

But the ankles were a constant worry.

That March, in the Division II district finals against Trotwood-Madison, Josh sprained his right ankle in the third quarter. He sat for the rest of the game with his leg propped on a chair and ice on his ankle. If this were Josh's sophomore year, Bacon might've lost. No, they *would've* lost. But that year, Josh's junior year, the Spartans had improved. They were more balanced. After an 0–3 start, Bacon finished the regular season 13–7 and was named city champion by the *Cincinnati Post*. The Spartans had good players, young players, players who were still getting better—Beckham Wyrick at the four, Monty St. Clair at the five, Frank Phillips at the three and Dave Johnson at the point.

And none were seniors.

Even without Josh, an all-state selection that year, Bacon beat Trotwood-Madison 77–64 and then knocked off Columbus Mifflin 63–45 in the regional semifinals. Frank scored a game-high 14. Beckham and Monty combined for 15. Dave hit three three-pointers. It was a team effort.

Bacon was back in the regional finals for the third time in five years and for the first time since Brandon and Eugene were seniors. But facing league rival Alter for the third time that season, the Spartans lost 58–54. Josh, still favoring his sprained ankle, didn't start. He gutted his way through 21 minutes and scored a team-high 15 points, but it wasn't enough. Bacon made just one three, missed eight of its first 15 free throws and trailed the entire game, falling four quarters short of Columbus once more.

Bacon, which lost all three of its games to Alter by four points that year, finished the season 18–8. Alter, meanwhile, went on to win the state title—its second in three years—blowing out the competition in the state semis and state final by a combined 32 points. Josh, as had become the annual custom, was on hand to see it.

"I wouldn't say I was rooting for them," Josh said of Alter. "I was rooting for the conference because I believe in the GCL; it's the best conference in the state. But they were such a big rival. Maybe it was jealousy, but I kept thinking, 'That should be us.'"

For the Spartans, knowing how close they came to advancing to—and probably winning—a state championship only made their loss in the regional finals hurt that much more. After that game, however, Alter coach Joe Petrocelli was impressed by what he saw from a young, scrappy—and most importantly, talented—Bacon squad.

"It's my personal feeling," Petrocelli told the *Northwest Press*, a community paper in Cincinnati, "that they'll be back here next year."

WHILE ALTER WAS BUSY winning a state championship, and as coaches throughout Ohio settled into the offseason, Bill was already thinking about next year. It was rumored that a team up north, Akron St. Vincent–St. Mary, might be jumping from Division III to Division II due to a surge in enrollment. Perhaps a reason for that surge was SVSM's suddenly must-see basketball team, which had just won its second consecutive state title.

The Irish, coached by Keith Dambrot, went 53-1 in that two-year span, their only loss coming by a point to perennial power Oak Hill Academy, a program repeatedly in the hunt for the national championship.

Even more impressive was the fact that SVSM was so young; the Irish started three sophomores in the 2001 state final—Sian Cotton, Dru Joyce and a supremely talented prodigy named LeBron James, who scored 25 points in a 63-53 win over Casstown Miami East. In fact, LeBron also scored 25 points in the state final as a freshman. In two years, he had twice been named first-team all-state and state tournament MVP. In two state finals, he shot a combined 21-of-26 from the floor. *Athlon* had rated him as the top sophomore in America; *The Sporting News* ranked him second. Barely old enough to drive, LeBron was already well-known throughout Ohio and was being described with those two magical words: *can't miss*.

SVSM's potential division switch meant one thing to Bill: if the Spartans were to win a state championship the following season—and they were set to return all five starters from an Elite Eight squad—there was a good chance they'd have to beat LeBron James and Akron St. Vincent–St. Mary in the state final. If that would be the case, Bill wanted to see SVSM before March. He wanted to see LeBron James. Most important, he wanted to see how his team stacked up.

One May afternoon, Bill sat with Brian Neal in the coaches' office waiting for the Ohio High School Athletic Association to release its enrollment numbers for the following year. When the numbers came out, Roger Bacon and SVSM were almost identical, and Bill and Brian were extremely confident SVSM would jump to Division II. With Bacon needing one more game to complete its 2001–02 schedule, Bill immediately called Keith Dambrot.

He got him on the first try.

"Hey, we wanna play you guys," Bill said. "Do you have a game left?"

"We don't have a game left," Brian recalls Dambrot saying, "but we're playing in this event in December, and we don't have an opponent yet. Here's the info for the event coordinator. Call him. We'd love to play."

The event was called the Tramonte Prep Classic. It was scheduled for December 22, 2001, at Kent State University. Bill called the event coordinator.

He got him on the first try.

"Yeah, we'd like to play," Bill told the coordinator. "St. Vincent needs an opponent."

Done. Booked. It was that easy. In the span of about 15 minutes, Bill called Keith Dambrot and the event coordinator, got both on the first try, and filled the last remaining vacancy on both SVSM's schedule and his own.

It was perfect.

It was May 2001, and six months before the first ball was tipped, Bill had everything he would need for that next season.

"You don't know it at the time," Brian Neal said, "but looking back, that was probably the smartest thing Bill ever did."

CHAPTER THREE

THE SPECTACLE

When the time came for Roger Bacon to see firsthand the spectacle of LeBron James and Akron St. Vincent–St. Mary, Peggy Brewer couldn't help but wonder:

Is this kid really *that* good?

It's hard to fault Peggy for wondering such a thing. As the wife of a coach, she knows a lot of players get a lot of hype, and many of them—maybe almost all of them—get too much of it. But hype is one thing; the hoopla surrounding LeBron was historic—and, it could be argued, justified. On December 21, 2001, the *Cincinnati Post* ran a game preview of the Bacon/SVSM matchup with the headline "Teen superstar: The Next Jordan?" For many, the headline probably seemed preposterous.

The next Jordan? Sacrilege. Blasphemy. Excrement.

But as you read the story, there's little wonder how LeBron—who at the time was around 6-7, 215 pounds—became the first sophomore to ever win Ohio's Mr. Basketball award. In two-plus seasons, SVSM had gone 57–1. The Irish, ranked No. 4 in the country by *USA Today*, were 4–0 on the season with three wins coming against nationally ranked opponents, including a 90–69 drubbing of Louisville Male in which LeBron had 37 points, eight assists, five steals and five rebounds.

The statistical trajectory of James' career was downright scary—18 points and 6.2 rebounds as a freshman, 25 points and 6.7 rebounds as a sophomore, and now, four games into his junior year, he was at 32.3 and 9.4. Already, not even halfway through his junior season, speculation swirled that he would forgo his senior year at SVSM and declare for the NBA Draft.

And then there was the photo accompanying the story. It was of LeBron, of course, appearing as so many photographers had captured him—dangling from the rim with both hands and letting the breakaway dunk linger, as if contemplating a pull-up for good measure.

But Bill didn't need the story or the photo to address Peggy's question.

"Is this kid really *that* good?" Peggy asked.

"Yes," Bill said. "He's *that* good . . ."

Bill didn't stop there.

". . . but we're the better team."

Bill was confident—and it wasn't just because he'd be going against a first-year coach. Keith Dambrot, who helped Bill schedule that regular-season game, didn't stick around to coach it. He left SVSM after three seasons—during which he went 69–10 and won two state titles—to become an assistant coach at the University of Akron. Several Irish players were reportedly upset at Dambrot's departure, but they couldn't have asked for a better replacement. SVSM's new coach was Dru Joyce III. Aside from serving as an assistant each of the previous two years, Joyce had coached several members of the team, including his son with the same namesake, in AAU. So even though he was a first-year coach, Joyce already knew the team well and had great rapport with his players.

As confident as Bill was, he was also cautious. He knew playing this game could help his team—that's why he had scheduled it seven months earlier—but he also knew it could be dangerous.

"My whole theory was, you're on their home court, so you're not going to win the game," Peggy said. "But keep it close so you can prove to these guys that you can play with them. If it's a massive blowout, there's no way of coming back from that psychologically."

Technically, the Irish weren't playing on their home court, but the game, the nightcap of the Tramonte Prep Classic, was played on a neutral court in name only. When the Spartans took the floor for warmups at Kent State's Memorial Athletic and Convocation Center, the crowd was overwhelmingly pro-SVSM. A devoted contingent of Bacon supporters—mainly the families of players—made the four-hour trek to Kent State and settled into their seats. For Bacon's players, the familiar faces were nice to see, but it still felt like Rocky versus Drago in Russia. Even fans from the earlier games—Walsh Jesuit versus Stow and Detroit Country Day versus Hudson—stuck around to see the fourth-ranked team in the country. They stuck around to see LeBron.

Most of Bacon's players, at least initially, were out of their element.

"I just remember being overwhelmed by the hype of LeBron—what he's done, what he can do, how he's going to the NBA," said Frank Phillips, who started for Bacon at small forward that year. "Before that game, I didn't really know too much about him. But when we got there, all the hype came true."

Phillips, a 6-3 senior, wasn't the only one. Jon Newton—a 6-3, 250-pound two-way lineman on the gridiron—never felt intimidated by anything, but even he was taken aback by LeBron.

"Here he comes to the middle of the floor," said Newton, a junior that year, "and you feel like you're a foot tall."

Said Leonard Bush, also a junior on that team, "We knew he was a good player, but just how big he was, how fast he was—I had never seen anything like it."

The only Bacon players completely immune to the hype were juniors Dave Johnson and Monty St. Clair, both of whom had seen LeBron or played against him numerous times on the AAU circuit.

"The first time I realized LeBron was going to become who he became, we were playing at nationals," Monty said. "The buzz was blowing up that summer going into freshman year. But Dave and I had been playing against all these guys—LeBron, Dru Joyce, Sian Cotton—since fourth or fifth grade."

Dave echoed that sentiment.

"LeBron wasn't LeBron until ninth grade," he said. "Me and Monty knew who he was growing up. We didn't necessarily play him every summer, but we knew who he was."

Even if this had been Monty's first time seeing LeBron, he insists he wouldn't have been awestruck. Monty is the kind of guy who walks past a celebrity and doesn't do a double-take. But what about the rest of the Spartans?

Josh Hausfeld, who had watched LeBron at the state tournament but had never played against him, wasn't intimidated—true Golden Boys never are—but he remembers LeBron signing autographs and posing for pictures before the game, even with the referees.

"I remember thinking, 'What in the world is going on?'" Josh said.

And then came warmups.

"I was watching him at halfcourt and thinking, 'Wow, he's the real deal,'" Tim McCoy said. "He was throwing balls off the backboard, doing windmills—just not touching the rim. It was ridiculous. He had everyone's (attention), all eyes on him—even our team."

Even when the Spartans dribbled in for a layup or tried to focus on a jumpshot, they could hear the *oohs* and *ahhs* of the crowd reacting to what LeBron was doing.

The awe, of course, was not reciprocated by SVSM. And why would it be? The Irish were getting national attention. Their schedule was loaded with powerhouses—Oak Hill Academy, St. Louis Vashon, Detroit Redford. Frankly, playing close to home against a little Catholic school from Cincinnati probably felt like a night off.

In fact, when each starting five met at midcourt for the opening tip, LeBron made it clear he didn't hold Monty—or Roger Bacon in general—in high regard.

And in less than a second, awe turned into anger.

• • • •

JOHN MONTGOMERY ST. CLAIR was in kindergarten or first grade—he can't remember which—when it happened. There were four or five other boys in his class who all shared the same first name—his first name, Johnny. To avoid confusion, one of the boys told his teachers and classmates to call him by his middle name, Montgomery, but that was far too formal for a 5-year-old. "Montgomery" quickly became "Monty."

The name has stuck ever since.

Funny how big men tend to go by one name. Shaq. Kareem. Wilt. For a select few, one name will suffice. For almost everyone else, no dice. Tim McCoy isn't Tim; he's Tim McCoy. Matt Reed isn't Matt; he's Matt Reed. But Monty? He's just Monty. If you say his first name in a conversation, everyone knows who you're talking about. It's the same deal with Beckham Wyrick, who was also a big man.

But it wasn't just his name that made Monty recognizable. Some people, maybe most people, blend in with the crowd. They walk through the hallway or down the street just like everyone else, with no distinguishing physical characteristic. Monty wasn't like that. Monty was 6-8.

"He's so tall," Beckham said. "But he was afraid of being that tall. He always kind of walked with his head down."

Monty was shy and quiet, as if silence would make him inconspicuous. But Monty couldn't escape it. He was tall, and everyone knew him for that and because of that. That was his blessing. That was his curse.

It's not like Monty had a huge growth spurt in high school, either. He was always tall, so basketball was always what he did. He grew up playing with Dave Johnson. Monty and Dave were best friends and had known each other almost their whole lives. They went to kindergarten together, they went to grade school together, they played AAU together; including their time at Bacon, they played on the same basketball team for more than a decade. They knew everything about each other, and they were both quiet, laid-back guys. They didn't take much seriously, but they took the right things seriously. School. Basketball. They were easy to be around.

Monty and Dave may have had similar personalities, but there was one glaring physical distinction—height. Monty was almost a foot taller than Dave. It may have seemed an amusing pairing, but no one could argue its effectiveness. For opposing coaches, especially, it was a nightmare of a two-man game. Monty and Dave were both smart. They were both skilled. One was big, one was small. One was a center, one was a point guard. Monty could score on anyone. Dave never turned the ball over. They won multiple AAU state titles in grade school. They grew up together as winners. It was the perfect combination.

Monty and Dave were so close that they chose Roger Bacon together. They could have gone to Wyoming, their local public high school, but Wyoming's basketball program wasn't in the same class as Bacon's—nor that of any other GCL school. And even though they were a year younger, they knew Josh Hausfeld. They knew the guys from St. Bart's—Beckham, Nate Wyrick, Tim McCoy and Matt Reed ("The Quartet," as they became known). Monty and Dave played against them in grade school. They respected those older boys, and those older boys respected them. By going to Bacon, Monty and Dave knew they would all be in the same program, and eventually, on the same team. That's what they wanted, so that's what they did.

Bill, naturally, was on Monty from the start. Monty was only a freshman when he had his first encounter with Bill; he wasn't on varsity yet, and in fact, the run-in had nothing to do with basketball. One day during the 1999–00 season, Monty, while listening to his teacher lecture, casually started playing with a rubber band. A little too casually. The rubber band accidentally flicked off his hand—and hit his teacher square in the chest.

"Who did that?" the teacher demanded.

Monty was instantly scared. He was a quiet, fearful freshman, never in trouble, and he wondered just how bad the potential punishment might be if he turned himself in.

"Who did that?" the teacher repeated, even more annoyed.

Monty remained quiet a little longer before eventually giving himself up.

"You shouldn't have lied," the teacher admonished, more perturbed at Monty's initial silence than his actual transgression. "That's a JUG."

JUG. Justice Under God. Also known as detention in the Catholic high school mecca that is Cincinnati. Monty didn't mind the JUG as much as he minded what the JUG meant—that he'd be 20 minutes late to basketball practice. What would he tell the coaches? Would Bill find out? The more Monty thought about it, though, the more he figured he'd be fine. At that point in the season, he was still practicing with the freshman team, and Bill never came to freshman practices.

Well, he did that day—and he pulled Monty out of a drill and into the hallway.

"What the fuck was that about?" Bill demanded.

"It was an accident!" Monty insisted, startled that Bill knew of the incident and even more surprised at how mad he was.

"Bullshit!" Bill snapped in an enraged hush. "You expect me to believe that?"

Monty didn't know what to say. It really was an accident, but Bill didn't believe that, and truthfully, he didn't care if it was. If you're in class, you shouldn't be playing with rubber bands. You should be listening attentively and taking notes. Monty hobbled back into practice, tail between his freshmen legs.

That was Monty's first run-in with Bill Brewer, and it was probably beneficial—because from that moment on, Monty knew one important fact: anything he said or did that was remotely bad, whether it involved accidentally flicking a rubber band or getting stuck behind a train, Bill Brewer was going to find out about it.

And there would be consequences.

Overall, though, Monty fared well as a freshman. So did Dave. They both dressed varsity toward the end of the year and eventually started as sophomores. Dave manned the point; Monty patrolled the paint. Monty, however, wasn't a classic big man. He was a finesse guy, a shooter. Banging the boards and taking defiant ownership of the post just wasn't his style. Maybe his passive style of play went back to his desire to blend in. Off the court, Monty would sometimes walk with his head down hoping not to be noticed. But on the court, a place where everyone was already watching his every move, maybe Monty wanted to blend in there, too. He wanted to score and rebound, but maybe he wanted to score and rebound in an understated fashion, as if his opponent somehow wouldn't know he was there.

On the trip to Savannah in 2000–01, the one in which Josh dunked all over Orangeburg-Wilkinson, the Spartans decided to shave their heads for team unity. It was Dan Huerkamp's idea, the same Dan Huerkamp who once vomited on the court because Bill refused to call timeout to get him a sub. Dan was a senior that year. A good leader. Tough. He thought shaving heads would bring the team closer together. Everyone was on board. Everyone except Monty.

"He liked his hair too much," Tim McCoy said. "And he thought he'd look stupid, being as tall as he was. But after everyone else did it, it was kind of like, either you're doing it, or you're getting it done to you."

And that's what it came to. Several Spartans held Monty down and were able to nick his head just enough before he broke free. All the guys were laughing and carrying on, but Monty wasn't laughing. Monty was pissed. He flat out did not want his head shaved. He went to a barber to see if the damage could be fixed, to see if his hair could be salvaged. But it couldn't. Monty shaved his head. Bacon kept that tradition through the 2001–02 season, even after Dan Huerkamp graduated. But whenever it came time for the team to shave, Monty was always the last do it—by a couple of days. Being 6-8 made him noticeable enough; being 6-8 and bald was his worst nightmare.

That was Monty—always wanting to blend in, never wanting to be the center of attention.

And that, in part, was why Bill was on him every day. Bill didn't understand how a kid so big and so gifted could be so reluctant to mix it up in the post. He didn't understand how a kid that big ended up on the floor all the time while playing defense or trying to get a rebound. During Monty's sophomore year, he would win just about every shooting drill in practice. He had great fundamentals and an array of post moves, but he wouldn't impose his size or will on anyone. He wasn't tough. He wasn't strong. He'd lift as much as he could, as often as he could, but he couldn't put on weight. Simply put, Monty was meek. He avoided contact. He kept shooting jumpers.

He was . . . *soft*.

"Monty was a big guy, but he played almost like a guard," Josh said. "He could shoot the three, he would post up and do headfakes— he was notorious for his headfakes and up-and-unders—and he just had a lot of good fundamentals. He was never a center who was gonna drop step and dunk on you or get a rebound and scream. He just wasn't that type of player. But Brewer rode him for being soft. He knew that would get to Monty."

Did it ever. One day it got so bad, Monty almost quit basketball. He went home and told his parents how miserable he was. He didn't cry, but he came as close to crying as a person can without actually doing so. That was the thing about Bill. He could break you down and reduce you to tears whenever he wanted. And Monty was just about broken. He had lost his confidence—and he wasn't overconfident to begin with. Monty was a great basketball player all through childhood, but unlike a lot of kids with his talent, Monty never had an inflated ego. He was always humble. His father, Mark, wouldn't have had it any other way. Mark was never a star athlete. In fact, he couldn't play sports growing up due to a health condition, one that was not passed on to Monty.

Because Mark was never a star athlete, he never raised his son like one. He never fed him the "you're better than everybody else" mantra. No matter how tall Monty was, he always stayed grounded. Mark had a lot to do with that. So did Bill.

"Playing for him kept (just) about anybody humble," Monty said. "And if you weren't humble, you either became humble or (you) weren't on the team."

But despite Bill's tough love, Monty didn't quit. He kept working. He kept trying. He was averaging seven or eight points per game during his sophomore year, and then one day against McNicholas, Monty became a little more aggressive. He didn't just score double figures; he broke 20 points. Scouts from Miami of Ohio and Ohio University were at the game getting a look at Josh, and they ended up offering Monty a scholarship within a week. That gave him the confidence to stick with it. He started believing in himself more. He knew how good he could be.

But he was still shy in the paint. He still avoided getting his hands dirty. Compared with other guys on the team—guys like Tim McCoy, Jon Newton, Leonard Bush and Matt Reed, guys who were all football players and who loved contact—Monty remained in their eyes and in Bill's eyes, soft.

And if the 2001–02 Roger Bacon basketball team was to accomplish anything of note, that softness was something Monty would have to remedy. And fast.

FIRST QUARTER

Monty and LeBron meet at midcourt for the opening tip. Monty, who has an inch on LeBron, crouches so low that his head hovers near LeBron's elbow. He looks like a 6-8 grasshopper eagerly waiting to spring to life and pop toward the rafters. LeBron leans forward at a slight angle, peering down at his opponent. The referee walks between more than 13 feet of humanity, pauses, and gives the underhanded, straight-up-and-down finger roll. As soon as the ball leaves the ref's hands, LeBron flinches, fakes his ascent and drifts back on defense. Monty elevates and taps the ball to Josh Hausfeld.

Bacon's bench is livid.

"That was LeBron's way of saying, 'It doesn't matter; you guys can have it,'" Tim McCoy said. "I could tell by the crowd's reaction that he had done that before."

Common practice or not, LeBron, by not jumping for the tip, has just shown up Monty. He has just shown up Roger Bacon. He has just shown up the entire GCL—and in the GCL, that's not something you do. Teams in the GCL don't always like each other, but they never show each other up. The GCL is about respect, and Roger Bacon just got disrespected.

Tim McCoy, watching from the bench, is seething.

The first possession doesn't help matters. Monty gets the ball on the block with a distinct height advantage over Sian Cotton, who stands 6-3. Monty spots Frank wide open under the rim, but the pass is picked off by—who else?—LeBron James, who races downcourt before being wrapped up by Dave and Josh. Foul on Bacon.

This would be a theme.

After a SVSM turnover, the Irish apply their press. Cotton, who also plays defensive lineman for SVSM, is nimble with great lateral quickness. He and Dru Joyce, a speedy 5-9 point guard, crowd Dave, who lobs a pass to Beckham. Beckham dribbles toward the bucket and finds Josh wide open in the corner for three. 3-0, Bacon.

Josh Hausfeld says the public address announcer.

SVSM looks immediately to push the tempo. Joyce shoves a long pass to LeBron, who tries to answer with a three of his own. Brick. Josh sprints ahead of the pack but his reverse layin is no good. Out of bounds. SVSM ball. LeBron finds Joyce open for a three on the wing. Tie game, 3-3.

DRUUUUUUUUUUU JOYCE FOR THRRRRRRREEEEEE! screams the announcer.

Beckham dribbles the length of the court and flips a floater in the lane. Foul, and-one. Beckham misses the freebie. 5-3, Bacon.

Cotton rebounds and outlets to LeBron, who tries to dribble through three defenders and loses the ball. Monty works Cotton on the baseline, goes left, extends and drills a turnaround. 7-3, Bacon.

Monty St. Clair.

And it's around this time that it happens. It's around this time that one of the refs approaches Bill.

"Bill was always pacing the sidelines," Cork said. "And a couple minutes into the game, a ref came over and told him to sit down. He said, 'I'm not gonna have you pacing the sidelines the whole game.' Well, the game just started. There were some college coaches behind our bench, chuckling, and they said, 'There's no way you guys are winning this game.'"

SVSM swings it around. Josh crowds Chad Mraz, a deadly three-point threat, 40 feet from the basket. The whistle blows. Foul on Josh.

Joyce finds LeBron, who misfires on another three. Dave corrals a long rebound and finds Josh sprinting upcourt for an easy layin. 9–3, Bacon.

LeBron is double-teamed in the corner and finds Mraz at the top of the key. Josh drifts toward the three-point line to contest the shot. Mraz lets it fly. After the release, Josh's left hand grazes Mraz's stomach. Mraz collapses and the whistle blows, just as the ball caroms off the rim. Foul on Josh. Three free throws for Mraz.

Bacon's best player already has two fouls.

Mraz hits two of three from the line. 9–5, Bacon.

Dave feeds Monty for a 15-footer on the baseline. 11–5, Bacon.

LeBron attacks the rim and dishes to Sekou Lewis, a 6-5 senior post player who can't handle the catch. Off his legs and out of bounds. Frank rebounds Beckham's errant floater and gets fouled on the put-back attempt. He hits both freebies.

13–5, Bacon.

Joyce misses a three and Frank boards it. He pushes and dishes to Beckham, who gets called for a carry. Mraz looks for LeBron. Turnover. Frank drives baseline on Romeo Travis for a layin. 15–5, Bacon.

LeBron dribbles to the baseline and takes a tough step-back jumper from 17 feet. 15–7 Bacon.

LEBROOOOOOOOOOON JAAAAAAAAMES!

It's LeBron's first bucket. Suddenly he's in rhythm. He swaggers back on defense.

Beckham swoops in to clean up a miss by Monty and sticks the layin. 17–7, Bacon.

Beckham Wyrick.

Mraz penetrates and flips it to Joyce, who drills it from three feet behind the arc. 17–10, Bacon.

DRUUUUUUUUUUU JOYCE FOR THRRRRRRRREEEEEE!

Dave finds Beckham for a floater in the lane. 19–10, Bacon.

Cotton in-bounds to Joyce, who takes one dribble and throws a cross-court heave to LeBron. Beckham is slow to get back on defense.

LeBron streaks past Bacon's bench, catches the pass, races to the right side of the rim and throws it down with his right hand.

LEBROOOOOOOOOON JAAAAAAAAMES!

It's LeBron's first highlight-reel play. 19–12, Bacon.

The Spartans answer immediately. Leonard Bush finds Monty on the baseline for another jumper. 21–12, Bacon.

Joyce tries to shake-and-bake Dave, but Dave sticks with him. Joyce feeds Romeo in the paint, and Frank rotates over to contest the shot. The whistle blows. Foul on Frank. The entire Bacon bench erupts in disbelief. Bill throws both hands in the air, does a pirouette and lightly stomps the court.

Romeo makes one of two. 21–13, Bacon.

Nate Wyrick checks in for his cousin, Beckham.

Monty squares up LeBron on the block. He takes one dribble left, spins back toward the paint and tosses up a hook shot in the lane. Pretty move.

23–13, Bacon.

Romeo stands with the ball at the top of the key and floats a pass toward LeBron, who is posting up Frank on the block. Nate leaves his man and comes over to help before the pass even arrives. LeBron sees it, leaps and rifles a touch pass in mid-air to Jermeny Johnson, who is now alone under the basket. Johnson flushes the easy deuce.

23–15, Bacon.

Nate leads Monty with an over-the-head pass. Monty converts the floater. He has 10 quick points.

25–15, Bacon.

LeBron glides upcourt and goes hard left against Frank toward the baseline. The whistle blows. Another foul on Frank.

LeBron misses the first and makes the second. 25–16, Bacon.

Nate misses a three. LeBron faces up Beckham at the top of key and works around a pseudo-pick. Neither Beckham nor Frank stays on LeBron, who dribbles around them for a baseline dunk. 25–18, Bacon.

Beckham drills a three to atone for his defensive lapse.

28–18, Bacon.

LeBron dribbles baseline. The whistle blows. Foul on Beckham. No free throws. Chad Mraz hoists a contested shot at the buzzer. No good. The first quarter ends. Bacon, stunningly, leads by 10.

"People expected us to be scared, but that really wasn't what happened," Monty said. "We weren't scared at all. We came out and punched them in the mouth. I think we were the only ones not surprised."

While the score may have been surprising, something happened midway through that first period that wasn't. It was something routine, something expected, something that three seasons earlier no one would've believed.

Nate Wyrick came off the bench.

● ● ● ●

THAT JOSH HAUSFELD WAS the best freshman in Bacon's 2002 class is beyond dispute. But Nate Wyrick wasn't far behind.

In the summer of 1998, Nate practiced varsity alongside Josh—and for good reason. Nate was a special grade school player at St. Bart's. He'd score 20 like it was nothing. Range like you wouldn't believe. If Nate crossed halfcourt unchecked, opposing coaches would yell to their players—"Get on him!"—and flail their arms like island castaways trying to signal a passing ship on the horizon.

Just how good was Nate?

"Back in grade school, I looked at Nate as the best player," Josh said. "*I want to be better than Nate Wyrick.* That was my motivation."

Nate was going to have himself a fine career at Roger Bacon. He'd play varsity as a freshman, probably start as a sophomore and then put up gaudy numbers as a junior and senior. But here he was, five games into his senior season, and things hadn't quite played out that way.

Nate was also a football player. Pretty good quarterback. Not the most mobile guy in the world, but he was accurate. As a freshman, Nate would go from school to football practice, football practice to home. But once he got home, once his day was done and he had time to unwind, he forgot to do one important thing—homework. Not enough of it, anyway. By the end of football season, he had two F's, and when basketball started, he couldn't play—not because of injury, but because he was academically ineligible.

Nate was in shock. He'd sit in the stands as a freshman and watch Josh play varsity. He'd watch Bacon struggle. He'd watch Bacon lose. All the while, he knew he could have been out there helping those guys.

"Really, I was just lazy," Nate said. "The worst thing was, I let a lot of people down. Some people were looking forward to me taking the next step and being on varsity. It just didn't happen."

Even if Nate had played as a freshman, Bacon didn't have the talent to win state. A nice tournament run, maybe, but Columbus was out of the question. What really hurt Nate, though, was not being able to play. He had all the momentum in the world going into that freshman season, but before he could play even a single game, that momentum flatlined. He was destined to dance under the lights of GCL varsity basketball. Not many get to do that. Almost no one does it as a freshman. If you play against the best players in the city—players who also happen to be three and four years older than you—you're bound to get better. Nate couldn't do that. He would go to his local rec and play pickup games, but it wasn't the same. The competition wasn't the same. His skills, once on an upward trajectory, tapered.

But it wasn't just about what happened—or didn't happen—on the court. Whether Nate would have averaged double figures as a freshman or merely played mop-up time for the upperclassmen was immaterial to Bill. It was the principle of the matter. *Here I am*, Bill thought, *giving this kid an opportunity, giving this kid the privilege to practice and play varsity as a freshman, and what's he doing with it? He's wasting it.* That angered Bill. He wasn't the type of coach who would jeopardize the long term for the short term. If playing varsity as a freshman would impede a kid's development—even if a kid could perform a role or fill a void—Bill wouldn't bring him up. With Nate, Bill had confidence from the start. Nate could shoot, and he had the tools, the size (6-3 as a freshman) and the fundamentals to hold his own on the court. More important, Bill thought Nate could hold his own off it, but the maturity just wasn't there yet. It may not be there for a lot of 14- and 15-year-old kids, but the fact is, Nate had a chance as a freshman to impress Bill Brewer, and he ended up letting him down.

Despite not playing as a freshman, Nate actually put together a solid sophomore season. He played varsity. He got decent minutes. He produced. He even started a few times. But when AAU rolled around in the spring of 2000, Nate, who was also a standout volleyball player, had a choice to make: he could play Roger Bacon volleyball, or he could play AAU basketball. For many athletes, this isn't even a question. Basketball, no doubt. But the thing is, Nate was good at volleyball. Really good. By the time he graduated from Bacon, he was a three-time player of the year in the GCL. He was all-city. He was all-state. The way he saw it, playing volleyball for Roger Bacon—which, to him, meant representing his school and not turning his back on his teammates—was more important than playing AAU basketball. *Besides*, Nate thought, *I can play AAU over the summer once volleyball season is over*. So that's what he did.

Bill wasn't a fan of that choice. He never told Nate to quit volleyball, but according to Nate, it was implied. Beckham also played volleyball at Bacon, but when given the choice, he chose AAU. Beckham didn't play volleyball as a junior or senior, either. Nate never faulted Beckham for doing that, but if there's strength in numbers, Nate didn't have any. He was alone.

Nate believes his decision to stick with volleyball hurt his relationship with Bill. First, he was academically ineligible as a freshman, and then as a sophomore, he refused to focus on basketball full time. Nate thinks that deep down—and maybe not so deep down—Bill questioned his commitment to the sport, to the team and to the program. The bond and trust between player and coach began to erode.

By the time he was a junior, Nate—the player who was practicing varsity fresh out of eighth grade—wasn't even starting. Nate wondered if this was, in part, personal. He wondered if it was Bill's way of getting back at him. Nate felt Bill had lost faith in him; that he had to constantly prove himself to Bill; that his leash was a little too short; that if he made a mistake in a game, any mistake, he was benched. Nate felt a certain uneasiness on the court. His confidence deteriorated.

There were days in practice when Nate couldn't miss. In practice, he felt free. The game flowed. The game came to him. If he messed up, so what? Bill wasn't going to kick him out of Fogarty for making a mistake. He might make him run, but really, what was the worst that could happen? In games, though, that wasn't the case. In games, Nate would sit on the sidelines wondering when he'd get to go to the scorers' table and check in. Once he did, the pressure to perform was often too great. *You make a mistake, you're on the bench*—that's how Nate saw it. That fear of messing up, of being taken out, showed in Nate's play. It didn't matter that he was one of the first guys off the bench—usually *the* first guy off the bench. He didn't play with confidence. He played tense, like a boxer forgetting to breathe.

Even when Nate did something right, he didn't. During a game against GCL-South rival St. Xavier, Bacon had possession with about 15 seconds left in the first half. Nate took a pass on the baseline. He was wide open. Shooters always think they're wide open, but Nate really was. So he took the shot and made it. He felt good about it. He contributed. He helped the team. But when he got to the locker room, he remembers Bill chewing him out. Conventional wisdom is to hold for the last shot. That's true at any level of basketball—particularly in high school, where there's no shot clock—but it's especially true for the GCL. The GCL is about grinding it out and executing in the halfcourt. It's not uncommon for GCL teams to hold the ball for more than a minute at the end of the half. It's all about slowing the game down and putting a premium on every possession. GCL coaches typically want their best player near halfcourt with ball in hand until there are five or six seconds left—and then he can attack. But to put up a jumper with 15 seconds remaining? It didn't matter whether Nate made it. It also didn't matter whether St. X scored on its ensuing possession to end the half. For Bill, that was all irrelevant. He wanted things a certain way. If you didn't like his way, tough. If you did it your own way, you felt his wrath. And that night, Nate did.

But Bill's biggest issue with Nate wasn't his shooting; it was his defense. Forget being ineligible. Forget refusing to give up volleyball. The biggest between-the-lines knock on Nate was defense. It's not so much that Nate couldn't play defense; it's just that, at times, it seemed like he didn't want to. His man would beat him downcourt for a layup. His rotations would come a second late. Instead of playing sound, solid defense, Nate would reach around and try to tap the ball away for a steal. There were days when Nate's lack of desire on defense—his lack of effort—drove Bill crazy.

Here's a kid who's 6-4, Bill thought, *who, in theory, could guard any position on the floor, and all he can think about is when he gets to shoot again.*

Bill had no patience for that. Thus, the minutes weren't always there in bulk for Nate. The substitutions, the ones in which Nate would be leaving games, came a little quicker than he liked. Some games, Nate would play well; the next game, he felt like it took forever to get off the bench. The divide between coach and player grew larger.

"For us to be good, you've got to play well," Bill would tell Nate.

"For me to play well, I've got to play," Nate would counter.

It wasn't all bad with Bill and Nate. Bill liked and respected Nate as a person. He knew Nate read the sports section every morning. Read? Studied is more like it. Nate would stroll into practice Saturday morning and hear Bill talking about an upcoming opponent. "I wonder how they did last night," Bill would say to an assistant. Nate didn't wonder. Nate knew. He'd tell Bill who won, what the final score was, who scored, how many points they scored—everything. Bill was always impressed by that.

But again, it always went back to defense.

If anything could explain Nate's struggles on that side of the court, perhaps it's his childhood. He and Beckham grew up together. They were best friends. Still are. But growing up, Beckham was never pushed to play sports. Nate was. For Beckham, childhood was fun. For Nate, it was work.

During the summer, Beckham and Nate would visit their grandpa's farm in Kansas, but even that wasn't a vacation. Nate's father, Tom, gave Nate strict orders to run at least a mile every day and told his grandpa to make sure those orders were followed. At home, Tom would make Nate jump rope with weighted shoes for a half hour to improve his vertical. Nate would jump up and down and drip in the summer haze. Tom would sit close by with a clock and time him.

Tom Wyrick had good intentions. He wanted the best for his son. He wanted Nate to do things athletically that he never got to do. He wanted Nate to be the best. And for a time, he was. But the constant conditioning took a psychological toll on him. Nate loved sports. He loved basketball. But some days, he just wanted to go outside and play. Some days, he just wanted to go down to the creek with Beckham and Matt Reed and Tim McCoy. Some days, he just wanted to be a kid.

Nate never complained to his dad. Never said a thing. Running didn't frustrate him. Jumping rope didn't frustrate him. He would do that. But having no say in the matter? Never being asked for his opinion? Never talking about what he wanted and didn't want? That was frustrating. It wore on Nate. It wore on him like old gym shoes left on the lawn, faded and soggy in the rain.

As much as people expected Nate to be a star at Roger Bacon—as much as he expected that from himself—the fact is, by the time Nate got to high school, he was a little burned out. It's often said that defense is about desire; well, Nate's desire wasn't as strong as it once was. That doesn't show on offense. On defense, it does.

"Nate wasn't the worst defender; he wasn't," Tom Thompson said. "But you couldn't make a mistake effort- and attitude-wise with Bill. He'd see it."

As much as Nate questioned Bill's intentions, as much as Nate and Bill sometimes clashed, teammates and coaches agreed that Bill never would've sacrificed the good of the program to disgruntle a player. To them, Nate's career to that point was his own doing, and if he was going to make something of himself that year, it would be on him to do it.

SECOND QUARTER

Dave, Beckham, Nate, Leonard and Monty take the floor for Bacon as the second quarter gets under way.

SVSM's strategy is simple: get the ball to LeBron.

LeBron backs down Leonard, a burly, tough defender. But at 6-1, he's giving up half a foot to LeBron. He can't do much with him. The whistle blows. LeBron heads to the line for the one-and-one and hits both. 28–20, Bacon.

SVSM scrambles into its press, and LeBron pokes the ball away from Beckham near halfcourt. Joyce scoops it up, attacks the tin and finds LeBron for an easy dunk. The ascent seems effortless. Maybe because it is.

28–22, Bacon.

Bill, angered, calls timeout.

SVSM presses again. Bacon breaks it and Nate shoots a wide open three. Brick.

LeBron misfires on a fallaway jumper from the baseline. Nate and Sian fight for the rebound. Jump ball. Possession arrow Bacon. SVSM pressures, but Dave breaks it on his own, which leads to an uncontested layin for Beckham.

30–22, Bacon.

Joyce one-hands another full-court heave to LeBron, who is in the clear. Beckham races frantically to contest the shot. He sprints past two teammates and pulls even with LeBron like a thoroughbred barreling down the final straightaway. He swats the ball out of LeBron's hands just as he goes up for the flush. The whistle blows. Bacon's bench hops and fidgets in frustration.

LeBron hits the first free throw and misses the second. 30–23, Bacon. SVSM snares the offensive board and works it to Joyce, who misses a three. LeBron muscles up the put-back. Monty denies him once but not twice.

30–25, Bacon. LeBron has scored all seven second-quarter points for the Irish.

Monty converts a layin and gets bumped by Sian. And-one. Monty hits the free throw. 33–25, Bacon.

Mraz misses a three. Bacon's ball.

Josh tries to break the press but carelessly dribbles behind his back in traffic. Turnover. Joyce finds Mraz streaking in for a layin.

33–27, Bacon.

Josh, looking to atone for his miscue, searches for daylight but sees only shadows. Mraz sticks to him like honey on a hive. Josh doesn't care. He dribbles left and pulls up for a jumper just inside the arc. Buckets.

35–27, Bacon.

Joyce finds Romeo slicing past Nate down the middle of the floor. Nate lunges for the block, but Romeo absorbs the contact and converts the right-handed layin. And-one. The free throw is no good.

35–29, Bacon.

Nate finds Monty for another short jumper from the right corner. 37–29, Bacon.

LeBron takes a three. No good. Josh draws a double team and flips a pretty drop off to Monty, who botches the floater, gathers his miss and converts.

The lead is back to double digits; 39–29, Bacon. Monty has 17 points.

Mraz misses a three but gets a steal on Bacon's ensuing possession. He takes it coast-to-coast and showcases his hang time with an acrobatic floater over Monty.

39–31, Bacon.

Nate shot fakes and drives to the paint. He tries a wrap-around pass to Monty, but no one's there. Turnover.

Sekou Lewis converts a put-back.

39–33, Bacon.

Josh takes a wild left-hander that doesn't draw iron.

Joyce pulls up in transition three feet behind the arc and lets it fly right in Dave's face. Splash.

DRUUUUUUUUUUU JOYCE FOR THRRRRRRRREEEEEE!

It's a 7–0 run for the Irish, who trail just 39–36.

Josh zips a pretty pass to Leonard, who is fouled near the basket. He misses the first free throw and makes the second.

40–36, Bacon.

Sekou Lewis extends over Dave and drills a three.

The lead is down to one; 40–39, Bacon.

Frank misses a layin but sticks the put-back. 42–39, Bacon.

LeBron gets fouled by Monty but misses the bunny. He slaps his hands in disgust before bricking the first free throw and hitting the second.

42–40, Bacon.

Frank takes it strong to the hole and gets fouled. He converts both free throws. 44–40, Bacon.

LeBron explodes to the paint and jump stops for an easy layin. 44–42, Bacon.

Dave shoots a quick three that smacks the back iron. Mraz rebounds to LeBron, who finds Joyce wide open again.

DRUUUUUUUUUUU JOYCE FOR THRRRRRRRREEEEEE!

SVSM has its first lead of the game, 45–44.

Leonard throws up a contested jumper at the buzzer. Air ball.

It's halftime. Bacon heads to the locker room happy on one hand, disgusted on the other. Why happy? It's a one-point game. Why disgusted? The Irish drilled five threes in the first half (four alone by Joyce), threw home four dunks (three by LeBron) and converted six layups. The Spartans, which led by 10 at the end of the first quarter and halfway through the second, are shooting 64 percent from the floor—and yet they are losing.

If Roger Bacon would have any chance to win this game, if it would have any chance whatsoever, it would have to shore up its defense. The Spartans have allowed just 51.8 points per game on the young season, but SVSM has almost equalled that in the first half alone. LeBron has scored 17 points, including 15 straight in the paint or at the foul line. In the locker room, Bacon asks itself two questions: How can we contain LeBron down low, and how can we neutralize Joyce from distance?

The Spartans look at each other, knowing that if they accomplish those objectives, they are going to beat the fourth-ranked team in the country.

THIRD QUARTER

Bacon's five starters—Josh, Beckham, Frank, Monty and Dave—return to the floor, as the second half opens with Romeo Travis missing a three. The ball trickles out of bounds. Bacon takes over.

SVSM applies its full-court press once more, and once more Dave breaks it. Josh hoists a three from the corner. No good.

LeBron misses another bunny. Josh draws another double team. Romeo and Mraz converge on the Golden Boy, who makes an immediate bounce pass to Monty for the layup.

46–45, Bacon.

Joyce throws another Hail Mary to LeBron, who goes up like a wide receiver in double coverage and brings it down between Beckham and Dave. LeBron puts his head down, spins left toward the paint and barrels into Frank, who beats him to the spot and extends both hands straight in the air. Frank falls to the floor. LeBron collapses upon contact. No foul call. Bacon fans groan. There is a scramble for the loose ball. The ball appears to hit a SVSM player before rolling out of bounds. The whistle blows. SVSM ball, the ref signals. The groans grow louder.

LeBron drives right on Beckham, draws a double team and dumps it off for Sekou Lewis. Another dunk.

47–46, SVSM.

Dave and Beckham break the press. Frank converts a crafty layin. 48–47, Bacon.

LeBron works around a pick, and Monty switches with Beckham. LeBron sizes up the 6-8 center. He dribbles between his legs, crosses

Monty over and pulls up for a jumper at the elbow. Bottoms. 49–48, SVSM.

Josh curls off a screen and drills a three. And-one. Bacon's bench players pump their fists. Josh completes the four-point play.

52–49, Bacon.

The Irish turn it over, but their pressure is effective. Dave is whistled for a 10-second violation. LeBron draws Monty again on a switch and shoots a three. No good.

Frank attacks the rim, misses, grabs the board and gets fouled on the put-back attempt. He makes both free throws.

The Spartans have breathing room once more; 54–49, Bacon.

Mraz shoots another three. The whistle blows. The shot is no good. Foul on Beckham, his third. Mraz drills three free throws.

54–52, Bacon.

Monty gets swatted. LeBron attacks in transition. Beckham picks up the blocking foul, his fourth. LeBron makes the first free throw and misses the second.

54–53, Bacon.

Frank misses a shot down low. Joyce is errant on a three. Frank goes up for a layin and has his shot blocked. He gathers the ball, goes up again and converts.

56–53, Bacon.

SVSM pushes the tempo. Joyce finds LeBron, who dribbles hard to the bucket and tries to split Dave and Monty. LeBron elevates, hangs in the air and releases the shot as he begins his descent. Josh appears out of nowhere and emphatically swats the ball out of bounds near the Irish cheerleaders. Bacon fans spring to their feet and roar their approval.

Mraz in-bounds from the baseline and lobs a pass in front of the bucket for LeBron. Bacon sniffs out the alley-hoop, but LeBron catches the ball, comes down and out-muscles Frank for a layup.

56–55, Bacon.

Josh drives to the hoop and drops it off for Frank.

58–55, Bacon.

SVSM gets to the foul line but can't convert. Nate shoots a three that doesn't draw iron. The ball ricochets off the backboard. A scramble ensues. Frank grabs the ball and flips up a floater.

60–55, Bacon. Frank has 10 of Bacon's 16 third-quarter points.

Sian is fouled down low and hits both free throws.

60–57, Bacon.

Joyce hounds Dave, who tries to flip a pass to Josh, but LeBron picks it off inside the three-point line and is off to the races. Four dribbles later, LeBron takes flight in the paint—closer to the free-throw line than the basket—and flushes a dunk just as the buzzer sounds.

LLLLLLEEEBBBRRRRRRROOOOOOOOON JAAAAAAAAAAMES!

The crowd is in a frenzy. The Irish bench spills onto the court to greet LeBron, who walks powerfully, defiantly, to the sideline. 60–59, Bacon.

The first three quarters are in the books. Bacon owned the first, SVSM owned the second, and the third was played to a virtual standstill, with Bacon holding a 16–14 advantage. Eight minutes remain.

It's anybody's game.

* * *

SITTING IN THE STANDS at Kent State that night was a boy, a high school junior who, one way or another, was destined to be at that game.

Marcus Smith was born in Akron. When he was 2, he moved to Cincinnati with his mom and stepdad, but he returned to his hometown for the next dozen or so summers to spend time with his biological father, John.

Akron and Cincinnati may be in the same state, but for Marcus, they were two different worlds. In Cincinnati, he lived with his mother, Beverley, a physical therapist, and his stepdad, Bruce, who was an assistant football coach at the University of Cincinnati. Marcus enjoyed a comfortable middle-class upbringing, with his mom serving as the disciplinarian in his life. She set ground rules and expected them to be followed. She sent Marcus to private schools and expected him to do well. She was his driving force, and they had a close relationship.

Marcus was just as close to his biological father, John, but it was different. When Marcus lived with Beverley, it was during the school year. There was a routine. Every day had structure. John was almost like the weekend parent. For Marcus, going to stay with his father, who worked as a bus driver, was like going on vacation. They'd go to movies, they'd get ice cream—they'd do whatever they wanted. That was their time together, and they cherished it.

Marcus got into basketball at an early age. He was a product of the Michael Jordan era and grew up watching the Chicago Bulls win championships. That was a powerful influence on him. So, too, was what basketball symbolized to him as a young black male.

"In the black community, making it, especially for males, there's two dreams—music and sports," he said. "That's it. Sad as that is to say, that's it."

Marcus thought about pursuing football. He thought about pursuing cross country. But basketball was his love—not just for the game itself, but for what it could do for him. Marcus' parents, however, didn't raise him to think basketball was his only hope for success. The game Marcus loved so dearly would be a part of his life, a big part of his life, but it wouldn't be everything.

Still, it was on the basketball court where Marcus realized who he was, who he wasn't, and how lucky he was to have the life he did. Marcus loved seeing his father every summer, but John lived in a rougher neighborhood—"the ghetto," as Marcus described it. So going from suburban Cincinnati to urban Akron was a culture shock.

John put Marcus in summer camps, where he played basketball with inner-city kids. Marcus remembers how aggressive they were, how they cussed every other word, how they talked about sex. He felt different from the other boys and struggled to gain acceptance. It was rough, but he learned to cope, and it prepared him for what he encountered in high school.

Marcus wanted to attend Roger Bacon for one main reason, a reason paramount to his life as an eighth-grader: that's where his best friend was going. Beverley and Bruce considered sending Marcus to Winton Woods, a public school in Forest Park, but they thought Bacon could offer more academically.

Marcus' first two years at Bacon weren't easy. He found it hard to fit in. He felt as though Bacon's student body at the time could essentially be divided into two categories: middle-class white kids and less affluent black kids. He struggled fitting in with the white kids because he was black, and he struggled fitting in with the black kids because he was middle class.

"I didn't mesh with either group," Marcus said. "And they let me know I didn't mesh with them."

Even basketball was a struggle for Marcus. He made Bacon's freshman team, but in some ways, he was fortunate to not get cut. Of the roughly 15 guys on that freshman team, Marcus estimated he was among the bottom two or three in playing time. By his own admission, he was soft. For a while that freshman year, he didn't play or practice due to an injured ankle, but truthfully, the pain wasn't that bad. He could've played on it. He could've gutted through it. But he didn't.

He also had a peculiar problem of rolling his eyes. Like breathing, he would do it and not even know it. All through childhood, eye-rolling got Marcus in trouble at school. Teachers, coaches and authority figures in general took it as a sign of disrespect. One day during his freshman season, Marcus unintentionally rolled his eyes at Cork, who was the freshman coach. It wasn't the first time that had happened, and Cork was fuming. He got Bill and they escorted Marcus to a small, dark room connected to the coaches' office, a room that Marcus didn't even know existed. Cork and Bill stood there, berating him.

What are you gonna do? Are you gonna keep rolling your eyes? Are you gonna keep being disrespectful? Are you gonna keep not playing because of that injury? Are you gonna quit?

The questions fired at machine-gun pace. Marcus was scared. He was crying.

"I don't wanna quit," Marcus said through tears. "I love basketball."

Marcus stopped spending summers in Akron once he got to high school. If you want to be a serious high school basketball player, especially in Bill Brewer's program, you had to commit during the summer. Vacations, weeklong getaways, jobs—none of that was really possible. But Marcus still saw his father as much as he could, and basketball became a way for them to bond.

Being from Akron, John loved LeBron James. Still does. Back then, he was a SVSM season-ticket holder. When Marcus was a freshman, John took him to the 2000 Division III state final, where Marcus laid eyes on LeBron for the first time. SVSM was led that year by a senior, Maverick Carter, but John would point at LeBron and tell Marcus, "That's the guy you need to be watching." LeBron scored 25 points that game, but Marcus wasn't overly impressed. When he saw SVSM play in the state final the following year, however, he was. LeBron scored 25 in that game, too.

"I was like, 'Wow, this guy's good,'" Marcus said. "He's frickin' unbelievable."

Marcus rooted for LeBron. He rooted for the Irish. He was amazed at how good they were, how young they were, and he liked that he and his father could share that rooting interest.

Back at Bacon, Marcus kept at it. He tried to get tougher, and he tried to stop rolling his eyes. But when he was a sophomore, it happened. He failed biology and, like Nate as a freshman, became academically ineligible. Marcus' gut reaction was denial. He knew he was ineligible, but he hoped it would disappear. It didn't. He walked out of class one day, and Bill was waiting.

"You failed a class," he said. "You know you're ineligible, right?"

Marcus had worked so hard that offseason and thought he would start JV. But he never got the chance.

Losing eligibility can be disastrous for a high school player—on the court and off. But for Marcus, it wasn't.

"Honestly," he said, "that was the best thing to ever happen to me."

Marcus was in a hole and had to dig himself out. So he did. He improved his grades, he didn't fail any more classes and he kept working on his game. A lot of programs would have looked at Marcus as a lost cause. He barely played as a freshman, and he was ineligible as a sophomore. It would have been easy for Bill and the other coaches to part ways with Marcus, but they didn't. When Marcus was a junior, he started the season playing JV—not as punishment for being ineligible, but because Bacon didn't know what to think of his skills yet. He was a high school junior who hadn't proven anything one way or the other.

So when Roger Bacon played SVSM at Kent State that night, Marcus wasn't on the bench. He was in the stands, a junior still trying to find his way in the program. He watched his classmates go blow for blow with one of the best teams in America, a team from his hometown, a team that he and his father had rooted for—together. Marcus remembers a great deal about that game for those very reasons, but he also remembers it for another: that was the last Roger Bacon game he ever watched from the stands. Days later, he was promoted to varsity.

And his life would never be the same again.

FOURTH QUARTER

Frank opens the final frame by taking it hard to the hoop—a pretty crossover along the baseline. He can't hit the shot, but he gets fouled and makes one of two free throws. 61–59, Bacon.

Sekou Lewis counters with a hop-step and a bucket to tie the game at 61–61.

SVSM continues to press. Joyce is called for a touch foul on Dave, who misses the front end of a one-and-one.

Joyce looks for a post feed as Frank and LeBron battle for position. Frank reaches around to steal the entry pass but gets called for a foul. Disgusted, he puts both hands behind his head, bends over and slaps the floor with both palms. Leonard Bush checks in to body LeBron and—still giving up a good six inches—is immediately whistled for a foul. LeBron goes to the line and hits both free throws.

63–61, SVSM

Josh answers with a deuce down low.

Tie game, 63–63.

Joyce misses a three. Leonard is called for another foul while boxing out LeBron, who heads to the line and makes one of two free throws.

64–63, SVSM

Monty gets fouled on the other end and hits one of two.

Tie game, 64–64.

Joyce misses a three, and Josh grabs the board. Bacon passes beyond the arc as Josh curls around a pick, takes a pass from Leonard and pulls up for a quick jumper near the free-throw line. Wide left.

Mraz feeds Romeo for two.

66–64, SVSM.

Roger Bacon looks stagnant on offense. Bill calls timeout to regroup. Both teams miss several shots before Frank converts a swooping drive from the right baseline. Tie game, 66–66, with 3:42 remaining.

LeBron is called for a walk. Monty misses a jumper from the elbow. Joyce uses a screen to find space from distance. He pulls up three feet behind the arc, again, and splashes it home, again.

DRUUUUUUUUUUUU JOYCE FOR THRRRRRRREEEEEE!

69–66, SVSM, 2:34 to go.

Bacon turns it over. Joyce attempts another three, which hits the back iron. A three by Beckham rims awry. SVSM calls timeout.

Bacon still trails by three. Time is running out. The Spartans foul Joyce to stop the clock. Joyce goes to the line with 1:07 to go and hits both free throws.

71–66, SVSM.

With just over a minute remaining, Bacon faces its largest deficit of the night. Frank drives to the hoop looking to score, but Sekou Lewis pokes the ball away, gathers it, gets fouled and makes both free throws.

73–66, SVSM.

Seven points. Three possessions. The game is slipping away.

Bacon looks to Josh for some Golden Boy magic, but he mishandles the pass. Turnover. LeBron scoops it up, heads the other way and gets fouled. He makes one of two at the line.

74–66, SVSM. The Spartans are unraveling.

Beckham misses a three. LeBron is fouled. He misses the first freebie and makes the second.

75–66, SVSM. Fans file toward the exit.

Beckham hits a layup—his first points of the second half. 75–68, SVSM. Bill calls timeout, but it's too little, too late. Joyce is fouled and hits two more from the line.

77–68, SVSM.

Beckham misses a three. Tim McCoy sticks the put-back.

77–70, SVSM.

Joyce is fouled and hits two more. 79–70, SVSM.

The buzzer sounds. The game is over.

Bacon has lost.

The Spectacle • 113

IT'S A RARE ATHLETIC event in which stats don't explain the outcome. In the case of Roger Bacon vs. St. Vincent–St. Mary, one stat was all that mattered. It wasn't field goals made (Bacon made 28 to SVSM's 23), it wasn't shooting percentage (Bacon shot 49 percent; SVSM shot 45), it wasn't rebounds (Bacon had a 33–28 advantage), and it wasn't assists (Bacon doubled up the Irish, 14–7).

No, it wasn't any of those stats. Because anyone who looked at those stats might have thought the Spartans had won. And they might've—if not for one glaring discrepancy.

Free throws. SVSM shot 40 of them; Bacon shot 16.

Bacon's three senior starters—Frank Phillips, Beckham Wyrick and Josh Hausfeld—played some, or all, of the fourth quarter with four fouls. SVSM made 11 more free throws (27) than Bacon even attempted, Bacon was called for nearly twice as many fouls (25–13), and 19 of SVSM's 34 second-half points—including 13 of 20 in the fourth quarter—came from the foul line.

"I guess they could guard us, but we weren't allowed to guard them," Bill told the *Akron Beacon Journal*, which had a next-day headline of "Irish steal one from Bacon."

For Bill to say that, especially publicly, was telling of the injustice he thought was committed. Bill was a bottom-line kind of guy. He didn't make excuses. In fact, he credited SVSM for the win. "When the game was on the line," he told the *Akron Beacon Journal*, "LeBron and Dru Joyce made the shots and the plays, and we didn't."

Bacon couldn't blame the refs entirely for the loss. After all, LeBron, who scored 29 points, and Dru Joyce, who scored 21, combined for 50 points. As a team, SVSM had six dunks and nine layups. That's 30 points right there. And after shooting 64 percent in the first half, Bacon shot just 10-of-29 (34.5 percent) in the second.

But still, Bill, like any coach, felt a free-throw discrepancy that wide was inexcusable. Besides, maybe some of those Irish dunks and layups wouldn't have been there had Bill not had to go to his bench so early and for so long due to foul trouble. Maybe his senior starters could have played more aggressively if they didn't have four fouls.

Maybe that second-half shooting percentage would have been a little higher as a result. But it wasn't. Bill's hands were tied from the start.

"In a game billed as a possible Division II state final preview, the Irish needed a late surge to earn a 79–70 victory," read the *Akron Beacon Journal*. ". . . The Spartans, dogged by foul trouble throughout, fell to 4-1 but not before gaining some big-time respect . . . Roger Bacon . . . played a strong all-around game despite plenty of foul trouble."

Coach Dru Joyce, who had taken a day off work that week to drive to Cincinnati and scout Bacon, knew the Spartans would be a tough opponent. "I was telling our team all week what a disciplined team (Bacon) had," Joyce told the *Akron Beacon Journal*. "But sometimes it's hard to communicate that to them when we are playing all these nationally ranked opponents."

Said Bill to the *Akron Beacon Journal*, "No disrespect to Coach Joyce and their fine team, but our kids didn't come up here for a great effort. We gave them a good game, but I wouldn't say it was our best game. I'd love another shot at them."

So did Bacon's players, several of whom were irate in the locker room.

"I was mad," Monty said. "We had a chance to make a statement. We were up 10, and we were in control of the game. There wasn't a doubt in our mind that we could beat them."

One player who wasn't all that mad, surprisingly enough, was Jon Newton, an intense football player nobody messed with.

"I remember in the locker room everyone was pissed—and understandably; we wanted to go undefeated that year," he said. "But I remember looking at Josh and saying, 'We lost a game. So what? We're going to play them again, and we're going to beat them.' And everyone's sitting there looking at me like I'm crazy. Of course, I'm not the best player or anything. I'm just a bench player. But I knew we could beat them."

So did Bill. When he walked into the locker room that night, he didn't go off. He didn't yell about the officials. He didn't yell at his players. He simply looked them in the eye and had one piece of advice:

"Remember what this feels like."

Even though Bacon was out-attempted 40–16 at the free-throw line, the game was tied, 66–66, with less than three minutes remaining.

That tidbit wasn't lost on Bill. And it likely wasn't lost on SVSM. Less than a week later, both teams played in the same holiday tournament in Lewes, Delaware. They didn't play each other, but they were both in the same arena. When Bacon was warming up for one of its games, the Irish walked along the baseline under the Spartans' basket. And that's when he did it.

LeBron James gave Frank Phillips a nod.

It was a sign of respect.

Maybe it was obvious to the thousands on hand at Kent State that Roger Bacon and SVSM were the two best teams in Ohio. Maybe it was obvious that they had witnessed a preview of the state final. Maybe it was obvious that Bacon, if given another opportunity, had a real chance of beating SVSM. But on that December night in 2001, three days before Christmas, the Spartans didn't care what anybody in the stands thought. They knew what they thought of themselves—and that was all that mattered.

After the game, Beckham Wyrick, brash and blustery even in defeat, walked straight up to Chad Mraz and Dru Joyce and told them he'd see them in March.

"They were like, 'Yeah, all right,'" Beckham recalled. "I don't think they believed me."

CHAPTER FOUR

THE SWAGGER

There was something inherently California Surfer about Beckham Wyrick. Off the court, the 6-6 senior power forward was soft-spoken, easygoing, chill. Someone who didn't really care what you thought of him or didn't think of him. He was who he was. Not in a standoffish "take it or leave it" kind of way, but in a sincere "you know you like it, so just embrace it" kind of way.

But on the court . . .

Ask any member of the 2001–02 Roger Bacon basketball team about one of his teammates, and he'll tell you. Without pause, without change of expression, without altered tone, he'll tell you.

"Tim McCoy? Oh, Tim was fiery."

"Dave Johnson? Oh, Dave was quiet."

"Monty? Oh, Monty was quiet, too. He could be sneaky and sarcastic and play tricks on you, but he was quiet."

What about Beckham?

They pause. They grow silent. They bob their heads and grin. They stare off into the distance, as if recalling a fond memory. They search for the right words, and upon location, utter them in the most endearing way possible.

Outspoken.

In your face.

Cocky.

A prick.

"Beckham was the SOB of the group; he was the tough guy," Brian Neal said. "If there was ever a fight, he was gonna be the first guy in it. Off the court, he's the most pleasant, most polite kid you'll ever meet. On the floor, he had the toughness and confidence every team needs—and it wasn't a quiet confidence. It was a swagger."

But how? Why? Where did that alter ego come from?

Beckham was as unique as his name, which dated back to his great-grandfather, who was named after John Crepps Wickliffe Beckham, a former Kentucky governor. The turn-of-the-20th-century Wyricks admired the governor so much that they named a son after him. The name has been passed on to at least one family member every generation since, including Beckham's father, who goes by David to avoid confusion with his cousin, also named Beckham.

Like any kid named after a politician, Beckham seemed destined to do great things, and for him, that meant one thing—becoming a professional basketball player. It wasn't until late in high school that Beckham thought this was a genuine possibility, but as his family can attest, that was his goal since childhood—even though his aspirations probably seemed far-fetched at the time. After all, if any member of the Wyrick clan was going to become a professional athlete, it would be Nate. And among Beckham's closest friends, if it wasn't Nate, it would be Matt Reed or Tim McCoy, both of whom were standout baseball players.

Eventually dubbed "The Quartet," Beckham, Nate, Matt and Tim were inseparable throughout much of grade school. They were best friends. They did everything together. And of the four, Beckham was the smallest. By junior high, Nate, Matt and Tim were all bigger, stronger and had developed earlier. Physical stature notwithstanding, Beckham lacked something else that many standout athletes possess—an intense, unyielding, year-round desire to get better.

Beckham's childhood wasn't all about sports. In fact, it was never about sports. Beckham's parents were athletes in high school—his mom ran cross country, and his father dabbled in football—but they were never consumed by it. That carried over into parenthood. David Wyrick never once made his son play a sport. So Beckham wasn't running for miles in the summer heat to improve his endurance. He wasn't jumping rope with weighted shoes to improve his vertical. He wasn't running sprints to bolster his 40 time. He wasn't even playing AAU.

What was he doing? He was swimming. He was skateboarding. He was riding his bike to the woods. He was playing backyard football with his buddies. He was being a kid. For Beckham, playing sports was like apples in autumn; unless they were in season, he didn't crave them.

But even when a sport was in season, something was still missing. Something was holding Beckham back. His uncle, Rick Bierman, coached him in basketball. Rick was a good athlete in his day and was the starting point guard on Roger Bacon's 1982 state championship team. Starting at a young age, Beckham would watch the game tape of his uncle winning state.

"I think it made him realize that this thing wasn't so far-fetched," Rick said. "It's been done before."

Rick saw something special in his nephew early on, something that even Beckham didn't know was there. It's not that Beckham lacked intensity, Rick explained; he just never showed it.

So Rick decided he was going to bring it out of him. He'd yell at him. He'd bench him. He'd always try to get Beckham to flip his aggression into that last gear, but Beckham always resisted. Rick would drive Beckham home after a blowout win and nitpick every little thing he did wrong—or every little thing he could have done better.

Why didn't you take that one shot when you were open? Why didn't you pass the ball down low on that one play? What happened on that rebound? Why didn't you grab it?

Rick wasn't trying to make his nephew feel bad; he just wanted to bring everything out of him.

"He had so much potential," Rick said. "And I was scared to death he'd never let it out."

David Wyrick was okay with Rick's coaching methods, to a point. He knew Rick had good intentions. He didn't mind a coach instilling discipline in his son and striving to make him better. But eventually, it got to be too much. Beckham was just a kid—a soft-spoken, easygoing kid who just wanted to have fun and play basketball with his friends. One day, after Rick laid into Beckham long and hard once more, David approached Rick and let him know in not-so-subtle words that he had gone too far. Rick got the message. Always a vocal coach, he developed a new style of sorts. He yelled less, and Beckham was able to relax. It ended up being good for everybody.

But that was the thing about David Wyrick. He was happy his son wanted to play sports, but most of all, he just wanted Beckham to have fun. He never forced Beckham to do something he didn't want to do, and that was good for Beckham. He wasn't burned out by the time he got to high school. If anything, he was ready to take the next step. David did, however, have one requirement. If Beckham didn't want to play sports, then he was going to get a job. He was going to join a club. He was going to do *something*. Coming home from school and lounging on the couch all night wasn't an option. There were times Beckham would say, "You know, I don't think I'm going to play football this year." And David would say, "That's fine. It's your choice. So where are you thinking about getting a job?"

It wasn't long before Beckham was on his way to football practice.

When Beckham got to Roger Bacon in 1998, he played freshman basketball. He wasn't the worst player on the team, but he definitely wasn't the best. Beckham's sophomore year is really when the transformation started. At 6-1, he could've dressed varsity if he wanted, mainly because the team was so young and inexperienced, but he wouldn't have seen the court much. He decided to play JV because at least then he'd be playing every minute.

A lot of sophomores wouldn't have done that. They would have been wooed by the fanfare and brouhaha of playing varsity. But that was Beckham. Basketball was fun, and he wanted to play; he didn't want to sit on a bench. So he didn't.

Tom Thompson, who coached Beckham on JV during the 1999–00 season, was absolutely floored by his ability, especially on defense.

"Beckham Wyrick was the best defensive player I ever coached," Tom said. "I told him, 'Bill doesn't see it yet, but you can guard anybody in the GCL.' Beckham really bought into that. He believed he could shut down anybody defensively. By season's end, I told Bill, 'This kid can guard anybody on the varsity level. Anybody.'"

Bill listened. At the end of the year, he offered to let Beckham dress varsity for the postseason. Bill couldn't guarantee that Beckham would play much, if at all, but he extended the invitation nonetheless. There was just one problem. David Wyrick had scheduled a family vacation to Hawaii during the tournament. So Beckham had a choice: skip Hawaii, sit on the bench and pray for some varsity postseason minutes, or decline Bill's offer and start packing some luggage.

Beckham chose luggage.

"When was I gonna get a chance to go to Hawaii again?" he asked in a no-brainer tone.

Well, Bill didn't like that. No, Beckham probably wasn't going to get much, if any, playing time in that tournament, but dressing varsity was meant as a reward for a sophomore who worked hard, played well on JV and got rave reviews from an assistant. Even more important, Bill always wanted the program to take precedence over everything else—even family vacations, even family vacations to Hawaii. So Bill gave Beckham an ultimatum.

Either you skip the vacation and dress varsity, or I can't guarantee you a spot on the team next year. You'll have to try out all over again.

Most sophomores would have been scared. Startled at the very least. But Beckham, who by his own admission had a knack for questioning authority, was unfazed. He went to Hawaii, even after Bill made him relinquish his jersey.

"Beck and Nate both, you're not gonna tell them what they can and can't do," Matt Reed said.

But that summer, the summer before Beckham's junior year, something happened. Something unexpected. Something crazy. Beckham grew. He sprouted five inches, from 6-1 to 6-6, from perimeter guard to post anchor. In the fall of 2000, he showed up at Fogarty a man and tried out for varsity—and there was no way Bill could even consider cutting him. Beckham started that year and helped Bacon advance to the regional finals.

But that wasn't the end for Beckham. That was the beginning.

The summer before Beckham's junior year, he changed physically; the summer before his senior year, he changed mentally—and there's no debating which transformation was more important. As a junior, even as a starter, Beckham deferred to Josh. He deferred to Frank, to Monty. He deferred to the seniors and was willing to blend in and be a role player. That all changed when he, like several of Bacon's players, played AAU in the summer of 2001. Rules prohibited more than two players from the same high school team playing on the same AAU team. Beckham was put on one team with Frank, while Josh was put on another team with Monty. It was unspoken yet obvious that Josh and Monty were on the "A" team, while Beckham and Frank were on the "B" team.

"I think Beck and Frank were good enough to be on (the "A") team, but (AAU doesn't) want you to be basically practicing high school in the offseason," Monty said. "That's a storied program, Cincy's AAU team. The coach, Mike Price, got me 10 or 15 D-I scholarship offers from teams that never even saw me play. That's how highly he's thought of."

Well, Beckham didn't like playing on the "B" team. He saw all the attention the "A" team got. He saw how they were treated. Beckham knew then that he had something to prove. He had something to prove to the AAU coaches who didn't want him on the "A" team. He had something to prove to Bill, who doubted he could play varsity as a sophomore and who made him try out again as a junior. He had something to prove to everyone who thought he was too laid-back and unassuming to ever become great.

Something inside him snapped.

That summer, more than any summer in his life, Beckham worked to improve his game and his body. He lifted weights harder than he ever had. In AAU games, he started scoring. Then he started scoring more. He and Frank became the go-to guys on that team.

"If you're the go-to guy for 80 games, and if you play well in those 80 games, you're bound to build your confidence," Beckham said. "And, maybe, a little cockiness."

But by that point, Beckham was good. Damn good. And he knew it. And he'd let you know he knew it. And he didn't care that he let you know he knew it.

Finally, the intensity, the aggressiveness, the swagger that Rick Bierman always knew his nephew had, came out. Beckham would talk trash. For four quarters, for 32 minutes, for 1,920 seconds, he would talk trash. He'd initiate it. He'd goad you into it. It was always directed toward his man, and it was always about the game.

I'm shutting you down. You can't guard me. You're not scoring another bucket.

It wasn't pointless braggadocio, either. No, there was a method to Beckham's madness. He'd create whatever mental advantage he could over his opponent, and then he'd snatch it and refuse to relinquish it. Why? Because Beckham knew if he took his man out of the game, then that was one fewer player his team had to worry about. And if his team had one fewer player to worry about, the odds of his team winning got a whole lot better.

And that was all Beckham cared about. Winning.

Because of that, Beckham never let trash talk blur the focus of what he had to do on the court. He was never flamboyant about it. He never sought attention for it. He never got into it with fans. If a fan were heckling him, Beckham wouldn't stare or respond, for that would be to acknowledge it, and he wouldn't allow himself to get distracted like that. He knew he was better-served saving that energy for the real battle—the battle between him and his opponent.

Indeed, for Beckham, like Michael Corleone, it was never personal. It was strictly business.

"Some guys can be cocky and arrogant to make themselves be heard," Cork said. "Beckham just did it. And he could back it up. If you're gonna be cocky and you can back it up, what are they gonna do?"

Bill gave Beckham free rein, perhaps because he knew how important this newfound personality was to the team. A lot of Bacon's players—Josh, Monty, Dave—were quiet by nature. Suddenly, there's this combative, domineering personality in games and at practices. Suddenly, there's a guy who won't back down from any player or shy away from any fray.

Bacon needed that.

"Beckham's somebody you want to be on the court with because—as cliché as it sounds—you know he has your back," Monty said. "I was soft compared to him. He was the tough one. That's the kind of player he was—not that he took care of me, but he helped big time doing tougher, inside work."

It helped that Beckham could do what a lot of guys couldn't. He could check his drama at the door. When it was game time, it was game time. Anything going on in his personal life, anything going on at school, anything going on with a girl, didn't matter. He wouldn't let his non-basketball life interfere with basketball. Off the court, it was, "*Hey, what's up?*" On the court, it was, "*What the fuck are you looking at?*"

Beckham had tight end bulk and power forward sculpt. He could guard any position on the floor—and he would. You knew he was going all out when his cheeks got red. If Beckham's cheeks were red and puffy, his man didn't have a chance.

Even more perplexing than Beckham's alter egos was the speed with which they appeared and disappeared—and on at least one occasion, it rubbed some people the wrong way.

Growing up, Beckham never said to his father, "You know, I might not play basketball this year." It was always football where Beckham wavered. It's not that he didn't love football; he did. But he only loved it on Friday nights. As hard as he tried, as much as he wanted, an unrelenting passion for the game the other six days of the week just wasn't there. It wasn't the physicality that bothered Beckham, nor was it the one-on-one battles the game presented.

Beckham loved all that.

But quite honestly, there was one part of the game that Beckham disliked, one key component that he could have done without. His pads. Beckham hated them. Specifically, he hated putting them on and wearing them.

"Going into the locker room, putting all that heavy, sweaty, stinky stuff on . . ." Beckham said, almost embarrassed at his explanation. "I know it's a terrible reason not to do something."

Terrible or not, that's how Beckham felt. In the fall of 2001, he entered his senior year on the gridiron gushing with his newfound swagger from AAU. It helped that he stood 6-6 and weighed 220 pounds.

"I've known Beck since he was a little kid, and I couldn't believe it was the same guy," Tim McCoy, Sr., said. "He was absolutely the best tight end in the city—and really, the state. He was phenomenal."

Beckham was quick, he was strong, he could leap and he was durable. He was almost an unfair matchup for opposing secondaries, especially playing in Division II. But this wasn't a case of Beckham feasting on helpless high school kids and posting take-it-with-a-grain-of-salt stats. He would have put up numbers against anybody.

"Beckham could've gone to Notre Dame, (Southern Cal)—anywhere," Jon Newton said. "He could've played anywhere as a tight end, and honestly he'd probably be playing on Sundays. I played with (2007 Philadelphia Eagles fifth-round draft pick) Brent Celek at (the University of Cincinnati). Beckham Wyrick as a senior in high school was better than Brent Celek as a senior at UC. Without a doubt. Way more athletic."

Beckham received invitations to attend numerous football camps. Ohio State. Wisconsin. Big schools. BCS schools. But Beckham never went. He never filled out any questionnaires, and he never returned any letters. He knew he wanted to play basketball. He loved basketball. And with basketball, he didn't have to put on pads every day.

Beckham admits that the passion for football outside of Friday night just wasn't there, but something happened in the last game of his high school career that allegedly made a handful of teammates and coaches wonder if Beckham, crazy as it sounds, sabotaged the season. The Spartans went 8–2 during the regular season, qualified for the playoffs for the first time in several years and were seeded No. 2 in the Southwest region (the top four seeds get to host a first-round playoff game). Bacon played No. 7 Dayton Carroll and trailed 18–13 late in the fourth quarter. With time ticking away, the Spartans were driving in front of their home crowd for the game-winning score. On the last play—"It was 4th-and-12 or something," Beckham said—Bacon called a play for its stud tight end. Nate, who was under center, dropped back in the pocket, looked his cousin's way, and, in the face of defensive pressure, unwound. Beckham couldn't come up with the grab. Turnover on downs. Game over. Season over.

After the game, the team, as always, walked to the campus grotto to say a prayer. One of the captains said an "Our Father." But tonight was different. Seniors knelt, heads down, sobbing. The game was over. The season was over. And for the majority of the guys on the team, their athletic careers were over. There was no practice tomorrow; there was no next game to prep for. Soon, they would turn in their pads and be forced to move on with their lives. But the seniors weren't ready for it to be over. They weren't ready to let go. The pain lingered.

After about 15 minutes, Beckham stood up—the first player to do so—and commented on the great season the team had. Then he walked out.

It rubbed some people the wrong way, including Jon Newton, only a junior at the time. Newton still had another year of football left, but the seniors on the team, particularly his fellow linemen, didn't. They weren't going to play in college, either. Their careers had just ended. Newton thought Beckham should have been more sensitive to that fact.

Besides, some thought, *how can the guy who couldn't haul in a season-saving catch on the last play of the game be the first to leave?*

Newton was so angry that he almost went after Beckham, but a coach calmed him down—in that moment, at least. Newton was so offended by Beckham's comment and departure that he actually considered not playing basketball. He didn't want Beckham as a teammate.

"After that comment, I didn't like him for a little bit," Newton said. "I couldn't stand him. It took me two or three weeks to get what he said out of my head. I didn't like it. At all."

It didn't help that some of the players knew football wasn't Beckham's first love. Some supposedly suspected that he was just ready for basketball to start, that he didn't go all out on that last play, that he didn't catch the ball on that last play on purpose.

But those were the emotions of the moment. As competitive as Beckham was, as competitive as he became, there was no way he would intentionally not catch a pass and end what some guys, including himself, had worked four years for. Beckham wasn't capable of such ruthlessness. And it's not as though he had been wide open and dropped the ball; he was well covered. It would have been an impressive snare, to say the least. He just couldn't come up with it.

And yes, Beckham was sad to lose, but at the same time, he didn't see the point of kneeling in the grotto all night crying about it. Crying wouldn't change the outcome. If he insulted any of his teammates by leaving, he certainly didn't mean to. But that was Beckham. He was an all-out competitor during the game, but once it was over, it didn't take long for him to decompress.

When Beckham pursued basketball after high school, some wondered whether he made a mistake. Even Beckham wondered. When he entered his freshman year at the University of North Carolina Wilmington, he encountered another Brewer-like coach in Brad Brownell. Three-hour practices twice a day. Always getting yelled at. As a freshman, he had no rights. *Do what coach says, do everything he says, and don't say a word.* That was hard for Beckham. This was the same guy who was never intimidated by authority, who scoffed at the threat of having to try out again if he went to Hawaii. And here he was, a college freshman at the bottom of the basketball totem pole, away from home for the first time, one year removed from guarding LeBron James.

It was hard.

And that's when Beckham started writing letters to football coaches.

"I was writing letters to all these schools—UC, Miami of Ohio," Beckham said. "I was like, 'Hey, I made a mistake. I wanna come back home and play football.'"

But by then it was too late. No one responded. Beckham doesn't even know if the letters got through. Still, he couldn't help but think he made the wrong choice and wondered what he should do. Should he return home? Should he walk away from basketball? Should he keep reaching out to football coaches?

During Beckham's senior year at Bacon, however, college was still a ways off. He was focused on shutting down every opponent he faced—whether it was a league rival's best player or the greatest player in the history of prep basketball.

But something happened on January 11, 2002. Something stunning, something inexplicable, something that Beckham was right in the thick of that would forever alter the course of that season.

And make life as a Spartan a whole lot tougher.

# CHAPTER FIVE

THE CJ GAME

Ask any player on the 2001–02 Roger Bacon basketball team about "the CJ game," and reactions range from smiles to laughs to looks of sheer terror.

It's irrelevant that Roger Bacon played Chaminade-Julienne twice that season; utter those three words, and every player instantly knows which one you're referring to—not because of what happened during that game, but because of what happened after it.

Said Tim McCoy, "That's my biggest memory from that season."

Exactly halfway through the year, the Spartans were 8–2. Their only two losses were to nationally ranked teams, one of which boasted the best prep player on the planet. Based on that information alone, most would think Bacon was having a pretty good season. Bill, of course, didn't see it that way. In his eyes, his team—a unanimous preseason city No. 1 with five returning starters—wasn't playing to its potential.

"Expectations are a funny thing; it's great that people think highly of your team, and it's great that your players are confident in their ability and that people think you can do special things," Brian Neal said. "But it's also dangerous. It can be dangerous when it seeps into the work ethic, when it seeps into the teamwork, when it seeps into the fabric of what you believe in. And sometimes it's not even consciously. Sometimes it's just something that evolves. Sometimes the expectations weigh you down. We tried to talk (that year) about being in the moment and not thinking about what was going to happen in March, but I don't know if you can ever just get that out of your head. You can try to dismiss it and focus on the now and focus on the moment, but who's to say these 16- and 17-year-old kids weren't always talking about March in their spare time? So from that standpoint, it seemed as though nothing mattered (to the players) except for the tournament—

and at times, especially early that year, we played like it. And that frosted Bill. That did not sit well with him. He was a guy who thought, 'We're going to commit to excellence, and we're going to be good every day we step in this gym.'"

Sometimes records don't tell the whole story. That year for Bacon, even at 8–2, was one of those times. Sure, there was the season-opening 63–38 drubbing of North College Hill at Xavier University's Cintas Center, a game in which Bacon led 22–4 after the first quarter. An impressive performance, yes, but one many might expect when playing an undersized team from Division III.

The Spartans then traveled to McNicholas for their first conference game of the season. Playing league games on the road, especially in the GCL, is always a tough task, and in those games, records and rankings don't matter. Those games are personal. It's all about pride. That said, McNicholas had just two players—senior co-captains Geoff Hensley and Brian Chrin—with anything resembling significant varsity experience. Nevertheless, McNicholas jumped on Bacon, hitting three three-pointers in the first quarter to take a 20–10 lead.

"I wasn't surprised because they have good players," Bill told the *Cincinnati Post*. "*Angry* is a better word. We want to pride ourselves on defense, and in the first quarter, it looked like we had never practiced."

Bacon came back to force overtime, and a slashing layup by Frank Phillips with 32 seconds left gave the Spartans a 63–61 lead; they held on for a 64–61 win—despite not making a single three-pointer the entire game.

"We didn't shoot well, and we didn't guard well," Bill told the *Cincinnati Enquirer*. "I don't know why a mature group like ours would come out like that."

Bacon followed with a 61–53 home win over GCL rival Purcell Marian a week later. Mike Pilgrim, who would play for Cincinnati and Seton Hall, was Purcell's best player, but the Cavaliers weren't all that balanced. Purcell entered the game ranked fourth in the city in Divisions II-IV but dropped to 1–3 with the loss. So Bacon's eight-point win, while nice, wasn't by any means impressive.

Bacon improved to 4–0 with a 71–55 win at Elder on December 18, four days before taking on the Irish at Kent State. Whenever a Division

II team beats a team from the GCL-South, especially on the road, it's a big deal, particularly when the margin of victory is 16 points. After all, that was only Bacon's second win at Elder since 1980, and SVSM head coach Dru Joyce, scouting for his team's upcoming game against the Spartans, was on hand to see it.

But if there were ever a time to take a win over the GCL-South with a smidgen of salt, this was it. Elder—coached by Joe Schoenfeld, who has a state title on his résumé—had graduated its all-senior starting lineup from a season ago, a starting five that carried the Panthers to the Division I state final, where they lost 49–46 to Cleveland St. Ignatius. The Elder team that Bacon beat was largely inexperienced. In fact, the Panthers, whose loss to Bacon was their third straight home defeat, fell to 1–4 on the season. Granted, they wound up going 13–3 the rest of the way—with those three losses coming by a combined 11 points—and winning the GCL-South. But five games into the season in mid-December, Elder, with five new starters, was still finding its way.

Then, of course, came the game against SVSM. The suspect foul calls and the free-throw discrepancy notwithstanding, Bacon led by 10 after the first quarter and had the lead—albeit by one point—entering the fourth. The game served as validation for the Spartans should they see LeBron and SVSM in March, but it was still a tough loss, one that Bill, despite his "Remember how this feels" sentiment, struggled to accept.

"Bill was bummed on the way home," Peggy said. "That was a long, quiet drive."

After the game against SVSM, the Spartans traveled to Lewes, Delaware, for the Slam Dunk to the Beach Holiday Tournament. They beat Philadelphia Archbishop Carroll 70–60 and Brooklyn's Bishop Loughlin 62–51. Bacon was feeling pretty good about itself, especially since Bishop Loughlin had Curtis Sumpter, who would go on to earn All-Big East honors at Villanova.

But against Tabor Academy, a school from Massachusetts ranked fifteenth in the country, Bacon was embarrassed—well, as much as a team can be for leading 39–35 entering the fourth quarter. The Spartans were outscored 24–10 in that final frame, they lost 59–49, and Torin Francis, who would go on to star at Notre Dame, destroyed Bacon inside. He outscored Monty 30–0. To lose to a good team is one thing, but to get manhandled, especially inside, especially with Bill at the helm, was unthinkable.

Back in Cincinnati, two blowout wins over struggling teams did little to temper Bill's rage. The Spartans beat Badin 72–48 and then destroyed 1–7 Northwest by a final score of 83–29 for a two-game onslaught of 155–77. Halfway through the regular season, the Spartans were 8–2.

And then . . .

. . . along came CJ.

Bacon and CJ had played some epic games over the years, including Josh Hausfeld's 42-pointer two seasons earlier. They had forged an intense rivalry. Bacon hated playing at CJ. Long drive to Dayton. Small gym.

"Every time we went up there," Josh said, "it was, 'Let's just try to get a win and get out of there.'"

CJ's head coach, Joe Staley, graduated from the school in 1972 and had led his alma mater to two state Final Fours, including a runner-up finish in 1991. He was a good, experienced coach whose 2001–02 squad was not without talent. Top players were Mark Johnigan, Richard Poole, Jermiel Atkins and, perhaps most notably, Nathan Peavy, a 6-6 center who would play collegiately at Miami of Ohio and professionally in Germany. His father, Terry Peavy, played in the NBA.

In short, CJ had some good players—but they were young players. Peavy, Poole and Atkins were all juniors. In many respects, that CJ team was still a season away from being truly dangerous—and in fact, the Eagles went 22–4 the following year and won a district title. But that was the following year.

"CJ had a good team in '01–02," Brian Neal said. "But certainly that wasn't one of the best teams they had had."

That showed in the first quarter against Bacon. In a game played at CJ on Friday, January 11, 2002, in the middle of a blizzard, the Spartans came out scorching. To CJ's fans, that first quarter probably felt like the most lopsided eight minutes in program history. Indeed, this was not at all like the McNicholas game in which Bacon played a league rival on the road and trailed by 10 after the first quarter.

No, a slow start wasn't the problem in this one.

BACON CONTROLS THE OPENING tap, and Beckham hoists the first shot of the game, drilling a three from the corner. Dave follows with a three from the wing on the Spartans' next possession. On the next, it's Beckham for three again, this time from the opposite corner. After a blocked shot by Monty, Dave pushes the ball and finds Beckham in the corner for another three. Buckets.

The game is barely two minutes old, and already Bacon has hit four threes and leads 12–1.

It doesn't end there. Frank zips a pass down low to Beckham, who pump-fakes, gets fouled and converts the layin and the and-one. Beckham returns the favor soon after, finding Frank in rhythm for a short floater. Then it's another layin from Frank and another three from Beckham, who has already hit four from downtown. Frank splashes a jumper from the left baseline. Josh gets in on the act, nailing a three from the corner.

CJ manages to hit a few buckets here and there and somehow only trails 27–15 at the end of one. But Bacon's ball movement those first eight minutes was exquisite. The Spartans zipped the ball crisply across the court. They hit six threes. They were on pace to break 100 points. It was a thing of beauty.

And it didn't last.

The second quarter opens with Josh botching a layup on one end, and Mark Johnigan drilling a three on the other. Five-point swing. Bacon's next three possessions are beyond forgettable. Turnover, turnover, air-ball. CJ follows with a layup. After several trips to the foul line for both sides, the Spartans lead 31–25 with 2:44 left in the second quarter. Their 12-point lead has been cut in half.

A minute later, another three by Johnigan. 31–29, Bacon. Beckham misses from the outside. Bacon has scored just four points in seven minutes. Dave gets a steal and takes it all the way for a layin. Beckham does the same on the next play. 35–29, Bacon. Finally, breathing room once more. But CJ's Richard Poole knifes through the lane for a layup just before time expires. Bacon, outscored 16–8 in the second quarter, leads 35–31 at the break. But it doesn't feel that way. In just one quarter, the feeling went from, *Wow, how are we only up by 12?* to *Wow, are we really still winning?*

Monty opens the second half with a jumper. Johnigan responds with a jumper of his own. Back to Monty. Foul. And-one. Three-point play. 40–33, Bacon. Two free throws by CJ. Monty with an up-and-under. 42–35, Bacon. A jumper for CJ. Frank with two free throws. Back and forth it goes. Dave hits a wide-open three from the top of the key. Bacon leads 47–38 with 4:30 left in the third quarter. This is more like it.

On defense, Frank rotates to take a charge and gets stampeded. He splats on the court like roadkill. The whistle blows. Blocking foul on Frank. Dave and Monty, in utter disbelief at the call, grab their heads with both hands. Bill goes crazy. The whistle pierces the gym once more. Technical foul on Bill. Johnigan makes one of two free throws.

47–39, Bacon, with 3:19 left in third.

Both teams exchange sloppy possessions. CJ pokes the ball out of bounds. Bacon basketball. Only it isn't. The ref blows his whistle. Another technical foul on the Spartans, this time on the bench. CJ gets two free throws and the ball.

"To this day, I still can't tell you what that one was for," Brian Neal said.

Johnigan hits both free throws. 47–41, Bacon. Nate with a layin. 49–41, Bacon. Two free throws for CJ. 49–43, Bacon.

Coast-to-coast layup for CJ. And-one. The free throw is no good. Rebound CJ. Another foul on Bacon, another free throw for CJ. Less than 10 seconds remain in the quarter. Beckham looks to in-bound the ball. Like a quarterback in the pocket, he surveys the court and eyes Josh streaking down the right sideline 20 yards ahead. Beckham unwinds. The ball sails past halfcourt but gets broken up at the three-point line. CJ recovers the loose ball and attacks. A floater clanks off the back iron, but the put-back is true as time expires.

Bacon, which scored just two points in the last four minutes and 30 seconds of the third quarter, clings to a 49–48 lead entering the final period. CJ closed on a 7–0 run and for the second straight quarter hit a shot just before time expired. After scoring 27 points in the first quarter, Bacon has netted just 22 in the second and third quarters combined.

Bacon has the ball to start the fourth. Turnover. Nathan Peavy with a layin. The Eagles' cheering section erupts. CJ, up 50–49, has its first lead of the game.

The Spartans answer right away. Josh drives and finds Monty, who flicks up a shot and gets the bounce. 51–50, Bacon. Bacon goes to a 1-3-1 zone and forces a travel. Monty is fouled and makes both free throws. 53–50, Bacon. Bacon stays in the 1-3-1, contests a three and gets the rebound. Beckham curls around a screen, flashes to the foul line, gets a pass from Josh and takes it in for a layup. 55–50, Bacon. A 6–0 run.

Maybe things are going to be okay.

Foul on Bacon. Two free throws for CJ. 55–52, Bacon.

Beckham travels. A foul on Monty. Two more free throws for CJ. 55–54, Bacon. Foul on CJ. Frank hits both ends of a one-and-one. 57–54, Bacon. Less than two minutes remain. Peavy scores off an out-of-bounds play. 57–56, Bacon, 1:48 left. Frank takes it to the bucket and gets fouled. Two free throws. 59–56, Bacon. Foul on Beckham. Two free throws for CJ. 59–58, Bacon. Frank dribbles off his foot. Loose-ball scramble. Dave recovers it and gets fouled. He makes the first, misses the second. 60–58, Bacon, less than a minute to go. Layup, CJ. Tie game, 60–60. The Eagles' bench leaps. Their fans frenzy.

Frank drives to the basket once more and is fouled once more. Two free throws. He bricks the first. A CJ player walks right up to him and claps in his face. Frank doesn't notice. He wipes sweat from his brow and stares at the rim. Money. 61–60, Bacon. CJ walks the ball up the floor and calls timeout.

12.3 seconds to go.

A CJ floater rims out. Touch foul on Dave. Two free throws. CJ drills the first. Tie game, 61–61, with 6.0 seconds left. The second freebie hits the back iron, ricochets to the front and bounces out. The ball is tipped several times before Beckham corrals it in the paint. He looks to advance the ball upcourt to win the game. Dave is on his left. Frank is on his right. He wants to pass to one of them, to give them a chance to score and sneak out of Dayton with a win. But he can't. He doesn't. Before he can even pick up his dribble, the ball bounces awkwardly out of his grasp. No CJ player pokes it away, no CJ player pressures him, and the ball doesn't bounce off his shoe. It just spurts out of his grasp, seemingly on its own, as if Beckham had no say in the matter.

As if it were meant to be.

CJ's ball. 3.9 seconds left. Bacon calls timeout.

It has come to this.

In one huddle, there's Bill, imploring his players to get a stop and force overtime. He has but one message: Switch everything. Don't fight through picks. If there's a pick, switch. No one gets a clean look at the basket. No one. No matter what happens, switch. Switch, switch, switch. Switch everything.

In the other huddle, Joe Staley draws up a play to win the game, a game his team has led for a total of less than 10 seconds.

Ten players walk onto the court. One side of the gym excitedly hopes for the best; the other timidly worries for the worst. Bill goes man-to-man with Frank, Beckham, Josh, Monty and Nate. Josh sticks Mark Johnigan, who has scored a team-high 13 points. Johnigan stands toward the left side of the paint about five feet from the basket as CJ prepares to in-bound. Johnigan jogs toward the foul line and lays a half-hearted screen on Beckham at the elbow. And that's when Beckham does it. He turns right.

And he fights through the pick.

Beckham stays with his man, who runs toward the basket. Josh abandons Johnigan at the foul line and switches down to seal the paint. Beckham's man is now double-teamed, meaning someone—Mark Johnigan—is now unguarded.

It takes Beckham all of about two seconds to realize this, which, in an end-of-game scenario, is two seconds too long. By the time Beckham turns around, Johnigan has already curled left inside the key and beelined toward his bench to accept the in-bounds pass. He has squared up on the wing, just behind the three-point line. Beckham races from under the basket to contest the shot. Frank sees what has happened and fights through his man to do the same. Neither he nor Beckham arrives in time. Johnigan, wide open, lets it fly. The attempt is so uncontested, the look so clean, the form so pure, that you almost don't even have to look. You just know.

Hell, the ball doesn't even touch the rim.

64–61, CJ. Frank looks to an official to call timeout. So does Nate. But it's useless. There's no time. The buzzer has sounded. The game is over. CJ's players and coaches rush the floor. Their fans, delirious, spill onto the court, and five shell-shocked Spartans plod to their bench in disbelief.

• • • •

Peggy and the girls didn't go to the game that night. It wasn't often that Peggy missed a game, but it was in Dayton, there was a snowstorm and she was tired from a long week at work, so she decided to sit this one out and stay in with her daughters.

Besides, she figured Bacon would win.

Bill's parents braved the blizzard. Whenever Peggy missed a game, she'd ask them to call afterward and let her know what happened. She was curious about the outcome, of course, but she also wanted to know what kind of mood Bill would be in when he got home. Bill took every loss seriously, and Peggy never second-guessed what he did on the sidelines. She learned not to. Early on in Bill's tenure at Bacon, she asked him after a loss why he didn't call a timeout during what she thought was a critical juncture in the game.

"Which way was the possession arrow pointing?" Bill asked.

Peggy didn't know.

"Were they in the bonus?" Bill continued. "Were we?"

Bill spat off about a dozen questions. Peggy's response to all of them was, "I don't know." From that point on, Peggy realized she should leave the coaching to Bill. If he needed to vent, she would listen. If he wanted advice on a player, she was there. Otherwise, Bill just wanted support, win or lose. And Peggy always gave it.

When she got the call from Bill's parents the night of the CJ game, when she found out the Spartans had lost and that they had lost on a three at the buzzer, she was speechless. Just dead silent. The girls wanted to know what happened.

"Let's get to sleep," Peggy told her daughters. "We'll talk to daddy in the morning."

That was probably a wise choice.

Bill stood in CJ's gym that night, not understanding what he had just witnessed. His team had scored 27 points in the first quarter but just 34 thereafter. The Spartans made seven threes for the game but only one after the first eight minutes. They led by double digits in the first quarter and by nine in the third and couldn't hold either lead. They made just three field goals in the final 12 minutes and 30 seconds of the second half. For three straight quarters—the second, third and fourth—CJ hit a shot at or near the buzzer, including the game-winner to give the Eagles their biggest, and only their second, lead of the game: three points.

Bill couldn't get that last shot out of his head.

What happened? Where was the switch? I told them to switch everything. I specifically told them one thing to do, they didn't do it, and we lost the game. What the fuck's going on?

"Those guys had a great junior year, everybody was coming back, expectations were high, we almost beat LeBron—they thought they were going to waltz their way to whatever," Brian Neal said. "And Bill thought, 'Enough's enough. I've lost their attention. I've lost my grip on this team—and I'm gonna get it back right now.'"

Bill had a rule for his players, a rule his players knew never to break. When a game had ended and the team went to the locker room to hear Bill's postgame thoughts, they didn't remove anything. They didn't untuck a jersey, they didn't untie a shoe, they didn't un-velcro an ankle brace. It was for one reason and one reason only—when the coach is talking after the game, you give him your full attention. You listen. You're not going to be distracted, however much or little, by taking care of your personal business while the coach is talking. No matter what.

"That's another thing I loved about him," Marcus Smith said. "He knew how he wanted everything. There was a set way to do everything. It was a command. When the game was over, you didn't take shit off until things was carried out. There wasn't any question about how you were supposed to do things or what the Bacon way was. It was, 'This is how we do things.' That's why I loved him. He gave me that structure in my life that I needed at the time."

Once Bill was finished talking, he would leave the locker room, and players were free to shower. When they were showered and dressed, Bill would re-enter the locker room and go over upcoming announcements about the next practice, the next game, the next whatever. On this night, while the players were showering, Bill stuck his head in the locker room. He didn't see the players, and the players didn't see him. He simply stuck his head in just to listen, just to see what he could hear.

And what he heard was laughter.

"Frank and Leonard were laughing and carrying on about how much CJ celebrated, storming the court like they had just won state," Marcus said. "(Coach Brewer thought) we were laughing as though we weren't taking the loss seriously, but that wasn't the case."

Bill didn't know the reason for the laughter. He couldn't hear the words being said. He didn't even know exactly who was doing the laughing. He didn't care, either. All he knew was, his team had just lost a game it had no business losing—to a league rival, no less—and now, instead of being sad, instead of being angry, instead of being embarrassed at their lackluster performance, they were laughing in the showers.

Bill took every loss hard. Every loss. Well, almost every loss. If his team lost by 15 or 20 points, "then their Xs are better than your Os," he would say. But a two-point loss? A three-point loss? Bill always felt that was on him. In his mind, if your team loses by one possession, then you, as a coach, could have—and should have—done something differently to alter the outcome of the game. Bill saw it as his job to find the answer as to what that something might have been; that way, he wouldn't make the same mistake again.

Against CJ, the answer, in theory, was clear. Bacon was whistled for two technicals—one on Bill, one on the bench—that resulted in three CJ points. Bacon lost by three. Case closed. But that wasn't it. On this night, that wasn't the answer. On this night, the onus wasn't on Bill.

"Even with the technical fouls, even with CJ playing at their place, Bill felt the game shouldn't have been that close," Brian Neal said. "He felt the guys just weren't playing to their potential. They're not playing with urgency. They're not showing that they understand this is their last go-around."

Going undefeated in the GCL, which hadn't been done by any GCL team since the mid-1970s, was one of Bacon's preseason goals.

Five league games into the schedule, that was no longer possible. Did the players realize that? Did they even care? Bill was at his breaking point. Not sustaining leads, not listening in the huddle, giving up three buzzer-beaters in one game, laughing after a loss—for Bill, this was proof that he had lost his team. And he knew what he had to do.

After the players had showered and dressed and gathered together, it began. What they thought would be a couple of quick closing remarks ended up being a tirade that lasted close to an hour and a half. Bill called out everyone, starting with Tim McCoy.

"He asked me if I liked winning," McCoy said. "He said I was the only one who he thought was competitive and cared about winning. That obviously wasn't true, but I think he was just trying to use me as an example because I'm kind of a fiery guy myself. I remember he asked what we needed to do to be more competitive. I didn't have an answer."

Bill then called out Josh, who had just played one of his worst games of the year. Josh usually kept his mouth shut when he was getting torn into, but on that night, he didn't. Just as he had done when Brian Neal urged him at practice to take the ball up with more authority, Josh snapped back—and he snapped back disrespectfully.

"A lot of times when Coach Brewer gives it to you, you just take it," Josh said. "For whatever reason, I felt like I needed to speak up and get everything out there."

That only incensed Bill more.

"Brewer just went off on him," Jon Newton said. "It was like a father and son going back and forth and getting into it—only with 20 guys watching."

That night, it wasn't Josh's turnovers that got Bill's goat. It was his scoring—or lack thereof. Josh hit a three in the first quarter, and that was it. Three points. Three points for the entire game. How does the same kid who dropped 42 on CJ as a sophomore only score three as a senior? Where was he that night? What was going on?

Monty got it, too. After the game against Tabor Academy—the game in which Torin Francis outscored him 30-0—Bill blew up at his junior center. Monty had a great game a few days earlier against Curtis Sumpter, one of the best players in the country, and was getting all kinds of attention from elite programs, including ones from the Big East. Monty was pretty pleased with himself. But two days later, in Bacon's last game of the tournament, Monty got manhandled by Francis.

"Well, Monty," Bill yelled in the locker room after that game, "you might as well accept your scholarship to Mount St. Joe (a Division III school in Cincinnati) because you fucking suck!"

That was the last time Monty went scoreless in his prep career.

"That's just him keeping me grounded," Monty said. "I came off that game a couple days before, there was a lot of buzz going—and he knew what was happening. So he made sure he got me back real quick to where I needed to be."

The night of the CJ game, Bill tore into Monty once more. It didn't matter that Monty chipped in with 11 points and had several timely baskets. Bill was frustrated, frustrated because his players weren't taking every game as seriously as they needed to be taken, frustrated because they weren't playing at a high level consistently, frustrated because they didn't *get it*. He went down the line. No one was spared.

Not even Frank. Bill loved Frank. Frank always did what he was supposed to do. He always busted his butt on defense. In the 16-point win at Elder, Frank had one of the most impressive plays of the season. After a careless crosscourt pass got intercepted, an Elder defender casually took the ball the other way, thinking he had an easy breakaway layup. But Frank, who was responsible for the turnover, refused to concede the two points and sprinted back on defense. Just as the Elder player went up for the finger roll, Frank came out of nowhere, pinned the ball against the glass, came down with it and fired a full-court bullet to Josh, who dunked it on the other end.

"Sweetest play all year," Jon Newton said. "Frank was running so fast, you would've thought his shoes were on fire."

Bill had gotten up to yell at Frank for the turnover, but after seeing the way Frank hustled, after seeing the way he didn't give up on the play, after seeing the way he turned two points for Elder into two points for Bacon, he didn't say a word. How could he? And with that, Frank Phillips did what no Roger Bacon player had ever done.

He silenced Bill Brewer.

But the night of the CJ game, not even Frank was pardoned. Bill laid into him. He laid into everyone. Minutes passed. It was tirade, silence, tirade, silence. Wash, rinse, repeat.

"You kept thinking, 'When are we gonna leave?'" Monty said. "Because when you're 16, 17, 18, that's all you care about. This guy just needs to shut up and let us go home. And of course he knows that's what we're thinking, so he's gonna do it just to spite us."

At one point, one of Bacon's players slyly glanced—or at least tried to slyly glance—at his watch. Bill saw it.

Oh, I'm sorry. Am I wasting your time? Is there someplace more important you have to be? Is that it?

"WE CAN SIT HERE ALL FUCKING NIGHT!" Bill snapped, frothy spittle spraying the locker room floor.

Rule No. 1, high school basketball players: never give a madman more ammo.

The tirade continued. Bill laid into his players for being too worried about their girlfriends, for not being focused enough on the team, for having their mommies and daddies call and ask about playing time. He went off on anything and everything, on anyone and everyone.

"Keep in mind we're in Dayton and our parents are upstairs waiting," Josh said. "Coach Brewer didn't care about any of that. He was going to unload on us, and we were gonna figure things out right then and there. He was gonna say or do whatever it took to move the season forward after that loss. This was that make-or-break, do-or-die moment that you have in life."

At one point, Dave Bidwell heard a knock on the door. It was one of CJ's janitors.

"Give me the keys," Bids said. "I'll lock up."

Eventually, after an hour and a half, it was over. Bacon's players and coaches exited the locker room into total darkness. The lights had been turned out. Every fan had left. No one, save for a few Bacon parents, was there, not even the janitors.

But Bill, it seems, made an impression on his players.

"(The CJ game) was maybe one of those times where confidence turned to cockiness," Monty said. "Everybody by that time knew we were good. We had just gone to Delaware and beaten some really good teams. People started to know who we were, and that's when it turned to cockiness."

Said Dave Johnson, "We let that CJ game slip away. We didn't play our best and probably didn't try our hardest. That's probably what set Bill off because there was no way we should have lost that game."

Of course, if any of Bacon's players thought the tirade was it, if any of Bacon's players thought the tirade was their punishment, they were deeply, deeply mistaken. Before dismissing the team, Bill offered one final ominous declaration:

"We'll see you first thing in the morning."

It was past 1 a.m. by the time the team drove back to Cincinnati and got home, and they needed to be at Bacon a little after sunrise. Josh wondered if he should even bother going to sleep, if he'd be better off staying up through the night and crashing after practice. But in the end he chose sleep.

Wise choice.

The players remember that practice more than the tirade itself, but that's not surprising. Bill had a way of making practices unforgettable. On the average team, maybe a lot of players would have been angry at Frank and Leonard for carrying on in the shower that night at CJ, for laughing and causing Bill to react the way he did. But no Bacon player was. Maybe's Bill blowup was inevitable. Maybe it was for the best. But as far as Frank was concerned, no one—not Josh, not Beckham, not Dave, not Monty—could get mad at him. Frank was just being Frank. And that was a good thing.

Because without him, there's a good chance that season unfolds a little differently.

CHAPTER SIX

THE TRANSFER

In the summer of 2004, two years after graduating from Roger Bacon, Frank Phillips came home from college and ventured across the state line to Covington, Kentucky. It was here, along the banks of the Ohio River, that he was seen not as a ball player, a man or even a human, but was instead swept up in a monsoon of malice, swallowed whole by a tsunami of scorn.

In a way, in a sad, sad way, Frank was lucky. He had made it the first 20 years of his life without feeling the wrath of racism, 20 years without feeling the tempest of oppression drench his skin. But eventually, inevitably, he felt it.

Frank grew up in Bond Hill, a predominantly African-American neighborhood in Northeast Cincinnati. It was a rough part of town. Guns, drugs, violence. Frank was exposed to this lifestyle at an early age, but thanks to his older brother, Marcus, he was in many ways shielded from it. Frank's mother, Jerelene, who goes by "Jerry," knew what the neighborhood could do to Frank. She knew because she saw what it did to Marcus. So did Frank's uncle, Jerome Harris.

"Marcus was my first Frankie," Jerome said with a tinge of sadness. "I taught him every sport—football, basketball, wrestling. He was so good at football."

Marcus, nearly a decade older than Frank, played football for CAPE—the now defunct Cincinnati Academy of Physical Education, which opened in 1977 and boasted one of the state's best small-school football programs in the 1980s and early '90s. CAPE won several state titles before eventually closing.

"They promised to stress academics," Jerome said, "but they never did."

CAPE drew kids—many of whom came from low-income, single-parent households—from all over the city. One of those kids was Marcus Phillips, who was a standout athlete. But that didn't matter. He got sucked into the street life. He got sucked into Bond Hill. He stayed out late, he drank, he got into drugs, and, despite urgings from his mother, he never went to college.

"Marcus was just enjoying life," Jerry said. "I wanted him to get a trade, but he wasn't interested in doing that. Making that fast money got him hooked."

Said Frank, "Marcus was kind of like the nice guy. He did have another side to him, he did get in a lot of trouble growing up—but he was in no way like anybody around the neighborhood."

Jerry knew that, too, but she saw what happened to Marcus anyway. That's when she knew she had to get Frank out of Bond Hill. She feared for his future. She feared for his life. So Jerry sent Frank to schools outside the district, schools that were predominantly white.

Like Marcus, Frank was a good athlete. He excelled in baseball and football, but basketball, thanks to Jerome, was his best sport—not to mention his true passion. Jerome spent many years as a volunteer coach at Friars Club, which uses sports to reach at-risk youth and provide a positive outlet in their lives. Jerome, who played high school basketball at Walnut Hills in Cincinnati, pushed Frank to succeed on the court. He had Frank dribbling with his left hand before he could even dribble with his right. Jerome would call Frank every day after school and ask him the holy triumvirate of questions.

Did you eat a snack? Did you do your homework? Did you do your dribbling drills?

Frank would go out on the front porch and dribble. If it was raining, he'd go in the basement. Sometimes he'd go in the basement anyway.

The basement was safer.

Either way, Frank did his dribbles every day. Right hand, left hand, crossover, crossover. By the time Frank entered Roger Bacon as a junior, Moeller basketball coach Carl Kremer, who has won multiple Ohio Division I state titles, said Frank had the best crossover first step he'd ever seen.

That was because of all the hours Frank put in—and the hours Jerome made him put in—years earlier. Starting in second grade, Frank would play at Friars on the weekends and stay with Jerome. He averaged around 18 points per game in third grade playing for a team that averaged around 25. He'd rip a rebound and go coast to coast. And the scary thing was, he'd pass. That was a product of Jerome, too. Jerome wouldn't let Frank become like so many selfish players he had seen and coached in the past.

"My uncle gave me my basketball knowledge," Frank said. "He had me in the gym all the time. Left-handed layups, left-handed dribbles. After practice, I was doing stuff for hours on my own—shooting, dribbling. The little things. I give all credit to him."

For all intents and purposes, Jerome was the father figure in Frank's life. Frank's biological father, Franklin, was around in some ways, not as much in others. When it came to basketball, he was there for his son. Oh, was he ever. He was that loud, proud parent who would cheer Frank's every move and jeer every perceived injustice. As a son, Frank misses those days.

But what he doesn't miss are the sleepless nights he spent lying awake in bed listening to his parents argue. Outside of basketball, Frank didn't have a strong connection with his father. According to Jerry, it's not that her husband didn't want to be there for Frank; it's just that he didn't know how. He didn't have a strong connection with his own father, so when the time came to build a bond with Frank, he wasn't quite sure how to do that. Rather than teach his sons how to be men, he preferred they learn on their own.

"He didn't teach them how to mow the grass or work on cars—things I wanted him to teach," Jerry said. "He was a good father and husband, but not the the type of father and husband I wanted to be with long term, I guess because I fell out of love."

Frank could tell at a young age that his parents weren't happy, that they tried their best to be happy for his sake. But Frank didn't want them to do that. Many kids might not understand why their parents argue; they think they should just be together and be happy no matter what because that's how it's supposed to work. Frank, however, could see the truth. He knew his parents shouldn't be together, which is why he doesn't remember being too distraught in eighth grade when they separated or when his father didn't come around to see him much.

"I really wasn't mad, and I didn't care, either," Frank said. "I think I was just a mommy's boy. (I told my mom), 'We won't need him. I can do this. I'll clean. I'll fix this. I'll do whatever he was supposed to do.' It was fine with me. I wasn't in need of a dad."

Jerry, however, recalls a slightly different picture. After the separation, she moved out of Bond Hill. She let Frank stay with his father for the remainder of eighth grade but made it clear he'd be moving in with her that summer. Had Jerry stayed in Bond Hill, she likely would have sent Frank to Withrow or Woodward, two public high schools about which she hadn't heard great things. Jerry wanted Frank to stay focused on school and basketball and keep his grades up. Most important, she wanted him to fall in with a good crowd. She saw with Marcus how a bad crowd can corrupt a good person, so she moved to Forest Park, where Frank enrolled at the local public high school, Winton Woods. Despite the separation, Franklin still wanted to support his son. He would send money whenever he could, but he wouldn't drop by the house to spend time with Frank. He wouldn't pick him up and take him places. During that time, Frank's freshman year of high school, his grades dropped significantly.

"I knew something was going on," Jerry said. "I kept trying to talk to Frank, but he never really wanted to talk and tell me how he felt. I kept assuring him that we loved him and that the separation had nothing to do with him. But it hurt knowing the family wasn't together. When parents go through divorces, kids go through it, too."

So Frank, as he had done all his life, devoted himself to basketball even more. Basketball was his happy place, his safety net, just as it was in Bond Hill, where he was in many ways shielded from the realities of the neighborhood.

For starters, Frank was a charmer. He always had that smile, that toothy ear-to-ear grin that would have made even the Grinch jealous. Frank was physical on the basketball court but easygoing off it. He wasn't the aggressive type. He wasn't the type to start anything with anyone. But he could flat out play ball. When he was younger, he and Marcus played a lot of one-on-one. Marcus was older, taller and stronger, so eventually, mercifully, the two stopped playing each other.

Because Frank started to win. And win convincingly.

Marcus' friends loved that. They respected Frank for it, which was a good thing because they were seen as enforcers in Bond Hill. Messing with Frank meant messing with Marcus, and messing with Marcus meant messing with Marcus' friends. And no one wanted to mess with Marcus' friends. So Frank could go outside to the concrete courts and play basketball with relative peace of mind that nothing bad would happen to him. Frank, in essence, had protection.

Frank played all the time growing up. He played Friars. He played AAU. He played for Winton Woods. But playing in Bond Hill was where Frank got his swagger. It was where Frank got his fearlessness. Frank was never afraid to be in the spotlight—and that's why playing for the Winton Woods Warriors was so frustrating.

In a three-year span from 1999–2000 to 2001–02, the Warriors went 68–4 and won three city titles with stars such as Robert Hite, who played for the University of Miami and in the NBA with the Miami Heat and New Jersey Nets; DeForrest Riley, who played for Penn State University; and C.J. Anderson, who played for Xavier.

But Frank was not a part of that success. Even though he felt he had the talent to play varsity in ninth grade, Winton Woods put him on the freshman team. Jerome didn't mind that so much; he was okay with Frank getting acclimated to high school basketball. But when Frank didn't make varsity as a sophomore—he played JV, started, and was the best player on a team that went undefeated—Jerome felt it was an injustice. So did Frank, who quickly became disenchanted with the program.

To make matters worse, Winton Woods, despite all its success in the regular season, had a series of early round playoff exits. The Warriors went undefeated during the 1999–00 regular season but then lost in the second round of the playoffs to Hamilton. All the while, Frank, playing for an undefeated JV team, kept wondering the same thing.

When do I get my chance?

Those two years were rough on Frank. He had moved to a new part of town, he started going to a new school, he didn't have his father around, and on top of all that, he felt he was getting swindled on the basketball court, which, at the time, was one of the few positive outlets he had in his life. It was sad. Jerry could see the sadness in Frank. She could see the sadness in his eyes. Frank was somebody who was always smiling, always laughing. Sometimes, he and Jerry would be driving somewhere and they'd hear a song on the radio that they both knew and liked and they would just start singing together. Jerry loved Frank's smile, and she always did whatever she could to keep it on his face. But those days, Frank's smiles were few and far between. He just wasn't himself.

"He never came to me and complained," Jerry said. "But I could just tell."

Frank wasn't growing as a player at Winton Woods. He wasn't growing as a person. His grades dropped. Then they dropped some more. Frank had keys to Jerome's house, which was located near Winton Woods. One day, Jerome intentionally came home from work early as a test and caught Frank having sex with a girl. Jerome, who took it upon himself to set boundaries in Frank's life, saw this as an overstepping of boundaries, a betrayal of trust. He banned Frank from his house for a month. Jerome just didn't understand. Frank was a great kid. Always had been. But Jerome, little by little, saw that slipping away.

"Being a stud athlete can bring the worst out of any person," Jerome said. "I've never been the stud, but I played sports all my life, and I've been around stud players. They can just become assholes. I saw some of that coming out in Frank and I thought, 'That's not my nephew.'"

So Jerome told Jerry that Frank needed a change. He needed a new school. They looked into a handful of schools in the area—at least one of which made it clear it would love to have Frank in its basketball program—but Jerome kept the search open-ended. And along came Roger Bacon. Bill talked to Jerome about what Bacon could do for Frank as a person and never once mentioned basketball. Jerome was impressed, but he did want to know how Bill ran the basketball program. Was it clean? Did Bacon recruit?

"Brewer said, 'No, we don't do that here. We don't have the finances to do that, and we just don't do that here,'" Jerome recalled. "That won me over right away. I loved that. Brewer said, 'We don't do that here.' I smiled. I said, 'What can you do?'"

Bill made some calls and determined that Jerry was eligible for financial assistance. After grants, Jerry would need to pay approximately $300 per month to cover tuition. So she did. Frank's father helped, too.

"She didn't even blink," Jerome said of Jerry. "That led to her working two jobs. She didn't have to do that. I thought I was going to have to foot the bill. But she started working nights, and she covered it."

It wasn't just Bill that drew Frank to Bacon. It was Josh Hausfeld. Josh and Frank played on the same AAU team the summer after eighth grade and remained the best of friends. During his time at Winton Woods, Frank often vented to Josh about his varsity playing time—or lack thereof.

"I'm not getting the time I deserve," Frank would tell Josh. "And I feel like I'm putting in the work."

Josh would always listen, and in the summer before their sophomore year in 1999, he told Frank something Frank won't ever forget.

"If you come to Bacon," Josh said, "we're going to win state."

Win state? Frank had never even thought about winning state. He had been so fed up at Winton Woods that he forgot that winning a state title, in theory, is the ultimate goal of high school athletics. He was so focused on just getting some playing time, on just getting an opportunity to succeed, that he forgot what actual success entailed.

Josh's mother, Mary Beth, put in a good word for Frank at Roger Bacon, and Bill had heard nothing but positive things about him through ties at AAU. With Jerry bridging the financial gap, it was a done deal.

"I was so excited the day he transferred," Josh said. "I remember thinking, 'We really do have a chance to be special.'"

• • • •

FRANK ENTERED HIS JUNIOR year in 2000–01 as a Roger Bacon Spartan. For the average kid, the transition Frank made—going from a public school to a private one, predominantly black to predominantly white, less affluent to more affluent—would have been difficult. Unimaginable, even.

"I would tell Frank, 'If you have any problems, if there's any racism going on, if you feel anyone is saying something you don't like, tell me,'" Jerry said. "And he'd always say, 'No, mom. Everything's fine.'"

Indeed, for Frank, there was no culture shock.

"I grew up in an all-black neighborhood, but my mom sent me to schools outside the neighborhood," Frank said. "I was familiar with being around mostly white people. It wasn't a shock at all."

Frank's beaming smile and engaging personality served him well at Roger Bacon, and the Spartans connected with him almost immediately, especially outside of basketball.

"Frank was my guy," Beckham said. "If he wasn't riding with me, I was riding with him."

Of course, it helped having Josh and Mary Beth Hausfeld. Since the Hausfelds lived right down the street from Roger Bacon, Frank spent a lot of time at their house. Several other players did, too, but Frank damn near lived there. He'd be there before practice, after practice; Mary Beth would cook meals for him; she'd give him rides if he needed to go somewhere; she'd let him sleep over, even on school nights.

"Oh, he lived at my house," Mary Beth said with pride. "His mom's a single mom, Jerome had twins—Frankie had nowhere to go, basically. By being here, he could get to everything on time."

Frank and Josh breathed, ate and slept basketball. They were competitive with each other. Both 6-3, they would play one-on-one and just go at it. Frank would always get on Josh for not playing defense, and Josh would get on Frank for not having the best jump shot. Basketball was their life, and they just wanted to make each other better.

But it went deeper than that.

Frank was Josh's alter ego—extremely outgoing, always cracking up, biggest smile in the world. He brought out the playfulness in Josh. As for Josh, well, he knew that Jerome made sure Frank was on the right path. But when Frank was hanging out in St. Bernard or sleeping over during the week or on weekends, Josh and Mary Beth took on that role, too.

And it had nothing to do with basketball.

"Me and Frank, we were like brothers," Josh said. "It was a natural fit."

If Jerry or Jerome couldn't do something for Frank, Josh or Mary Beth would do it. Mary Beth was a second mother. Frank would buy her birthday cards. He'd buy her Mother's Day cards. Sometimes, he'd even call her "mom."

Jerome would try to slip Mary Beth money for everything she did—from the time commitment of caring for Frank to the sheer financial burden of feeding another mouth. Mary Beth wouldn't take it.

"My family loves Frankie," she said. " Always has."

Frank's old spirit was back. Yes, Bacon was tougher than Winton Woods academically; it was also more strict. But Frank's smile was back. There's no denying Frank made the right decision off the court; on the court was no different. He went from varsity benchwarmer as a sophomore at Winton Woods to starting as a junior at Roger Bacon. That year, Winton Woods once again went undefeated in the regular season and once again lost in the second round of the playoffs, this time to Western Hills. Frank, meanwhile, was a key starter on a Bacon squad that finished regional runner-up.

Finally given a chance to showcase his skills at the varsity level, Frank played with Friars toughness and Bond Hill swagger. If Josh Hausfeld was the Golden Boy, and if Beckham Wyrick was the California Surfer, then Frank Phillips was The Hustler—in the street sense.

"Frank did nothing pretty on the court—nothing," Marcus Smith said. "He wasn't shooting threes. He wasn't shooting jumpers. He wasn't doing too much of anything, but he would just nickel and dime you to death. He'd pick your pocket, he'd get a steal, he'd get a rebound, he'd drive right by you—little stuff. And you can't do nothing to stop it."

"He was just so consistent," Marcus continued. "Whenever we needed a play, that was the guy. That was the guy. He had a nose for the ball. He just found it. He just found it. We would call plays for Beckham; we would call plays for Josh. Frank would just score. Frank would just get it done—a crucial stop, a crucial rebound. Whatever plays needed to be made, Frank was there. He was doing all the dirt. All the dirty stuff we needed, he was doing. To me, he was the most important piece. He was the backbone. He was cocky, and he was arrogant. He gave the team what we needed."

Frank learned that on-court cockiness from Jerome. If Frank drove to the basket on his man and scored, Jerome would yell for his nephew to do the same move over and over until the opposing coach made an adjustment. "Frankie, he can't guard you!" Jerome would yell. Jerome worked to instill that confidence in Frank, and eventually, he did.

"I'm super humble everywhere else, but the arrogance on the court? I'm proud of that," Jerome said. "I coached that. I still coach it. Is Frank cocky? Totally. Arrogance—it's what separates players. Name a great player who's not cocky. If a great player isn't cocky, then he needs to work on that. You got to have arrogance. You got to have cockiness."

And Frank had it. Like Beckham, he talked trash. Like Beckham, he was good at it. And like Beckham, he backed it up.

Said Dave Johnson, "Frank was that player we needed. Extremely versatile, crafty. That's how I always described him. I always gave him shit for not having the best jump shot, but you couldn't stop him from going to the hole. He's tall, skinny, long and extremely crafty with the ball. He always used his pivot real well, he shot-faked real well, he got a lot of stick-backs—he always got to the hole."

Frank knew he didn't have a pure jump shot, but then again, he never really needed one. He was taller than most boys growing up, so he always played in the post. When he stopped growing at 6-3, he played small forward and was often matched up with players who were undersized or who weren't comfortable playing down low. So Frank would post them up or use his quickness and length—not to mention his craftiness and guile—to drive right by them and score. And even if Frank wasn't having a good day offensively, he still played lockdown defense. Defense was his pride and joy.

"I wasn't a great shooter," Frank said, "but I made up for it on defense—because my man wasn't scoring."

There's that light-hearted confidence, that self-aware swagger. Frank brought plenty of both, but that wasn't all he brought.

In December 2001, at the holiday tournament in Lewes, Delaware, the Spartans shared a team bus with Winton Woods, which was also playing in the tournament. Both teams would ride back and forth from the hotel and the arena together. The Bacon players sat in front, quiet and orderly. Left, right, left. The Winton Woods players sat in back, yelling and laughing and acting wild.

"Frank brought just a little bit of that, that wildness," Marcus Smith said. "And we needed it. He made us go."

It was a curious pairing, Bacon and Winton Woods. It was also potentially volatile. A bit of a rivalry had developed between the two programs, as they were both ranked No. 1 in the city in their respective divisions. Both were loaded with talent, and despite a series of early round playoff exits by Winton Woods and repeated regional-finals heartbreak by Roger Bacon, both were considered favorites to get to Columbus. In the preseason, in fact, Bacon and Winton Woods scrimmaged each other, and a brawl broke out between two players—Frank and Robert Hite. Frank and Robert had developed a bit of a rivalry;

it wasn't an unfriendly rivalry, Jerome explained, but it wasn't exactly friendly, either. And on that day, two competitors got caught up in the heat of the moment.

The scuffle didn't last long, but when it ended, Frank discovered that his team had his back—literally. He turned around and saw Beckham, Tim McCoy, Leonard Bush and Jon Newton, among others, ready to go to blows on his behalf if need be. It didn't matter that Frank came from a public school. It didn't matter that he had only been at Bacon for a year. It didn't matter that he was one of two black players on a mostly white team. His teammates considered him one of their own.

"We took him in," Jon Newton said. "He knew he had us behind him."

• • • •

IF THERE WERE ONE night when Frank's former teammates weren't there but wished they were, it would be that summer night in Kentucky in 2004, the night that changed Frank's life and career forever. Frank had a successful sophomore season at the University of Findlay, one in which the Oilers went 25–7 and won the Great Lakes Intercollegiate Athletic Conference Tournament. He returned home to Cincinnati that summer, and on his first night back, he ventured across the Ohio River to Covington with his girlfriend. They went to one of the more popular clubs in the area, one that catered mainly to the 30-and-younger crowd.

As Frank recalls, he was the only black person in the club that night. His girlfriend, Ashley, was white. In some parts of this country, even in the 21st century, that's a no-no; one of those parts, apparently, was a club in Kentucky in the summer of 2004.

Frank remembers being on the dance floor late that night with Ashley when suddenly two or three bouncers started bumping into him, pushing him. Frank could smell the alcohol on their breath, the drunkenness wafting from their mouths. Frank was confused.

What's going on? Why are they coming at me? Do they think I'm with somebody who started something?

Immediately, Frank's instinct was to protect Ashley, to shield her from any potential harm. And that's when he was ambushed. A bouncer grabbed Frank from behind, put him in a choke hold and slammed him against a wall. Frank tried to get away, but two other bouncers held Frank's arms stationary against the wall, one on each side, while the first pelted Frank with fists to the face. Even as he was getting pummeled, even as he squirmed to get away, Frank remembers several other bouncers grabbing Ashley and yelling at her. He remembers the words they said, the slur they uttered.

"NIGGER LOVER! NIGGER LOVER!"

Frank wanted to break free. He wanted so desperately to break free. He wanted to break free and grab Ashley and get her to safety. But he couldn't. He was powerless. And that's when it happened. Frank remained plastered to the wall when another bouncer approached him and knelt down, stabilizing his shoulder against the side of Frank's left knee. Once stable, the bouncer jerked Frank's leg as hard as he could, as close to a 90-degree angle as possible, as if he were giving one last heave-ho to a lawn mower that just wouldn't start.

The bouncers let go. The damage had been done. And he knew. Frank knew. He heard the pop. He heard all the pops. He lay on the ground, bawling, his leg dangling helplessly amid the late-night stupor of hip hop and liquor. In that moment, Frank knew his career was over. He wondered if he'd ever be able to walk again, let alone play basketball. Somehow, Ashley helped Frank outside before he collapsed on the sidewalk. They sat on the pavement, crying, not knowing what to do. Frank called his mom.

"Mom!" Frank yelled. "They broke my leg! They broke my leg!"

Jerry's worst fear had come true. Interracial couples were nothing new in her family. She didn't mind Frank dating Ashley at all. She liked Ashley. But she made it clear to Frank that he might encounter people who didn't feel the same way.

"When they started dating, I told him, 'You might end up going through a lot of different problems with racism,'" she said. "'But if this is what you've got to do, you have to stand up for yourself, and you've got to go through it.'"

But even Jerry didn't imagine this happening. Luckily, someone at the club who witnessed the incident offered Frank and Ashley a ride to the hospital, where Jerry, along with Frank's father, met them in the middle of the night. Frank had torn or damaged his ACL, MCL, PCL and meniscus. Everything. Frank's doctor said that in his more than 20 years as a surgeon, he had never seen a knee as bad as Frank's. He said there was a chance Frank might walk with a limp, and that it'd be by the grace of God if he ever played basketball again.

Jerome got the news. It was perhaps the worst moment of his life.

"I felt helpless," he said. "I just felt so helpless."

Frank, Jerry and Jerome decided to pursue legal action. Jerome spoke to a close connection he had through Friars—a lawyer, who, after some investigating, determined that the case would become a he-said, she-said affair, and that some were prepared to say Frank started the fracas. The lawyer said he was still willing to pursue action—and even offered to do so for free—but Jerome declined.

"It was a lost cause," he said.

To anyone who knew Frank, the notion of him randomly starting something with anyone was crazy, even to Mary Beth Hausfeld.

"Being married to a police officer, you learn there's always two sides to every story," she said. "But Frankie's not a fighter. He's a lover. He's got that smile, and he just charms everybody. Frankie's the guy who could have 50 million girlfriends. It's just the way he is."

Marcus, always the protector, was irate. Within days, he desperately wanted to drive to the club with his boys from Bond Hill. He knew he'd end up in jail if he did anything, but at that point, he didn't care; he just wanted to avenge what had been done to his little brother. Somehow, Frank convinced him not to go. But even Jerry, a self-described "church-going person," struggled to control her anger.

"I felt really . . . I can't think of the word," she said. "If there was something I could do to the person who did it, I felt like I would want it to be done. Frank is my son, and any time someone hurts your child, it puts you on the defense. As time went on, I prayed to let it go. With that person, justice will be done. When you do something like that and you hurt another human being, justice will be done. So I had to let it go. And I told Frank to let it go."

But Frank couldn't. He was devastated. He replayed the incident over and over in his head, struggling to move past what happened in the club—and struggling even more so to move past what happened while he was sitting outside on the sidewalk with Ashley. As he writhed in pain on the pavement, tears glistening his cheeks, Frank looked over and saw one of the bouncers taking trash to a dumpster. After a few seconds, Frank realized it was the bouncer who had shattered his knee. The bouncer noticed Frank. Their eyes met. And then the bouncer did something Frank won't ever forget.

He winked at him.

And then he laughed.

"I won't ever forget that," Frank said. "That hurt worse than my knee."

Frank was on crutches for eight months. It was a year before he could start running again. He redshirted what would have been his junior season. That year, in 2004–05, Findlay, a Division II school, went 30–4 and advanced to the Elite Eight, which at the time was the best season in program history—and all Frank could do was watch. In his opinion, the only thing that team was missing was a versatile wing player, a player who could drive to the hole and play lockdown perimeter defense. The only thing that team was missing was Frank. And if Findlay had him, it might have won the national title.

"Could you imagine not being part of that?" Jerome asked. "That killed me."

From the start of rehabilitation, Frank was told he wouldn't be able to play basketball again. The goal was simply to make sure he didn't walk with a permanent limp or hitch. But jumping? Cutting? Ripping a board, going up top and stuffing it home? Forget it. For Frank Phillips—the boy who learned to dribble in his basement, the boy whose father wanted to be there for him but couldn't, the boy seen one summer night in Kentucky as less than human—those days, sadly, were over.

CHAPTER SEVEN

THE SCRAPPERS

The Spartans arrived at practice not knowing what to expect. Mere hours removed from the meltdown at CJ, they wondered what kind of mood Bill would be in. But they already knew. They just wondered how bad it would be.

The players changed into their shorts and shirts, slipped on their ankle braces and laced up their gym shoes. No one said much. The more the players shot around to get loose, the more tense they felt. There was a nervousness, an uneasiness, that permeated Bacon's gym that January morning. The Spartans weren't laughing or cackling or carrying on. They weren't shooting trick shots or fallaway jumpers or one-handed threes. Absent was the unrestrained cadence, the iambic flow, the capricious whimsy by which ballplayers light-heartedly float from one floorboard to the next, unencumbered by time, demand or purpose. Instead, the players shot sedately, delicately, quietly, as if taking a test in a library. Their shots caromed off the iron; their shots tickled the twine; their shots collided and plummeted to the floor like dead birds. And suddenly, the doors to Fogarty flung open. In walked Bill.

"All right," he said casually, "let's get some stretches going."

For a brief instant, peace washed over the players. Stretches? That was normal, everyday, status-quo practice stuff. Suddenly, they felt safe. It was like acing an exam they thought they failed. Maybe things were going to be okay.

And then again, maybe they weren't. Before the players had time to get up, before they even had time to react and carry out Bill's order, the whistle blew.

"Not fast enough," he said bloodlessly, without conscience or regard for humanity. "Get on the line."

Get on the line.

Those were Josh Hausfeld's four least favorite words in the English language.

Any sense of peace among the players vanished. Sullen and somber, 13 Spartans trudged toward the baseline like prisoners on the way to execution. Fear filled their faces. Silence consumed the gym. The players looked to each other for help, but no one could offer any. No one had any answers. They watched as Bill carried a garbage can to midcourt.

"If you have to use this," he said, "use it."

Well, fuck.

And with that, the whistle shrieked and pierced the gym. Sneakers squealed. Stampedes started, stopped and started again. Sprints, suicides—the players did it all but could do no right. Nothing was fast enough. Nothing was as Bill wanted. He issued commands impossible to fulfill. Twelve lengths in 30 seconds. Sixteen lengths in 45 seconds. If even one player failed, and all of them did, everyone was back on the line. Do it again, fail again, back on the line. Do it again, fail again, back on the line. The players were pushed until psychologically broken, beaten until bereft of moxie.

It was a fucking track meet.

"Oh, it was bad," Jon Newton said. "That was the worst practice I've ever been to in my life."

Jon Newton played Division I college football.

But the Spartans had come to expect this. Practice was purification for sins committed in games. Once, in the week leading up to a game against St. Xavier, Bill warned Tim McCoy that the player he would guard, Steve Gay, had one go-to move—a back cut. Every day at practice that week, Bill kept telling Tim, "He's gonna back cut! That's all he's gonna do! Whatever you do, don't let Steve Gay back cut you."

Well, Tim subbed in late in the second quarter against St. X and manned up on Steve Gay. On the first possession, Gay faked to the three-point line, back cut and took a pass for an easy layin. But that's not all.

Tim fouled him for the and-one.

To make matters worse, this all happened right before halftime. Bacon jogged into the locker room for the break, and Tim knew what was coming. He sat on a bench, waiting. Bill stomped in.

"HOW THE FUCK ARE YOU GONNA GET FUCKING BACK-DOORED BY STEVE FUCKING GAY?" Bill snarled, breaking his clipboard in the process.

Tim didn't have any answers, so he did what any of his teammates would have done in that situation. He just sat there and took it. Bill scolded Tim on how bad of a basketball player he was, on how he never listened, on how he cared about everything except basketball, the team and winning. Bill knew none of that was true. He knew Tim cared. But mental breakdowns like that drove Bill crazy. After he left the locker room, it was silent. The players just sat there, stunned, looking at Tim. All of a sudden, Leonard Bush leaned close to Tim and asked, "Man, how you gonna let him talk to you like that?" The players all laughed, but that was a one-sided tirade none of them will ever forget.

Of course, it wasn't just Tim who made mistakes. During one game against Moeller in 2000–01, Beckham was set to guard the Crusaders' best player, Matt Sylvester, a future Ohio State standout best known, perhaps, for hitting a game-winning three in March 2005 to beat Illinois, which entered the game 29–0. In the days leading up to the game, Bill told Beckham repeatedly how Moeller's first offensive possession would unfold. Sylvester, a 6-7 post player, would run to the elbow, fake as if he were to receive a pass, and back cut. Bill called it exactly. Unfortunately for Beckham, he fell for the fake, giving Sylvester a clear path to the basket. Bucket, foul, and-one. 3–0, Moeller. Bill yanked Beckham 10 seconds into the game.

It was perhaps the quickest non-injury substitution in the history of basketball.

And Beckham paid for it in practice. They all did. That is where the purging of trespasses occurred. There was nothing the players could do about it, either. Bill wouldn't allow insubordination. During practices—or any time, really—players couldn't back-talk or cuss. Bill could cuss, but players couldn't. If a player cussed, he was running. If a player cussed while running, he was running longer. Bill was like a drill sergeant, a prison warden. He made his players work. And if they stepped out of line, there would be consequences. That was just part of the deal.

The penance during the practice after the CJ game went on and on and on. Bill had no remorse. He felt no guilt. He watched and waited until he saw his players had nothing more to give—and then he made them give more. But Bill knew running could only do so much. Running would improve fitness, but fitness wasn't an issue. Running might make his players hate him, but Bill didn't care. All he wanted was to make his team more competitive. All he wanted was to make them tougher. Could running do that alone? Bill didn't think so.

But he knew what would.

• • • •

BILL BLEW HIS WHISTLE, temporarily stopping the madness. The players were dying. They stood bent over, hands on their knees, panting like dogs in summer. They gasped for air and suppressed their vomit while trying to focus as Bill introduced a new drill. It was a toughness drill. The rules were simple: five-on-five, halfcourt, no shooting.

Each player's eye brows crinkled.

What? No shooting? How do you score? How do you win?

"If Team A completes five passes in a row, Team B runs," Bill said. "Oh, and by the way, no fouls."

Jesus Christ.

"It was just an all-out war," Tim McCoy said. "If you tackled somebody, Brewer might break it up. But he wasn't calling fouls."

That five-on-five toughness drill wasn't the only one Bill had. There were others. For one drill, Bill divided his players into four groups of three. Two of the groups would play each other. The first team to score, stayed; the group that got scored on exited the floor, while the next three-person team scrambled into the mix, sticking whoever was closest to them. Why? Because the team that just scored didn't have to wait for the new defense to get set. They could grab the ball after a made basket, clear it beyond the three-point line and try to score again as soon as they could. The first three-person group to score five baskets won. All of the losers ran.

But they didn't just run. They *ran*.

Bill didn't have the attitude of, "Well, you guys tried really hard there, and it was close, so just give me one suicide." No. It was serious running. It was, "You just lost, and losing is not okay, so this is your punishment." That fear Bill created ensured that everyone always took each drill seriously, that everyone always tried his hardest.

For every drill, there was constant movement. There was constant communication. There was high energy. There was high pressure. That's what Bill wanted, and that's what he got. Bacon's players learned early on to do everything the right way as soon as possible, because if they didn't do things the right way, they weren't going home. Bill didn't care if practice lasted six hours. He didn't care if the girls team was waiting outside to use the gym. And as the father of three girls—and as a coach of girls basketball—there wasn't a shred of sexism in making the ladies wait. Bill just wanted his message clear: you weren't going anywhere until you got it right.

For another drill, Bill divided the team into three groups of four. Team A would play Team B on one half of the court. If Team A scored first, it would gather the ball and dribble to the other side of the court, where Team C was already waiting to play defense. Teams A and C would then play in the halfcourt, and whichever team scored first would gather the ball and go back the other way, where Team B was set to play defense. There were no fast-breaks. There couldn't be. It was all about grinding it out in the halfcourt—because Bill knew that's where games would be won or lost. Whichever four-person team scored five buckets first, won. And if you lost?

"Shit," Marcus Smith said. "You'll die."

●　●　●　●

IF THE PLAYERS HAD a get-out-of-jail free card of any sort, it was Bill's daughters—Katie, Abby and Maddy. The players were so happy when Bill brought his girls to weekend practices. When they were around, Bill had an off switch. He didn't yell. He didn't cuss. Sometimes he didn't even coach. He'd sit off to the side, play with his daughters and let Brian Neal run practice. Katie, Abby and Maddy were like headache medicine. Instant relief.

"Those girls were our shields," Monty said. "If you went to practice Saturday morning and those girls were there, it was a weight off your shoulders. He loved those girls so much, and you could tell the different side of him. Usually he was the toughest person in my life in terms of yelling and cussing at me. And then you see him with those girls, and he's a completely different person. (I would ask myself), 'Who is this guy?'"

Most of the time, though, Bill's daughters weren't there, so the players did whatever they could to ease Bill's mood before practice. Monty and Tim McCoy, in particular, would try to get Bill to smile, something he rarely did. Peggy wishes Bill would have done that more. She loved his smile. But even when Bill was happy, he usually didn't flash a full-blown grin. It was similar to Peggy asking him every preseason how the team would be. "We'll be all right," Bill would say, even if he knew they'd be exceptional. That was part of who he was. That was the competitor in him. He downplayed everything. He never showed his hand.

But the players always tried. They didn't just want Bill to smile; they wanted him to show his teeth—"get Brewer to bare all," they called it.

"It wasn't very often that you saw all his teeth," Tim McCoy said. "If you did, it was going to be a good day at practice."

It would also be a good day if Bill shot free throws before practice. He'd ask his players why they were only shooting 70 percent from the foul line, and then he would proceed to shoot free throws with his eyes closed—and make them. "Look how good I am!" he'd joke.

"If Brewer was baring all and shooting free throws," Tim said, "it was going to be okay."

But a lot of days, most days, there was no joking. There were no free throws. Most days, Bill wasn't baring all. He was by himself and looking serious, looking angry. Just not in a good mood. On those days, there was no hope. Practice was going to be rough, and there was nothing anybody could do about it. As soon as that first whistle blew, it was going to be three hours of blood and guts.

"Walking down the hallways at school, you'd almost be afraid to approach him," Dave Johnson said. "It was just like, I'm gonna stay away from him because I'm gonna have to deal with him at practice. He was that intense. Almost scary."

● ● ● ●

OVER THE COURSE OF the 2001–02 season, something happened within the confines of Fogarty. Something extraordinary. Something . . . *special*.

When Bill stepped back, swallowed his whistle and let his players scrimmage—when he let them go five-on-five, full-court—he discovered that he could do something not a lot of coaches can do. Something almost unheard of.

He had the ability to let his starting five play together against his bench, and somehow, still have the scrimmages remain competitive.

Extremely competitive.

"As the season evolved, we had our starting five, and we knew it wasn't going to change; those were our five guys who fit the best together and who were probably our five most talented players," Brian Neal said. "But one of the challenges that every coach has is, how can we allow our starters to play together in practice yet also create a competitive environment?"

Brian Neal has coached teams at Roger Bacon where scrimmages between his starters and his bench have gotten ugly. Instant blowout. Some coaches will stack the deck against the starters and opt for 5-on-6 or 5-on-7. That can be useful, but it's a far-from-perfect approach, mainly because it doesn't simulate realistic situations. Bill wanted his five starters—Josh, Beckham, Frank, Monty and Dave—not only to play together in practice, but also to play their hardest while still being challenged. Luckily, Bill had one of the best benches in state history—maybe not in terms of raw talent (though some of those players were quite good), but in terms of sacrificing, forging an identity and buying into what Bill wanted, or better yet, what that team needed.

And over time, it happened. It evolved. A group of benchwarmers, most of whom didn't get significant playing time, were so dedicated to advancing the cause of the 2001–02 season that they took it as a personal challenge to make the lives of the starting five miserable.

They became known, derisively yet affectionately, as the Scrappers.

The Scrappers were anyone who wasn't a starter. They were, by and large, players whose best sport wasn't basketball, but rather, football or baseball; players who were tough-minded, who loved contact and were ultra-competitive. Bill let his players scrimmage every day, and every day it was almost always starters versus Scrappers—Josh, Beckham, Frank, Monty and Dave versus some combination of Tim McCoy, Leonard Bush, Nate Wyrick, Jon Newton, Marcus Smith, Matt

Reed, Zach Gruenwald and Kevin Waymire. For the Scrappers, practices became their games. If the starters entered those scrimmages not ready to play, if they weren't all-in mentally, they would lose.

"There were times when they kicked our ass," Josh said. "There were days when Tim McCoy would be on fire with his threes and wouldn't miss. Newt would be a force down low. Those guys were absolutely vital to our success. Everybody brought it every day—and if you didn't bring it, it wasn't going to be pretty. You were going to be left behind."

The Scrappers gave maximum effort every scrimmage, in part because Bill planted the seed.

Hey, you guys can't beat our starters. They're too good for you.

Motivational ploys aside, every Scrapper knew that if one of the starters got hurt, there would be a starting spot up for grabs. And even if a starter didn't get hurt, the Scrappers knew that pushing the starting five to their limit every day would prepare them better for the next game, and that, in turn, would make the team better.

"Even though our starting five was probably a little bit better—probably a lot better—than the next five or six, it was still very, very competitive," Brian Neal said. "And the credit goes to the depth of that team. We could have played more guys and not seen a huge drop-off."

Bill, of course, had a way of bridging the talent gap. He'd let the Scrappers foul the starters. He'd let the Scrappers mug the starters. In fact, he'd *tell* them to mug the starters. And when they did, he wouldn't blow his whistle. But if a starter committed a touch foul, guess what? Two free throws. Nothing angered the starters more than that. They'd get hacked to hell on one end with nothing to show for it and then get whistled for cheap ones on the other. And it wasn't just fouls. If a Scrapper shuffled his feet on a drive to the basket, Bill would let it slide. But if a starter shuffled his feet? Traveling. The starters didn't understand.

How come they get to foul and we don't? How come they get to travel and we don't? This isn't fair!

But that was entirely the point. Sometimes in games, you get called for fouls you didn't commit. Sometimes you get fouled and the refs don't see it. Sometimes an opponent travels but doesn't get called for it. But guess what? You have to play through it. You have to stay poised. You have to stay focused on the task at hand.

Other times, Bill would tell the starters to run a specific play, and then he would call timeout to tell the defense what was coming and what option he wanted them to take away. It was all a test for the starters. Bill wanted to see if they could adjust on the fly and, like a quarterback, make the right read. The starters could handle that. They welcomed that. But the fouls? Not so much.

"Brewer would take me, Leonard and Tim to the side and say, 'Foul them. Do what you want,'" Jon Newton said. "I loved it. Hell yeah. I'll do whatever. We basically lowered our shoulders and did whatever we wanted. Oh, the starters used to get so frustrated. But the Scrappers had that mentality. And we didn't care. We didn't want any of the limelight. We didn't want none of that. If our jerseys were ripped at the end of practice, Brewer was happy with us."

Said Frank, "Brewer let them hack us. It'd be a fast break one-on-one, and they would take our whole arm out. We'd look over at coach for a foul, and he's just shaking his head no. And we knew we couldn't yell at Brewer, so we had to take it out on the players."

Yes, even though Bill was prone to calling touch fouls on the starters, some days he didn't. Some days, maybe even most days, it was anything goes. Tempers flared. Verbal altercations ensued. Physical ones, too. Guys would bump each other, push each other, almost come to blows with each other. Guys would have to be held back, pulled apart, broken up. If a defender reached in for a steal, he'd get his hand slapped away. That taught players not to reach. It taught them to get back to basics and play solid, fundamental defense. Some players, like Leonard, didn't like being crowded when they had the ball. There were times in practice when a defender would get up on Leonard, crowd him so much that he couldn't even hold the ball in front of his chest; he'd have to hold it above his head. But Leonard, who played linebacker for Bacon, didn't throw elbows to clear space. No, he'd take the ball and, while maintaining possession, slam it against the top of a defender's head. That had a way of clearing space—for a few seconds, anyway.

"Some of the practices were like street fights," Leonard said. "Lots of physical scuffles, trash talking. That's what it was."

Bill loved that. He lived for that.

"Bill was a coaches' coach," Frank said. "No way was he a players' coach. Maybe off the court he'd relax a bit with some of the seniors and be nice, but he wasn't a players' coach that everyone loves. He was more Xs and Os. Just playing strong. Never backing down. Never being late to practice. Running a lot. Just very precise with things. He was very smart. He saw a lot of good things in us that we as players didn't see."

• • • •

THE SCRAPPERS EMBRACED THEIR role. Hell, they came up with a damn nickname for themselves.

"When Brewer found that out, he loved it," Monty said. "Brewer had that smile. When he found out, he bore all."

But if one individual personified exactly what it meant to be a Scrapper, it may have been Tim McCoy. The self-declared "Captain of the Scrappers," Tim was fiery and intense. A hothead. Beckham could turn the switch on and off. So could Frank. Tim couldn't. For him, the switch was always pointed up. For him, everything was a competition. For him, everything was full throttle.

When Tim was a kid, he'd get up early in the summer and round up the neighborhood kids to play ball—any kind of ball. Baseball was his best sport, but he didn't care what game they were playing as long as it was competitive. They'd start early in the day and play for hours. But when the other kids would quit or go home for lunch or dinner, Tim would get so mad. If it were up to him, they'd play all day until bedtime.

"He was always that way," said his father, Tim Sr. "Still is. He'll drive you crazy."

Tim physically matured earlier than most boys. He was a developed kid by seventh grade and was Bacon's varsity starting point guard as a sophomore. He was a good player, but then something happened. He stopped growing. He stopped getting bigger. Guys started catching up with him in size and skill, and then they surpassed him. Tim took it to heart. Before Tim's junior year, Bill told him that Dave Johnson, a sophomore, was going to replace him as starting point guard.

"I remember Brewer telling me I was going to play behind Dave, and I remember that being an issue for me," Tim said. "I thought, 'Who the hell is this sophomore? All he did was play freshman basketball last year.' But I knew he was good, and then he got better and better. He was just a better ball player than I was all the way around. He could shoot better. He could handle better. He was just better."

But the demotion was still difficult to accept, and in some ways, Tim never did. He often opened up to his dad about it. He wanted to be a part of that starting five in the worst way. He knew Dave was better, but whenever Tim got on the floor, he didn't want to come off. Tim never told Dave of his anger, but he showed it. At 5-11, Tim wasn't much taller than Dave, but he was stronger. So in practice, Tim would be extra aggressive. What he lacked in skill relative to Dave, he tried to make up for in physicality. So he'd body him. He'd push him. He'd try to provoke him. Dave usually kept his cool, but sometimes Tim went a little too far. Jon Newton would have to grab Tim by the neck and pull him away.

"To this day, no one hates losing more than I do," Tim said. "That's what Bill said at our senior banquet. I remember him saying he'd never met someone who hated losing more than he did—until he met me."

And that's why it was so hard for Tim to accept the reality of the situation.

"As a father, you want your son to play; you want him to be the star," Tim Sr. said. "You kind of die with him when he's not playing because you know it's bugging him. But it made you feel better—and it made Tim feel better—to know that Brewer thought so highly of him."

Tim always carried a little chip on his shoulder against Dave, but he still liked and respected him. It helped that Dave never rubbed anything in Tim's face. It helped that he never showed Tim up at practice. He just went about his business.

"Tim was the aggressive macho man, and Dave was just smooth," Beckham said. "Tim would start yelling at Dave, and Dave would just turn around and walk back up the court. Dave wasn't the type of guy who would go out there and try to embarrass people or make you feel bad. He was just playing ball. Just a nice guy. Humble. Damn good basketball player."

In many ways, Dave Johnson was a genetic enigma. His father, who played high school basketball at Withrow, a public school in Cincinnati, was 6-4; his grandpa was 6-5. Dave was 5-10. Something didn't add up—literally. But Dave embraced being short. He knew he wasn't going to grow, and he was okay with that. He never saw it as a disadvantage.

Dave may have been the quiet guy in the corner, but he could lead. He was smart. He was calm. He was one of the best ball-handlers in the state. After a foul, he'd gather the starters together under the basket and shout instructions. He was a 5-10 junior gathering Monty, who was 6-8, and three seniors—Josh, Beckham and Frank—ranging in height from 6-3 to 6-6. Some point guards would be intimidated by that. Some would be afraid to speak up. But there was Dave—grabbing jerseys, giving orders, making you look him in the eye. *Listen up. We're going to a 2-3 zone. Hey, we're going to a 1-2-2.* Dave knew how to take control. He never said much, but when he talked, teammates listened.

Dave was a pure point guard, a pass-first point guard. He never shot the ball unless he was wide open. Wide. Open. Virtually every player on Bacon's team knew his role; Dave's role was to take care of the ball, get it up the floor and get it into the hands of the scorers. It's not that Dave couldn't score, but for a team to be successful, it doesn't need all five starters looking for their own shot. The Spartans had Monty scoring on the block. They had Josh coming off screens and shooting jumpers and driving to the bucket. They had Frank taking it to the hole and sticking put-backs. They had Beckham scoring from every which angle. The fact is, after the other four starters, there weren't really a lot of shots to go around. And Dave was okay with that. As long as the team was winning, he was okay with that.

Of course, there were times when Dave was given wide-open shots by design. He was never the recipient of much trash talk, but he did get a lot of trash attitude. He was the shortest guy on Bacon's team and the shortest starter by five inches. By extension, opponents assumed he was the weak link. They figured he probably couldn't shoot and probably couldn't handle pressure from bigger guards. Those assumptions were wrong. Dave could shoot. He could handle pressure. He played great defense. He could keep up with quick guards. And he never turned the ball over. Never. He just didn't do it. He was a one-man press break. Get the ball to Dave and give him room to operate; that was Bacon's press-break strategy.

"Everyone assumed Dave was the weak link," Brian Neal said. "Well, he was the link that held everyone together."

During a game against Moeller that year, the Crusader defense absolutely disregarded Dave. Didn't even try to check him. They double-teamed Josh and left Dave wide open. They weren't daring Dave to shoot; they were daring Bacon's other four starters just to pass him the ball, which they did—and Dave started lighting up Moeller from distance.

"We all remember that Moeller game well because they would leave him alone; a lot of teams would leave Dave alone," Josh said. "We needed Dave to score when the opportunity presented itself, especially when teams weren't going to guard him. And Dave always came through, especially that Moeller game. He was wide open and shooting and hitting—and then he kept hitting."

Dave made four three-pointers that night, forcing the Crusaders to switch their defense, which led to more opportunities for Josh and the other starters. That was Dave. He loved facilitating, but if an opponent left him open, he wasn't afraid to let it fly.

"Next to Steve Callahan, Dave's the best pure point guard that I've seen in the last 20 years," Jerome said. "And Callahan was the truth."

Callahan—whose father, Bob, coached Roger Bacon to a state title in 1981–82—was a starting point guard at St. Xavier. As a junior in 2000, he guided the Bombers to a 25–2 record and a state championship—the first hoops title in school history. He went on to play four years at Dartmouth. At 6-3, Callahan was bigger than Dave, but the similarities were there—smart, always made the right choice, never turned the ball over, good shooter, sound defender.

"Dave never screwed up," Monty said. "He never made a bad decision. He was just so solid. And solid can be underrated because solid is what we needed."

That was another reason why it was impossible for Tim to dislike Dave. He knew how valuable Dave was to the team. Tim might have carried a chip on his shoulder for losing his starting job, but everything he did to Dave in practice, justified or not, made Dave a better player. And it made Tim a better teammate.

"Brewer knew what he was doing," Tim said. "Dave turned out to be great."

TIM MCCOY MAY HAVE been captain of the Scrappers, but Jon Newton wasn't far behind. A junior who became Bacon's starting power forward the following season, Jon Newton was a bruiser. Plain and simple. He didn't have a lot of pure basketball talent, but he was 6-3, 250. Much of it was muscle—and whatever wasn't was pure will and resolve. Newton, referred to as "Newt," was there for defense, rebounding and the occasional put-back. He scored when opportunity met hard work. Bacon didn't run plays for him. It was never, "Hey, let's set a screen and get a shot for Newt at the elbow." No, there was none of that. Newt was a bulldozer.

"Just huge," Tim said. "He was as tough a kid as you were gonna find in the city that year."

Newt, who played defensive lineman at Cincinnati, was never supposed to be a college football player. In fact, he was never supposed to be a football player, period. He wanted to play in grade school at St. Clement, but he wasn't allowed—not because his parents were overprotective, but because he was over the weight limit. When Newt was in fourth grade, his mom would get phone calls from other parents saying they didn't want Newt to play because they didn't want their kids getting hurt. And these weren't parents of fourth graders; these were parents of eighth graders. Newt could make that weight limit, but the other parents didn't care. They were just looking out for their sons and didn't want them getting hurt by an oversized 10-year-old.

It was frustrating for Newt. He wanted to play football and be out on the field with his friends, but he couldn't. So one year, he decided to be a water boy. He'd run onto the field and bring water to his friends, most of whom he dwarfed in size. By the time Newt was in eighth grade, he was 6-1, 220—still way over the weight limit. Newt wondered if some sort of arrangement could be made. If allowed to play, he promised he wouldn't run the football and would exclusively play offensive or defensive line. But it never happened. No exceptions were made.

By the time Newt got to high school, he was a big, raw bundle of gridiron badass—and he was eager to unleash it. Finally, there was no weight limit holding him back. Finally, there were no pesky parents calling his mother. Finally, he would get a chance to play. There was just one problem.

He had absolutely no idea what the hell he was doing.

As soon as the ball was snapped, Newt would try to bull his man to the ground and hit somebody. He had no technique whatsoever. Bacon's coaches, salivating at his size, put Newt on varsity for two-a-days, but he played just one game of JV before being sent down to the freshman team. That was all it took. Coaches realized Newt needed to learn the basics, so they taught him. Results were favorable.

Bacon was happy to have Newt. It wasn't always assumed that he would go there, but it was never really in doubt, either. His grandpa went to Bacon. His mom went to OLA. His dad went to St. Bernard. Like Josh, Newt's family was one of public service. Firefighters, police officers, corrections workers. It was a no-nonsense, duty-first household. And like Josh, Newt had a teammate who practically lived at his house, a teammate whom he treated like a brother.

That teammate was Leonard.

Growing up, Leonard never knew he would attend Bacon. In some ways it's almost surprising that he did. His sister went to Purcell Marian. One of his best friends went to Moeller. But Leonard chose to become a Spartan, and that's how he met Newt. Newt and Leonard both loved basketball, but they were football players at heart. They played all four years together and anchored the defense. They were leaders on the team. No matter the season, they were always around each other.

"We had that special bond," Leonard said. "And we had pretty much the same attitude: *Don't back down from anybody.*"

That attitude carried over to the court. Leonard, one of three black players on the team, wasn't much of an offensive threat—and he never tried to be. If an opportunity presented itself, he'd take it, but he knew scoring wasn't his niche.

"When I got on the floor," Leonard said, "my job was to get a steal or beat somebody up."

Newt was the same way. If Tim McCoy's fiery personality made him perfect for the Scrappers, so too did Newt's work ethic. If jerseys had sleeves, Newt would've rolled his up.

Newt's job at practice was to body the bigs—Beckham and Monty, especially. Whenever Beckham posted up, Newt would lay a beefy forearm into his lower back and push him away from the bucket.

"I hated that," Beckham said. "I would go down there banging as hard as I could, but he's a defensive lineman. You're not moving him.

And he was quick, too. I would keep going, but I would be hurting. Bruises on my back, bruises on my rib cage. He was the one guy who was just as tough as me who I couldn't move or push around."

Newt relished those forearms to the back, especially in the wake of Beckham's quick departure from the grotto the night Bacon's football season ended. It was great therapy, and Newt finally let go of his anger a few weeks later.

Beckham's comment alone, however, wasn't what almost made Newt sit out that year. In fact, Newt had already considered giving up basketball to focus entirely on football. He had scholarship offers from Cincinnati, Minnesota, Louisville and North Carolina, and he wanted to do whatever he could to procure the next big one. When he turned his pads in after the season, some of the football coaches recommended he do just that—quit basketball and focus squarely on football. They said it'd be better for him to concentrate on getting bigger and stronger. Newt agreed, but he also knew basketball would improve his footwork, speed and agility. Beckham's comment, though, had sent him over the edge.

Days later, Bill approached Newt before algebra class and told him to take a week off before coming to practice so he could let his body heal from football. Newt got quiet.

"It might be longer than that," he said.

"What do you mean?" Bill asked.

"I'm not sure, coach. We'll have to talk about this later."

"We'll talk *right* after class," Bill said sternly.

Bill let class out five minutes early that day. Everyone left. Everyone except Newt.

"What's going on?" Bill asked. "Are you banged up? Do you need two weeks?"

Truthfully, Newt did. He was a two-way lineman and played special teams. He played 80 or 90 snaps a game. His feet and knees were sore, and going straight from grass to hardwood didn't help. The first two weeks of basketball practice were always hell for Newt.

"No, it's not that," Newt said. "I'm not sure if I want to play this year."

Bill couldn't believe it.

"Jon, you're sixth man," he said. "You're the first guy off the bench. You're Monty's guy. You're Beckham's guy. They go down, we need you."

"I just don't know if I want to play, coach."

Bill looked Jon square in the eyes.

"We need you," he said. "You're playing."

So Newt played. He took a week off and Bill worked him slowly back into the mix. It was good having Newt, whose true Scrapper value wasn't in beating up Beckham; it was in beating up Monty.

Newt and Monty were always partners for Bill's loose-ball drill. Two players would line up at the baseline, Bill would roll the ball toward the opposite basket and each player would race to get it. Fought is more like it. Fouls didn't exist in this drill, either. It was anything goes. Get the ball no matter what. Monty had five inches on Newt. He had a longer stride than Newt. But Newt was heavier, stronger and used his lower center of gravity to muscle Monty out of the way. Monty usually fell over, and when he did, he would get mad and frustrated. Newt usually got floor burn, but he didn't care.

He liked it.

Other days, Newt would guard Monty down low. He'd push him, elbow him, blatantly foul him—as though Monty were nothing. Bill, of course, never called anything. Instead, he'd rip Monty for being soft and question his toughness in front of everyone. Monty took a beating, physically and verbally, every day.

"Honestly," Newt said, "there were probably only five to 10 practices that year that Monty did not walk out with a bloody nose. That's not me punching him. That's just elbows (being) thrown. And that's before black eyes or busted lips."

It may have been harsh, but it got Monty ready for games. If he could survive Newt, he could survive anybody. And eventually, slowly but surely, Monty began to retaliate.

"There were practices when I was like, 'Damn, that hurt. I'll stop hitting you if you stop hitting me,'" Newt said. "He finally came back. And I was like, 'Wow, now I feel bad. Now I know how it feels.'"

Said Monty, "That's where I really think I started to get more toughness throughout the year—in practice against the Scrappers."

Newt deserves most of the credit for that, but not all. Sometimes someone else would guard Monty, someone who most people would least expect, someone who didn't have a prayer of matching up with him.

Someone named Matt Reed.

• • • •

MATT REED PLAYED BASKETBALL for four years at Roger Bacon. He didn't score many points, and he didn't play many minutes.

But he stuck with it.

A lot of high school athletes wouldn't have done that, especially high school athletes who were standouts in other sports. Matt was a starting linebacker on the football team. Imagine playing virtually every play during one sports season and then being a complete afterthought the next.

Only Matt Reed wasn't an afterthought.

Matt always won attitude awards. Every sport, every year. That was it. Best attitude. It made sense, too. Matt always had that energy, that spirit. He was the kind of guy who didn't need an alarm clock to wake up at sunrise. He'd pop up ready to go as if he'd just gotten 14 hours of sleep.

In terms of pure basketball talent, Matt Reed was the Rudy of the team. By all accounts, he had the game of a 7-footer trapped inside a 5-11 man's body. He couldn't shoot, he couldn't dribble and he didn't have good hands.

"He had no reason to be on the court—none," Newt said. "He had nothing to give physically. He had nothing to give athletically. Nothing at all. But he knew his job."

That job was to work his ass off. Matt's motor was set to one speed—all out, all the time. He knew he wasn't going to see the floor unless Bacon was up 20 with a minute to go, but he didn't care. Matt was a great guy to have around. He pushed his teammates. He kept everyone loose. He kept spirits high.

"I was just there to give good energy, give good effort in practice and maybe provide some comic relief when anxiety was high," Matt said in a self-aware tone.

Playing high school basketball—especially for Bill Brewer—was a big commitment. It's six days a week during the season. Practice for hours on end. Games during the week, games on the weekend, games out of town. Individual summer workouts at 7 a.m.

It's a lot to ask from a kid who's not going to play.

Bill would ask Matt in the preseason, "Matt, are you sure you want to do this?" Matt was sure. He never once considered quitting. He just loved being around his teammates. He loved being around his friends. He loved winning. And that was one thing about Bill. If a kid didn't have much talent but truly wanted to be in the program, if he stuck with it and showed up and did what he was told and didn't defy the coaches, Bill wasn't going to cut him. So that's what Matt did. Practices, games, summer workouts—he was there for all of it.

"I don't know if I got better," Matt said. "But I was there."

Whether Matt got better was irrelevant. Sure, Bill wanted him to get better, but that wasn't his primary concern—because Matt, even though he didn't know it, kept everyone on the team humble. One day at practice, Newt was complaining to Tim McCoy about how he wanted more playing time.

"This is bull crap," Newt said. "I'm working just as hard as Monty. I know Monty's better, but I should be getting more minutes."

Then Newt looked at Matt Reed, who was as eager as could be waiting to check into a starters-versus-Scrappers scrimmage. And that's when Newt realized: Here was a kid who came to practice every day, who gave everything he had all the time, who endured—just like everyone else—the wrath of Bill Brewer, and who knew he'd be fortunate just to get a garbage-time minute or two in the next game. And despite all that, Matt never said a word and never complained. He was just happy to be there.

Wow, Newt thought, *I should probably just shut the hell up.*

And it wasn't just playing time. It was work ethic. Any Spartan who ever thought about dogging it at practice just had to look at Matt. Granted, if Bill saw a player dogging it, he had ways of fixing it. But so did Matt—the only difference was, he could do it without a strong word or a stern look.

"If the least skilled player in the gym is working his ass off," Beckham said, "you damn sure better be working yours off, too."

Matt was comfortable with who he was. He was into the arts. There were times when he was out with friends on the weekend, and he'd call it an early night; he had to be up early the next morning for choir practice. Matt was interested in singing by the time he was in middle school. His older sister, Erica, was in Bacon's choir and graduated in 1997. Matt would be at home cleaning the house with his family and they'd listen to ballads and show tunes and sing along. Matt enjoyed it so much he decided to join the choir. All the guys on the team ridiculed him endlessly for this, but Matt didn't care. He'd just laugh it off. And before one game, he joined the choir in singing the national anthem. After that, Bill, genuinely impressed, always wanted to know if and when Matt would do that again.

Matt, more than anybody else on the team, wanted so desperately to be taken seriously. But no one could take him that way. At one practice, Josh grabbed a rebound and flung a one-handed bullet toward Matt, who had leaked out for a fast break. All Matt had to do was catch the ball and take a few dribbles. Easy layin. But the pass blistered through Matt's hands and hit him square in the face, knocking him over in the process. Not one single player chased after the loose ball.

They were all too busy laughing.

Even Bill couldn't contain himself. And if Bill was laughing, it was funny.

Matt looked around, embarrassed and annoyed.

"Why are you guys laughing at me?" he demanded. "It's not funny!"

But the guys kept laughing. How could they not? Matt was funny even when he wasn't trying to be. Anything he did, the guys couldn't help but smile. Matt just brought out that side of everyone—and everyone loved him for it. There were days Matt walked into practice and Bill would just smile. He wouldn't bare all, but he'd smile—because he knew something funny was about to happen.

"I think Matt Reed was Coach Brewer's favorite player of all time," Tim McCoy said.

And it wasn't just for the laughs. It was for the hustle, the work ethic, the great attitude. It was giving everything he had to the program and expecting nothing in return.

"Matt was that guy," Josh said. "He knew his role. Probably better than anybody else on that team, he knew his role. Whenever I looked at him, I just thought of positive things. I never thought he felt sorry for himself. He just knew his role and was so happy to be part of the team. He did whatever he could to help us prepare. He knew he didn't have as much skill as some of the other guys, but for love of the game—and for love of us—he went out there and did the best he could during practice so we could do our best during games."

Never was Matt's selflessness more apparent, perhaps, than during the 2000–01 season at the tournament in Savannah, Georgia. It was at that tournament that Matt Reed, then a junior, almost died.

As soon as the team left for Savannah, Matt began having terrible stomach pains. Sharp, crippling stomach pains that just wouldn't go away. He was unable to go to the bathroom, so Bill gave him laxatives, which, as they would later find out, was the worst possible thing they could have done. The team went out for dinner one night, and Matt, while waiting to be seated, hunched over in excruciating pain and fell to the floor. Bill, seriously alarmed, told Matt he would arrange for him to be flown home. Matt refused.

"Heck no," Matt said. "I'm here with all my friends! This is like vacation! I don't want to leave!"

That was Matt Reed.

Matt stayed, but he wasn't himself. He didn't have the energy and excitement he always had. He tried to practice and play through the pain, but something wasn't right. He got in toward the end of one of the games, and as he was going for a layup, he collapsed on the court.

"It was bad," Newt said. "We didn't know it was as bad as it was."

Matt got back to Cincinnati and went to the hospital, where doctors told him immediately what was wrong. His appendix had exploded. Luckily, the infection was so big and so rampant that it walled itself around the burst appendix, thereby preventing anything from spreading. Matt's doctors couldn't believe that he went an entire week playing basketball with a burst appendix. Matt needed two surgeries—one just to remove the infection and another to remove the appendix. He was in the hospital for about a week. He lost 35 pounds and went from a burly 200 to a gaunt 165. It was sickly how much weight he lost and the speed with which he lost it. He missed a couple of games but still went to practice to sit and watch. When he returned to action, he would get winded pretty quickly, but he eased back into it and worked his way back up to 200 pounds heading into his senior year.

His teammates didn't forget those handful of games he missed as a junior, though. Some bench players, you can't tell when they're not there. But the void Matt left was apparent—and his teammates couldn't wait to get him back. It wasn't because they needed his scoring. It wasn't because they needed his rebounding.

It was because they missed his spirit.

Matt may not have gotten much playing time, but games consume only a few hours of any given week. What about the other 90 percent of the time? It was during that chunk, especially, that Matt was missed, that he was needed, that everyone realized just how indispensable to the team's success he really was.

"If that had happened to Dave, Matt—if he could—would go inside Dave's stomach, take it out and put it in his own stomach," Newt said. "Just because he knew it'd be better for the team. And because he didn't want to see anyone go through pain. He'd rather take it himself. That's Reed. He was the heart of the team. I was probably the enforcer. I wouldn't let anything happen to anyone. But Reed was the heart of the team. Everybody knew that."

One of Tim McCoy's fondest Matt Reed stories occurred on Senior Night in 2002. As is customary, Bacon trotted out an all-senior starting five that night. Matt was one of the five. It was, in his last home game, the first varsity start of his career. Because of that, most people would think Matt would do anything he could to stay on the court as long as possible. Odds are, he's getting subbed for a minute or two into the game—or the first dead ball. Whichever comes first. But Matt was so hyped to be starting—and not just starting, but starting on a Friday night in front of a packed house in Fogarty—that his adrenaline wore him out almost immediately. He ran up and down the court a few times before motioning toward the bench—about one minute into the game—for someone to sub in for him. That was Matt. Always excited, always going 100 miles an hour.

"For me, Matt was inspirational," Newt said. "For him to do what he did just shows how much of a man he really is. He didn't care about minutes or numbers or press clippings. He didn't care. He just wanted to win. He wanted to be in that locker room. He wanted to be on that bench. He wanted to be on that team. He wanted to be Matt Reed."

EVEN WITH TIM HOUNDING Dave, even with Newt matching Beckham's intensity, even with Matt Reed inspiring everyone in the gym—and even with Bill letting them get away with fouls and the occasional carry—the Scrappers still needed to score. And on days when they did beat the starters, it was usually because of Nate. Nate was a shooter, and some days, maybe a lot of days, he'd catch fire from distance. One three after another.

"There were so many days," Josh said, "when he was the best player on the court."

Leading the Scrappers to victory, however, wasn't a source of pride for Nate. Rather, it was a reminder of his frustration. It was a reminder that he wasn't a starter.

"Tim is proud to be head of the Scrappers," Nate said. "I hated it. I wanted to be on the other side. Even in practice, I wanted to be with the starters."

But he wasn't.

"Nate was really good in seventh and eighth grade—like, really good," Monty said. "He just maybe never turned the corner. Still a good player. Any other team, he's playing a lot. Had he played for Purcell Marian, he's scoring 15 a game. But with what Brewer wanted, it maybe wasn't the perfect fit. Those other guys (on the Scrappers) were not that skilled, but they were tough as hell and did all the things Brewer wanted. Nate was really skilled but maybe didn't do all the other stuff."

Tim, Newt, Leonard—they were Bill Brewer personified. He rewarded them with minutes because they took on his personality. Hell, they *were* his personality. They practiced defense more than offense. When they were in, Bill didn't have to worry about anything. He knew there wouldn't be defensive breakdowns. But with Nate, Bill wasn't always so sure.

"Nate was one of the best players on that team; he's 6-4, can nail a three, finish and shoot free throws—but he didn't play defense," Jerome Harris said. "Leonard played defense like a football player—and that's what Brewer wanted. He figured he had (all the scoring he needed from his starters). But I didn't think Nate, as frustrated as he was, was ever envious. Those were his teammates. Those were his friends. He was proud of them. Sure, he wanted to play more, but he genuinely liked those guys."

Nate really did. He was never jealous of the starters, but he almost always wanted—and felt he deserved—more minutes than he got.

"There were guys in front of me—Beckham, Josh, Frank—that were better than me; I'm not gonna play ahead of them," Nate said. "But I could still bring certain things to the table. I viewed myself as by far the best shooter on the team. There was no one on that team who was as consistent of a shooter as I was. But when I got in the game, I don't know if it was confidence or whatever, I just couldn't get it together. Brewer wanted to mold me into something I wasn't and never was. I was never gonna be a defensive guy giving you 10 rebounds a game. Beckham is like that. He's big and athletic, never afraid to do the dirty work. I was never gonna do that. It wasn't in me."

Therein lay the problem.

"There's no compromising with Brewer," Marcus Smith said. "Brewer was defense-oriented. He doesn't care that you can shoot. Even if you can shoot 50 percent from three, which is unbelievable, he'll go with a guy who shoots 30 percent from three but who does things Brewer's way. If you're smart, and you wanna play, that's what you gotta figure out. I don't care what I *think* I am. I can be the best shooter in the world, but if defense is gonna get me on the floor, I'm gonna start playing defense. Then maybe he'll let me shoot a couple—instead of (thinking), 'Oh, he needs to let me play because I'm a good shooter.' That's just not how Brewer was. He was a dictator."

• • • •

Every time the practice doors closed, Fogarty became a fortress of fortitude. Players could enter; coaches could enter. By and large, that was it. No students, no girlfriends, no parents. For several hours each day, the Spartans lived in their own 4,700-square-foot world. They lived and breathed and governed by their own rules. Time had no purpose. Money lost all meaning. Everything that occurred outside was irrelevant. Everything that occurred inside remained only for them to see and know and feel.

And that's where it came from—the bond, the kinship.

"Practice is where we made our team," Leonard said. "The dedication we had for the game and for each other, Bill instilled that. He brought out the best of everybody. It was a competition, but at the end of it, we were a family. That's Bill Brewer."

Yes, despite the daily battles that were the starters-versus-Scrappers scrimmages, there was a brotherhood at every position. Newt was there for Monty and Beckham. If an opposing player started something with either of them, especially Monty, Newt was there. Leonard was there for Josh and Frank. Tim was there for Dave. Same deal. If someone tried to rough up Dave, if someone tried to cheap shot him, Dave might let it go unpunished. Tim wouldn't. As much as he'd harass Dave in practice, he respected him. He loved him. If somebody messed with Dave, Tim wouldn't stand for it. No Scrapper would. Yes, they tussled with the starters for playing time, but they never lost sight of the bigger picture. No one did.

"You couldn't put anything between us," Newt said. "We were all brothers."

There are some days you might hate your brother. You might get in fights with him. You might say or do things you don't mean. But when an outsider hurts your brother, when an outsider tries to harm someone in your family, those disagreements, those squabbles, don't matter. Loyalty supersedes all else. Rule No. 1: Protect your brother; be loyal to your family. That was it. Every player on that team knew it, and every player on that team practiced it.

That's how that team became close.

That's how that team became great.

* * * *

THE PRACTICE AFTER THE CJ game lasted an hour. Tops.

"It was the shortest practice of the season," Marcus Smith said, "but it was the longest practice of the season."

Sprints, suicides, toughness drills. Bill spared no expense. Whenever there was a down moment, the verbal blasting from Friday night resumed. One by one, Bill tore into his players once more. It was as if they were right back in CJ's locker room being scolded like children, and waiting, just like the janitors, for permission to go home.

And then it happened. Bill, disgusted beyond comprehension, picked up a basketball and punted it toward the scoreboard. Direct hit.

"GET THE FUCK OUT OF HERE!" he barked at his players.

Now, normally when a coach says this, it's a test, a test of a player's will and commitment to the team. The coach doesn't actually want his players to leave. In fact, if a coach angrily yells for his players to get the fuck out of the gym, getting the fuck out of the gym is about the worst thing those players can do—and the Spartans knew that. But on that January morning in Fogarty, they went against conventional wisdom. They didn't wait for Bill to calm down or see if there was anything else he needed to say. They didn't wait for him to formally dismiss them. They didn't stick around to work on free throws as they usually did. Instead, they grabbed their gear and skedaddled skittishly to the parking lot.

"Everybody just wanted to get out of there," Newt said.

Some people might say Bill overreacted. The postgame tirade, the early morning practice, the track meet, the toughness drills, the punt. Some people might say, "Hey, you lost a league game on the road. That happens." Or, "Oh well, you'll get 'em next time."

That's not the attitude Bill had.

"It taught us how much losing wasn't okay," Monty said. "Losing is absolutely not okay. It's gonna be hell. If you didn't want to win, Brewer was gonna make you want to win."

It was mid-January, barely halfway through the regular season. Bacon was 8–3. The Spartans would play 17 more games that year, and for every one of them, the CJ game—not to mention the practice that followed—wasn't far from their minds.

CHAPTER EIGHT

THE COVER

The next month unfolded spectacularly for the Spartans of Roger Bacon. They left little doubt in the two games following the debacle in Dayton, dismantling league rivals Alter and La Salle by a combined 40 points.

"I felt sorry for our next opponent," Josh said. "There was no way we were losing."

After a closely contested 51–48 home win against St. Xavier, Bacon reeled off three straight double-digit victories against McNicholas, Purcell Marian and, once again, Alter. Two impressive road wins followed, as Bacon earned a hard-fought, four-point win at Badin and blew out, thanks to four three-pointers from Dave, typically tough Moeller 74–46 in the Crusaders' brand new gym. How bad did the Moeller game get?

Matt Reed played the final minute.

Wanting, as always, to show his appreciation to Bill, Matt played with typical Matt Reed vigor. With Bacon up 30 points with about 30 seconds to go, Matt dived wildly out of bounds trying to save a loose ball. He collided with a cooler of Gatorade like a baserunner barreling into a catcher for a play at the plate. The cooler toppled, and Gatorade gushed all over Moeller's new floor. Matt lay sprawled out of bounds before picking himself up, dusting himself off and hustling back on defense.

That was Matt Reed.

"Brewer was just dying laughing," Monty said. "That's the thing. Brewer was always so serious and yelled so much, but when he laughed, he had a good sense of humor."

But wins at Badin and Moeller were mere appetizers for the main course that was the regular-season finale. Bacon's opponent? CJ. The showdown, like the one 35 nights previous, came down to the final seconds. CJ post player Jermiel Atkins hit a short jumper to put the Eagles up 37–34, but Josh Hausfeld, as he had done throughout his career at Bacon, led the Spartans to victory. He answered Atkins' jumper with a jumper of his own. After a steal by Frank, Josh scored on a layin to give Bacon a 38–37 lead. He scored a game-high 11 points that night, and Dave hit two free throws with 2.4 seconds left to seal the 40–37 win.

To make matters worse for CJ, two key seniors were kicked off the team the following week for an off-court incident. Bacon thought all along it would have to face CJ en route to Columbus, which was cause for concern since both regular-season games were decided by three points. But CJ's postseason run ended before it started.

That was fine with Bacon. The Spartans, finally playing with the tough-minded urgency Bill so desperately desired, won their final nine games of the regular season, including six by double-digits. They gave up just 42.7 points per game during that stretch and allowed only one opponent to break 50.

Bacon was balling.

Then, three days after beating CJ, something happened—something that raised the stakes irrevocably, something that would forever alter the life of one boy, the lives of those close to him and the lives of those who sought to defeat him.

LeBron James was unleashed by the national media.

And the season would never be the same again.

• • • •

IF ANY PERSON—SPORTS DIEHARD or otherwise—in this vast land didn't know who LeBron James was already, then on February 18, 2002, there was a good chance he or she found out. Because on that day, perhaps the greatest prep basketball player in history appeared on the cover of perhaps the most reputable sports publication in the world—*Sports Illustrated*.

There was LeBron. The 17-year-old prodigy palmed in his right hand a basketball, a glowing orb faintly illuminating the gold of his Irish jersey. His eyes widened; his lips puckered. He possessed a now-you-see-it, now-you-don't expression, one conjured by only the most mesmerizing of magicians. His left arm reached out to touch you, his hand frozen in shadows. Across his body read the words, "The Chosen One." The subtitle? "High school junior LeBron James would be an NBA lottery pick right now."

If the cover seemed over the top, the story explained why it wasn't. *SI* writer Grant Wahl chronicled the quaint yet extraordinary spectacle of LeBron engaging in small talk with Michael Jordan in a tunnel at Cleveland's Gund Arena, which later became Quicken Loans Arena. It was that surreal, singular scene when soon-to-be past collided with on-the-rise future—only the future was now. The on-court laurels came fast and furious. Comparisons were made between LeBron and the greatest of greats, between LeBron and the most titanic of titans. People all across the country—from the Indiana farm boy to the New York street baller in Rucker Park—read fervently of the boy wonder. This was huge. This was beyond huge. This was Beatlemania multiplied by Jesus Shuttlesworth. LeBron was the talk of the town—in every town.

"I won't lie; my first thought was, 'That is pretty darn cool,'" Josh Hausfeld said of the cover. "Here's a guy, basically my age, and he's on the cover of *Sports Illustrated*. You know that's a big deal because they don't put just anybody on that cover. I knew at that point that his fame and the admiration people had for him was on a whole other level. But in the back of my mind, I couldn't help but think, 'This is gonna make our rematch even sweeter.'"

The cover was everywhere.

"We were reminded of it every day, all the time," Frank Phillips said. "It was in cafeterias, it was in hotels, it was in busses—I don't think our own students thought we could beat them."

Even if the Spartans wanted to get away from the cover, they couldn't. Fellow students taped it on a couple of the players' lockers as a joke. Local media asked the Spartans what they thought of the cover and of LeBron and what a potential rematch would mean. For the last two months, Roger Bacon had operated with the quiet conviction that it belonged on the same court with LeBron James and SVSM. When the *SI* cover hit newsstands, when the players got their copy in the mail or saw it plastered to their lockers, it would have been easy for them to lose the psychological confidence—not edge, but confidence—they had in potentially facing SVSM again. Suddenly, everything seemed bigger. The balls bounced a little crisper. The lights shined a little brighter. If Bacon were, in fact, to play LeBron again, the entire nation, the entire basketball world, would be watching. That's when the Spartans realized this wasn't just Ohio high school basketball anymore.

This was history.

It's one thing to face a highly touted teenager who many feel has a bright future ahead of him. It's another to see him on the cover of *Sports Illustrated*. It's another to see him with the words "The Chosen One" attached to his name—words that imply this boy wonder is in some way majestic, in some way destined, in some way appointed by a higher roundball power to fulfill a prophesy spurred by the basketball gods.

Roger Bacon wasn't in Kansas anymore.

Maybe he's gotten a lot better in the last two months. Maybe we caught him on an off night. Maybe he wasn't trying his hardest. Maybe we were lucky the game was that close. Truly, what is this kid capable of?

It would have been easy for the Spartans to think that. Some of that. All of that. But those thoughts never crossed their minds—not even the mind of Marcus Smith, who watched from the stands when his team almost beat the fourth-ranked team in the country.

"Just from my experience playing, no matter what a magazine or TV says, I was just up close and personal with this guy," Marcus said. "We just played toe to toe, nose to nose. That outweighs anything anyone can tell you."

Personal experience trumps hype, but there was no denying that the hysteria surrounding LeBron and SVSM for the rest of the season was in many ways uncharted territory. As seen in *More Than a Game*, the Irish were seemingly living the life of NBA All-Stars. Wherever they were became the place to be. Whoever they were with became the person to see. Their home games had been moved to the University of Akron to accommodate SVSM's ever-increasing fan base. Game tickets were going for hundreds of dollars. People flooded hotel lobbies. Girls tried sneaking up to the players' rooms. Hundreds of people begged for autographs before games, after games. They all wanted to witness greatness, to touch it and be a part of it. Junior point guard Dru Joyce likened the experience to being in a rock band, with LeBron as the lead singer.

Everybody was talking about The Chosen One. Michael, Kobe, Shaq—*everyone*. No prep basketball player had ever gotten this much attention, especially not before his senior year. That made everything LeBron did that much more special. David Letterman was calling SVSM for interviews. Everybody wanted a piece.

And the Irish, understandably, ate it up. These were high school kids thrust into the national spotlight. People knew who they were. The players watched their game highlights on team bus rides, almost marveling at what they could do and at just how good they were. After a dunk or pretty play, LeBron would sometimes shimmy his shoulders. He'd flex. There was attitude behind it.

It was irresistible.

Brian Neal doesn't envy in any way the challenges that Dru Joyce likely faced that season, especially as a first-year coach. Taking over a program with a history of success, especially recent success, is tough enough. But to do it with the whole country watching your every move? That's not easy. How does a coach manage the hype? The attention? The expectations? How does he prevent complacency among his players?

"I don't care who you are, what your background is or what people tell you," Brian Neal said. "When you're a 17-year-old kid on the cover of *Sports Illustrated*, you can't tell me it doesn't affect you. You can't tell me it doesn't affect your work ethic. You can't tell me it doesn't affect what you do on a daily basis. Our guys were typical high school kids—going to class, studying when they got home, practicing at our gym, not playing at (Xavier's) Cintas Center. We were just going about our daily business. Our guys lived in the gym. That's part of the reason we were so good. Guys wouldn't leave. Guys would stay in the gym and shoot. If they needed to work on free throws, they'd stay and work on free throws—not because Bill told them to, not because I told them to, but because that's part of the make-up of that team. We had guys who were committed to being really good (because we) had a chance to do something special. We just went about our business. And I'm sure that *SI* thing affected (the Irish) in ways they didn't even know at the time."

Oddly enough, SVSM lost two games—one right before, one right after—the *SI* cover hit newsstands. The first setback came against perennial power Oak Hill Academy, which, like SVSM, boasted a top-five national ranking and one of the best players in America—a senior named Carmelo Anthony, who in a little over a year would lead Syracuse to the 2003 national title. LeBron outscored Anthony 36–34, but Oak Hill won 72–66 in a game played at Sovereign Bank Arena in Trenton, New Jersey. The next loss came against George Junior Republic, a physical team from Grove City, Pennsylvania, that bested SVSM 58–57 in overtime. George Junior Republic limited LeBron to 20 points and held the Irish to their second lowest scoring output of the season.

SVSM had now lost consecutive games for the first, last and only time in LeBron's prep career. Nevertheless, the Irish won their final two regular-season games and finished No. 1 in the final Ohio state poll with an overall record of 17–3. Their only other loss that season, also by a point, occurred in December at the Slam Dunk to the Beach Tournament in Lewes, Delaware. The Irish lost 84–83 to Long Island Amityville, a public-school power from New York. Amityville was led by McDonald's All-American and Villanova-bound big man Jason Fraser, as well as Connecticut-bound guard A.J. Price, who made the game-winning free throws in the final seconds. LeBron, playing on his 17th birthday, netted 39 points—this despite suffering from the flu—and converted a four-point play with 5.4 seconds left to give the Irish an 83–82 lead, amazing given that SVSM was out-rebounded 49–23. But Price's two free throws gave Amityville the win.

Thus, entering the state playoffs in 2002, LeBron's career record at SVSM was 70–4. Three of those losses were by a point. Two were to Oak Hill Academy.

LeBron and the Irish had still never lost to a team from Ohio.

• • • •

IF THE COVER AFFECTED the Spartans in any way, it strengthened their resolve.

"Honestly," Newt said, "I don't think I ever read it. I looked at the cover, but I don't think I even read the story."

Then again, Newt probably didn't have to. The Spartans knew who LeBron was. They knew who he would become. But they wouldn't let him—or the hype surrounding him—affect their goals. The cover made them want LeBron that much more. If he was going to be dethroned, they wanted to be the ones who did it. They might not make *Sports Illustrated*, but they didn't care. They remained undeterred.

"Outside our locker room, there were probably a lot of doubts," Josh said. "But inside our locker room, we knew what we were capable of."

Dave Johnson and his parents hosted several team dinners that year. Players and parents would convene to talk, eat and grow closer together. After dinner, the players would hang out in Dave's basement—playing pool, playing darts. Taped to the front of that dart board was a cover from *Sports Illustrated*, a cover dated February 18, 2002, a cover adorned by the greatest prep basketball player the world had ever seen.

The Spartans took turns casually chucking darts at The Chosen One—not in anger, annoyance or animosity, but in playful confidence, knowing that soon, very soon, in a little over a month, the rematch of all rematches would be theirs.

CHAPTER NINE

THE DOG DAYS

Even though the Spartans won their last nine regular-season games, even though they avenged the loss to CJ, even though they felt confident heading into the state tournament—*SI* cover and all—one unspoken question remained.

Was something wrong with Josh Hausfeld?

Throughout his career, Josh had established himself as one of the premier scorers in the city, if not the state. But as his senior season wore on, Josh simply wasn't playing like the offensive force he had been his entire life. Through the first 10 games of the regular season, Josh averaged right around 16 points, which was certainly nothing to scoff at. But over the final 10 games, he averaged just over 11. Included in that second-half funk was a brutal four-game stretch in which he scored three points or fewer on three occasions.

It all started with the loss to CJ, a game in which Josh scored just three points—and none after the first quarter. He did follow that quiet night with a trio of treys and 14 points in a home win against Alter, but the ensuing two games were inexplicable. He scored just three points at La Salle and none—*none*—in a 51–48 home win against St. Xavier. As Josh recalls, his future college coach at Miami of Ohio, Charlie Coles, was in attendance that night against St. X.

"I don't know if I had a lot on my mind or if I was nervous because he was there," Josh said. "When I look at that stretch, I look at it as I was just in a slump. There was something going on in my mind. I was in a rut. I wasn't as confident as I normally would be."

Not as confident? The Golden Boy?

When asked that season by the *Cincinnati Enquirer* of his string of quiet performances, Josh replied, "It's not that I was missing but that I wasn't shooting much."

The best of scorers, especially in high school, will have off nights. Tough crowds, hostile environments, scouts to impress—it can be a lot of pressure for a kid. Some nights the shots just don't fall. Stress at school, problems with a girl, fatigue in the legs—any number of things can contribute. Missing shots? That happens.

But not shooting much? The kid who practiced varsity right out of eighth grade, the kid who started varsity as a freshman, the kid who dropped 42 on CJ as a sophomore, the kid who was league player of the year and all-state as a junior . . .

. . . *wasn't shooting much*? As a senior? Against CJ and two GCL-South opponents?

It didn't make sense.

Granted, senior year is when Josh's body truly began turning against him, especially his ankles, which would plague him throughout his career at Miami.

"Josh always had ankle injuries—rolling, twisting," Dave Johnson said. "I feel like it was like that his whole career. He had to sit out practices sometimes. He probably played through a lot of pain that year."

Indeed, the spring in Josh's step that once came so naturally just wasn't there.

"I never had a knee problem my whole life, but I always sprained my ankles—that was my thing," Josh said. "Senior year, it took a turn for the worse. I couldn't jump as high. I had to do things a little differently than I was used to."

But still. Goose eggs?

No, this went deeper than ankles.

• • • •

THE BATTLES AT PRACTICES weren't just between the starters and Scrappers. They were also between Bill and his players. Mostly, they were between Bill and Josh.

As Brian Neal attested, it's hard being a head coach; if you want to win a popularity contest, coaching isn't for you. Decisions aren't always easy, especially when they involve improving the team at the expense of one of its players.

"Josh was kind of—I don't want to say the whipping boy," Neal said, "but sometimes as a coach, you have to get on somebody so the other players know you're serious."

For Bill, that somebody was Josh Hausfeld. Had to be. Part of it was because of Eugene Land. Part of it was because of the football coaches. But forget the psychology of it all. When a player is as good as Josh was, the hounding and harassment are just part of the deal. It comes with the territory of being the best player. The best player might not always like it—he might never like it—but sometimes, like a pro athlete signing an autograph at a restaurant, he has to oblige, even if he'd rather be left alone.

Bill never left Josh alone. Not for one second.

Every practice, every practice for four years—but especially once Josh was an upperclassman—Bill almost always gave him some variation of the same message.

Well, Josh, you scored 20 but you gave up 30! You don't play defense! You gotta play defense! You don't rebound! You gotta rebound! You gotta put a body on him! You gotta stop turning the ball over! What the fuck was that, Josh? What the fuck's going through your mind when you make a pass like that? Someday there's gonna be a banner in this gym—Most turnovers in a career: Josh Hausfeld.

Four years. Four God damn years.

Film sessions were particularly brutal. Every Saturday, the team would gather to watch its game from the previous night. Win or lose, whether Josh scored three or 30, Bill would go out of his way to point out Josh's defensive deficiencies, pausing and rewinding the film time and time again to harp on every blunder in basics, on every faux pas in fundamentals.

It was caustic. It was biting. It was embarrassing.

"I knew it was a learning point, but I almost never learned from it because I would do it every game," Josh said. "It was something I thought about and worked on, but every Saturday it would be the same thing. He would pause the film and say, 'Look at Hausfeld.' I wasn't trying to not be a good defender, but for whatever reason, I didn't develop all the skills there that I needed."

Frank's uncle, Jerome Harris, had a theory. He had coached players similar to Josh—outstanding scorers who were quiet by nature and not exactly known for their defensive tenacity, which is something Bill repeatedly tried to hammer into Josh.

"Josh was always a great talent, so he didn't have to play defense," Jerome said. "No matter how much Brewer tried, it's just not gonna work. You can't yell and make a guy play defense. All you can do is permeate an environment where you get the most out of him. Was Josh a great defensive player? Not at all.

"But here it is," Jerome continued, leaning in and lowering his voice, as if preparing to divulge a secret. "He didn't know how. It wasn't in his DNA. I understood the Joshes of the world. I was never a Josh. I was a Dennis Rodman in high school. I'm a role player. As a role player, I understood my friends. You need me to play defense because that's just not in your DNA. (Players like) Josh, it's not in their DNA. All their lives they're told, 'Don't get into foul trouble. Don't dive for loose balls. Don't get hurt. Let the role players do it.' Well, now you got guys around you just as good. That team evolved around Josh, but now it's in Frankie's hands, it's in Beckham's hands, it's in Dave's hands. It really hurt Josh's confidence."

Josh admitted Jerome's star-scorer theory is spot on.

"I've seen it many times; there's definitely truth to that," Josh said. "For the longest time—in grade school and high school—I was able to get away with my natural ability and scoring. I knew I was a great scorer and could do a lot of things, so I took defense for granted. But once Coach Brewer got a hold of me, he was the first person to really be all over me about defense. But growing up, it was something that I didn't necessarily need in order to play in games. No one ever said to me, 'You're not gonna play unless you play defense.'"

If a player isn't a great defender, teammates and coaches will look past it—provided the player is just that good on offense. And for the first three years of Josh's career at Bacon, he was. But entering his senior year, Josh knew he didn't have to score 20 points a game for Bacon to be successful. He didn't need to average the 18 and change he averaged as a sophomore. Even as a junior, when he still averaged close to 15 points, it was different. Frank had transferred from Winton Woods. Beckham was on the precipice of a psychological revolution. Monty and Dave were starting as sophomores and quickly developing. Josh had a lot of talent around him, so even then, he didn't have to score 20 points for Bacon to win. There were games when he still did put up that many, but he didn't have to. He had the option, the luxury, of deferring to his teammates. It was the same thing senior year—only more pronounced.

Balance was good for Roger Bacon, but was it good for Josh? Better yet, was it good for Josh's personality?

"As good as Josh was, if you could put a little bit of Beckham into Josh . . . ," Mitch Perdrix said before trailing off. "He's just too nice a guy. And it's all the reasons you love him as a person that hurt him as a player—and I shouldn't say it that way because he was a phenomenal player. He was the best player on that team. He was just too nice. Anybody who plays will tell you, being nice doesn't get you very far. Beckham's one of the nicest guys; you put him between those four lines, he's a raging dickhead. And that's an M.O. for anybody who's good. You almost had to remind Josh sometimes, 'Hey, you're the best guy on the floor.' Beckham thinks it even if he's not. You put Beckham on the floor with LeBron James, and Beckham's going, 'I'm the best guy on the floor.' Away from the game, he knows LeBron James is LeBron James. But when you put him out there, it's, 'This guy's nothing.' That's the mentality you have to have, and Josh just didn't have that. I can remember being in warmups sometimes, going, 'You gotta pull the trigger. You're the best guy out here.' That was the one fault Josh had. He didn't have that killer instinct. But in life that's why everybody loves him. He's such a good guy."

That year, in 2001–02, the Spartans had Frank, who averaged nearly 13 points per game. They had Beckham and Monty, who each averaged more than 10. They had Dave, who hit three or more three-pointers in a game four times that season. In short, they had a lot of quality players, all capable of scoring.

"Josh wasn't the kind of guy who would say, 'I'm the best. Give me the ball,'" Mitch said. "Sophomore year, he had to (be the go-to guy). If he didn't do it, no one's going to. But if you're out there with four guys who can do it . . ."

Mitch and the other coaches tried to instill that killer instinct in Josh. They tried to get him to take over games, to be more aggressive, to demand the ball and make things happen. But it didn't work. If Josh had been unselfish in grade school, where the talent gap between him and everyone else was particularly pronounced, he wasn't going to suddenly become selfish on varsity, where the talent gap had bridged however slightly or greatly.

"It just wasn't me," Josh said. "It wasn't in my nature."

Coaches know which kids they can yell at, and if they don't know, they find out. Some adjust, some don't. Bill was who he was. With Josh, he remained overbearing, unrelenting—about defense, about rebounding, about turnovers. But senior year was different. It used to be that Josh, in Bill's eyes, could do no right—but he was still scoring 20 a game. Senior year, Josh still wasn't doing anything right, but now he was merely one piece of the puzzle—a big piece, maybe still the biggest, but the pieces around him had all become far, far bigger.

No matter. Josh still bore by far the biggest brunt of Bill's snarl.

"There were times," Brian Neal said plainly, "when Bill was not very nice to that young man."

Some, like Josh's mother, Mary Beth, insisted that even though Bill was hard on Josh, it was never to the point where it bothered him.

Not everyone remembered it quite the same way.

"It was a father-son thing," Newt said. "They had a love-hate relationship. They'd love each other one moment and then absolutely hate each other the next. You yell at me or Tim, we'll take it. We'll take it and laugh. You yell at Josh, he's muttering under his breath. It takes him a couple of minutes to calm down."

And it wasn't just during the season.

In the summer of 2000, Josh—along with Frank, who had recently transferred from Winton Woods—were a few minutes late to Bacon's first summer-league game. Some coaches would've let that slide. It's summer. It's the first game. Josh and Frank were probably busy being kids and simply lost track of time.

Bill didn't see it that way. He sat Josh and Frank for the entire game. *The entire game.* But that wasn't all. He told them—point blank—that if Bacon lost, it would be their fault. Any time something went wrong in that game—a missed shot, a turnover, if someone didn't get a rebound—Bill turned to Josh and Frank, yelled at them and said it was because of them.

Welcome to Roger Bacon, Frank.

As for Josh, no exceptions were made—not even for the leading scorer in the GCL.

"It goes back to Bill's discipline," Bobby Holt said. "He had the ability to push guys out of their comfort zone so they could be ready for any situation that could occur. He was trying to make Josh mentally tough."

Sure, all the players had something Bill would pick at.

Monty, you're not tough! You're soft! You're 6-8 and you're soft! Get stronger! Get tougher! Get your ass off the floor! How the hell does your ass end up on the floor so damn much?

"Some of them would take it in different ways," Cork said. "Beckham was the only one who heard it, filtered it in, kept what he wanted to hear, and filtered the rest out."

But that's just it. Josh wasn't Beckham—and even Beckham conceded that playing for Bill was hard. It's a long season. Riding somebody that hard for that long can take a toll on a person. And many saw it take a toll on Josh.

By the time Josh was a senior—and as that senior year wore on—he appeared, according to some, burned out. Burned out on Bill. Burned out on basketball. Burned out on having to be The Guy. Josh had been the face of the program for four years, and everyone knew that to beat Roger Bacon, you had to contain Josh Hausfeld. The game plan—whether Bacon's or the opposing team's—always revolved around him. *How can we make it easy for Josh to score?* versus *How can we stop Josh from scoring?*

Those were the questions. Every game. For four years. And now, with the postseason approaching during Josh's senior year, here he was lacking confidence, questioning himself, not pulling the trigger.

"I think he was done being the star," Tim McCoy said. "I think it just wore on him over the years."

Monty, who went on to play with Josh at Miami of Ohio, noticed a change in him that year but didn't sense the burnout some of the others did.

"Josh's problem was he was so good so early that he didn't have much room to get better," Monty said. "If he would've gotten any better, he would've gone to the NBA. Brewer stayed on him until the day he graduated. And Josh isn't dumb, but especially in high school, he did a lot of dumb stuff. All those turnovers.... For a player with his talent to make those types of decisions, that can drive a coach crazy—and it drove Brewer to get on him even more. I got yelled at because I was soft, and Brewer thought I was talented so he needed to toughen me up. With Josh, Brewer needed to make sure that he didn't get too far ahead of himself mentally. I think Josh mellowed out more as a senior, (but) I wouldn't say he was broken down. He had to battle more. He had a more constant battle than probably everybody else did, but I don't think he was burned out. It maybe wore on him a little, but even if he could change it, I don't think he would."

It wasn't just teammates who noticed a change in Josh that year. Bill had a rule about parents at practice—meaning, they weren't allowed to attend—but Jerome Harris, perhaps because he was Frank's uncle and not his father, witnessed his fair share of Bacon practices. Even he detected a difference in Josh.

"Basketball wasn't fun anymore," Jerome said. "Senior year, which was supposed to be the happiest year of Josh's life, wasn't fun anymore. He's happy because of his teammates. He's proud because of the success. But there's no way he had fun. I watched him every day. I never saw Josh and Brewer (talking). Every practice, every game, Frankie and Brewer were always laughing—and Brewer didn't laugh. Josh is the nicest kid in the world. I used to say hi to him. He'd say, 'What's up?' And he was quiet—but he used to be quiet with a smile."

"Was Josh cocky?" Jerome continued. "No, not at all. Not at all. Josh was so humble. But he was an introvert, and that's where I think Brewer broke him. Brewer lost confidence in Josh all the time. He rode him so unfairly. Just rode him so unfairly. That was Brewer's style—to break guys down. But Josh isn't Frank. He's not Beckham. I love Brewer to death, and I thought Brewer was a great coach. But great coaches make mistakes. And I'm a yeller, but I can't yell at (certain players). I can't. I held (them) accountable. There's a difference. You can hold Josh accountable. You just can't yell at him. Some people are sensitive. It doesn't make them a bad person; it definitely doesn't make them a prima donna. Josh had no prima donna in him. (But) he was scared—of Brewer, of turning it over, of missing shots. Josh just lost his confidence. Brewer was overly harsh on him. Could he have handled it differently? Yes. Was he wrong? No, he wasn't wrong. Bill was phenomenal, and he was a hell of a lot better coach than I am. He was breaking Josh down to build him up. He just never built him up."

But maybe he did. Maybe he did and others just didn't know it.

Josh always tried to take Bill's riding in stride. In fact, early on in his career, he learned to understand it, to appreciate it—and it wasn't just because of the annual trips to Columbus he and Bill took together. No, there were times when the coach, unbeknownst to anyone else on the team, would let his best player know why he was the way he was.

There was a game during Josh's sophomore year, for instance, when Josh broke down. He made a terrible play, prompting Bill to bench him and lay into him for all the world to see. It's tough for a stud to take that, especially in front of everyone. Josh sat on the bench, feeling horrible.

"He was being so hard on me," Josh explained, "and I just wanted to be so good for him and for the team."

After the game, Josh was alone thinking of the mistakes he'd made, thinking of how he'd let the team down. He became emotional. And that's when it happened.

"I remember Coach Brewer, for the first time ever, coming over to me—and it was just me and him; no one else was there," Josh recalled, "and he just looked at me and said, 'You know I love you, Josh.' I was in shock. And he said, 'I'm so hard on you because I think you have a chance to be great.' Just hearing those words from him, him actually saying that to me, I had a different perspective on why he was giving me a hard time. He saw something in me."

When Josh was a senior, Bill gave him a ride home after Bacon's 16-point win at Elder—the game right before the Spartans played SVSM at Kent State.

"Josh, you played well tonight," Bill said before letting his star player out of the car. "You did good."

Josh was caught completely off guard. That's not how they normally operated. Usually, Bill would get all over Josh, and Josh would search inside himself to respond as best he could.

Not that night. On that night, Josh got his due.

"There were very few occasions like that Elder night where he said, 'You did good.' That just wasn't his style with me," Josh said. "But I knew in my heart that he loved me."

• • • •

Perhaps Josh's relationship with Bill is common between a head coach and a best player. Maybe with inherently competitive people, that's just the way it has to be. A coach needs his best player to play well to win, so he'll push him to maximize his ability; the best player, meanwhile, needs his coach to have his best interests at heart, to help him reach his potential and prepare him for everything he'll encounter.

It's give and take. It's mutually beneficial. It's common.

"He wanted me to be the best player in the GCL," Josh said. "He made me earn everything. Nothing was ever given to me by Coach Brewer. He rode me and rode me and rode me. But even when you were getting chewed out, you respected him because you believed in what he was saying."

Because you believed in what he was saying.

No doubt there was a change in Josh senior year. As tough as Bill was, though, maybe he wasn't the cause of it. And maybe the game that Josh grew up loving wasn't the cause, either.

Maybe it was everything that the game suddenly meant.

On the one hand, Josh was the best player on the team. St. Bernard, born and bred. The St. Clement stud. Pickup basketball at the Pavilion. The hopes of a hometown thrust on its hero.

Who wouldn't want that?

On the other hand, Josh was the best player on the team. St. Bernard, born and bred. The St. Clement stud. Pickup basketball at the Pavilion. The hopes of a hometown thrust on its hero.

Who would want that cross to bear?

"People know who Josh Hausfeld is," said Newt, who was a year behind Josh at St. Clement. "They know who he is. I think he felt uncomfortable to the point where people almost knew more about him than he knew about himself. They know him as that star. He wanted to be the star, but he didn't want to be everything else that came with it. He'd take some of the responsibility, but he didn't want it all on his shoulders, which I think, to a point, wore him down. It got pretty heavy on him. Josh had that chip on his shoulder that he didn't want to fail. He wanted (state) more than any of us. He just didn't know how to handle it."

It's not that whether Bacon won or lost hinged entirely on Josh, but sometimes that's how Josh felt. Freshman year, Josh got his feet wet. Sophomore year, he was unreal but the team wasn't. Junior year, he was still great, and now so was the team—but it was a young team, a team left knocking once more on the state door, just as two of Bill's previous teams had. Now Josh was a senior. Last chance for the last dance. All five starters back. High expectations. LeBron James. *Sports Illustrated*.

Everything was magnified.

"There was a lot of pressure on him, and it seemed like the pressure was getting to him," Bobby Holt said. "But back then, I never really talked to him about it. Even though we were close, I tried to step back and let him figure it out on his own."

There were times that year when Josh would think about life as an eighth-grader, about watching Brandon and Eugene lose in the regional finals. Josh remembered how disappointed everyone was; he remembered how sad. He didn't want his hometown going through that again. He didn't want to let anyone down.

"I put more pressure on myself than anybody could put on me," Josh said. "I felt a lot of pressure to take our team to state. I knew it was our last year. I think my ankle, my body—there were times when it got to be a lot, and I would think, 'Man, I just wanna win so bad.' So I'm sure I wasn't the same. I wouldn't say I was depressed, but as far as being totally different . . ."

There's a pause.

"I don't know," Josh said. "I don't know."

Josh was no longer the player he used to be. His personality wouldn't allow it. Neither would his ankles. Still, there was a sense, an inkling, a sneaking suspicion that if the Spartans were going to win state, the old Josh Hausfeld would have to reappear.

And reappear with a vengeance.

CHAPTER TEN

THE TRAGEDY

It was Saturday, March 9, 2002, and Beckham Wyrick drove to Roger Bacon feeling good. And why wouldn't he? True, he was on his way to one of those classic, early morning Bill Brewer practices, but seniors have a way of embracing everything, of savoring even the harsh and the grueling, when time dwindles and the end is near.

It was March. Bacon had won four yawner playoff games by an average of 29 points. The *SI* cover had only made the Spartans that much more steadfast in their goal. For six of them, this was their last run, their last chance. They had a legit shot at state. They had a legit shot at LeBron.

Life was good.

But when Beckham pulled into campus that morning, he quickly realized something was wrong. He saw Josh propped against his car with sadness in his eyes and tears on his face. It's rarely a good thing when a player sees a teammate in tears. Countless thoughts and questions will converge in the player's head at that very moment, the moment when curiosity meets fear. *Just how bad? Just how bad is it?* Beckham swung out of his car and approached Josh to see what was wrong and to determine what, if anything, he could do to fix it. But there was nothing Beckham could do.

It was Meg. There had been an accident.

* * * *

MARGARET ELIZABETH GUTZWILLER WAS born on May 31, 1982. Her older brother, Matt, remembers that day clearly. He was too young to remember when his other sister, Katie, was born, but he remembers Meg. It was early in the morning, real early, 5:30 or 6, and when Meg was brought home, there was a buzz in the house, an energy.

Of course there was. For Meg, there was always an energy.

Meg was the baby of the family, the underdog, the long shot. Her three older siblings—Katie, Matt and John Jr.—were separated by a combined seven years; then there was a five-year gap, and then there was Meg. Katie always wondered if Meg was an accident—not simply because of the interlude between pregnancies, but because her mother, Karen, was pregnant with Katie five years earlier when she found out she was diabetic. When Mr. and Mrs. John Gutzwiller discovered their fourth child was on the way, they were in their mid-to-late 30s. Mrs. Gutzwiller's age, but more so her diabetes, worried doctors that complications could arise if the pregnancy were carried to term. The doctors were so worried, in fact, that they advised Mrs. Gutzwiller to not have the baby.

They advised, in essence, an abortion.

John Jr. was only 10 or 11 at the time, but he remembers vividly the hours and days and weeks after his parents were given such bleak counsel. He remembers the sound of his mother weeping in her bedroom and how she hoped in vain that a closed door could hide her sorrow. But it couldn't. For Mrs. Gutzwiller, maybe it was the shock of the advice, maybe it was fear for her child, maybe it was fear for herself. Maybe, in some roundabout way, it was guilt. In any event, she didn't heed her doctors' advice. She never even considered it.

But already the theme had been set. In the womb, it had been set. Extenuating circumstances. Second guesses. *Maybes* and *what-ifs*. These were fixtures of Meg's life. These were fixtures of her death.

· · · ·

ALL OF THE GUTZWILLER children played sports—the boys played football and baseball, the girls played soccer and basketball—but Meg was the best athlete. John, more than a decade older, was part-brother, part-father to her. He would drive Meg to practice when she was little, and he would sit and watch. Whether on the court or the pitch, his baby sister was always the most competitive girl out there.

In their backyard at home was a hoop, a court, where Mr. Gutzwiller painted free-throw and three-point lines. Meg would play Katie one-on-one and was able to hold her own despite being five years younger.

And Katie was talented—she was a starter on Bacon's undefeated state championship team in 1995, the team for which Brian Neal was an assistant—but Meg was quick, she was feisty and she was left-handed. She would steal the ball before her opponent even had it. Some days, Katie would get so frustrated she'd insist on playing H-O-R-S-E. Meg was a good shooter, but at least that way she couldn't steal the ball.

But it wasn't just Katie, and it wasn't just against other girls. Meg would challenge John to free-throw shooting contests. Because John was about a foot taller, shooting free throws was one of the few basketball activities he and Meg could compete in where the playing field was level.

Even more than winning, Meg loved competing—even if she was alone. When she was in junior high, her parents were at Roger Bacon for an end-of-the-school-year party—the entire Gutzwiller family attended Bacon (except Mrs. Gutzwiller, who attended OLA) and Mr. Gutzwiller taught there—when Meg got the itch to play basketball. Unfortunately, one of the family cars was parked right in front of the hoop. Seeing that, the average 12- or 13-year old would wait for a parent to get home and move the vehicle. Or just go on to something else and forget about it. Maybe play tomorrow.

But Meg was someone who always knew what she wanted and when she wanted it. So, she hopped in the car, slid it in neutral and let it roll down a hill until it stopped—by slamming into a tree. Meg bounced out unscathed. And then she played basketball.

That was Meg. Meg always found a way.

Meg was a phenomenal athlete. When she was a senior at Bacon, her best friend, Emily Holt—the same Emily Holt who grew up playing backyard basketball with her best friend and cousin, Josh Hausfeld—needed another player on her summer team for Youth Basketball of America. "Sure," Meg said. "I'll play." But Meg didn't just fill a roster spot and ride the bench. She was a starter and helped the team qualify to a national tournament in Florida, where she was named to the all-tournament team. As for the tournament? Yup, Meg's team finished first. National champions. Not bad for a last-minute fill-in.

Meg was good at basketball, but soccer was where she truly shined. She played midfield at Roger Bacon and led her team to the state semi-finals as a junior and senior in 1998 and 1999. The '99 team was especially young and started several freshmen, but Matt, who attended the state semis, remembered how fast Meg was, how intense she was, how unafraid she was of getting in her opponents' faces. She was a spitfire blur of a midfielder, and the whole team played around her. Bacon, however, lost on penalty kicks.

"Them damn shootouts getcha," Mr. Gutzwiller said.

Matt never forgot that game and how impressed he was with what he saw. But then again, he was always impressed by Meg. Even though he was older, and even though little sisters tend to think the world of their big brothers, Matt was the one always trying to impress *her*, always trying to get her attention, always trying to make her laugh. Once, when Matt was home on break from college—he attended Ohio State—he challenged Meg to a race. Meg was running just about every day for soccer and was in extraordinary shape. But Matt, like a lot of college guys, thought that a girl, especially his baby sister, was no match for him.

"I can still beat you," Matt said.

So Matt and Meg mapped out a course around their neighborhood and stood in front of their house. Meg went one way; Matt went the other. Each had to run a mile. When Matt got back to his street, he was huffing and puffing and gasping for air as he came down the final straightaway. And that's when he saw her. Meg was reclining on their front porch, legs up on a ledge, relaxed as could be. She had run the mile. She wasn't breathing heavy. Her heart rate had already slowed to normal.

"Where you been?" Meg asked, reveling in her victory.

That was Meg.

"Meg never said, 'I can't do something,'" Mr. Gutzwiller said. "If you wanted her to do something, all you had to do was tell her she couldn't do it, and she'd say, 'I'll prove you wrong.' And she would."

When Meg got to college at Tiffin University, a liberal-arts school in north-central Ohio about three hours from Cincinnati, she wanted to start on the soccer team as a freshman. During the first few weeks of soccer practice, most teams don't actually practice soccer; they get in shape. Tiffin was no different. The summer after Meg graduated from Bacon in 2000, she ran every day—45 minutes to an hour, rain or shine, whether it was 80 degrees or 100. When she showed up to practice at Tiffin, she was in the best shape of anyone and won every conditioning drill. Tiffin's coach approached Meg.

"So, Meg," he said, "what do you wanna play this year?"

"Midfield," Meg said in a what-else-would-I-play tone. "I've always played midfield. That's what I know how to play."

"Well, I don't need a midfielder—I got plenty," the coach said. "If you want to play midfield, you can sit on the bench. I need a sweeper."

Meg thought for a few seconds.

"Okay," she said. "I'll play sweeper."

Meg had never played sweeper. She'd have to learn it on the fly—in her first year of college ball, no less. None of that mattered. Meg played sweeper. She was All-American that year.

That was Meg.

Meg loved her brothers. John would take her to movies on her birthday when she was little. One year, he took her to see *The Land Before Time*. When Meg got older, they branched out a bit. John would take her to Reds games. One year, he took her to a game against the Phillies, and it started pouring. The game was delayed, and John knew the delay would be long. He knew the game might even be postponed. But he refused to take Meg home. They waited out the storm together and stayed for the whole game. By the time they got home, it was well after midnight. Mr. and Mrs. Gutzwiller weren't too happy about that, but Meg thought that was the neatest thing, staying out late with her big brother.

Meg didn't like it when John started dating his eventual wife, Kari. It had nothing to do with Kari as a person; Meg just didn't like competing with another girl for John's attention. So, early in the relationship, Meg curled up next to John, looked Kari in the eye and said, "I don't know who you are, but you need to stay away from my brother." John and Kari laughed. Eventually, Kari and Meg became close, in part because Kari let her watch *Beverly Hills 90210* with her.

But that was Meg, fiercely loyal.

Meg was always popular with the boys. She was 5-6 and slender with brown eyes and long, thin legs. Her chestnut hair flowed casually past her collarbone. Her smile was warm, inviting. Still, she could be shy with guys. She worried about what they thought of her and whether they would approach her. But there was at least one guy she never had to worry about.

His name was Josh Hausfeld.

* * * *

EMILY HOLT ALWAYS HOPED that her two best friends would hit it off. What could be better, she figured, than if Josh and Meg dated and got married? Eventually, Emily got her wish—well, half her wish.

Because the Gutzwillers lived in Forest Park, it didn't make sense for Meg to come home in between school and practice for whatever sport she was playing. So, she'd stay in St. Bernard and hang out with Josh and Emily. Meg loved St. Bernard. She begged her parents to move there, but they never did.

Meg, like a lot of teenage girls, always wanted guys to pursue her—and not the other way around. But she had no problem pursuing Josh, who was two years younger and shy. They started dating when Meg was a senior at Bacon. They would talk on the phone for hours about anything and everything—always smiling, always laughing.

"She was always so nice," Josh said. "Just a fun person to be around. Great heart."

Josh and Meg bonded over sports, among other things. Josh would go over Meg's house to watch movies, hang out and act silly. He would tease her about her dad's eagerness to hand out JUGs at school.

"If your dad gives me a JUG, I'll need you to pull some strings," Josh would joke.

Meg took Josh to her senior prom. After graduation, though, she moved away to college with Emily, who also went to Tiffin. Meg, who would be busy with school and soccer, had to move on to the next stage of her life. She and Josh broke up, but they kept in touch and emailed each other quite a bit.

"The dating thing didn't really work," Josh said. "We were always better friends."

* * * *

IN THE FALL OF 2001, Meg entered her sophomore season at Tiffin eager to repeat as an All-American, but she never got the chance. In the third game of the year, she broke her leg and wound up redshirting. After her leg healed months later, she couldn't wait to play spring soccer and work her way back into the game.

That March, in 2002, while Bacon's basketball team was in the midst of its playoff run, Meg returned home for Spring Break. She, along with most of the soccer team and dozens of other Tiffin students, planned to spend the week in Florida. So Meg came home Friday, March 8, to pack and do her laundry, and Katie took her shopping for Spring Break essentials.

That day and night, Meg wasn't feeling all that well, so Katie, ever the big sister, pushed her around the grocery store in a cart and got her Chinese takeout for dinner. After dinner, Katie helped Meg finish packing. Meg's teammate and roommate, Beth Snyder, was swinging by the Gutzwillers' house around midnight to pick up Meg and join the rest of the team. The girls planned to drive through the night—three cars, three girls per car, as Mr. Gutzwiller recalled—and in the morning, voilá. Good times and sunny skies.

Beth arrived at midnight as scheduled, and that's when it happened. Before getting in the car to leave, Meg turned toward Katie, walked up to her, hugged her and said, "I love you." Katie couldn't believe it. She and Meg were close, as was the whole family, but they weren't the type of family that often expressed that closeness in hugs or words. For them, that care, that tenderness, didn't need to be said. It was shown. It was implied. It was understood.

"That night was one of the only times she ever did that," Katie said. "That's something I'll never forget."

That was the last time Katie saw her sister alive.

· · · ·

EMILY HOLT MET MEG in the eighth grade while attending a summer basketball camp at Roger Bacon, but it wasn't until their sophomore year that they became inseparable. They were both so similar and yet so different. Meg was equal parts tomboy and girly girl. Guys were drawn to her, in part, because she was that rare female who was competitive and loved sports yet also took time to do her hair and makeup. Emily, tomboy through and through, didn't have an older sister to look up to, so when it came to mascara and nail polish, she looked to Meg and took cues from her.

Emily drove to Toledo to be with Meg the night she broke her leg.

She slept alone in the visitors' room. When Meg got out of the hospital, Emily helped her with everything—laundry, shopping, chauffeuring. The cast went from Meg's toes to her hip. Walking was interesting. Maneuvering was amusing. Going to the bathroom was an ordeal. But Emily was there throughout. And she was almost with Meg the night she died.

Emily was invited to go on that Spring Break trip but decided against it. She still remembers the last time she saw Meg. It was at Tiffin. Meg was in her car, just about to leave for Cincinnati.

"The last thing I said to her was, 'Call me when you get to Cincy, or I'll call you,'" Emily said. "I never called."

• • • •

KATIE GUTZWILLER CAN STILL hear the sound of the phone dropping and rolling across the floor. If there's one distinct memory she has from the early morning hours of March 9, 2002, that's it. Katie, then 25 and only a few years removed from college, was on her way home after a night out with friends when her father called around 5:30 a.m.

It's Meg. There's been an accident.

Katie called her brothers to break the news. John was speechless. He wanted to talk—he tried to talk—but he couldn't. He can't recall if Katie alluded to the fact that Beth Snyder had been killed instantly. He can't recall if Katie was even aware of that at the time. But when he found out Meg was in the hospital, the phone wobbled out of his quivering hand and splattered on the floor like a bomb detonating over a tranquil town that would never know true harmony again.

In that moment, hearing her oldest brother react the way he did, any optimism Katie possessed vanished. She drove home to her parents' house. Matt and John joined her. The Gutzwillers didn't know what had happened or what was happening, and the hospital wouldn't release any information over the phone regarding Meg's status. All anyone knew was that there had been an accident, that it occurred on Interstate 65 in Tennessee, and that Meg had been taken to Vanderbilt University Medical Center in Nashville.

Mr. and Mrs. Gutzwiller couldn't sit around and wait. They needed to know what was wrong with their child. They got in their car and began the five-hour trek to Nashville. Katie started getting calls from Meg's friends. *It's bad*, they said. *You need to come.* Katie packed her mother's diabetic medicine and headed to the airport with Matt. John and Kari, meanwhile, chaotically arranged for someone to watch their daughter, Leah, while also trying to get updates on Meg. Once they procured a babysitter, John and Kari got in their car and raced to Nashville.

Mr. and Mrs. Gutzwiller arrived at the hospital while Katie and Matt were in the air. The two siblings landed and were trying to find their way out of Nashville International Airport when Matt got the call from his dad.

She's gone.

Thousands of people scurried about the airport in Nashville that morning—booking flights, catching flights, missing flights. Somewhere amid the flurry, Matt and Katie Gutzwiller found out that their baby sister, like the whirlwind of faces streaming by and known only for an instant, was gone forever. The ensuing moments were a blur of shock and sadness.

"I remember Matt saying to my dad, 'I can't tell her. You have to,'" Katie recalled. "And he handed me the phone. That's all I remember."

Matt and Katie grabbed a cab to the hospital, while Mr. Gutzwiller called his oldest son, who had just crossed into Kentucky with Kari. John doesn't remember a whole lot from the last four hours of that car ride. Maybe he thought of *The Land Before Time*. Maybe he thought of the rain delay at Riverfront Stadium. Maybe he thought of the soccer ball Meg had given Leah for her first Christmas just a few months earlier, and how Leah would grow up never knowing her Aunt Meg. John can't remember. He felt both pain and numbness as worry gave way to woe.

One by one, Meg's immediate family arrived. The hospital provided them with information on grief counseling, but in that moment, no one really cared about grief counseling. They just wanted to see Meg. Only two visitors were permitted in the intensive care unit simultaneously, but that didn't stop the whole family from entering. Meg lay in her bed, helpless. She was there, but she wasn't. Aside from a tiny cut on her forehead, no one would have guessed that she had been in an accident. But even with a ventilator, Meg's organs were already shutting down. There was no brain activity. There was no hope.

Katie knew that Meg supported organ donation. Over the years, Meg had made that clear, and Katie tried to convince her parents that's what Meg would want. Some of Meg's organs, like her heart, were too damaged to be donated. Others were still viable, but time was of the essence. After deliberating, Mr. and Mrs. Gutzwiller acquiesced—on one condition. The doctors could take anything they wanted, anything at all—but not the eyes. Not the eyes.

Meg's were beautiful.

And Mrs. Gutzwiller just couldn't give those up.

• • • •

Josh was downstairs in his bedroom that morning, and Frank, as he did so often during his two years at Roger Bacon, had slept over. Mary Beth came downstairs and told them that Meg had been in an accident.

There was shock. There was sadness. There were tears.

"It was horrible," Josh said.

Elsewhere in St. Bernard, Emily Holt sat in her parents' house, powerless. She didn't know whether Meg would make it. When Katie called to tell her that Meg had died, Emily wondered whether she should drive to Nashville to say good-bye. Katie advised against it.

"You don't want to come," Katie said. "You don't want to do this."

So Emily didn't.

She went to Bacon's parking lot to see Josh before practice. The two cousins sat there and tried to console each other.

"It was a long, sad day," Josh said. "Losing your best friend is never easy."

• • • •

Meg Gutzwiller rode shotgun in what was the last car ride of her life. Beth Snyder sprawled in back. The driver, according to police, fell asleep at the wheel of her 1995 Geo Prizm and lost control of the car around 5 a.m. in Lewisburg, Tennessee, about 50 miles south of Nashville. The car flipped several times, and Meg and Beth were both thrown from the vehicle. Meg landed in the middle of the highway, while Beth was tossed into the brush. The girls in the other cars pulled over, hysterical.

An approaching truck driver witnessed the accident and feared for Meg's body lying helplessly on the road. He positioned his semi in front of her, blocking traffic and shielding her from cars blazing by in the middle of the Tennessee night. He noticed the girls shaking and crying and went over and calmed them down. He made them feel like everything was going to be all right. Then he walked over to Meg and knelt on the highway, holding her prostrate body in his arms until the ambulance arrived.

Meg had crushed her cerebellum, yet somehow she was still breathing. She was put on life support and taken to the hospital, where doctors cut a hole in her head to relieve the pressure on her brain. But it wasn't enough.

Meg died. She was 19.

• • • •

Mrs. Gutzwiller wanted Meg's organs, the ones that could be donated, to go to as many young people as possible. She wanted people who would live the longest to benefit the most from Meg's passing. A girl around Meg's age later wrote the Gutzwillers and thanked them because Meg's kidneys saved her father's life. The Gutzwillers took solace in that. They knew that as long as people were alive because of Meg, Meg would in some way be alive, too.

The visitation took place March 15 in Mt. Healthy. Thousands of people stood in line for hours waiting to see Meg and to spend a few moments with her family. Tiffin students were there. Roger Bacon students were there. The basketball team was there, too. Josh was quite close with the Gutzwillers. When he got to the casket, when he saw Meg lying there, he broke down. He sobbed uncontrollably.

"It was too much to handle," he said.

At one point, Mr. Gutzwiller noticed a man standing in line with a boy who looked like he was around Meg's age. Mr. Gutzwiller had never seen them before and noticed that they kept getting in and out of line whenever someone got behind them. It was as if they wanted to be the last ones to offer their condolences—and that's just what they did. They sat and waited and let others pass. At the end of the layout, the man and boy rose as one and approached Mr. and Mrs. Gutzwiller.

"You don't know me, but I have to thank you for Meg," the man said. "She saved my son's life."

Mr. and Mrs. Gutzwiller listened as the man spoke. His son, apparently, was a classmate of Meg's at Roger Bacon. He had been a troubled boy, a depressed boy. He was a loner and didn't have any friends. He had attended several high schools and found it hard to fit in at all of them. The boy had seen numerous doctors over the years to seek treatment for his depression, but none of them could help. The boy had even talked of killing himself.

One day at Roger Bacon, Meg noticed this boy sitting all by himself during lunch. She saw him again the next day. And the next. Always alone. So Meg, always surrounded by friends, got up and walked over to the boy. She sat with him and had lunch with him. Eventually, she invited him to go places—basketball games, parties. The boy went home and talked excitedly to his parents about a girl named Meg who had befriended him. The boy started going out, meeting up with Meg and her friends and becoming more social.

At the layout, the boy's father explained that his son had been in college for two years and was doing just fine. He had at last found happiness in his life. Without Meg, the man said, that wouldn't have been possible. His son might have taken his own life. But he didn't—because Meg reached him, because she saved him, because she did what doctors couldn't.

And she did it just by being herself.

● ● ● ●

MEG'S DEATH, LIKE HER birth, was influenced by a perfect storm of circumstances. A few weeks earlier, Meg was experiencing pain in her midsection. She saw a doctor, who discovered cysts on her ovaries, and was given medication for the discomfort.

"You know, you don't have to go to Florida," Katie told Meg while pushing her around in the grocery cart the night she died.

"I'll be fine," Meg kept saying.

"Meg, please," Katie said in her big-sister tone, "just be careful."

"It's okay," Meg said. "I'll take my medicine, pass out in the car and sleep."

Then there's the seatbelt. Meg was always adamant that people wear them. With her, there was no dallying. If you got in a car and didn't put your seatbelt on right away, she'd ask you to put it on. Command is more like it. But driving to Florida that night, Meg didn't wear hers. Throughout the week, seatbelts had been rubbing against her and causing irritation, and she couldn't bear the thought of wearing one through the night.

If Meg hadn't been taking medication, maybe she wouldn't have been so drowsy. If she hadn't been so drowsy, maybe she wouldn't have fallen asleep. If she hadn't fallen asleep, maybe she would have been carrying on a conversation with the driver. If the driver had been engaged in a conversation, maybe she wouldn't have fallen asleep at the wheel. And if the driver hadn't fallen asleep, maybe the car wouldn't have crashed. And even if it would have, maybe Meg wouldn't have been thrown through the windshield because she would have been wearing her seatbelt like she did on any other car ride. Maybe she'd still be alive. But she isn't.

It's as if her death were destiny.

Meg's death reminded John of the stories he heard in the days following September 11—stories about people who called in sick that day or who were normally in the World Trade Center but, for whatever reason, weren't inside when the planes hit.

"You don't hear the story of the person who just happened to be there and was unlucky," John said. "Some people were saying, 'I'm so lucky I survived. I was so fortunate.' Well, it can happen just the opposite. Is that fate? Or is that just how things work out?"

For a long time after the accident, John felt strong anger, especially toward God. When John was younger, he once prayed for the outcome of a sporting event—Reds or Bengals, he can't remember which—but he remembers being reprimanded by his mother.

"You don't pray for something like that," she said. "You pray for something that's important."

That advice stuck with John. He stopped praying about sports. Instead, he prayed for one thing and one thing only—the safety of his younger siblings. When he and Kari gave birth to Leah, he added his first child to the list. But for several years, his prayers centered on Matt, Katie and Meg. It made him feel as if their safety was in his control, that if he prayed hard enough and long enough and for only one thing, God wouldn't let him down. After Meg died, John was angry.

I pray for one thing, he thought, *and you can't even deliver on that?*

Over time, John let go of his anger toward God. He also let go of his anger toward the driver. He and Matt didn't want her at Meg's visitation or funeral—they were too angry to look at her—but that anger has subsided. None of the Gutzwillers can even remember her name. For some people, that's a name you can't forget. It's a name you can't forget even if you want to. But the Gutzwillers can't recall it.

"You know when people say your heart hurts?" Katie asked, her voice cracking. "It physically hurts for a long time, and I never knew what that was until Meg died. I wasn't mad at the driver. Being mad at anyone wasn't bringing Meg back."

The funeral Mass was held at St. Clement. Josh, of course, wanted to attend, but he couldn't. Neither could the rest of the basketball team.

They had to play in the regional finals.

Meg often begged her parents to move to St. Bernard because that's where she was happiest. She got her wish in death.

Margaret Elizabeth Gutzwiller was laid to rest in St. Mary's Cemetery, right down the street from Roger Bacon High School.

• • • •

THE GUTZWILLERS HEARD ALL sorts of stories about Meg in the weeks and months after she passed, including one about the truck driver who stopped on the highway to help Meg that night, who shielded her from traffic and knelt beside her, holding her in his arms. Meg's friends were grateful for everything the man did. Before parting ways, the girls wrote down his name—Mr. Gutzwiller can't remember the last name, but his first name was "Elvis"—his trucking company and his license plate. The girls planned to track down this truck-driving samaritan and thank him for his help, and they spent the next several weeks trying to do just that. They made phone calls. They contacted the Tennessee Highway Patrol. They did all sorts of things. No luck.

The mother of one of the girls happened to have a brother who worked for the FBI. So the mother gave her brother the information the girls had gathered, and he said he'd see what he could do. A few weeks later, the brother reported his findings: There was no one in the country with that name, no such trucking company existed and the license plate number had never been issued. No one knows who that man was, and he was never seen or contacted after that night.

"Strange story," Mr. Gutzwiller said. "But you find out all kinds of weird things after Meg died."

Meg, like her father, was a gifted artist, and after she passed away, one of her teachers at Tiffin drove to Cincinnati and dropped off all of her artwork. One of Meg's paintings—the last one she ever did—was of a forest. It was a lush, green forest with a little stream running through it. It was serene. It was beautiful. But in the foreground of that painting was one dead tree—brown, black, branches all broken.

The forest, like Meg, was teeming with life, and the one dead tree, like the tiny cut on her forehead, was but the one puzzling blemish on a masterpiece.

⬥ ⬥ ⬥ ⬥

BEFORE THE TOURNAMENT BEGAN, Emily wrote a letter to Josh. She can't remember what it said verbatim, but it was motivational in nature.

This is it. This is your season. This is your year. You're going to do it. I never did it. Do it for us. Win state. I love you.

Josh put the letter in his shoe before Bacon's first playoff game. He did the same thing for the next game, and for the next and the next. It was a constant reminder of his mission, of what he needed to do. Four games into the postseason, Bacon hadn't been challenged. But now, the girl Josh once dated, the girl who remained one of his close friends, was dead.

Did basketball still matter as much? Did it matter at all?

A lot of Bacon's players knew Meg. Many of them didn't know her all that well, but they all knew who she was, and they all knew Josh was close to her.

They knew he was devastated.

So they supported him as best they could. They wrote messages on their shoes like "RIP Meg." Newt wrote Meg's name on rubber bands he wore on his wrists.

"It was rough," Newt said. "It was hard for a lot of guys. We drove up to Wright State for our next game, and it was one of the few quiet car rides we ever had. It was pretty somber. It was one of those games you just couldn't get up for. It was like, 'All right. Let's go. We know what we gotta do. Let's just get it done and go home.'"

Bacon defeated Bishop Watterson 51–39 in the regional semifinals on March 13, four days after Meg died. It was, at the time, the Spartans' closest win of the tournament.

On Saturday, March 16, as Meg was being buried, Bacon played in the regional finals for the fourth time in six years and sought to advance to the Final Four for the first time in Bill's tenure. The Spartans played Badin, a team they had beaten by just four points one month earlier.

They knew they'd be in for a dogfight.

Beckham hit a three-pointer on Bacon's first shot of the game. He scored eight points in the first eight minutes and finished with 13. Monty scored 14. Frank scored 15. Dave added seven. Josh had a quiet game—nine points, five coming from the foul line—but it didn't matter. His teammates picked him up and found a way.

Bacon won 61–47.

"It was nice to be able to do that, to maybe bring a little positive back to the school because everyone was so upset," Monty said. "But winning a regional championship and going to state was probably the second thing on everyone's mind that week."

Nevertheless, Bacon had done it. The regional-finals curse had been lifted. But beating Badin, which the Spartans had already done twice that year, was in many ways expected. In a few days they would leave for Columbus, where the competition would be decidedly stiffer. There was no way the Spartans could put Meg's death behind them, but could they play through it?

"When tragedy strikes, you never know how it's going to affect things," Brian Neal said with solemnity in his voice. "Even though Meg was out of school, the guys still knew her. We felt it was important to let them grieve the way they felt they needed to. So writing messages on their shoe, making a point to recognize what had happened, it was good for them. But we were apprehensive. How would it affect them? And how would it affect Josh especially?"

In exactly one week, Brian Neal and the rest of Bacon's coaching staff would have their answer.

CHAPTER ELEVEN

THE MOMENT

Nine years. For nine years, Bill Brewer waited for the opportunity to have this moment, and dammit, he was going to have it.

Bill's favorite movie was *Hoosiers*, which should come as no surprise. That film encapsulated everything he could ever want in life—a tough-minded coach, a group of underdogs, a state final and a team that was supposedly unbeatable. If ever a film was made that Bill could relate to, especially during the 2001–02 season, *Hoosiers* was it. For Bill, it was always about the journey. The destination, of course, was a state championship. Always had been, always would be. He knew that; so did his players and assistants. But for Bill, the destination was nothing without the journey. The journey was paramount.

You couldn't blame Bill if he did some reflecting in the week leading up to Columbus. Maybe he thought of his first year at Roger Bacon back in 1993–94, when his first daughter was born; when he offended Spartans both young and old with his unbridled sideline language; when he was called into Father Roger's office thinking his first game at Bacon would be his last. Or maybe he thought about the gold uniforms and the Fab Five and Mitch Perdrix, the hardest-working kid in the gym. Or maybe he thought about Brandon and Eugene and how they brought respectability to the program. Or maybe he thought of that regional final in '98 and how, in his eyes, he had let that team down. Or maybe he thought of Josh Hausfeld and the struggles the St. Clement Golden Boy had to overcome as a freshman. Or maybe it was his run-ins, both good and bad, with Beckham and Nate. Or maybe it was all the hours he spent yelling at Monty and calling him soft, trying to bleed every ounce of toughness out of a tall guy who didn't like being tall. Or maybe he thought of the players who resisted being pushed, the players who were afraid to be pushed, the players he had broken and built up and built up and broken. Or maybe he thought of the CJ game and his postgame tirade in the locker room and how Bacon was a perfect 15–0 ever since. Or maybe he thought of Meg.

Bill probably did a lot of reminiscing that week. But now, nine years after coming to Roger Bacon, he had started a family and watched it grow—both at home and in the program. After pushing players mercilessly for close to a decade, he had led Roger Bacon to the Final Four. It was the Spartans' fourth trip to state in school history and their first since 1982.

Quite a journey, indeed.

Twelve games would be played in a three-day span that week in Columbus—two semifinals and one final in all four divisions—and Roger Bacon would lead things off against Columbus Beechcroft on Thursday, March 21, at 11 a.m. The other Division II semifinal, Akron St. Vincent–St. Mary versus Poland Seminary, would follow thereafter.

But that was Thursday.

The team drove to Columbus that Wednesday in time for Bill to have the *Hoosiers* moment he always dreamt of having. When the Spartans arrived in Columbus, they checked into their hotel and ate dinner at The Old Spaghetti Factory. Afterward, Bill took his players and assistants to Ohio State University's Value City Arena. Also known as the Jerome Schottenstein Center—or simply, "The Schott"—this would be the site of the state tournament. Bacon's game wasn't until the next morning, but Bill needed his players to see something. He needed to prove something to them. And he made arrangements to make that happen.

The team entered the arena and walked through winding tunnel after winding tunnel until suddenly the court was upon them. The stands were empty. The lights were dimmed. It was just St. Bernard Roger Bacon and the eerie calm of dust and floor boards.

There's a certain sadness to an empty arena. There's a certain loneliness, the kind that fills classrooms in summer. Many of Bacon's players had seen this same arena on television—some had even seen it in person—but none had seen it like this. There was no action on the court, no player to watch, no ball to follow. The cameras had been turned off, the loudspeakers silenced. The Spartans beheld a sanctuary stripped to its core, its essence, and awe spurred their sneakers along a sacred ground both nostalgic for its past glory and eagerly awaiting its next moment of triumph and grace. A scene so accustomed to the throngs of thousands cheering at displays of valor and vigor remained silent for but a few more hours and aged gracefully in its sleep.

"You wish you had that moment back," Newt said. "Just one more time. You didn't think it then, but now that Brewer's gone, it's one of those moments that's surreal. That's when it hit us. *We're here. We made it.*"

No one said much—not the players, not the assistants, not Bill. Bacon had played in college arenas before, but none as big as this. The reverence they felt was real, the awe so palpable they could grasp it with their fists. But as Bill led his players along the floor and toward the seats by the baseline, wonder and worship gave way to feelings of familiarity. The floor was just like the floor in Fogarty. So was the net, the backboard. Everything was the same. It felt like home.

"I hear the rims are 12 feet high here," Cork said, breaking the silence and drawing a chuckle from the players.

But Bill's moment, the moment he waited nine years for, had served its purpose. The Spartans basked in the glory of what it meant to get to Columbus—something neither they nor Bill had ever experienced until now. And as they sat and took in the scene, any jitters the players might have felt the next morning vanished before they could arrive.

"We're just thinking, 'Wow, these stands are going to be full tomorrow,'" Matt Reed said. "And it wasn't because of us."

● ● ● ●

THE TOP DRAW THE next day—the top draw that whole weekend—was LeBron James and Akron St. Vincent–St. Mary. Record crowds didn't flock to the Schott to see Poland Seminary, they didn't drive in droves to see Columbus Beechcroft, and they certainly weren't aching to see Bacon. No, they came from different cites and different states, all with the same purpose—to see the next Michael, the Cover Boy, the lead singer of the hottest rock band this side of Liverpool in the last half century.

They came to see LeBron.

Of course, the Spartans knew that with one more win, they'd see LeBron, too. Up close and personal. Again. But they also knew—better yet, they were told—to forget about LeBron. If they didn't get past

Columbus Beechcroft in the state semis, there would be no LeBron. There would be no rematch. The season would be over.

The Spartans had several days to prepare for Beechcroft, a team that was a bit of a mystery. The Cougars, 18–8, had taken a curious route to the Final Four. Unranked in the final state poll, they defeated eighth-ranked Dover in the regional semis and third-ranked Washington Court House in the regional finals—two teams with a combined record of 46–1. Washington Court House, in fact, was 25–0—and got blown out, 80–51. To beat a previously unbeaten team is one thing; but to beat a previously unbeaten team by 29?

Something didn't add up. Either Beechcroft played an ungodly under-the-radar schedule and was extremely battle-tested, or Dover and Washington Court House were vastly overrated. Or, maybe Beechcroft just got hot. The Spartans knew they would have their chance to solve this riddle, but in the meantime, they were a little uneasy—and Bill didn't do much to quell their fears. Actually, he was responsible for them.

Beechcroft displayed brilliant balance in the regional finals, placing five players in double figures, including post player Mike Brown, who scored a game-high 23 points. Brown, a 6-2 senior, averaged 21 points and 11 rebounds that season and had scored more than 1,000 career points. The way Bill talked about him, the players almost wondered if Brown—and not LeBron—had been on the cover of *Sports Illustrated*.

Bill hyped Mike Brown so much that he implemented an entire new defensive package for the Beechcroft standout called "Star." That week at practice, Bill called for the usual starters-versus-Scrappers scrimmages, but he designated Nate as "Star." Any time Nate touched the ball, he was to be trapped immediately. The idea was to get the ball out of his hands. If Nate so much as attempted a shot—regardless of whether it went in—the Scrappers were awarded two points and the starters had to run. That's how hell-bent Bill was on sending his message.

"We can't let this guy shoot," Bill ordered. "We can't have the ball in his hands."

Wow, this guy must be the real deal, Matt Reed thought, *and I've never even heard of him*.

Bill, always the planner, drew up practices like lesson plans. The week of the state tournament would be no different.

SPARTAN BASKETBALL
Practice #76
Monday, March 18, 2002

- 2:50 Meet and go over Beechcroft scouting report
Scrappers gave great effort last Thursday and Friday
Team Attitude and Enjoy
How long have you thought about this???
- 3:10 Run
- 3:15 Form and partner shooting
- 3:25 Ball toughness drills
    1. Square up
    2. Straight line drive
    3. Back tips
    4. Split trap off dribble
    5. Split trap off pass
  We need offense to try to get to the basket hard (out of control)
- 3:35 2v2 Help and recover on a side
- 3:40 3v3 Help and recover (ball on top)
  3v3 Mix in ball screens and cross screens
  3v3 Help the helper
- 3:50 Diamond shell—Must finish with a block out
    1. No movement
    2. Penetrate and kick
    3. Cross screens and ball screens
    4. Fist Star (Double #5 NATE—also step out and make plays)
       **2 on the ball 3 guard the basket then out INSIDE—OUT, we are trying to get it out of his hands
- 4:05 Free throws
  Talk to Scrappers about presses and zones
    1. 1–2–2 trap over halfcourt
    2. 2–2–1
    3. 1–3–1 trap the corners and play the skip
    4. Diamond
- 4:10 5v4 Convert
  Press on makes, know ahead of time
- 4:20 6v5 Press break after free throws and makes—Start with Beechcroft set FIST Star on the way back
- 4:35 Free throws

4:40 5v5 All Sets vs Pressure Defense
4:55 :55 shooting
5:10 Pressure free throws and conditioning
Announcements
Tomorrow Practice 3–5
Take a copy of agenda

The "#5 NATE" was code for Mike Brown, whose jersey number was five. But who was Beechcroft besides Mike Brown? The Cougars, coached by Kent Burgert, were a member of the Columbus City League. They started one sophomore, Sirjo Welch, and four seniors—Brown, Josh Rohrbacher, Josh Moore and Kevin Stewart.

Bill, who had coaches scout potential opponents two or three games in advance, had plenty of material on Beechcroft. Here is some of what his assistants came up with:

STARTERS

#5 Mike Brown: 6-2 Sr. Center; 20.8 ppg, 11.2 rbpg, 59.6 FG%

Best player; very, very athletic; big leaper; keep him off the glass; will not shoot the three—has not made a three all year; excellent passer; makes strong moves to the rim and finishes; turns to his right in the post every time; in-bounder after makes; doesn't leak out; only weakness we saw is he tries to block everything, so look to shot-fake him <Beckham>

#12 Josh Rohrbacher: 6-1 Sr. Guard; 7.9 ppg

Very good shooter, so close out on him; likes the corner; give no open looks; did not see him penetrate that much; not as quick as others; runs point if no pressure; suspect handle; looks to pass first, especially off the dribble <Josh>

#3 Josh Moore: 6-0 Sr. Guard; 7.6 ppg

Quick; doesn't look to score from the perimeter; looks to drive and dish a lot; gets out of control at times; likes to run a two-man game with Brown off clear-outs; good defender; poor free throw shooter <Frank>

 # 24 Sirjo Welch: 5-10 So. Point Guard; 9.2 ppg

Good handle; runs the point vs. pressure; pushes the ball hard; looks to split defenders on penetration; goes right most of the time; will shoot the three; very good on-ball defender <Dave>

#20 Kevin Stewart: 6-1 Sr. Post/Wing; 7.6 ppg

Solid jump shooter; looks to score a lot; will shoot it from anywhere; quick; goes to offensive glass real hard <Monty>

SUBS

#21 Raylon Almon: 5-10 So. Guard; 6.4 ppg

Shoots mostly threes (43%)

#22 Damien Harris: 5-10 Sr.; 5.5 ppg

Good shooter; gets one three a game

OVERVIEW

If we handle their pressure, I do not think we will have problems scoring. They are very athletic and go after the ball hard but do not block out that well. They did not look very physical.

Defense

They will play whatever defense they think it will take to win, but they are not real good at any of them. They are very quick with quick hands. They will reach around, slap the ball and take a lot of gambles. Back cuts will be there. Look to shot fake on the inside. They switch ball screens.

Speculation: They will either try to stop us in the backcourt with pressure, or zone us in the front court to neutralize the size differential with Monty.

Offense

They are not real organized vs. Man. They will run motion. They will all shoot it, but they want (Brown) to get the ball every time down the floor. They like to run a two-man game with (Moore) and (Brown) with a pick and roll. Mostly all penetrate and dish. We must contain the ball, give early help and contest all shots. We will start straight up. We will double the post on the pass if needed.

Transition

They are very good from defense to offense. We will start getting two back to limit their easy baskets. (Rohrbacher) usually trails for the three.

KEYS TO WINNING

1. Contain the ball
2. Contest every shot
3. Rebound and rebound position
4. Handle their pressure
5. Get the ball to the basket

Armed with this information, Roger Bacon prepared to crack the code that was Columbus Beechcroft and sought to stop the unstoppable Mike Brown. At practice that week, Bill, perhaps not surprisingly, called out his players—not individually, but as a team. He questioned his players' desire to bring home the trophy. He questioned whether they were content just making it to Columbus. The players took umbrage at the verbal prodding. They didn't need any added motivation, but Bill and his staff weren't convinced—that's the impression they gave, anyway.

"The practices that week were intense," Matt Reed said. "Some of the coaches who weren't normally as vocal, were vocal. The reserve team wasn't playing anymore; the freshman team wasn't playing anymore. The whole coaching staff was there coaching—and being very vocal."

When the Spartans trotted out for warmups in the state semifinals, they got at long last a glimpse of the mythical Mike Brown and Columbus Beechcroft. Within seconds, several Spartans thought the same thing.

This is them?

Bacon knew it would have a size advantage over Beechcroft, but this was almost unfair. The Cougars didn't roster a single player taller than 6-2. Bacon had seven, including Beckham and Monty, who were 6-6 and 6-8, respectively. Bill, by his nature, would never let his players underestimate an opponent, but anyone watching warmups that day had to know that the first game of the 2002 Ohio High School Athletic Association State Boys Basketball Tournament might get out of hand.

Beechcroft certainly didn't do itself any favors by jawing with Bacon before the game.

"They were talking so much trash in warmups—'We're gonna beat the shit out of you,' 'Fry the bacon,' and all that stuff," Monty said.

"Every time I went back to the layup line, it was someone new saying something to me. They were so cocky, which made it fun."

But it wasn't just fun. It was history.

* * * *

EACH STARTING FIVE MEETS at midcourt. The four tallest players on the floor are Spartans.

Monty and Mike Brown jump for the tip. Monty wins it, and Bacon seeks immediately to impose its size. On the first play of the game, Frank sends a beautiful lob into Beckham for an alley-hoop, but Beckham bobbles the catch. Turnover.

This blunder, however, would only delay the inevitable.

On the other end, Beechcroft's Josh Moore tries to drive on Frank. Frank blocks the shot.

This would be a theme.

Bacon pushes the ball and somehow Sirjo Welch, all 5-10 of him, ends up guarding Monty in the post. Monty demands the ball. 2–0, Bacon. Beechcroft, after passing around the perimeter, settles for a contested jumper by Kevin Stewart. Air-ball. Frank outlets to Josh. 4–0, Bacon. Moore fires a jumper for Beechcroft. Iron.

Josh turns it over. Bill sighs.

Moore penetrates the lane and gets swatted by Monty. Mike Brown gets swatted by Frank. That's three blocks in three minutes. Beechcroft is 0-of-5 from the floor.

Josh with a three from the corner. 7–0, Bacon. Stewart, at 6-1, drives left toward the foul line and puts up a shot against Monty. Blocked. Bacon pushes the ball. Monty with a layup. 9–0, Bacon, 4:21 to go in the first quarter.

Timeout Beechcroft. Four of the Cougars' six shots have been blocked. Already their trash talk has ceased. Already their huddle has grown weary. Bacon's student section booms amid the hush of desperation.

WHY SO QUI-ET? WHY SO QUI-ET?

When the action resumes, Josh Rohrbacher fires a three. Clank. All five Cougar starters have taken at least one shot. None has fallen.

After a missed floater by Beckham, Beechcroft sophomore Raylon Almon tries a desperation heave from five feet behind the arc. Has it come to this? Already? Frank contests the shot, which hits the glass about six inches to the left of the rim and bounces straight back to him. Frank races ahead for the layin. And-one. 11–0, Bacon. Frank mercifully misses the free throw.

Mike Brown drives right and puts up a shot just inside the free-throw line. Miss. Almon tries to tip it, but the shot doesn't even touch rim. He tries again. Blocked by Beckham. Josh finds Leonard, who banks in a short jumper. 13–0, Bacon. Moore with an air-ball. Senior Damien Harris tries to tip it. Nope. Rebound Josh. Beckham misses a three. Monty with the rebound. Rohrbacher, at 6-1, is guarding him. Monty with the stick-back. 15–0, Bacon. Sirjo Welch dribbles past the timeline and throws up a three. Nope. Dave finds Beckham for a dunk in transition. 17–0, Bacon.

Timeout Beechcroft. There are 38.5 seconds left in the first quarter. Both teams have attempted 12 shots. Bacon has hit eight; Beechcroft has hit none.

Nate enters the game, and Bacon comes out in a zone for the first time. Damien Harris receives a pass just beyond the arc. Nate is unable to close in time. 17–3, Bacon.

"If you had seen Brewer's reaction on the bench," Matt Reed said, "you would've thought that shot just tied the game."

Tim McCoy checks in for Nate. In terms of total seconds played, the speed of the substitution rivals that of Beckham getting yanked after the first play against Moeller. Nate makes his way to the bench. It doesn't matter that Bacon still leads by two touchdowns; you miss an assignment, you're sitting. Period.

Frank throws up a runner that hits the iron as the buzzer sounds. No matter. The Spartans lead 17-3 despite not forcing a single turnover the entire first quarter. They out-rebounded Beechcroft 13-4. The Cougars, which average 71 points per game, are on pace for 12. Five of their 13 missed shots were blocked.

The game is over. It's not, but it is. Harris drills a three to pull the Cougars within 17–6. Irrelevant. Sophomore Tyler Perry fires a three, hoping to sustain the magic. The shot is nothing but net. The only problem is, it didn't go through the hoop first. Another and-one layin for Frank. Another Beechcroft miss. A free throw for Josh, two for Monty. 22–6, Bacon.

Mike Brown gathers a missed shot and banks it home. 22–8, Bacon. These are Mike Brown's first two points. They would also be his last.

On the other end, Frank skies for a put-back. Harris drills yet another three for Beechcroft. 24–11, Bacon. Harris is now 3-of-4 from downtown; the rest of the team is 1-of-18 overall. Bill calls timeout to change up the defense on Harris. It works. Harris doesn't attempt another shot the rest of the game.

Beckham hits a jumper in the lane. Beechcroft junior Wayne Dudley throws up an awkward runner over Monty at the foul line, a prayer that gets answered. 26–13, Bacon. Beechcroft has life for an instant—and then Bacon squashes it. Another and-one layin for Frank, who follows with an and-one dunk. He buries the free throw.

The rest of the half is more of the same. Dave drills a three just before the buzzer to cap a 12–0 run. The Spartans lead 40–15 at the break. It's the largest halftime margin at the state tournament in five years.

Interestingly enough, much was made that week of Beechcroft's vastly improved defense. The Cougars, which allowed an average of 66.8 points through their first 22 games, had yielded just 45.8 in their previous four. Bacon's players and coaches remember reading that every time the Cougars held an opponent under 50, head coach Kent Burgert rewarded them with a pizza party. Under 50.

Bacon had 40 at halftime.

The third quarter is a blur of embarrassment for Beechcroft, which gets outscored 28–7. The Spartans lead 68–22 entering the final frame—and yet they continue taking charges and diving out of bounds for loose balls.

With 7:10 remaining in the fourth quarter, Bill sends in the Scrappers, who extend the lead against Beechcroft's starters. Matt Reed scores two points, both from the foul line.

Bacon led 80–28 with a minute to go and won 82–31. The 51-point win was the largest margin of victory in the 80-year history of the state tournament, while Beechcroft's 31 points were the fewest ever scored by a team from Division II. All 13 Bacon players saw action. Eleven scored. Five scored in double figures, including Monty, who had a game-high 18. The Spartans shot 56.7 percent from the floor, including 57.1 percent from three.

Stat of the game: Frank made four and-one field goals in the first half; Beechcroft's five starters had just three total field goals in the entire game combined.

No Beechcroft starter made more than one shot, and 19 of the Cougars' 56 shots never even hit the rim. As for Mike Brown, he finished with two points on 1-of-11 shooting.

In the waning moments of the blowout, with Bacon's starters on the bench and the outcome beyond decided, Beckham almost felt sorry for Beechcroft. Thirty-two game minutes earlier, this team was talking smack in warmups about the beatdown it would soon deliver. Now, by and large, those once-mouthy players sat on their bench weeping in defeat.

Beckham wasn't too upset, though. The way he saw it, the story of the game could be summed up in eight words, so he looked playfully at Monty and uttered them.

"They ain't gettin' no pizza party this week."

• • • •

THE GAME AGAINST BEECHCROFT was thorough, unadulterated, take-'em-behind-the-shed domination from start to finish. No one, absolutely no one, could have anticipated that game would unfold the way it did to the degree it did.

Well, almost no one.

After Bacon beat Badin in the regional finals, Bill told his staff not to celebrate too much; they needed to hit the road and drive three hours east to Athens to scout the regional final between Beechcroft and Washington Court House. Mitch Perdrix couldn't believe it. He figured all along that beating Badin would mean punching Bacon's ticket to the state final, that the state semis would be mere formality. But Mitch begrudgingly drove to Athens to get a look at Bacon's next opponent. At the end of the game, he showed Bill his scouting report.

"All it says is, 'These teams are terrible,'" Mitch said. "We knew we were going to kill them. But to Brew's credit, he's thorough."

To be fair, Beechcroft and Washington Court House both advanced to the Elite Eight; terrible teams don't advance that far in the tournament. But relative to teams like Bacon and SVSM, they were simply outclassed. And, as Mitch observed, Bill was thorough.

It was always about the journey.

The scare tactics Bill employed at practice that week may not have been necessary, but no one can question their effectiveness.

"Brewer was always good at hyping someone up and making you think they were better than they were," Marcus Smith said. "If you look at that score, (Beechcroft) was nothing compared to what we were. But I remember going into that game a little fearful."

So did almost every other Spartan.

"I thought we were going to have a tough game; I thought we were going to have a tough time scoring," Monty said. "Brewer knew that we wouldn't, but he did a good job scaring us. It made us take that whole week seriously. We had gotten better all year, and even then, he wanted us getting better."

And they did. That's what the Star defense was all about. It wasn't for Mike Brown. It was for LeBron James.

"I'm a smart guy; I should have known better," Monty said, smiling and shaking his head as if he'd just fallen for an April Fool's Day prank. "Brewer was just getting us ready for LeBron."

Ah, yes, LeBron. SVSM dispatched Poland Seminary with ease, 76–36, before a state tournament record crowd of 18,371. LeBron had 32 points on 14-of-21 shooting to go with six assists. Like Bacon's win, it was domination from opening tap to final buzzer. LeBron opened the game with three consecutive jumpers and had 24 points by halftime. At times, Poland Seminary seemed so in awe of LeBron that it did more watching than playing.

"He's the best I've ever seen," Poland Seminary head coach Ken Grisdale told the *Cincinnati Enquirer*. "He may be the best we've all ever seen."

Interestingly enough, SVSM's 40-point margin of victory was the second largest in Division II semifinal history. The largest? St. Bernard Roger Bacon over Columbus Beechcroft.

"I don't think there's any doubt who the two best teams in Ohio were that year," Brian Neal said. "And that made it special."

It was March 21, 2002—almost three months to the day since the Spartans fell to SVSM at Kent State. And now, after a quarter of a year of waiting and wishing and hoping, the rematch was upon them. Truthfully, Roger Bacon wasn't all that wowed by LeBron's performance in the semifinals. By then, they had come to expect such outbursts from The Chosen One. But what they didn't expect was what he did afterward. LeBron—or King James, as he became known—issued a decree as only a king can. It was a decree demanding homage.

Homage Roger Bacon wouldn't give.

CHAPTER TWELVE

THE
GUARANTEE

Roger Bacon had been there before. Once, anyway. There was a time, exactly 20 years earlier—two or three years before the players on the 2001–02 team were even born—when the Spartans engineered one of the most improbable runs to a state championship in Ohio history.

"I've witnessed eight miracles in my life," said Bob Callahan, who coached Roger Bacon from 1979 to 1985. "The births of my seven children—and winning that state title."

It was 1982. Bill Brewer would have remembered it well. He was a junior in high school, the same age LeBron was in 2002. Bacon was essentially a five-man team comprised of boys who had grown up playing together. No starter was taller than 6-3. The team's best player, Greg Schildmeyer, hoped to play college basketball, but no one wanted him. So he played football at the Naval Academy instead. Schildmeyer, as well as 6-3 center Bruce Knolle, 6-3 forward Rob Niehoff, 6-1 guard Mike Morrissey and 5-10 guard Rick Bierman—who was Beckham and Nate's uncle—played hard and played together. The only bench player who saw much action was 6-6 junior center Don Hausfeld, who would one day have a nephew named Josh.

The team went 16-4 during the regular season. All four losses were to league rivals, two coming against Elder. The Spartans beat local schools Milford, Turpin, Woodward and Lebanon to win a district title. And then it got hard.

In the regional semifinals, Bacon made all 10 of its fourth-quarter shots en route to beating Mt. Healthy, 69–67. Up next was Moeller, a team Bacon had beaten three times during the regular season. But this time the Spartans would have to face sophomore Byron Larkin, who had averaged 27 points in six games after getting called up to varsity. Larkin, who had a baseball-playing older brother named Barry, would become the all-time leading scorer at Xavier. But in the 1982 regional finals, Schildmeyer held Larkin to nine points, and Bacon won 54–53 thanks to a put-back layup from Knolle just before time expired. A similar story unfolded in the state semis. Knolle hit an eight-footer at the buzzer to give Bacon a 49–47 win over Lima Senior.

The Spartans had advanced to the state final for the first time since 1939, and to some, their run was beginning to feel like destiny. But not to Callahan.

"I just think we got more confident," he said. "We realized we could do this."

In the state final, the Spartans almost ran out of miracles against an aptly named foe, the Barberton Magics. Bacon led by as many as 13 points in the third quarter, but Barberton, making its third appearance in the state final in seven years, came back and sent the game into overtime. Schildmeyer, who scored 22 points and grabbed nine boards, had fouled out. So had Morrissey. But Don Hausfeld, with the score tied and 33 seconds remaining, calmly hit two free throws to win the game. Bacon held on, 71–67.

After four straight victories decided by four points or fewer, Bacon had won its first state championship trophy in the school's then 54-year history and joined Elder's 1973 and 1974 teams as the only Cincinnati squads to win Class AAA state titles. Even more impressive, the Spartans won state despite losing two key players late in the season; one of their top scorers was declared academically ineligible, and another player quit the team by not showing up to Bacon's first playoff game. Rick Bierman, however, took his place in the starting five, and the Spartans never looked back.

"Some people might say, 'Well, you guys weren't a great state championship team,' but I believe we were," Callahan said. "Were we as memorable as some of the great teams with Jerry Lucas? No. But we had great chemistry, we had a good balance between outside shooters and guys who could score down low, we were good rebounders and we were very good defensively. The ball bounced well for us those last four games—and each one could've gone the other way—but I truly felt those kids deserved it. They worked hard for four straight years."

After the win, Callahan had but one request for his players: No matter what happens in life, always keep your state championship ring.

If you're dating a girl and want to show her a sign of your affection, give her your class ring. If you want to show her she's really special, buy her a diamond. But keep the state title ring. Keep it, and keep it safe. That's something no one can ever take away from you.

Once you're a state champion, you're always a state champion.

• • • •

SIMILARITIES BETWEEN THE 1982 and 2002 squads were apparent. Guys who knew each other since childhood. Guys who weren't necessarily great basketball players. Guys who played hard, together. The fact that two key players on the 1982 team had a combined three nephews on the 2002 team was fitting for a school, for a community, as tight-knit as Roger Bacon.

But with all due respect to the Barberton Magics, they didn't possess a player like LeBron James—what team ever had?—and with all due respect to the '82 Spartans, they never had to face a player like LeBron James—but again, what team ever had?

Well, the '02 Bacon team, for one. On March 22, the day before the state final, the Spartans held a walk-through practice at nearby Ohio Dominican University. Guys were going at 50 percent. Nothing crazy. Bill didn't want injuries, and he didn't want his players wearing themselves out the day before the biggest game of their lives.

And that's when Matt Reed decided to be Matt Reed. He was guarding Monty—something he usually did whenever Newt wasn't.

"(Reed) would beat the shit out of me at practice," Monty said. "He played so hard. Brewer would stick him in the post—that's all you could do because he was so unskilled—but he was really physical."

Said Matt, "There wasn't a time when Monty wasn't getting fouled by me. And I didn't care. There were times when I was intentionally fouling him. I'm six feet tall. Monty's 6-8. I couldn't guard him. I always just fouled him."

So that day, Matt decided to do one of the craziest things ever done at a walk-through practice: he took a charge. Monty, not expecting this, toppled over and hit the deck. Hard.

"WHAT THE FUCK ARE YOU DOING?" Bill yelled at Matt.

It was one day before the state final. Tomorrow, the Spartans would face perhaps the best team in the country with unquestionably the best player in the country. And if they were going to win, they would need their starting center at full strength.

Matt felt terrible. He kept asking Monty if he was okay. Monty was fine, but he had a little fun with it.

"I don't know," Monty said with a fake grimace. "My wrist doesn't feel too good."

Some of the players recall Bill kicking Matt off the court and making him run. That way, everyone was safe as the team made its final preparations for SVSM.

"Brewer was mad," Monty recalled fondly. "But Reed always took it seriously. His career was over in one day. He wasn't fighting for playing time. But he always took it serious. That's how he was."

Bacon had scouted the Irish the day before at the state semis. It was the fourth time that year that the Spartans had either played or seen SVSM in person, and here is what they gleaned from those experiences:

ST. VINCENT–ST. MARY

Keys to winning:
- Rebounding—no one out-rebounds us
- Guarding in the halfcourt. Be attentive to what they are doing to hurt us
- Aggressive composure on offense
- Defensive transition—limit their easy buckets
- Handling and attacking their pressure

Personnel
- #23 **LeBron James**—plays everywhere; takes a big jump stop in the lane—take a charge on him every time. Our goal is to limit him to his 25 points and only one shot per trip
- #12 **Dru Joyce**—point guard—(quick, good shooter)
- #5 **Chad Mraz**—2 guard—runs point sometimes—deadly shooter
- #24 **Romeo Travis**—very solid player; good athlete and long, good rebounder
- #34 **Sian Cotton**—big and physical

Defense
- They will probably press us the entire game
- Mostly man-to-man full court and halfcourt

- 1–2–1–1 Full court and halfcourt
- They really pressure the ball well and deny passes (be strong with ball)
- Help side is not great—hedge screens
- Usually trap up (look sideline, basket)

Offense
- They run the floor from defense to offense very well
- UCLA High 2–1–2 (2–3) post offense vs. zone they will run a 1–3–1 set and James will run baseline
- Will run James off screens in motion
- High screen and roll (hedge but no trap)
- Mostly isolations
- Not a very good free-throw-shooting team

Our defense
- We will start in 12, with Beckham guarding James. We will look to help on him but not double. Beckham will deny everywhere at first. We must get back to the shooters. When your guy screens for James, make sure to help. We must have good ball pressure.
- If that gives us problems, then we will go to doubling him—STAR
- We will also play some zone and 22 because he will run the baseline.

Our offense
- If we execute, we should be able to score. They are very aggressive and pressure the ball very well. Make sure to attack the basket and get second shots.

We must:
- Only give one shot per possession
- Limit penetration with great help (but) recover to Joyce
- Limit their run-outs—sprint to paint—funnel to Joyce
- Handle their pressure aggressively without turning it over
- If we don't get a great look in transition, be patient; make them guard
- Get the ball inside (especially from the top); shot-fake Travis
- Execute our stuff—screen our people
- Have confidence

Bacon's coaching staff—per Bobby Holt's recommendation—decided to make one additional adjustment for the state final. Frank, and not Dave, would guard Dru Joyce. In the regular-season game, Joyce burned Bacon for five three-pointers. Dave was a good, quick defender, but at 5-10, he didn't have the length to bother Joyce, who was essentially the same height. Bobby figured that Frank, at 6-3, had a better chance of limiting and contesting Joyce's looks from deep.

And with that, Bacon was ready. It's appropriate that the last piece of advice the coaches had for the players was, "Have confidence." That's something the Spartans already had plenty of. But when they got back to the hotel, that sense of assurance skyrocketed. That's when they found out what LeBron had said.

And no one could believe it.

• • • •

THERE WAS A CURIOUS contrast between the two teams in the two days leading up to the state final. After the rout of Beechcroft, Bill insisted that Bacon wasn't trying to run up the score or send a message to SVSM. He remained fairly guarded in his comments about the rematch but did tell the *Cincinnati Enquirer*, "I don't think they got our best shot last time."

Perhaps Bill didn't want to give the Irish any added motivation. Or maybe he just didn't have the energy to get into a war of words. Bill had a stomach flu that entire week—so did Peggy, Katie, Abby and Maddy. In fact, when Peggy drove her daughters to Columbus for the state semis, they all held Ziplock bags in their laps in case they got sick in the car. Bill started to feel a little better that Friday, the day before the state final, but staying in the same hotel room with Peggy and the girls made it difficult to get away from the stench of flu and vomit.

Bill scheduled a team meeting at the hotel for Friday night. Minutes before it was slated to start, Tom Thompson, Creegs, Bids and the rest of the coaching staff knocked on Bill's door only to discover that he was asleep. If they hadn't woken him up, Bill would've missed the meeting—the very meeting that he scheduled. Bill shook himself awake and staggered to a room where his players sat waiting. He leaned against a wall for support.

"All right, you guys know what we gotta do tomorrow," Bill said. "Let's get it done."

And with that, Bill walked out and went back to bed. That was the meeting. That was his speech. There was no "win one for the Gipper" about it. It was the eve of the state final. Tip-off was a little more than 12 hours away, and those were his words of wisdom, his words of inspiration. Bill was never the most rah-rah coach, but the brevity and simplicity of his oration was an indication of just how bad he felt. Besides, his players knew what they had to do. He didn't need to get them riled up. He needed sleep.

Even if he felt fine, though, there was a pretty good chance Bill wouldn't have said anything inflammatory after the Beechcroft game. He didn't want to ruffle SVSM's feathers. Even Bacon's players were hesitant to comment. When a reporter from the *Canton Repository* asked Frank and Monty for their thoughts on the rematch, the two Spartans looked at each other and smiled. Neither wanted to respond.

Why anger a sleeping giant?

• • • •

WHEN THE PLAYERS RETURNED from practice, they checked their email and settled in to watch the NCAA Tournament. At one point, the local news replayed LeBron's highlights from the state semis. That's when Bacon came across the words that made a passionate pregame speech from Bill unnecessary; LeBron did the honors himself.

When asked at a press conference about the rematch, LeBron, as replayed in *More Than a Game*, had this to say:

> "We the defending state champion, you know? They gotta come get us. . . . I'm guaranteeing I'm not gonna let my team lose. I don't want my team losing, and I know they don't want to lose—and I ain't gonna let it happen."

Roger Bacon had been pining for a rematch with SVSM for three months, and now that it was finally about to happen, LeBron James publicly guaranteed that Bacon would lose.

The Spartans, winners of 16 straight, were pissed.

Excuse me? What was that? You're guaranteeing victory? We played you guys down to the wire in December, on your turf, in a game in which your team shot 40 free throws, and now, after we just set a record for the most lopsided win in state tournament history, you're gonna sit there and guarantee a win? Do you think you're THAT much better than us? Do you have THAT little respect for us? Do you really think we don't belong on the same court as you?

From a disrespect standpoint, this was reminiscent of LeBron not jumping for the opening tip at Kent State—only about a thousand times worse.

"Once he did that," Beckham said of The Guarantee, "we knew we were gonna win."

Several Spartans were particularly irate, including Leonard, who in many ways was the team's emotional leader. If he got excited, everyone else usually did, too. When Bacon played at Badin during the regular season in early February, the JV game went into overtime. The Spartans, eagerly awaiting their turn to take the floor and warm up, had already lined the hallway leading to the court well before the end of regulation. Leonard, a compact 6-1 ball of energy, couldn't bear the thought of waiting five more game minutes to run under those GCL lights and beat a rival on its home court. So he started bouncing a basketball. Then he started bouncing it hard. Then he started slamming it. And then he started screaming.

"THIS IS OUR HOUSE! THIS IS OUR CRIB! WE GONNA MAKE THIS OUR CRIB! WE DON'T LOSE IN OUR CRIB!"

"Leonard went crazy," Tim McCoy said.

The cuckoo was contagious. The Spartans began jumping up and down, pushing and hitting each other like a football team—maybe because many of them were football players—and began shouting, "OUR CRIB! OUR CRIB!"

A pregame ritual was born.

When news of The Guarantee broke, Leonard was just as rambunctious. He began tackling his own teammates, saying, "OH, YEAH, HE'S GONNA GET IT NOW!"

"It was a slap in the face," Leonard said. "This guy's gonna guarantee a victory? They barely beat us the first time. Just hearing him say that was a sign of disrespect. We kind of took it personal."

Newt, a Scrapper through and through, was ready to play. *We'll play right now*, he thought. *We've got sandals on, and we'll play right now.*

"You want a guarantee?" Newt asked, explaining his mindset. "Well, I'll guarantee this: you'll be hurting after this game. He's 17 years old and guaranteeing a win. You're not in the NBA yet, LeBron. Slow down. You haven't played a bunch of Catholic boys from Cincinnati just yet. *Know your role—because we'll take you there.* That was our mentality."

As Mitch Perdrix watched the players react the way they did, he couldn't help but think back to his junior season eight years earlier in 1993–94—Bill's first year at Bacon—and marvel at how far the program had come, at how far Bill had brought it. Mitch thought of all the times Bill laid into him, of all the times Bill laid into his teammates, trying to get them to care more about the team than anything else in life. Mitch thought of Bill's halftime fury that year at Badin: "*God dammit! You guys can't play like this all fucking night!*" And then he thought of the response after Bill stormed out of the locker room: "*We're not playing all night, are we?*"

"You go from that to guys who said, 'Fuck LeBron. Bring him on,'" Mitch said. "That's a coach's dream."

Granted, not everyone was quite as mad as Leonard and Newt.

"I wasn't pissed, but I remember people were," Monty said. "It got a lot of play. The media did a good job of playing it up. I don't know the point of (making a guarantee), and I didn't know the point at the time. But I already knew what I wanted and what I came there to do."

The players called their parents and delivered the news.

"Mom, LeBron guaranteed his team a win," Josh told Mary Beth.

"How do you guys feel about that?" Mary Beth asked. "Are you nervous?"

"We're not nervous at all. You don't need to worry about it. We're gonna win."

Tim McCoy, Sr., got a similar phone call.

"I said, 'What do you guys think?' And Tim said, 'You can tell everybody we're gonna win this game tomorrow. We're gonna shove that cover up his ass. There's no doubt about it.'"

One of Bacon's players, it seems, felt a need to make that fact known not only to family, but also to strangers. The Spartans went out for dinner that night. At one point, Beckham, in typical Beckham fashion, got up and approached numerous people at surrounding tables.

"Do you know who LeBron James is?" he asked.

Everyone said yes.

"Well," Beckham said, "we're gonna beat him tomorrow."

Classic Beckham. It should come as no surprise, then, that it was Beckham Wyrick, who, before the next sunset, would do something so stunning, so jaw-dropping, so perfectly fitting, that anyone who attended the state final—anyone who actually saw what Beckham did—would never forget.

CHAPTER THIRTEEN

THE REMATCH

Most of Bacon's players didn't sleep well that night. They weren't up late watching television, playing cards or goofing around—actually, lights were out pretty early—but knowing they were mere hours from their rematch with the most talked about team and player in America made sleeping difficult. And truthfully, the Spartans didn't want to sleep. They wanted to be on the court. They wanted to play. Most of all, they wanted to take LeBron's guarantee and shove it up his ass.

The most important day of their lives began with a wake-up call—not from the hotel front desk, but from one of their own, Joe Corcoran, who made the hallway rounds at 7 a.m. He tapped each door one by one and waited for a player—there were two to a room—to inch it ajar. Once Cork had full attention, he smiled and proceeded in sing-song baritone.

"Rise and shine. It's state title time."

What started as one player soon became many. They stood and stared, one foot in the hallway, the other still in their room. Sporting their boxers and socks, they stood and stared, confused, knowing neither the time nor what was happening.

"Rise and shine. It's state title time."

The game wasn't for four more hours.

"Come on, Cork!" came the whines of sleep-deprived teenagers. "What are you doing? Let us sleep a little longer!"

Cork was unyielding. He went to the next door and the next and the next.

"Rise and shine. It's state title time."

As much as the players wanted a little more shut-eye, getting up at 7 a.m. on a Saturday probably felt like sleeping in. They were used to getting up well before then and having to be *at Bacon* at 7 for all those early morning practices Bill scheduled, especially the ones after those Friday-night parties, parties most guys left way early or didn't even bother attending. And on those days, the Spartans didn't just practice; they *practiced*. If the Spartans had anything to worry about that day, being alert and mentally ready by game time wasn't one of them.

Four state finals would be played that day, but the one people were talking about the most—Roger Bacon versus LeBron James and SVSM—was up first. Tip-off was slated for 11 a.m. The Division I state final, which interestingly enough featured Winton Woods, the team Frank left when he came to Bacon, wasn't scheduled to start until 8:30 p.m. For the Spartans, the idea of sitting in an arena all day and watching every other team take its crack at the title while waiting to take their own sounded dreadful. No thanks. An 11 a.m. tip-off was fine and dandy.

The players ate breakfast at the hotel, returned to their rooms to dress and were soon on their way to the arena. The team arrived two hours before tip-off, and already the parking lot was packed. Scalpers were everywhere. Hundred-dollar tickets for a high school basketball game. Two-hundred-dollar tickets. Maybe three. A state tournament record crowd of 18,375 piled into Value City Arena—and almost all of them, just as they had for the state semis, came to see LeBron and SVSM. Beckham's parents, David and Jill Wyrick, pulled into the parking lot and stopped to pay the attendant.

"Hey! You coming to see LeBron?" the attendant beamed. "You coming to see LeBron win?"

He must not have noticed their Roger Bacon apparel.

• • • •

EMILY HOLT DROVE TWO hours from Tiffin to watch Josh play in the state final. This was what they had dreamt of as children more than a decade earlier—a chance to play in the state championship. Finally, the day had come.

And it came seven days after they buried one of their best friends.

Had Meg been alive, there's a good chance she would have been in Columbus that day. She would have been riding in that car with Emily. But she wasn't.

The Gutzwillers remained in Cincinnati and watched the game on television—well, everyone except Mr. Gutzwiller. He was too nervous to watch. He paced in his basement for the duration of the game, thinking of Meg and missing her and praying that Bacon would win.

Everyone, including the coaches, worried about Josh. The Spartans had been more or less unchallenged the entire postseason, winning every game by double digits. But they knew that wouldn't be the case in the state final. For the Spartans to have any chance of winning, they would need Josh Hausfeld to have the game of his life.

The previous night, with the rematch looming and all the commotion about The Guarantee, Josh knew he wouldn't be able to sleep. He wandered down to see Bobby Holt and asked if his wife, Amy, had any Tylenol PM. She did. Josh had never taken Tylenol PM, so he didn't know quite how his body would respond, but given the circumstances, it was a risk he was willing to take. He wound up sleeping just fine.

Before going to bed, however, he sat with Bobby and Amy and reminisced about all the great times they had shared. The games at St. Clement. Driving to Fogarty and throughout the city as members of the Tue/Fri Club. They relived those wonderful memories and discussed both the peril and promise of what lay ahead.

"We knew tomorrow was one of those days that could change our lives," Josh said.

Eventually, Josh went back to his room and said a prayer.

Thank you, God, for this unbelievable journey. I am so blessed. I'll remember tomorrow for the rest of my life. Thank you.

Please, Meg, watch over us.

Josh lay in bed thinking of the journey, of the state final, of Meg. He thought of the state tournament program and how the school was listed not as Cincinnati Roger Bacon, but as St. Bernard Roger Bacon. That was always a source of pride for Josh, and he was reminded of the famous quote he first heard from former McNicholas head coach Jerry Doerger:

Good, better, best,
Never let it rest,
Until your good is better,
And your better is best.

"I just remember thinking we were gonna have that opportunity," Josh said. "We were gonna have that opportunity to be our best."

The next day during warmups, Josh reflected on all those trips to the state tournament he went on with Bill, Brian Neal and the other coaches; on how he always watched from the stands and decided as a freshman to go to state every year until he himself was playing in the final. Now he was.

It didn't seem real.

Mitch Perdrix, of course, took to his pregame ritual of reminding Josh that he needed to be The Guy—especially now in what, win or lose, would be his last game as a Spartan.

"I was worried about him," Mitch said. "Big stage, big opponent. LeBron guaranteed the win. But I remember Josh being really confident before the game, and I thought, 'I really hope he means that.'"

• • •

INSIDE, THE ARENA LOOKED nothing like it had three nights earlier. Replacing the silence and loneliness and nostalgia were lights and music and people who had gathered together for the annual pomp and circumstance. Student sections were saturated. Stands overflowed with humanity. More than 18,000 people were on hand, but for Bacon, it might as well have been a million. The Irish were used to this setting; the Spartans weren't. Still, there was no intimidation. There was a buzz, an electricity. The lights were blazing. The juice was flowing. The players could feel it. Everyone was amped up—even before tip-off.

"I remember bumping into Chad Mraz pretty hard when we were going out to warmups," Matt Reed said. "I wasn't gonna move, and neither was he. I think I gave him a pretty good blow, and we both stopped and stared at each other for a little bit. There was nothing said. It's an ego thing. No one was going to step to the side."

During warmups, cameramen zoomed in on Monty, who led Bacon in scoring against Beechcroft.

"It just had that big-time feel already," Monty said. "You look up and it's sold out. You don't question yourself, but you wonder how you'll react. We played big games in Cincinnati, but this was a whole different level."

And the Spartans knew it wasn't because of them. All week, all season, the story was never about Roger Bacon. It was about LeBron James. It was about LeBron James on the cover of *Sports Illustrated*. It was about Beechcroft's pizza party. It was about The Guarantee. And now, as tip-off approached, it was about catching a glimpse of the next Michael; it was about seeing a shooting star before it streaked past the horizon; it was about sucking in the spectacle so years later you could say you saw the greatest basketball player ever way back when. That morning, the *Columbus Dispatch* ran a nearly full-page photo of LeBron dribbling. Beneath his shorts read the words: "If you thought Michael was hot, wait until you see LeBron."

Needless to say, there was no mention of Roger Bacon.

"He was the story," Monty said. "But I knew it'd be our story if we won."

• • • •

It was barely past 10 a.m., and the greatest prep basketball player ever looked a little tired.

"He kind of seemed disinterested during warmups," Beckham said. "He was biting his nails and yawning. He just didn't seem too focused."

Said Josh, "I remember him being kind of lackadaisical. I remember him trying to do trick shots, almost. It struck me as, 'They're not taking this serious,' or, 'Maybe that's just what they do.' But I remember thinking, 'Well, that's different.'"

Even some of LeBron's teammates, according to the Spartans, appeared to be going through the motions.

"That was their persona," Brian Neal said. "They were a turn-it-on, turn-it-off team. Because they were so good, they could usually just turn it on and win."

But this day, perhaps, was different. Coach Joyce, as seen in *More Than a Game*, gave his players an earful in the locker room that morning. Joyce tried to hammer home that hunger and humility—not complacency and arrogance—were the true hallmarks of the Irish. As Coach Joyce talked, Willie McGee wore headphones and bobbed his head to the beat. Dru Joyce? Head phones. Sian Cotton? Yawning. LeBron James? He seemed unconvinced, as if his entire face were doing an eye-roll. Of those shown in the documentary, the only player appearing to be listening with conviction was Romeo Travis.

It was a stark contrast to Bacon's locker room, which was relaxed, loose, ready.

OUR CRIB! OUR CRIB!

Cork was jumping up and down and bumping into people, just as the players were.

OUR CRIB! OUR CRIB!

Even Bill was smiling. He wasn't baring all, but he was smiling.

OUR CRIB! OUR CRIB!

Then it grew serious. Bill made the final pregame preparations. He talked strategy once more. The team said a "Hail Mary." There was silence. And then Newt shattered it.

"HE GUARANTEED IT?! OH, HELL NAW!"

Newt sprung to his feet and skipped rhythmically out of the locker room, a defensive lineman celebrating a sack. The rest of the team followed into the tunnel, energy and exuberance surging through them. And that's when Bill gathered his key Scrappers and delivered the news.

"I was walking out of the tunnel with Nate and Leonard," Tim McCoy recalled, "and Coach Brewer told us, 'I'm just gonna warn you guys right now: You're not gonna play today unless we're getting whopped or there's foul trouble. I'm keeping the starters in there as long as I can.'"

It's hard for any player to hear that, especially a senior, especially one like McCoy, who played in all 27 of Bacon's previous games that season. Sometimes it was two minutes; sometimes it was eight minutes; sometimes it was substantially more. But he played in every game. He was always ready. Whatever Bill needed, Tim was always there. But in the state final, the last game of his career, Tim McCoy never saw the floor.

"I remember telling Brewer, 'I don't care,'" Tim said. "'I just want a ring.'"

• • • •

"*St. Vincent–St. Mary will throw their high-powered offense up against a team that prides itself on defense,*" play-by-play announcer

Marty Bannister says. *"Bill Brewer's Roger Bacon Spartans are a team; they'll get after you defensively, and that's the strength of their game."*

The camera pans to Bill. Ninth season. A career record of 134–83. A .618 winning percentage.

"I think we guard very well," Bill said in a taped interview, wearing a white shirt and yellow tie against a pitch-black background. ". . . Our shooting percentage against is in the high-30s. You know, we're giving up 45, 46 points per game, so I think these guys have done a good job of guarding. That's one thing we hang our hats on is playing defense."

In fact, in the Spartans' previous 16 games—the 16 games they played after the debacle at CJ—they allowed only one team to break 50. That team was GCL rival McNicholas, which scored 52 and lost by 15. This was a stark improvement over the first 11 games of the season, when eight teams broke 50 on Bacon. Four broke 60. And one, SVSM, broke 70—and came within one point of 80. Clearly, Bacon's defense had improved.

A practice like the one after the CJ game can do that for a team.

As for Bill's yellow tie, it wasn't his. He was so sick when he packed for Columbus that week that he forgot to bring one. Of course, even if he hadn't been sick, he might have forgotten one anyway. When Bids, Creegs and Tom Thompson would pick Bill up at his house for those Friday-night games at Bacon—when Bill would come to the door barely awake from his pregame nap, hair sticking straight up in the air—it wasn't uncommon for him to be on the way to the game before realizing he'd forgotten his tie. So inevitably, some member of his staff would be scrambling around St. Bernard trying to find him one. That week in Columbus, though, there were more important things to worry about. So Bill borrowed a tie—a yellow one from Bobby Holt. Bill never wore that tie again.

And Bobby never got it back.

• • • •

BILL MIGHT'VE BEEN SUPERSTITIOUS about pregame meals and naps, but Peggy was just as superstitious about during-game apparel. Specifically, if a shirt said "Roger Bacon" on it, she wasn't wearing it. She learned early in Bill's tenure that if she wore Roger Bacon shirts to Roger Bacon games, Roger Bacon would lose. When Bill went to Princeton, she tried to start a new trend. She wore Princeton attire to the first two games; Princeton lost both. So instead of a Roger Bacon shirt, Peggy always wore University of Dayton attire. That year, in particular, she had worn the same UD shirt to every game, and Bacon won every game that she attended. The only loss Peggy saw in person was the regular-season game against SVSM—and she wasn't wearing her UD shirt that night; she had forgotten to bring it. But even though Peggy was dressed in her trusted UD cotton for the state final, she struggled to control her emotions walking into Value City Arena that day.

"I was literally shaking," said Peggy, who clasped a rosary in her hands the entire game. "I remember thinking, 'There's not a darn thing I can do to change the outcome of this game. Bill's either going to win and be euphoric for the next six months, or he's going to lose and be miserable for the next six months.' I obviously wanted it to go the right way, but truly, my fate was in the hands of 17- and 18-year-old boys."

• • • •

FOR THOSE ON HAND that day in Columbus and for those watching at home on the Ohio News Network, the differences between Roger Bacon and SVSM, even before tip-off, were apparent. Yes, there was the racial element; 10 of Bacon's 13 players, including four starters, were white, while the majority of SVSM's 14 players, including four starters, were black.

But far more telling, perhaps, were the introductions. When their names were announced, some of the Irish exchanged extravagant handshakes—routines full of flair and panache, of style and swagger. Dru Joyce brushed his shoulder. LeBron shadowboxed with Sian Cotton and then slid his arms across his body like a referee signaling an incomplete pass.

The commentators, Austin Carr and Marty Bannister, couldn't help but chuckle.

"*Well, it's certain that LeBron has the pregame introduction down,*" Bannister jokes.

On the other end of the floor, Bacon's starters—sans glitz, sans glamour—burrowed past the Scrappers and collided with Newt, who lowered his shoulder as if they were linemen in the way of the quarterback. There was no style; only substance. The Spartans had no use for theatrics. They just wanted to get down to business.

"You could tell the difference between the teams just by watching that," Tim McCoy said. "They had all these elaborate handshakes. When they announced our starters, me and Newt, we'd hit each other with forearms. It was GCL, not GCL; tough, not tough; tough versus flashy. You guys want to look good, but we're gonna hit you. We're gonna grind it out."

The Spartans stood in a circle in front of their bench and dived toward the floor in unison. Thirteen heads clustered in the center. Twenty-six legs sprawled on the outskirts. They looked like wrestlers killing time before a meet. It was in this scrum that the players soaked everything up one last time—every hope, every dream, every wish. They lived. They lived completely and fully in that moment. Nothing else mattered. Nothing else mattered not even for a second. The lights shone upon them. That wonderful feeling of youth and invincibility washed over them. They felt like they could do anything. They looked at each other. Hearts were racing. Exhales came heavily. Sweat seeped through their jerseys. They were ready. They knew it.

It was their time.

FIRST QUARTER

Each starting five trots to center court, and Beckham's alter ego has arrived. All five Spartans know who they're guarding—this has long since been decided—but just in case any memories need refreshing, Beckham struts toward the timeline and cries out, "I got The Chosen One! I'm guarding The Chosen One!"

Already Beckham is trying to get under LeBron's skin. Already he is mocking him. Already he is showing no fear.

"Just trying to be a smart-ass," Beckham said. "That's the way I was."

Monty and LeBron convene for the tip. This time, LeBron actually jumps, and SVSM, like it would have done in December, easily controls the tap. This time, LeBron isn't messing around.

And then . . .

. . . it happens.

As Dru Joyce corrals the tip, Beckham eyes LeBron, who peers off to the side as he jogs into SVSM's first offensive set. Suddenly, the energy, the intensity, the 18-year-old adrenaline that has been coursing through Beckham's body all morning reaches its peak. It cannot be quelled. The boy once criticized for not showing enough aggression, the boy who chose Hawaii over sitting varsity, the boy who didn't pursue big-time college football because he couldn't stomach the rank aroma of football pads, sticks his right forearm up and buries it fiercely into LeBron's sternum, freezing the prodigy in his sneakers. It's a bold blow to the chest, a brutal bullet fired with fury from a .357 magnum at point-blank range. More than one Scrapper sees LeBron's arms squirm and flail backward. They sit in stunned silence.

"He's coming down the court and I (thought), 'You ain't gonna get farther than right here,'" Beckham recalled. "And I just put my arm up and stopped him. I don't know if he flopped or if my adrenaline was going, but it almost ended up making him fall over."

It was quintessential Beckham. Perhaps the most highly anticipated game in state tournament history. A sellout crowd, a record crowd. The best prep player ever. And on the first play—before the first play could even develop—Beckham delivered a body shot before the opening bell had even finished ringing. It was a *fuck you* with a forearm.

And the message had been sent.

I'm here, LeBron. I'm right here. I don't care who you are or how good you are. I'm gonna be on ya. I'm gonna be on ya all day. So get ready.

It's conceivable that in the history of high school basketball, no greater message had ever been sent. None, surely, had ever been sent in a more high-profile setting. And the crazy thing is that almost no one saw it. Most of Bacon's bench didn't see it. Most of the people in the stands didn't see it. And perhaps most important, none of the refs saw it.

"When we came back down on offense after that possession, (Coach Joyce) was going absolutely ballistic on the sidelines," Creegs said. "He's just right in the ear of this official, and I'm like, 'What the hell is his problem?' And then we found out later."

Said Brian Neal, "None of us saw it. We were watching the ball like the rest of the officials."

It's easy to get pumped up at what Beckham did, but as a coach, even as a teammate, part of you worries. Your best defender, the guy on your team most capable of matching up with LeBron, risks getting an early foul, a silly foul. Maybe worse.

Said Mitch Perdrix, "That should have been a flagrant right off the bat."

But forget about fouls. You risk pissing off LeBron James. You risk pissing off the greatest prodigy in the history of prodigies. There was courage in what Beckham did; pride, too. But there was also recklessness, rage, and in some ways, insanity. No one knew Beckham was going to do that. Not even Beckham. It just happened.

And it set the tone.

•   •   •

THE FIRST PASS OF the game goes to—who else?—LeBron James, who catches the ball on the right wing. He immediately goes to work on Beckham, backing him down toward the paint. But he doesn't shoot. He passes to Romeo Travis, who misses a jumper. Frank rebounds. He crosses halfcourt and eludes LeBron, who reaches in to poke the ball away. Frank maintains his dribble and finds Beckham streaking along the right sideline. Frank forces a pass that sails way over Beckham's head and out of bounds. SVSM ball.

Emotions are high in the early going. Everyone is amped.

LeBron gets the ball again, this time on the left wing. He goes left and lofts a layup over Beckham. 2–0, SVSM.

Beckham isn't worried.

"I was just out there playing," he said.

SVSM applies a full-court trap. Joyce and Romeo converge on Dave, who, as usual, breaks the press by himself. He finds Frank, who hits Josh for a layin. Tie game, 2–2.

"*What I noticed there,*" color commentator Austin Carr says, "*is LeBron was late getting down the floor. It was 5-on-4. He can't do that in this game. Not with this team he can't.*"

Romeo backs down Monty. The shot is no good. Out of bounds. Bacon ball. Dave breaks the full-court trap again. Beckham with a wide open three from the left wing. 5–2, Bacon.

Bill crouches down and settles into the trenches. He watches his defense. Joyce finds Chad Mraz open in the corner for three. Miss. Josh rebounds and takes a three on the other end. No good. Rebound Romeo. Sekou Lewis puts it up and in after a whistle. The basket is no good. Foul on the floor. On Josh. Already, a foul on Josh.

LeBron works the middle of the floor and passes to Joyce in the left corner. Frank can't fight through Sekou's pick. Nothing but net. Tie game, 5–5.

Already, a three from Joyce. In his two previous state finals, Joyce shot a combined 10-of-15 from beyond the arc, including a perfect 7-of-7 as a freshman. He drilled five threes against Bacon back in December. But Frank is undeterred.

"I was trying to get in his head that second game," Frank said. "I was telling him, 'You're not getting any threes off this game, and if you do, it'll be because I wasn't guarding you.' Me and him went at it a bit."

Beckham forces a three that hits the front iron. Rebound Romeo. LeBron dribbles left of the key, as Romeo comes over for the pick. No thanks. King James pulls up for three. Buckets. 8–5, SVSM. LeBron is 2-of-2 with an assist. He has had a hand in all eight SVSM points.

Josh takes a pass from Dave at the top of the key and slips through the lane. 8–7, SVSM. LeBron shoots a quick three off another screen. No good. Rebound Beckham.

Monty has isolation on Romeo. He thinks about a three but backs his man down instead. Spin move with the old up-and-under. Sekou rotates down to help but commits the foul. Monty hits both free throws. 9–8, Bacon.

That's three ties and three lead changes.

Romeo drives the lane and collides with Beckham. The whistle blows. Block on Beckham. Romeo converts both freebies. 10–9, SVSM.

Bacon breaks the press. Beckham with a running floater. 11–10, Bacon.

Joyce passes to LeBron on the right wing. LeBron puts his head down, goes left and drives into Beckham, who bodies him away from the rim. LeBron's fallaway from the elbow grazes the front iron. Rebound Frank. Josh takes a three. No good. Monty with the rebound and the put-back. 13–10, Bacon.

The Spartans have outscored SVSM 8–0 in the paint.

Joyce spots up from six feet behind the arc. In and out. Dave breaks the press again and races to shoot a jumper. Rebound Romeo, who flips to LeBron on the run out. It's one-on-two. Beckham closes in from the left, Dave from the right. They converge on LeBron, who begins his ascent one stride inside the free-throw line. The whistle blows. LeBron, sailing left, flips up an awkward shot with his left hand. Off the window and in. Foul on Dave.

"OHHH! OHHH! OHHH!" Carr screams. *"Folks, not too many people in this world have body control like that!"*

The crowd *oohs* and *ahhs*.

Wait a minute. Wait a minute. No basket. The foul was on the floor. It remains 13–10, Bacon, with 2:50 left in the first quarter. Timeout.

Tim, Newt and Matt Reed rush to greet the starters. Josh's chest heaves rapidly as he tries to swallow oxygen.

"You all right, Josh?" Newt asks.

"I'm tired as hell," Josh says worriedly between gulps of air and chugs of water. "I ain't gonna make it."

"Just remember," Newt said, "in the nose, out the mouth."

Josh nods.

SVSM comes out of the timeout and gets the ball to LeBron on the perimeter. Beckham suffocates him and makes him give it up. After a flurry of passes, the ball is back in LeBron's hands. He looks for Romeo, but Dave tips the ball away and tumbles out of bounds while diving to make the save. Bacon pushes. Monty finds Beckham in the post for what should be a wide-open layin, but LeBron closes like a safety and swats the shot out of bounds.

"When you have LeBron James and Romeo Travis lurking around, you've got to be aware of where (they) are," Carr says. *"You can't put up a weak shot like that!"*

Frank passes to Josh, who drives the left baseline on Chad Mraz and flips up a finger roll. Back iron. Joyce gathers the rebound and starts the break. LeBron finds Romeo in transition for a layup. 13–12, Bacon, 2:01 to go.

Beckham in-bounds to Dave, but the pass is stolen. Joyce flips it to Sekou, who misses a layin. Beckham recovers and pushes to Frank, who misses a layin of his own. The action has suddenly become fast-paced. Sloppy. Helter-skelter.

"This is just the game Roger Bacon doesn't want to play," Bannister says.

"Right, they don't want to get up and down the floor with this team."

LeBron works Beckham on the left block and spins right. Monty rotates over to seal the baseline. LeBron sees it, reacts and, just before fading out of bounds, fires a beautiful pass to a wide-open Romeo under the basket. SVSM regains the lead, 14–13.

"Super pass!" Carr says. *"I'll tell you—this young man can pass the basketball!"*

Bacon pushes the tempo, and Josh dishes to Frank for two. 15–14, Bacon, with a minute to play in the first quarter. Joyce finds LeBron in the corner for a spot-up three. LeBron rattles it home. 17–15, SVSM.

Both teams are shooting 6-of-13 from the floor. Frank with a turnover.

"So far, Bacon is playing the kind of game they want," Carr says. *"They take a few fast-break opportunities—not too many—and force (SVSM) to play in the interior."*

Joyce hoists a 30-footer as time expires. Air-ball. At the end of one, the Irish lead 17–15—a far cry from their 28–18 first-quarter deficit back in December. LeBron has eight points on nine touches and three assists on three double-teams.

"What I like about him, he's not afraid to give the ball up, and he doesn't hesitate," Carr says. *"He sees what's in front of him. He gives it up right away. He doesn't try to beat the double team. Kobe Bryant had a big problem with that when he first came into the professional ranks. He always tried to beat the double team instead of giving it up and letting the game come to him."*

Beckham leads Bacon with five points. The Scrappers again race onto the court to greet the starters. There wasn't a single substitution made in the first quarter. Newt notices that Josh's breathing is more controlled, more relaxed. He asks if he's okay.

"I'm good," Josh says. "I could do this all day."

SECOND QUARTER

It's Bacon's ball. Monty works for a look down low but has his shot blocked from behind. SVSM takes over. LeBron tries to drive on Beckham, but Beckham pokes the ball away. Monty scoops it and flips a quick outlet to Dave, who beats Mraz and Joyce for a transition layin. Tie game, 17–17.

"LeBron was very careless with the basketball," Carr says. *"(Bacon) stole the ball and got the opportunity. LeBron has to protect the ball. This (Bacon) team, on the defensive end, they're in-your-face-type defenders."*

Sekou Lewis works the post and finds Mraz open for three in front of Bacon's bench. 20–17, SVSM.

"That's the shot he looks for all the time," Carr says. *"He sits in that corner, and he waits for the penetration. They know where to find him because they just sling the pass over there, really, without looking sometimes."*

Josh counters with a midrange jumper. 20–19, SVSM.

Romeo answers with a midrange jumper of his own, this one over Monty on the baseline. 22–19, SVSM.

Bacon beats the trap. Wide-open layin for Frank. 22–21, SVSM.

"That time, again, LeBron was out of position," Carr observes. *"He went for the steal, he got caught in the middle, he didn't get back (and Bacon) got a layup."*

Joyce fires a three from the top of the key. It's pure. 25–21, SVSM. That's Joyce's second triple of the day and the twelfth of his state-final career. SVSM is shooting 5-of-9 from distance; Bacon is just 1-of-4.

Monty goes for a layup, but LeBron emphatically swats the ball against the backboard. There's a collective gasp from the stands, an "*OHHHHHHH!*"—as if a would-be tackler got blindsided or an out-on-his-feet boxer timbered to the canvas.

LeBron brings the ball upcourt and tries to thread the needle, but Beckham picks it off in the lane. Everything for the Irish is coming from the perimeter; the Spartans have outscored SVSM 14–4 in the paint.

Monty converts along the baseline against Romeo. 25–23, SVSM.

Romeo bricks one off the iron. Dave rebounds.

Bacon is hanging around.

"*(The Irish) have not lost a game to a team from the state of Ohio since the '98–99 season,*" Bannister reminds viewers.

"*Their experience is what (has) helped them,*" Carr says. "*They play so many good teams around the country that when they play against teams from Ohio, they really aren't bothered by the competition.*"

Monty misses a baseline jumper. Beckham skies over LeBron for a rebound, causing him to tumble out of bounds. The whistle blows. Over the back. That's two on Beckham.

"*That's a big foul right there,*" Bannister says.

"*Right, that will hurt him because he's a very physical player.*"

With 4:17 left in the first half, both teams make their first substitutions of the game—Newt for Beckham, Sian for Sekou.

Bill puts Frank on LeBron, whose three rattles out. Romeo outmuscles Monty for the rebound and stick-back. 27–23, SVSM.

Dave approaches the timeline and tries to loft a pass to Josh, who is standing right by Coach Joyce. LeBron reads it, strides forward and jumps at Dave as if sprinting off a rooftop. He tips the ball and chases it as it scoots toward the sideline. The ball rolls out of bounds, but LeBron keeps after it anyway and jumps effortlessly atop the scorers' table, seemingly because he can. Bacon fans serenade LeBron with a chorus of boos.

Official timeout. 27–23, SVSM, 3:45 left in the half.

"*(The Spartans) are really good at . . . getting everybody involved,*" Carr says, "*But . . . LeBron James, he's probably one of the best passers in the country, especially (at the) high school level. Runs the floor well. He's not afraid to give it up. That's one thing that I like about him because he's such a prolific offensive scorer, but he realizes he needs his teammates to get involved.*"

"*A lot of times, too often you'll see guys go into the air and not know what to do with the basketball when they get (there),*" Bannister says. "*A little different with James.*"

"*You're right. Well, he's always aware of where everybody is on the floor. Right now, though, he has to get, I think, more in the paint area. Too many outside shots. He has to get inside.*"

SVSM is shooting 4-of-6 this quarter. Bacon is shooting 4-of-7.

Frank gets the ball on the left wing against LeBron. Clear out. Frank stutters left, stutters right and freezes LeBron before exploding left along the baseline. LeBron recovers to make a play on the ball. The whistle blows. Foul on LeBron.

That's one.

"... They aren't afraid of LeBron James," Carr says. "One-on-one, isolated play, and (Frank's) taking him to the basket.... LeBron does not bend his knees on the defensive end. He stands straight up too much—and these guys know that, and they're going right at him."

Frank, a third-team all-state selection, goes to the line for two. He misses the first and makes the second. 27–24, SVSM.

Joyce bounce-passes to Sian, but Newt taps the ball away. Dave recovers.

The ensuing sequence is sloppy. Loose-ball foul on Mraz. Bacon in-bounds. Josh takes Mraz to the bucket. He has a good four inches on him, and Romeo and Sian rotate over to help. Josh pump-fakes and gets both defenders to bite, but he can't convert. Newt boards it and lofts a put-back. No good. Rebound Romeo.

"I'll tell you," Carr says. "Roger Bacon is getting a lot of good opportunities around that basket. Eventually, it's gonna wear V's down if they don't start getting inside themselves."

Right on cue, LeBron takes a pass from Joyce and drives along the left baseline. Monty rotates over, and LeBron gives it up to Romeo—but Frank stands tall in the middle of the paint. Romeo's right shoulder collides with Frank's chest, sending Frank to the floor. The whistle blows. The shot falls. LeBron, motioning with his right wrist and index finger, implores the official for the and-one. But it's all for naught. Offensive foul. Charge on Romeo. That's one. Exasperated, Romeo spins demonstratively and spreads both arms, staring at the official for an explanation.

"*Super pass by LeBron,*" Carr says, "but Phillips is standing right there. You can't go through him; you gotta go around him in that situation."

Instead of SVSM leading 29–24—with a chance at 30–24—it remains 27–24 with 2:36 left in the half. Dave dribbles upcourt and Romeo, the game's high scorer with 10 points, is still shaking his head in disbelief.

SVSM has four second-quarter turnovers; Bacon has none.

The Spartans run their offense. Newt sets a hard pick on Mraz, and Josh takes care of the rest. Floating behind the arc, he's already into his jumper when the pass arrives from Frank. Nothing, absolutely nothing, but net. Tie game, 27–27, with 2:20 left. It's a five-point swing and the sixth tie of the half.

"*Super outside shot!*" Carr beams. "*Ball movement again by Bacon. This team here is solid. I like what I see.*"

LeBron and Romeo work the pick and roll, but the 6-6 junior can't convert the bunny. Newt tries to feed Monty down low, but Romeo knocks the ball toward Mraz. Another pick and roll. LeBron drives on Frank and finds Romeo for a wide-open deuce. 29–27, SVSM. Ninety seconds left in the half.

The lead doesn't last long. Dave pushes the ball and finds Frank running up the left sideline. Frank dribbles left-handed toward the goal—just like Jerome taught him. LeBron cuts him off, but the defense is matador. Frank goes behind the back at the three-point line and dribbles in with his right hand. Romeo runs the floor and jumps for the block just as Frank begins his ascent. Frank's feet barely leave the floor. He absorbs the contact with his right shoulder, switches the ball back to his left hand and flips it off the glass. The whistle blows. The shot falls. Count it. And-one. Tie game, 29–29, with 1:24 to go. That's two fouls on Romeo, who must sit for the rest of the half.

"*You know, Marty, the more and more I'm watching this, LeBron let this play happen because on the defensive end he didn't go strong. He let the guy go right by him. His teammates have to suffer for the lack of intensity on the defensive end. He has to start challenging people on the defensive end. Otherwise, when he gets to the next level, he will get his heart broken a lot.*"

Willie McGee enters the fray for SVSM.

Frank, who is responsible for all three fouls on LeBron and Romeo, misses the free throw. LeBron pulls down the board—his first of the game—and finds Mraz in the corner. The senior sharpshooter pumps and drives the lane. Reach-in foul on Dave.

He and Beckham both have two fouls.

"*Bill Brewer talked about it prior to the game, Austin. He's concerned. He quizzed us continually about timeouts and how long they were because he's concerned about his depth.*"

Mraz makes the first free throw. 30–29, SVSM. Leonard Bush checks in for Newt.

"*Right,*" Carr says, "*and he knows that this team will wear you down worrying about trying to keep LeBron under control. . . . If you continue to get in foul trouble, which happened in the first game (between these teams) . . .*"

Mraz misses the second free throw.

Frank rebounds and outlets to Josh on his left. Josh goes crossover on LeBron, gets a step, drives to the hole and tries to dump it off to Leonard, but the pass goes out of bounds. Turnover. 58.2 seconds to play.

LeBron, with a four-inch height advantage, backs down Frank. The defense collapses. LeBron finds Mraz open for three. No good. Leonard with the board. Dave dribbles upcourt and finds Leonard in the corner. Leonard drives baseline on Willie McGee, as LeBron rotates down and extends to swat the shot. But somehow, Leonard, at 6-1, gets it off.

31–30, Bacon, with 21 seconds to go.

The Spartans lead for the first time this quarter.

"I knew time was winding down, and I was thinking aggressive," Leonard said. "When I got the ball on the baseline, that was my first thought. *Attack.* They were pretty much giving me the baseline, and I wasn't gonna back down. That was my personality. If (the shot) gets blocked, it gets blocked. But I'm gonna go up strong and try to score."

LeBron takes Frank one-on-one to close the half. He puts his head down as if he's going to the basket, but he dribbles back and shoots a fallaway three. Frank gets a hand in LeBron's face, and the ball smacks off the front of the rim.

Halftime.

The Spartans lead by a point, 31–30. In December, they trailed by a point at halftime, 45–44, after Dru Joyce made a three that gave SVSM its first lead of the game. Thus, the combined score of both first halves was 75–75. But today, Leonard's basket—his only basket of the game—ensured that Bacon went into the locker room with the lead. The Spartans didn't win either half in December, but they won this one.

Now they just needed to do it again.

Even though the game was as close as could be through 16 minutes, Bacon had reason to feel good. First, the combined 61 first-half points were a stark contrast to the 89 at Kent State. There were seven ties. There were nine lead changes. Thus far, the state final had been a low-scoring, back-and-forth defensive slugfest—exactly the kind of game Bacon wanted to play.

And then there was this: Somehow, LeBron James didn't score a single point in the second quarter. *Not one single point.* He scored eight in the first quarter, and he was stuck on eight at the break.

Bacon also controlled several key stats. SVSM shot 11-of-24 (.458) from the floor; Bacon shot 13-of-25 (.520). SVSM had 11 rebounds; Bacon had 14. SVSM made five three-pointers to Bacon's two, but both teams were shooting an almost identical percentage from distance (The Irish were shooting 38.5 percent, the Spartans 40). Bacon was also plus-four in points off turnovers.

But the most pivotal stat, without question, was points in the paint, where Bacon held a 20–10 advantage. The Irish had scored exactly one-third of their points in the paint. Not bad—until you consider that's where the Spartans scored *two-thirds* of theirs.

"That, to me, tells a big story," Carr says. *"And eventually, it will show up in that fourth quarter."*

That wouldn't be the only thing to show up in the fourth quarter—or the second half in general. No, something—or better yet, someone—was about to take over. Someone talented. Someone famous.

Someone determined to make good on his guarantee.

THIRD QUARTER

With the action set to resume, LeBron James sits on the Irish bench, gnawing at his right pinky.

". . . They've always talked about LeBron wanting his teammates to step up," Carr says. *"LeBron's gonna have to do the stepping up here in the second half if they want to win this game."*

Bill strategizes with Brian Neal on Bacon's bench. Coach Joyce takes a knee and sizes up his opponent. The second half gets under way.

The third quarter begins much like the first, with Joyce getting the ball to LeBron on the right wing. He immediately goes to work. Romeo sets a screen as LeBron goes left. Monty steps up to meet him, but LeBron has already crossed him over and split the defense. Frank reaches in to try and tip the ball away. Another crossover. Elevation. Two points. 32–31, SVSM.

LeBron has already equaled his points in the paint from the first half.

"What I'm looking to see is, is LeBron going to step out of the system to get himself going?" Carr asks. "Because he has to get going here in the third quarter."

LeBron looks angry. He barks at his teammates. A *Let's go* scowl flashes across his face.

Beckham doesn't seem to notice. Of course he doesn't. He inbounds the ball to Dave. Joyce closes in. Dave gives it right back to Beckham, who dribbles over the timeline and passes to Frank on the left wing. Ten feet beyond the arc, Beckham begins his take-off route down the runway. He starts slow but quickly gains speed. Then he gains more of it. LeBron backpedals. He turns around just in time to collide with Josh, who supplies a sturdy pick. Frank sees it the whole way. Chad Mraz, who is guarding Josh, sees it the whole way, too. He knows what's about to happen, but he can't do anything to stop it.

Frank lobs the ball across the court from the wing to the basket. Beckham skies, catches the floating orb with both hands and rattles the rim. He screams. He roars. He howls from within, from the gut, a visceral yawp of the unwavering and unvarnished. The Scrappers spring to their feet. They jump. Their hands hammer the air. Beckham struts back on defense, cheeks red and puffy, both fists raised. He pumps them off his head three times to crown himself—and mock King James. He smiles. He swaggers. He Beckhams. *What now, LeBron?* his face suggests. *What now?*

". . . (He's) able to answer the drive by James!" Bannister exclaims. "And Beckham Wyrick gets WAAAAY up into the air to send it down!"

Bacon has regained the lead, 33–32, but the score is irrelevant. Beckham, just as he did in the first half, has opened the second with a body blow—this one less literal—and has sent another message.

No matter what you do, LeBron, we're not going away. Anything you throw at us, we're gonna respond. Any problem you present, we're gonna have an answer. Your boys better be ready—'cause you're gonna need 'em.

Every Spartan—on the court or off—has a spring in his step. SVSM's next possession ends before it starts. Offensive foul on Sekou Lewis.

Bacon looks to extend the lead, but Monty turns it over. LeBron and Romeo work the pick and roll once more, and Romeo finishes with a dunk. 34–33, SVSM.

Frank sends a nice lob over Romeo's head and into Monty, but Joyce comes in to swipe it away. LeBron recovers the ball and looks for Romeo, but Dave tips the ball out of bounds.

Bill calls a 30-second timeout with 6:26 remaining in the third quarter.

"I think both teams have come out a little bit more resolved to get the job done here in the second half," Carr says. "It should be a barn-burner going down to the stretch here."

Both teams break the huddle. Mraz stands along the baseline looking to in-bound to LeBron, who jostles with Beckham for position. Even here, 90 feet from the basket, Bacon's senior won't concede an inch. He's so close to LeBron's cheek he might as well be kissing it. A ref steps between the two. Beckham keeps jawing anyway.

Another pick and roll with LeBron and Romeo. LeBron takes Frank left toward the baseline and drops it off for Sekou Lewis, who can't handle the pass. The ball goes right through his hands to Josh, who beats Mraz downcourt for a scoop-shot layin. 35–34, Bacon.

Frank sticks LeBron, who lobs it into Romeo. Romeo misses once but not twice. Foul on Beckham, his third. And-one. Romeo hits the freebie. 37–35, SVSM.

"Austin, that was a big foul on Roger Bacon. It was on Beckham Wyrick, their defensive stopper—his third personal foul."

"Right, and he's the one they definitely have to keep out of foul trouble because he has to take the brunt of guarding LeBron."

Bacon is undaunted. Dave zips a pass to Josh. Frank sets a screen on Mraz to give Josh some daylight, and Josh fires a three in front of his own bench. Nothing, absolutely nothing, but net. 38–37, Bacon.

All six third-quarter baskets—three by each team—have resulted in lead changes.

Joyce shoots a three. Short. Beckham rebounds, dribbles upcourt and looks to pass, but Romeo is tardy getting down the floor. Beckham takes it all the way in for two. 40–37, Bacon.

"That's just the cardinal sin in basketball," Carr says. "You never let a guy take the ball off the board and go all the way down through your defense like that. St. V has to tighten it up."

LeBron drives, draws two defenders and kicks it out to Mraz in the corner for three. Short. Frank drives on Sekou Lewis, spins right and is met by Romeo. Both defenders go for the block—and somehow neither gets it. Frank, crafty as ever, puts it up and in. 42–37, Bacon.

"Nice spin move by Frank Phillips!" Bannister says. "One thing you're seeing (is) no intimidation (by) Roger Bacon."

"(Bill Brewer) told us that before the game," Carr adds. "They're not afraid of LeBron James. He's just another player."

That's a 7–0 run in the last 1:03 for the Spartans, which have their biggest lead of the game.

Beckham mans LeBron. Frank comes for the double-team and reaches in. Foul on Frank, who smiles and claps. SVSM in-bounds. Frank and LeBron go at it. LeBron, using his size advantage once more, backs hard into Frank. All Frank can do is grab his arms. Another foul. LeBron is animated. He yells at his teammates and points violently at the paint. The scowl is back. His forehead crinkles.

"He understands the game of basketball," Carr says. "He knows what's going on. His team's getting beat up in the paint."

LeBron wants the ball. No, he demands it—and he gets his wish on the right wing. He immediately puts his head down and drives left. He gets to the paint, lowers his shoulder, collides with Frank and powers up a shot that banks off the window and in. The whistle blows. And-one? No. No basket. Charging on LeBron. That's two. LeBron extends both hands, palms facing up. He doesn't understand. He's frustrated.

There's 4:28 left in the third, and LeBron has just two points since the first quarter.

"Nice move inside," Carr says, "but he went forward (on the shot) instead of going up."

LeBron and Romeo have a combined four fouls. Frank is responsible for all of them.

Monty, as he did so often that December night at Kent State, hits from the baseline. 44–37, Bacon. A 9–0 run. Romeo in-bounds to LeBron like a softball pitcher. The underhanded scoop finds LeBron just before midcourt, where Frank picks him up. LeBron dribbles left and goes up for a layin on the left side of the rim. Monty rotates down to block the shot, but LeBron remains in flight, extending toward the other side of the basket. The right-handed reverse, however, hits the glass and caroms off the rim. Josh corrals the rebound and takes off.

Monty spins left against Romeo and flips up a right hook. No good. Josh rebounds and goes up strong. Blocked by Romeo. The whistle blows. Foul on Romeo.

That's three.

Romeo is irate.

"Emotions, emotions, emotions," Carr says. *"St. V is really getting taken out of their game."*

Official timeout. The Spartans, thanks to a 9–0 run, lead 44–37 with 3:58 left in the third quarter. LeBron works his fingers again, this time his left pinky. On Bacon's bench, meanwhile, the media timeouts are taking their toll.

"It felt like the timeouts would never end," Matt Reed said. "When we were making that push in the third quarter, I just kept saying, 'Don't let up! Don't think those guys can't come back! We shouldn't be happy with this lead! Keep putting it on 'em!'"

While some of the players grew anxious, Bill didn't.

"I remember how calm Brewer was," Monty said, his tone suggesting just how uncommon this occurrence truly was. "We had a lot of time in the huddle, but he was just so calm."

Josh comes out of the timeout and drills both free throws. The second one actually touches the rim on the way down. 46–37, Bacon. An 11–0 run.

Josh, who so often drew Bill's ire for his defense, slaps the court with both hands, imploring his teammates to dig in. Joyce feeds LeBron on the right block. LeBron backs Frank down again and spins left, where Monty stands, all 6-8 of him, hands straight up in the air. LeBron jumps toward the baseline and looks for a teammate. Romeo and Sekou loiter in the lane, but the pass goes right to Dave. Turnover.

"The other three guys are going to have to get involved for St. V to win this game," Carr says. *"Bacon is too solid as a unit."*

The Irish attempt an impromptu full-court trap, which Dave and Monty break. Frank takes a pass, dribbles to the lane and kicks it out to Beckham on the right wing for three. Way off. The ball bounces off the glass on the other side of the rim. Doesn't draw even a smidgen of iron. Several players have a crack at the rebound, but Beckham controls it and finds Josh on the wing. Josh delivers a touch-pass to Monty, who finds himself being guarded by Joyce, who is a foot shorter. Monty banks home an easy layin. The whistle blows. Count it. And-one. Foul on Joyce.

Bacon's bench and student section explode. Bill smacks his hands together. And Monty—the most stoic player on the team, the player who walked with his head down as if to be less noticeable—roars at his student section and punches the air with his right fist.

"People were still bringing that up months afterward," Monty said. "I would never show emotion, no matter what I was feeling. But when I made that, I just went nuts."

Bacon leads 48–37 with 3:26 left in the third. A 13–0 run. A double-digit lead.

Monty misses the free throw.

"Right now, I see two against five (with LeBron and Romeo)," Carr says. *"The other three guys for St. V are just out there. (They) have to get involved in this game. Otherwise, (SVSM has) no chance."*

LeBron dribbles upcourt and doesn't even think about passing. He attacks Frank on the right side of the paint, quickly backing him down, spinning right and putting up a floater that hits the back and front of the iron, bounces twice and falls through the net. The drought had ended. The deficit is back to single digits—48–39, Bacon, with 3:16 on the clock.

"Remember," Bannister cautions, *"(in) the first matchup between (these) two, Roger Bacon led by 10 points . . . before St. Vincent–St. Mary was able to rally back and win it."*

SVSM's Corey Jones subs for Sekou Lewis. Leonard subs for Beckham.

Josh drives past Chad Mraz, but Mraz pokes it away from behind. Joyce recovers. He feeds Romeo on the other end. Monty stands tall. Romeo misses. Frank rebounds. He drives past LeBron but gets swatted by Romeo.

SVSM has one basket in the last 3:30. The Spartans have outscored the Irish 30–18 in the paint and are out-rebounding them 21–13.

"One thing I've noticed about Bacon's defensive play, they don't go for the head-fake much; they stay flat on the ground," Carr says. *"They're forcing Romeo and LeBron to take tough shots over the top. . . . So far, their (defense) has been the key. . . . Again, everything is focused around the paint area for Roger Bacon."*

Josh drives on Mraz. Both players fall over. Offensive foul. SVSM ball. Joyce lobs one into the paint for LeBron, who takes it up strong. 48–41, Bacon.

Dave handles the pressure and zips a pass into Monty, who spins in the lane against Romeo. No good. Leonard grabs the board, hesitates and goes up with it against LeBron and Romeo. The whistle blows. Foul on LeBron, his third. Romeo is hopping mad.

"It looked like a good block," Carr says, watching the replay. "Ah, that was a tough call, but you get those in these type of games."

Leonard misses the first free throw but makes the second. 49–41, Bacon.

LeBron creates space against Frank, and Romeo delivers the ball for the layin. LeBron flexes and stomps defiantly back on defense. 49–43, Bacon.

Frank tries to answer. He drives baseline but travels. SVSM ball. Bill applauds the effort.

"St. V's is re-establishing themselves on the defensive end now," Carr says. "They're gonna make a ball game out of this, hopefully going into the fourth quarter."

The Irish fans rise to their feet. The comeback is on. A three would make it a one-possession game. Corey Jones feeds LeBron on the left block. LeBron takes one dribble and barrels into Frank, who falls to the floor. The whistle blows. Charge on LeBron.

That's four.

Frank has now picked up a combined five fouls on LeBron and Romeo and can sense LeBron's frustration mounting.

"In the third quarter, he was complaining about a call that was two or three possessions ago," Frank said. "I was like, 'Man, you can't keep complaining about that foul. That was three plays ago.' And he just politely told me to shut up. He told me to shut up, that I wasn't on his level and that I was shitty. And with that, I just kind of shut up. I was like, 'All right. You the man.' But I knew right then and there that I got in his head a little bit. I thought, 'Okay, he talks now. He wasn't talking before.' Once I heard that, I thought, 'We got him. He's done.'"

Well, not entirely done. Even with four fouls, LeBron stays in the game. Bacon, in typical GCL fashion, holds for the last shot. Tick tock, tick tock. LeBron walks past the key to greet Dave, who, 30 feet from the basket, looks at Bill and waits for the signal. With 13 seconds to go, Bill makes a circular motion with his right hand. *Go.* Dave, nine inches shorter than LeBron, takes one dribble left, fakes another dribble left—freezing LeBron for a split second—and then crosses over to his right. Austin Carr *ooohs*. So do people in the stands, incredulous at what they've just witnessed.

Dave Johnson has just crossed over LeBron James.

Dave has a step. He scurries into the lane; the defense collapses. He finds Beckham wide open for a 10-foot jumper on the baseline. The ball splashes the net and turns it inside out. 51–43, Bacon. Less than nine seconds remain in the third quarter.

The clock keeps ticking. LeBron gathers the ball and in-bounds to Joyce with four seconds left. Surely, SVSM won't get a shot off. Surely, the score will remain 51–43. Surely, Bacon will lead by eight entering the final frame. Surely.

But then it happens.

The magic of LeBron happens.

Joyce takes one dribble and gives it right back to LeBron. Three seconds. LeBron dribbles once and takes two steps—which, with his long stride, carry him from one end of the circle at halfcourt all the way to the other. The ball leaves LeBron's hands with 1.2 seconds left. He is eight feet inside the timeline.

Marty Bannister has the call.

"Good if it goes . . ."

The shot sails in the air, rising and rising before falling and falling. Irish players and fans watch in wonder and freeze as if pleading with a basketball deity. You can see it in their faces. *If only one basketball prayer ever gets answered*, they seem to be thinking, *please, let it be this one.*

The shot hits the window. And then, the unthinkable.

". . . IT GOES!"

No way. No *fucking* way.

LeBron James just banked in what was essentially a halfcourt shot. Frank, in pure disbelief, grabs his head with both hands. The lead is down to five, 51–46. The arena boils to a fever-pitch frenzy. LeBron marches to the sideline, where the Irish bench, injected with life, surrounds him and pays homage. On the Bacon sideline, Tim, Newt and Matt Reed, among others, rush the court to greet their teammates and lift their spirits.

"Hey! That's all right! That's all right! We still got the lead! One more quarter! One more quarter!"

But Dave, Beckham and the others are deflated. They're in shock. They walk in a stunned stupor. Like a dazed fighter trying to find his corner, Frank wobbles right past Newt. He doesn't even see him.

"The Chosen One chooses to go long distance and finish the third period!" says Bannister, animated.

The shot was shades of the CJ game—only worse. The lead went from eight to five in a flash. But it was more than the score; it was the momentum; it was the psychological impact. The guy who's supposed to be the best prep player ever just hit a halfcourt shot. In the state final. When his team needed it the most. Like it was nothing.

"I would go see LeBron play all these games when I was in Akron," Marcus Smith said. "And I'd sit there and think, 'Why is he shooting all these halfcourt shots in warmups? Why is he in the front row of the stands shooting with one hand?' I thought, 'He's cocky, he's this, he's that.' Well, he hit one in the state final. When that shot went in, the whole crowd was just, *oooooh*. You could feel it."

SVSM scored 16 points in the third quarter. LeBron scored 11 of them. He assisted on another two. He has personally outscored Bacon 9–3 over the last 3:16.

On the SVSM bench, there is instant belief. Guys are smiling. Guys are laughing. Some put their arms around each other. *Things are going to be fine*, their body language suggests. *We're only down five with eight minutes to go—and hey, we got LeBron. We got this.*

Even the announcers can sense it.

"The Chosen One answers the call (and) gets it to go down—bang!" Carr says, amazed at the replay. "And what's interesting about that shot—that was his only jump shot of the quarter. He's changed his game. He knows where he has to go now. He has to go to the well now to make it happen."

Eight minutes remain. It's anybody's game.

FOURTH QUARTER

LeBron sits and waits for the fourth quarter to start, patient yet jittery. He works his fingers again.

Bacon opens with the ball and goes to Frank. LeBron hounds him. He drapes against him like a curtain. It's all clean, but LeBron's urgency and intensity have magnified. Frank passes to Dave, who finds Monty in the lane for a turnaround hook. Air-ball. Beckham grabs the ball and kicks it out to Dave for three. Brick. Monty and Mraz give chase. They both hit the deck as the ball darts out of bounds like a squirrel pursuing a nut. Possession stays with Bacon. Mraz is visibly frustrated at the call. Romeo is hopping mad—literally—once more. LeBron pleads his case with an official but to no avail. Frank runs to Monty and helps his teammate to his feet.

The replay indicates the ball bounced off Monty's left shin. The refs got it wrong. SVSM is upset—and justifiably so—but something is becoming increasingly obvious.

"Right now," Carr says, "St. V's is getting a little bit too worried about what the referees are (calling)."

Beckham in-bounds to Josh, who takes Mraz left to the hole. Josh extends his right arm into Mraz's belly to create separation. Mraz falls down. Offensive foul. Bill can't believe it. He grabs his head with both hands and does a near-360. He shakes his head and smiles before applauding Josh's effort.

Bacon has nine offensive rebounds. SVSM has three.

The Irish pass around the perimeter and wait for LeBron to get open. He receives the ball from Joyce in front of the SVSM bench. Beckham gets in his stance as Romeo comes with another screen. LeBron splits Beckham and Monty. Frank rotates over to take a charge, and he and LeBron collide as the running floater is released. Both players hit the floor. The shot is short. Rebound Josh. LeBron sits under the basket and stares at an official, both arms in the air pleading for a foul. No call. Play on.

Bacon's possession lasts six seconds. Josh bounce-passes to Monty. Monty outlets to Dave. Dave takes one dribble and finds Beckham streaking past Bacon's bench to the bucket. Beckham takes one dribble and lays it in. The play was seamless. 53–46, Bacon, 6:53 to go.

"Bacon is not wasting any time getting down the floor!" Carr says. "You cannot be late. . . .You cannot sit around and wait for this Bacon team! They will score!"

Joyce races up the floor and lobs one over Beckham and into LeBron, who pushes off with both hands to receive the entry pass. No foul is called. Frank looks to help and closes in on LeBron from behind. LeBron, two feet from the rim, jumps away from the basket and contorts his body against Frank's chest to avoid the block. The shot hits the glass, bounces around the entire rim and falls out. No good. LeBron has shanked a bunny and fallen to the floor in the process. Beckham rebounds.

LeBron rises from the deck, stares at an official and shrugs both arms as if to say, *"Where's the foul?"* There was none. LeBron slowly turns his head around to see the action unfolding. Beckham is already at halfcourt. He zips a pass across the floor to Dave, who immediately bounces one to Monty on the baseline. There's no one in front of him. Suddenly, out of nowhere, LeBron sprints into the paint. Monty pump fakes. LeBron, with four fouls, runs right by him. Doesn't even jump. He can't. He can't risk it. Monty with the layin. 55–46, Bacon, 6:31 to go.

"That's what's hurting (LeBron); that's what's hurting him," Carr reprimands. *"You cannot sit back and watch! You have to get down the floor and get involved!"*

Said Josh, "They weren't getting back on defense very well, so we tried to push the ball whenever we could."

Joyce brings it up. LeBron and Beckham jockey for position. LeBron slips. The whistle blows. Foul on the floor. Foul on Beckham, his fourth.

Bacon is shooting 56 percent from the field; SVSM is shooting 47.

Joyce lobs it into LeBron again. Beckham, Frank and Dave all converge. LeBron hits the layin anyway. He has scored 11 straight points for the Irish. 55–48, Bacon, 6:01 remaining.

LeBron, who wants the and-one, looks at a referee and sighs. He is again tardy getting back on defense, and Dave doesn't stop to wait for him. He pushes the ball and finds Josh on a run-out. Josh dribbles left, gets Sekou Lewis to bite on a pump fake and hits a five-foot jumper just outside the paint. 57–48, Bacon, 5:53 left.

"You see, now, again," Carr says, *"(SVSM) can't extend back, complaining to the referees about calls."*

Joyce presses forward and finds Mraz on the left wing for three. Short. Romeo rebounds and banks home a put-back. The whistle blows. And-one. Foul on Frank, his third. Leonard subs in for Beckham, who is saddled with four fouls. Romeo has 19 points and eight rebounds. He misses the free throw, but Sekou Lewis, with a four-inch height advantage, extends over Leonard for the rebound. He puts it up and in. It's a four-point trip for SVSM. Bacon's lead has once more been cut to five, 57–52.

Josh tries to respond, but his jumper from just inside the key falls short. Romeo rebounds.

"St. V's is starting to establish themselves in the paint now—something they didn't do the whole first half," Carr says.

SVSM whips the ball crisply around the floor. Romeo to Joyce, Joyce to Sekou, Sekou to Mraz, Mraz to LeBron. Layup. 57–54, Bacon. The Irish have scored six points in less than a minute, and just like that, it's a three-point game.

And there's still 4:46 to go.

Timeout Bacon. The Irish bench runs out onto the floor. The comeback is almost complete. Over on Bacon's bench, Bill looks worriedly at Brian Neal, Joe Corcoran and Tom Thompson. Each carries a *"Well, shit"* expression. Bill gathers his team and shouts "Rebound! Rebound!" But rebounding isn't the problem; LeBron and Romeo are. LeBron has 23 points and six assists. Romeo has 19 points and nine boards. They've shot a combined 18-of-31 (.581) from the floor and have 42 of SVSM's 54 points, including 22 of 24 in the second half. LeBron has scored 15 points since the break—12 on dunks or layups.

"I saw a sense of urgency in LeBron," Josh said. "They started posting him up and lobbing him the ball. There were several plays where he just turned around and had a layup. For a while there, we really couldn't stop him."

Bacon comes out of the timeout in desperate need of a bucket. Remember the Spartans' 13–0 run? They've been outscored 17–9 since.

Frank drives to the hole and puts up a floater. Miss. Rebound Mraz, who outlets to LeBron at the timeline. LeBron spots Romeo sprinting on the opposite side of the court in transition. He lofts a pass that sails over Romeo's outstretched right arm. Turnover SVSM.

The Spartans need offense from someone, anyone. They haven't scored in more than two minutes. SVSM is on a 6–0 run. Dave works a bounce pass into Monty. Romeo tries to poke the ball away but gets nothing but forearm. The whistle blows.

That's four on Romeo.

Bacon is in the bonus. Monty drills both ends of a one-and-one. 59–54, Bacon, 3:50 remaining.

Official timeout.

Bill has a decision to make. His team is up five with under four minutes to go. LeBron has done nothing but attack the paint the entire half. Beckham has the size to man LeBron, but he also has four fouls. What if Beckham fouls out? What if the game goes to overtime? Who would guard LeBron then? Frank only has three fouls, and to his credit, he's done a good job guarding LeBron on the perimeter and defending the drive. But Frank doesn't have the size to match LeBron down low. LeBron has a good four inches on him and is posting up lower and lower each possession.

What should Bill do?

His assistants wondered the same thing the previous night. They sat at the hotel bar, knowing full well this problem could arise. *What if Beckham gets hurt or in foul trouble? What if Frank gets hurt or in foul trouble? What if we reach a point in the game where both players, for whatever reason, can't guard LeBron? Who do we turn to?*

Well, there was Leonard. Leonard was tough and physical and would play LeBron hard, but he was giving up half a foot; he would get destroyed in the post. What about Tim McCoy? Same deal as Leonard. Tom Thompson said Tim McCoy might have been the grittiest defender Roger Bacon ever had, but the size discrepancy between Tim, at 5-11, and LeBron, at 6-7, was too great to ignore. There was Newt. Newt was 6-3, 250 pounds. He had a low center of gravity. He could match wills with LeBron down low, no question, and if Newt fouled him, it was going to hurt. But there's no way that Newt, even with his quick feet, could hang with him on the perimeter; LeBron would drive right by him. The coaches briefly entertained the idea of a zone, but they decided almost immediately that would be a disaster. Joyce and

Mraz were dead-eye shooters, and Bacon didn't want to give LeBron and Romeo the ball in space.

And so, the question remained: What would Bacon do?

It was dead silent. Seconds became minutes. Not a word from anyone. And then, someone said it.

"How about Monty?"

Monty? The guy who got abused and outscored 30–0 by Torin Francis? The guy who Bill rode constantly for being soft, for ending up on the floor every other play? You mean that Monty? You want that Monty guarding LeBron James in the fourth quarter of the state final?

Yes. Yes, yes, yes. Monty was 6-8. He had the height to match LeBron in the post. As for the perimeter, if Monty got low and got wide and stuck his hands straight in the air, he could at least contest LeBron's jumpers. He would need help against the drive, no doubt; but truly, from a size perspective, Monty offered more than any Spartan not named Beckham or Frank. But it wasn't just size that Monty had.

Said Tom Thompson, "He had the heart of anybody."

The assistants had made their choice. Monty would be third on the "Who's Guarding LeBron?" depth chart. And they made a point to tell this to no one—not Bill, not the players and certainly not Monty.

"If Brew would've heard that pregame," Creegs said, "he would've looked at each of us and pointed and said, 'You're nuts, you're nuts and you're fucking nuts.'"

As for Monty?

"Why would we tell Monty that before the game?" Tom Thompson asked. "We didn't want him to play with crap in his pants from the start."

But now, with less than four minutes to play and the state final hanging in the balance, Bill turns to his assistants for advice. And that's when they tell him: put Monty on LeBron.

"We're in the coaches' huddle," Thompson said, "and Brew goes, 'WHAT?' Then he turns around and goes, 'Monty, you're guarding LeBron.' Monty looks at me, looks at Brew and looks back at me. And I said, 'Get down, get wide, and contain.'"

Bacon breaks the huddle. Five players from each team return to the court.

Monty St. Clair walks straight up to LeBron James.

"I think that was the defining moment of our team," Thompson said. "We had never asked Monty to do anything like that."

Beckham switches to Romeo. Frank switches to Sekou. The Irish don't waste any time. They get the ball to LeBron at the top of the key. It's a clear mismatch.

Or is it?

LeBron sizes up Monty, who crouches like a wrestler, his arms dangling in a circular motion as if he's contemplating a takedown—or maybe even a hug. LeBron wants to drive left. You can see it. But Beckham collapses down on that side of the paint. LeBron looks right. There's Frank, camped out in the middle of the lane. Either way LeBron goes, he must split the defense to get to the hole—and if he charges, he's out of the game. So LeBron does the only thing he can do. He jacks up a contested three that hits the front of the rim. LeBron gathers his miss near the baseline, and Frank comes over to trap. LeBron turns left and sees Sekou on the perimeter. He tries to get him the ball, but Monty, with his long arms, tips the pass and steals it. LeBron and Sekou trap him in the corner. Monty has nowhere to go. So he turns to an official and does something that no Bacon player has done all season.

He calls timeout.

Bill hated when his players did that, and as a rule, he strictly forbid it. Timeouts are a way to manage the game, Bill reasoned, and managing the game is the coach's responsibility. If you're a player, play. Let the coach worry about coaching. Whatever you do, don't you dare call timeout.

"Even if we were falling out of bounds, he never wanted us calling timeout," Monty said. "But I remember running over to the huddle after that play and Brewer looks at me and goes, 'Helluva call!'"

Indeed, Bill, the same coach who let a former player puke on the floor to avoid using a timeout, was going to let this one slide. It was Bacon's ball, 59–54, with 3:18 to go.

"I really like the way Bacon's defense collapses on you when you attack the basket," Carr says. "They don't give you many angles to get rid of the basketball. They are a solidly coached team, especially on that defensive end."

It's a tense game, one seemingly destined to go down to the wire. Neither team has been in many close games this year, but Bacon has fared better in tight situations. In games decided by five points or fewer,

SVSM was 2–2 with a pair of one-point losses. Bacon was 4–1, the only loss coming against CJ.

The Spartans come out of the timeout and break SVSM's full-court press. Frank passes to Monty at the free-throw line. Monty turns to kick it out to Dave, but the pass never makes it. LeBron tips it as soon as it leaves Monty's hands. He collects the ball at halfcourt with no one between him and the rim.

Showtime.

"I threw a terrible pass," Monty said. "That's the worst feeling. I felt awful about that."

It's back to a one-possession game—59–56, Bacon, with three minutes left.

Dave single-handedly breaks the press once more. Frank drives the lane, draws the defense and kicks it to Beckham on the right baseline. Beckham beelines toward the bucket as Romeo comes over to challenge. Beckham jumps. Romeo jumps. Contact. The shot is blocked. The whistle blows. Foul on Romeo, his fifth. It has happened.

Romeo Travis has fouled out.

The junior power forward cannot believe the call. He stands gaping at an official. His eyes widen in anger and astonishment. He acts as if he will slam the ball but thinks better of it. He untucks his jersey amid the theatrics and appears to mouth the words, "That's bullshit, man!" He stomps sourly off the court, his temper anything but tepid.

"He was going nuts," Monty said. "I still remember that look with his mouth open. He was just so shocked."

Looking at the replay, Romeo got the ball—but he got a whole lot of wrist first. The call appeared legit. Either way, Romeo is gone with 2:45 left in the game. He exits with 19 points and nine rebounds—this after scoring just three points against Bacon during the regular season. He paces along the Irish bench with the bottom of his jersey folded over his chest and stuffed into his mouth.

"Well, he had talked . . . going into this game (about how) in the first matchup he felt he played too passively, and (how) he was developing a mean streak," Carr says. "Well, unfortunately, he is done for the day."

It's a huge loss for SVSM. Romeo scored seven points in the second half. Aside from a layup by Sekou Lewis off a missed free throw, Romeo is the only Irish player other than LeBron who has scored in the second half.

Sian replaces Romeo. Beckham bricks the first free throw but hits the second. 60–56, Bacon, 2:45 to go.

LeBron goes to work at the top of the key with Monty dogging him. He drives left toward the paint and kicks it out to Mraz in the corner—this after catching Monty with a right elbow to the sternum. Monty falls down. LeBron follows. No call. Play on. SVSM works the ball to LeBron at the top of the key once more. This time he drives right, and the help defender never comes. LeBron absorbs the contact from Monty and banks it home. The whistle blows. Foul on Monty, his first. 60–58, Bacon, with 2:17 to go.

This is the closest the Irish have been since trailing 38–37 midway through the third quarter.

With 27 points on 12-of-19 shooting, LeBron heads to the line to pull SVSM within one. There's pep in his step and gusto in his gait. He looks determined, unstoppable. But LeBron, a 59-percent foul shooter, misses the free throw. Monty grabs the board in traffic and outlets to Frank. Joyce and Sekou trap immediately, as Frank looks in vain for an open teammate. He takes off to break the press himself and dribbles from the left corner of the baseline all the way across the court and up the right sideline. He gets past Joyce and Sekou, as LeBron approaches on his left shoulder to challenge for the ball. Just before Frank crosses halfcourt, LeBron reaches around Frank's back to poke the ball away, which he does. But LeBron doesn't graze even a shred of leather. It's all wrist. The whistle blows.

Foul. Foul on LeBron, his fifth. LeBron James has just fouled out.

Frank picks up the ball with his left hand and sprints downcourt with his right arm in the air, his fingers in a fist. He looks like Desmond Howard about to hit pay-dirt and do the Heisman.

"I remember that like it was yesterday," Frank said. "Running down the court like we won the game even though there was still time left. If LeBron was gone, I knew right away we would win. But then I turned around. I couldn't believe it."

No foul. Ten-second violation.

Frank is stunned. So are others. People in the stands thought LeBron had just picked up his fifth foul; the announcers thought LeBron had just picked up his fifth foul; even LeBron thought he had just picked up his fifth foul. But he didn't. Ten-second violation. Was it really? It's close. LeBron shot the free throw with 2:17 remaining. Monty controlled the rebound just before the clock ticked down to 2:16. By the time the clock keeper heard the ensuing whistle and stopped the clock, it read 2:07. Exactly 10 game seconds had elapsed between the free-throw attempt and the stoppage of play.

LeBron peers into the crowd, puts his left hand over his heart and takes a deep breath. His eyes bulge. Another deep breath. He knows that was a close one. Bill stands on the sideline, shaking his head in protest. LeBron got wrist, no doubt, but the 10-second call either came before the foul or during it. Either way, LeBron is saved.

Timeout SVSM. Bacon still leads 60–58.

Out of the timeout, Chad Mraz walks the ball past the timeline and passes to LeBron in the corner. With less than two minutes to go, Beckham is back on him, four fouls and all. LeBron dribbles toward the elbow and finds Mraz to the left of the key for three. Mraz lets it fly, hoping to give the Irish their first lead since it was 37–35. The entire SVSM bench rises as the shot is in the air. No good. Players fight for the rebound before Monty takes control. The whistle blows. Foul on Sian.

But wait. There's something wrong. Monty grabs his right shoulder and grimaces. He schleps gingerly to the foul line, his right shoulder dangling three inches lower than his left. Monty doesn't know it, but he has just sustained a tear in his shoulder. Will he even be able to shoot the free throws? He's in obvious pain, severe pain, but he ignores it. An entire season of practices at Fogarty has taught him to ignore it.

"Toward the end of the year before the playoffs, we did juniors versus seniors," Monty said. "That was the most heated practice. We played two eight-minute quarters, and the juniors won. No fouls. I still remember that. One of my favorite wins ever—and it wasn't even an official game. We went at it. Beckham beat the shit out of me."

Beckham. Newt. Matt Reed. Monty had endured pain and punishment every day for five months. He endured it every day for this moment. It was the state final. And there was no way he was leaving this game.

Monty has 14 points and three rebounds. A 73-percent foul shooter, he is 4-of-5 from the stripe on the day and hits the first free throw. 61–58, Bacon, 1:54 left. Monty misses the second, but Beckham bats the ball right back to him. Bacon passes around the perimeter in a controlled frenzy as the Irish trap aggressively. Franks flips up a shot from four feet. No good. Josh boards it and goes right back up. The whistle blows. The ball hits the back iron and bounces harmlessly to the floor. There is a collective "*OHHH!*" from the crowd. Foul on Sian.

"*They're giving up too much out front,*" Carr says of SVSM. "*They have to be focused more on what's happening around the basket. That's the way the whole game has gone. Right now, they're trying (for) too many steals (and) getting out of position. And Phillips goes in strong. Good second effort (by Hausfeld). That's what Bacon's been doing all (day)—going after the ball, getting second chances. (And Hausfeld) goes to the line for two.*"

Bacon has out-rebounded the Irish 31–17, including 13–5 on the offensive glass. Josh hits both free throws. 63–58, Bacon, 1:30 to go. The Spartans have scored their last six points at the foul line.

The Irish, meanwhile, need to score. Time is running out. Joyce pushes the tempo and passes to LeBron in the corner. Beckham lunges for the steal but arrives a step late.

Oh boy.

LeBron accepts the pass, turns and goes baseline. Frank rotates down to help, but LeBron treats him like a prop in a dunk contest, jumping over him and flushing it home with two hands. 63–60, Bacon, 1:23 left.

"*LeBron James glides to the baseline AND GOES AIRBORNE and finishes with a big-time flourish!*" Bannister exclaims.

Bacon breaks the trap. Frank drives to the paint and dumps it off to Beckham. LeBron challenges the shot. The ball hits the backboard and bounces three-quarters of the way around the rim. No good. LeBron boards it, dribbles upcourt and finds Corey Jones in the left corner. Jones gives it up to Joyce on the wing. Joyce penetrates the lane, but Frank reaches around to poke the ball away. It bounces right to Beckham, who chucks it toward Frank, already approaching halfcourt on the run-out. He beats Mraz to the hoop, takes two awkward dribbles with his left hand and goes up with his right.

"I remember going down there and thinking, 'Don't dribble off your foot. Don't dunk the ball. Just go and lay it up,'" Frank recalled. "I could barely jump. I felt like I had weights on my ankles."

It's a huge bucket. The lead is back to five. 65–60, Bacon. Forty seconds remain.

The Irish push quickly. Time is running out. LeBron gets the ball on the right baseline. Beckham bodies him. Monty looks on from the paint. He knows what's coming. LeBron spins away from the baseline, takes two hard dribbles with his left hand, puts his head down and barrels into the lane. Monty is there. He's been there, waiting, frozen like a statue, arms straight up in the air. LeBron bulldozes right through him and flips up a shot. Monty splats to the floor as if cut down by a sniper. The whistle blows. The shot falls.

LeBron James has just fouled out.

Only he hasn't.

Blocking foul on Monty. And-one.

The Irish bench jumps and claps. Bacon is in utter disbelief. The 10-second call could have gone either way; this was a blatant charge.

"Could have been an offensive foul there!" Carr says in a how-did-they-not-call-a-charge tone.

"It sure could have been!"

"Could have been an offensive foul there!" Carr repeats, still stunned.

Monty is speechless.

"He did exactly what I thought he'd do," Monty said. "And I didn't even flop. He rammed me over. Worst call I've ever seen."

A raging torrent of boos flood the floor. Every Spartan player, coach and fan in attendance is livid. Some, however, understand.

"In the state final, you cannot take out LeBron James," Jerome Harris said. "You cannot have him go out like that on a charge. It has to be a clear defensive foul. Everybody's here to see him. No one was there to see us. They're here to see LeBron James. I'm okay with that non-call."

Said Matt Reed, "That was a charge, but who's gonna call that? Who's gonna put the best player in America on the bench?"

LeBron stands at the foul line, both hands on his knees. Sian and Sekou are on opposite blocks, waiting for the ref to give LeBron the ball for his crack at the three-point play. The Irish grow impatient. Why the delay? Well, Bacon's five starters—Josh, Beckham, Frank, Monty and Dave—huddle smack dab in the middle of the paint, their arms around each other. They break on their own terms when they're ready, only after saying what they need to say to each other.

LeBron stands at the foul line and takes a few get-in-rhythm dribbles. He has scored 31 points on 14-of-21 shooting. He flicks his wrist. Thirty-two. 65–63, Bacon, 32 seconds to go.

Beckham in-bounds to Dave, and Dave gives it right back. Beckham dribbles twice and finds Josh at halfcourt. The Irish need to foul to stop the clock. Josh dribbles all the way to the baseline and kicks it back out to Dave. The whistle blows. Foul on Joyce.

Dave Johnson is going to the line for two.

There's irony in this moment. Dave, the shortest guy on the team, the guy who opponents would sometimes disregard entirely and dare to shoot, the guy who's had the same basketball role all his life—pass, pass, pass; facilitate, facilitate, facilitate—walks to the foul line, more than 36,000 eyes staring straight into his core and waiting to see if he can, of all things, put the ball in the basket.

How's that for poetic justice?

The game, to this point, has been quintessential Dave. He's played all 32 minutes. He has three assists. He's taken just three shots. He's scored just two points. And against constant full-court pressure, he hasn't turned the ball over once.

Not once.

These are his first free throws of the game. He steps to the line, a 63-percent foul shooter. He has a chance to increase the lead to four, to make it a two-possession game, to bring Bacon to the brink.

It's all on him.

He dribbles twice. The light reflects brightly off his bald head. He takes a deep breath and lets the first one go. It hits the back iron and bounces right to LeBron, who catches the ball and underhands it to a ref. Dave sighs in disappointment. The pressure has mounted. He needs this next one. Bacon needs this next one. Dave dribbles, looks up and stares at the rim. He lets it go. Bottoms. 66–63, Bacon, with 22.5 seconds remaining.

Timeout Bacon.

The Irish have a choice to make. Do they go for the quick two and foul, or do they try to tie the game with a three? Either way, everyone knows who is taking the next shot.

"*. . . Down the stretch, The Chosen One has stepped up for Akron St. Vincent–St. Mary to get them back in the game,*" Bannister says.

"*Well, that's why he's become The Chosen One—because he knows when and how to (win) the game. What I'm surprised at, though, is why he waited so long to get himself going. . . . He should have been (going to the basket) in the first quarter. It might not have come down to this type of situation.*"

All five Bacon starters have scored in the fourth quarter. In fact, Josh, Beckham, Frank, Monty and Dave have each scored at least one of Bacon's last seven points. SVSM, on the other hand, has been a little more forthcoming with its strategy; LeBron has scored 11 straight.

In Bacon's huddle, Bill strategizes with his players.

"Our message was simple," Brian Neal said. "Beckham's got LeBron. If they set a ball screen, guard it the way we always guard it— hedge it and push him and let the guy get through and help on the backside. And we said, 'Be ready to contest because LeBron's going to shoot.' Why would anybody else shoot it?"

In the stands, SVSM's comeback has taken a toll on Bacon's parents. For the entire fourth quarter, the clock couldn't have ticked any slower.

"I was petrified," Tim McCoy, Sr., said. "It was one of those things where you thought, 'We got this.' And then the next thing you know, they're down by three with 22 seconds left. And you just know LeBron's gonna take the last shot. You just know it. He's gonna bring the ball down, and he's gonna shoot it."

The players take the floor. The Irish prepare to in-bound.

"I remember coming out of the timeout, and that possession was everything," Monty said. "You're there. As cliché as it sounds, you go all year long, and if you get a stop here, you win the state championship. I still remember that feeling walking out of that timeout. It was probably the biggest possession of my career."

Bacon trots out its starting five. Bill got to the state final with these five guys, and he was going to win it or lose it with these five guys. All except Beckham have played every second. The Irish trot out LeBron, of course, along with Sekou Lewis and a trio of deadly three-point shooters—Chad Mraz, Dru Joyce and Corey Jones.

Mraz waits calmly on the baseline for an official to hand him the ball. LeBron is five feet away. Beckham, as he has all game, plants right up against him.

They are the only players within 40 feet of the baseline.

Beckham, if he wanted, could let LeBron catch the pass and bring the ball up the floor unmolested. But that wouldn't be any fun. He sticks to LeBron like honey on a hive and stares, his lips two inches from LeBron's cheek.

"I was just being a pest," Beckham said. "I was just in his face, in his ear, not even saying anything. Just annoying him."

LeBron breaks toward Mraz and accepts the handoff. He dribbles the ball upcourt through his own lane, as Beckham backs off a bit. Nineteen seconds. LeBron crosses halfcourt. Seventeen seconds. Beckham greets LeBron near the key. Josh guards Joyce. Monty takes Sekou. Dave gets Mraz. Frank sticks Corey Jones.

All five Spartans have at least one eye fixed on LeBron.

Since in-bounding the ball, Mraz has jogged up the right sideline and past both benches. He curls along the baseline and under the basket as Corey Jones sets a screen on Dave. Fifteen seconds. Mraz, who pointed at Corey for the pick, sprints out beyond the arc near the left corner.

LeBron sees it the whole way.

Chad Mraz, perhaps SVSM's best spot-up shooter, is going to be open for three—near the corner, no less. His money spot. So LeBron, despite scoring 11 consecutive points for the Irish, passes the ball. He fires it before Mraz has even reached the three-point line. The ball arrives almost perfectly, a little higher than chest high. Fourteen seconds. Dave goes right, then left, and fights around Corey Jones' pick. He scurries out to the three-point line to meet Mraz, who catches the pass and rises for the shot all in one motion. Dave takes two strides and lunges, his left arm extending as high and as far as his 5-10 body allows. When Mraz reaches the apex of his jump, there is the slightest hesitation, the slightest hiccup, as his upper body, fearing the blocked shot, fades backward at a slight angle.

But he gets the shot away.

The ball is sailing, sailing. This would tie the game. This could force overtime. This would erase what was once an 11-point lead for Roger Bacon. The Irish bench rises as one. Dave's momentum sends him toward the corner and out of bounds. Mraz lands and keeps his balance as he backpedals three steps out of his control. Dru Joyce stands on the right baseline. Corey Jones fades to the right wing. LeBron watches from beyond the foul line. Only Sekou Lewis crashes the paint for a potential Irish rebound. Monty follows him, with Frank camped out to his left and Josh camped out to his right. The shot is falling, falling. It clanks off the back iron and bounces right. Sekou fights for position, but he doesn't have a prayer. It's three-on-one. By the time he has cleared space to jump, Josh has already skied for the board, snatched it with his right hand and secured it with his left. Sekou reaches in and fouls Josh immediately.

"And to think, Josh of all people got the rebound," Monty said. "Brewer was always on him for not rebounding well."

The ball stutters out of Josh's hands after the foul and rolls directly to Dru Joyce, who scoops it up on the right block. Disgusted, the junior point guard winds up and chucks a fastball toward the basket like an unruly fan refusing to keep a home run hit by the visiting team. The ball hits the rim and bounces out of bounds. The whistle blows.

Technical foul.

Bacon will get four free throws—two for the foul on Josh, two for the technical on Joyce—and retain possession of the basketball. 8.9 seconds remain.

"For all intents and purposes, that put the nail in the coffin, I think, for St. V," Carr says.

Bacon's starters float down the floor, grinning.

"That's when you realize, 'Oh, shit, we just won the state title,'" Monty said. "But you can't really celebrate yet."

Bacon's student section glows and claps expectantly. Elsewhere in the stands, Peggy clutches her rosary and cries.

"Mommy, why are you crying?" Abby asks.

"It's over!" Peggy says. "Daddy's team won!"

Abby looks at the scoreboard.

"Mommy, there's still time left," she says, confused. "And why are you crying?"

Yes, the final 8.9 seconds appear mere formality, but Bill doesn't act like it. With perspiration staining his light blue dress shirt, he motions for his players to gather around. "Come here!" he shouts angrily. Bill, deadly serious, strategizes with his five starters, none of whom is smiling anymore.

In the regular-season meeting, SVSM put the game away at the foul line in the final minute. Dru Joyce, in fact, hit six free throws in the final 67 seconds that night. Now, with 8.9 seconds left in the state final, Joyce crouches by his bench with his right fist planted on the floor and his left hand covering his eyes. It's as if he can't bear to watch.

"*. . . A lack of composure down the stretch has hurt Akron St. Vincent–St. Mary,*" Bannister says.

Josh, a 77-percent foul shooter, heads to the line with a chance to seal the state championship, just as his uncle, Don Hausfeld, did 20 years earlier. Josh looks calm, confident. For the day, he is a perfect 4-of-4 from the line. The lane is empty. Players, coaches, refs, fans and media all look on. Arms intertwine on Bacon's bench. Josh holds the ball softly in his hands and looks at it. He rotates it. He finds the right grip. He takes two dribbles. His legs move in rhythm with each bounce. He flicks his wrist. Nothing, absolutely nothing, but net. 67–63, Bacon.

It's a two-possession game.

Bacon's bench leans back as one. They stomp excitedly. Josh waves both hands in the air, imploring Bacon supporters for more noise. Josh flicks his wrist again. The second free throw falls short. Two more coming. LeBron works his nails. Josh stands at the line, practicing his form. He takes the ball. Two dribbles and a flick of the wrist. The stomps become more pronounced. 68–63, Bacon. A cocksure smile finds its way on Josh's face. He looks toward the bench and utters three words.

"State champs, baby."

Bacon's bench eats it up. They shout back at Josh. They can feel it. Two more dribbles. Josh rattles it home. 69–63, Bacon. The Spartans retain the ball. 8.9 seconds left. Nate and Tim grin. Newt pumps his fist.

They know.

"(Bacon) played a solid game, a well-coached game; they weren't afraid of LeBron," Carr says. "I'm just surprised LeBron waited so long to get himself going. He should have been playing like this in the first quarter. . . . He acted more like he was bored and not really into the game until he absolutely had to (be). And you can't pull those kinds of miracles out of your hat all the time, even though you are The Chosen One."

Beckham tries to in-bound to Dave, but Mraz gets a hand on the ball and tips it out of bounds. 7.2 seconds left. Beckham lobs a pass to Josh in the backcourt. Joyce tries to foul, but Josh eludes it. Six seconds. He dribbles and passes to Monty. Four seconds. Monty dribbles once and passes to Frank. Two seconds. The Irish have stopped playing. Frank drives the baseline and throws down a two-handed jam as time expires.

71–63, Roger Bacon.

Bill, his assistants, the Scrappers—they all storm the court. Thirteen Spartans leap, hands in the air, pumping their fists in jubilee. Newt hoists Frank; Matt Reed jumps in Beckham's arms and screams.

A Scrapper lifts a starter.

A starter lifts a Scrapper.

Cork wraps his arms around Bill's neck and jumps up and down. Josh joins them for a three-way embrace.

LeBron works his nails again.

In Bacon's student section, bedlam. An army of teenagers exalt and shout like they've just won the lottery. They beam as if not believing what they've just witnessed. The Spartans push each other at midcourt, excitement and adrenaline surging through their bodies as they line up to shake hands with SVSM.

"Cincinnati Roger Bacon has upset Akron St. Vincent–St. Mary and won the Division II state championship," Bannister says. ". . . (Bacon) said coming into the game, 'We're not intimidated. We're not afraid. We're going to play our game—and play it to win.' And they did it today."

The Spartans gallop to their student section. Dave gets a kiss on the lips. Another girl plants one on Josh's bald head. Beckham, cheeks still red and puffy, stands amid his fellow students. Hugs and high-fives all around. Josh high-fives Bill. Matt Reed hugs Brian Neal.

The OHSAA arranges for each trophy presentation. One by one, the Irish receive their runner-up medals. Chad Mraz cries. Dru Joyce sobs. He uses his headband as a blindfold. LeBron receives his medal, still somewhat dazed. Romeo Travis receives his and immediately removes it. Sian Cotton consoles Dru. Bench players hug Chad Mraz. Coach Joyce accepts the runner-up trophy, disappointed yet gracious.

Tim McCoy, who as a senior played in every game except this one, is the first Spartan to receive his medal. Marcus Smith follows.

Then Nate Wyrick. Zach Gruenwald. Leonard Bush. Kevin Waymire. Jon Newton. Matt Reed.

"They never panicked; they stayed solid," Carr says. *"They had no fear of The Chosen One."*

Josh Hausfeld. Dave Johnson. Monty St. Clair. Beckham Wyrick. Frank Phillips. Arron Ranford. Brian Neal. Tom Thompson. Bobby Holt. Mitch Perdrix. Joe Corcoran.

Bill Brewer, holding Maddy, with Katie and Abby by his side.

The Spartans lift the state championship trophy and pose for photos, each player with an index finger pointing toward the rafters.

Afterward, Josh embraced Emily. Their childhood dream had come true. They won state. Josh worked his whole life for this. The boy born and raised in St. Bernard; the boy reared on Pistol Pete videos, UNC dreams and pickup basketball at the Pavilion; the boy who always knew he would attend Roger Bacon; the boy whom Bill Brewer rode harder than anyone else yet still loved; the boy whose ankles betrayed him but who made all-state anyway; the boy who wanted more than anything to deliver a state championship to his hometown; the boy who 14 days earlier lost one of his best friends and who seven days earlier couldn't be there to bury her—for him, this was his time. This was his moment.

"It was a feeling of happiness," Josh said, "that up until that point, I had never felt."

Josh, who was named the tournament's Most Valuable Player, dominated the state final the only way he knew how: quietly, subtly. For all the talk about LeBron—who he was, what he could do, who would guard him—Josh played the best game of his career on March 23, 2002. Who led Bacon with 23 points, including 14 in the second half? Josh Hausfeld. Who led with seven rebounds? Josh Hausfeld. With six assists? Josh Hausfeld. With five turnovers? Josh Hausfeld, of course. But that didn't matter. For four years, Roger Bacon took the best and worst of this quiet boy from St. Bernard, and on a March Saturday in 2002, his best, as it almost always was, was worth far more than his worst.

"Those first few seasons, he had unbelievable highlight moments," Brian Neal said. "But to me, the character of Josh Hausfeld—despite the fact that he was injured, despite the fact that he was hurting all year—when it mattered most, he was just great."

Josh didn't do what he did that day just for himself; he did it for his teammates; he did it for Bill and the assistant coaches; he did it for his family, for his friends, for St. Bernard. He did it for Meg.

"I didn't win state," Emily said. "But when Josh did it two weeks after my best friend died, it was amazing. He's a very motivational person—spiritual, you could say. With Meg passing and him being so dedicated and working his whole life at basketball, this was it. *I'm gonna win state. I'm gonna do whatever I can to help my team win.* Meg dying killed him inside. But instead of being sad and giving up, he took it the other way. *I'm gonna do this for her. We're gonna do this for her.* I know she was in the back of his mind every sprint he ran, every layup he hit. That's just Josh."

And it wasn't just him. It was Beckham Wyrick, the trash-talking SOB who had the courage and audacity to forearm LeBron; to crowd him and mock him and jaw with him the whole game; to counter jabs with haymakers; to never give homage—to never give homage for a second—and to instead demand it himself. It was Frank Phillips, the transfer who came to Roger Bacon in search of something better; who came in search of a chance, a chance to play with his best friend and to compete and win; who was enticed by the promise of a state title and who brought wildness and charm to a tough-minded team that accepted him regardless of race, background or any other distinction of inconsequence. It was Monty St. Clair, who toughened before Bill's eyes, who screamed when he got the and-one, who guarded LeBron when teammates and coaches looked to him for help, who injured his shoulder and never once considered leaving the game. It was Dave Johnson, the perceived weak link who sacrificed, who willingly took a back seat to every other starter, who made the free throw when it counted, who played 52 minutes in the state tournament and didn't turn the ball over once—*not once*—and whose end-of-game defense altered Chad Mraz's final shot just enough. It was Tim McCoy. It was Jon Newton. It was Leonard Bush. It was Marcus Smith. It was Matt Reed. It was every Scrapper who did what he was told, who never complained, who sought only to make the team better in any way he could.

It was them. It was all of them. This was their moment.

As the players celebrated, Bill made his way to the end of Bacon's bench and sat down, alone. The weight of a decade had been lifted from his shoulders and was soon replaced by the validation he had so desperately sought—validation for a coach who inherited a program without a pulse and injected life into it; a coach who three times came within one game of Columbus and who three times came up empty; a coach who kept at it despite the near-misses and the second-guesses and the *what-ifs*; a coach who changed, who adapted, who stayed the course and finally broke through; a coach who made his players adjust to him but who also adjusted to his players; a coach who loved the game—who lived it and breathed it and demanded that everyone around him do the same; a coach who never stopped believing; a coach who always dared to dream. On that day, as morning segued into afternoon, everything that he had ever hoped for or aspired to be came true. Aside from his wife, aside from his daughters, aside from his close friends and family, nothing in his life had ever meant more or would mean as much again. Finally, he had done it. Finally, he went the distance.

Bill Brewer was baring all.

CHAPTER FOURTEEN

THE AFTERMATH

Whenever Roger Bacon accomplished something of note athletically, Joe Corcoran had T-shirts made to commemorate the achievement. District titles. Regional titles. This, that and the other. The day before the state semifinals, Cork and Bids were exercising at the team hotel when Bacon's cheerleading moderator, April Taylor, walked in holding trash bags.

"Bob Meyer told me to give you this," she said.

Cork was confused. Bob was Cork's go-to guy for T-shirts, but Cork hadn't ordered anything. He got off the treadmill, opened the bags and was shocked by what he saw: state championship shirts and hats. Cork hadn't asked for these, but Bob made them on a whim and had them sent as a vote of confidence in Bacon. Cork appreciated the gesture, but part of him panicked.

"Bids, you need to put these in your car," he said. "We can't let Bill or the players see these."

Bids put the bags in his car and hid them in the arena the morning of the state final. After the technical foul on Dru Joyce, Bids, knowing the game was over, left Bacon's bench, retrieved the bags and brought them out onto the court. The Spartans sported the shirts and hats as they received their state championship medals, and more than a few spectators that day couldn't help but be amazed by one fact:

Roger Bacon knew it was going to win.

• • • •

IN THE SECONDS FOLLOWING the final buzzer, commentator Marty Bannister made a seemingly innocuous, irrefutable statement—that Cincinnati Roger Bacon had upset Akron St. Vincent–St. Mary. Technically speaking, Bacon's 71–63 victory was an upset in every sense of the word. The Irish were ranked No. 1 in the state; Bacon was ranked sixth. The Irish were ranked thirteenth nationally—this after losing a handful of games to other ranked teams toward the end of the regular season—while Bacon didn't even crack the Top 25. That, by definition, is an upset.

But if the Spartans knew they were going to win, was it? Even without the shirts and hats, several Bacon players called their parents the day before the game and said they were going to win, while Beckham made that fact known to strangers at a team dinner later that night. All of this begs the question:

Shouldn't underdogs be a little more guarded in their optimism?

Maybe. But then again, maybe the Spartans didn't feel like underdogs. It might sound crazy to just about everyone in the basketball world, then and now, but is it possible, is it even conceivable, that what occurred on the morning of March 23, 2002, at the Jerome Schottenstein Center in Columbus *wasn't* an upset? Is that even a question worth considering?

"To us, it wasn't an upset; we knew we were good enough to play with them, and everybody saw what happened," Beckham said. "But to everyone else who wasn't on our team and who didn't know how confident we were, then it was an upset for sure. They had LeBron—the superstar, the once-in-a-generation player—and we didn't have anybody who was going to go on to the NBA or anyone who was going to play in the ACC or Big East or Big Ten. But we had a bunch of guys who loved the game and who knew how to play with each other. That's a formula for success regardless of who you play."

Does that mean the Spartans think they could have beaten SVSM again?

"If we play them 10 times," Dave Johnson said, "it's probably 50–50."

Monty took it a step further.

"I think we would win seven or eight times out of 10," he said. "I honestly believe that. I think we were a much better team. I think they were more talented, but I think we would've beaten anybody. I think we were easily one of the best teams in the country that year. We just didn't have that McDonald's All-American. I wasn't surprised at what we did. I thought if we played well, we would win. To me, that's not an upset."

Bacon's players aren't alone. After the Spartans dismantled Beechcroft in the state semis, they settled into their seats to watch SVSM play Poland Seminary. That's when a strange thing happened. Two gentlemen approached Bacon's players and asked them to autograph their programs.

"They said, 'You guys are the only team from Ohio that's gonna beat LeBron James,'" Newt recalled the men saying. "'We're from Akron, but we know you're gonna beat them.'"

On March 24, 2002—the day after the game—the *Akron Beacon Journal* ran several stories pertaining to the Division II state final. One story described Bacon as a "physically superior opponent," "a big, strong, well-balanced team with interchangeable parts." As for the Irish, they were "a little too soft defensively" and "could not hit big buckets or rely on anyone other than James in crunch time." But the *Akron Beacon Journal* didn't stop there. It went on to say that "the better team won." Even Coach Joyce was quoted as saying the Spartans "were the better team."

Based on the box score, it's hard to argue with any of those statements. Bacon had four players reach double figures—Josh (23), Monty (15), Beckham (14) and Frank (13). SVSM had just two—LeBron (32) and Romeo (19), who combined for 51 of their team's 63 points—81 percent of the offensive output.

What happened to everybody else?

SVSM senior Sekou Lewis shot just 1-of-2 from the floor and finished with two points. Chad Mraz and Dru Joyce, meanwhile, took six and five shots, respectively. All 11 of their combined attempts were from outside the arc, and neither scored after halftime. In fact, LeBron scored 24 of SVSM's 33 second-half points, including 13 of 17—not to mention the final 11—in the fourth quarter

In short, Bacon was more balanced.

"We know they had a great player," Bill told the *Cincinnati Enquirer*, "but we thought we had a better team."

Looking beyond the individual scoring breakdown, one fact—one odd, downright eerie fact—suggests Bill's assessment was accurate: In both the state semifinal and the final, LeBron James scored 32 points on 14-of-21 shooting to go with six assists. In the semis, he had 24 points in the first half and eight in the second; in the final, he had eight points in the first half and 24 in the second. In essence, he was statistically identical in both games. Yet the Irish won one of those games by 40 and lost the other by eight.

How? Why? What was the difference?

"They had a player; we had a team," Newt said. "With LeBron, they had more talent. Without LeBron, it's us by far."

Said Matt Reed, "Take the matchups, guy for guy. You think Joyce is gonna beat Frank Phillips? You think Mraz is gonna match up to Josh Hausfeld? Take away Beckham and Monty; take away LeBron and Romeo. Who are the better guys left? In a game of three-on-three, I'll take Frank, Josh and Dave over Sekou, Mraz and Joyce every day of the week."

Delving deeper, the Spartans owned the boards, out-rebounding SVSM 32–18, including 13–5 on the offensive glass. They had more assists (16–13), more points in the paint (40–34), more fast-break points (16–4) and more points off turnovers (21–10).

And then there were the free throws—the very thing to which Bacon attributed its regular-season loss. In the first half of the state final, free throws were almost dead even; SVSM was 3-of-4, while Bacon was 3-of-5. But in the second half, Bacon was 13-of 19, while SVSM was 2-of-4. For the game, Bacon was 16-of-24, and SVSM was 5-of-8. Thus, in the state final, the Irish attempted 32 fewer free throws than they did against Bacon in the regular season.

And yet, despite all the numbers that lean in Bacon's favor—some of them heavily—the Irish had the ball, down three, 22.5 seconds to go, with a chance to tie the game. Bacon was convinced that LeBron would take the last shot; he'd either shoot a three or drive to the basket and hope to get fouled or convert a layup. In the timeout before that play, Bill, Brian Neal and just about everyone else in Bacon's huddle told the starters just that: LeBron was going to shoot. There was no way he'd pass.

But he did—to Chad Mraz. LeBron did the same thing in a similar situation when he was a freshman and Chad was a sophomore. It was the 2000 Division III regional finals against Villa Angela-St. Joseph, and the score was tied with about a minute to play. LeBron passed to Chad for an open three, and Chad nailed it. The Irish went on to win the game and their first of two consecutive state titles.

But March 2002 was a little different. It was an unusual week for Chad Mraz, who was admitted to a hospital the Sunday before the state semis. He had a horrible flu, was dehydrated and had to be given an IV. That Wednesday, he traveled to Columbus with the team, not knowing whether he would play in the state semis. He did. He gutted his way through 22 minutes and shot 1-of-2 from the floor, finishing with three points. When the state final rolled around, there was no way Mraz wasn't going to play, and there was no way he would let his recent illness affect his minutes. He was a senior. He played the entire game, the last of his prep career.

But even though Mraz was a good—if not great—shooter, even though he was money from the corners, even though he had hit big shots in the past for SVSM, no Roger Bacon player or coach thought anyone but LeBron would take the final shot. Whether Bill knew about the shot Chad had hit two years earlier in the regional finals is anyone's guess, but the end-of-game scenario, while similar, has a few key differences. This wasn't the regional final; this was the state final. The score wasn't tied; SVSM was down by three. And this was a game played before a record crowd; hitting a game-winner in a regional final is by no means easy, but it could be argued that the crunch-time pressure on March 23, 2002, in Columbus was far greater.

But beyond that, one thing that boggled Bacon's mind was this: how could LeBron James—the two-time state champion, the eventual *USA Today* and Gatorade Player of the Year, the *Sports Illustrated* cover boy, The Chosen One, the best prep player ever, the guarantor of victory—pass the ball with the game on the line to a teammate who had been in the hospital just days earlier and at that point was just 1-of-5 from the floor?

"LeBron's got to take that shot—even if it's a 25-footer with me guarding him in his face," Beckham said. "Maybe that was a sign of LeBron's unselfishness, and you still see that today—what a great passer he is in the NBA. But I think Coach Joyce and everybody in the arena would've rather seen LeBron try to create something. Maybe they would have had a better shot (of winning) if he did, but he's an unselfish player, and that showed then—maybe to a fault."

Coach Joyce, however, told reporters after the game that he was fine with the way his team's final possession unfolded. "We didn't set up the play for any certain individual and we knew what Roger Bacon was going to give us at the defensive end," he told the *Akron Beacon Journal*. "I have no regrets that Chad took the shot. He's a senior and he's hit those shots before in big games. He got a good look and that's what we wanted."

Even LeBron didn't regret his choice. "I wasn't necessarily looking to take the shot myself," he told the *Akron Beacon Journal*. "I have faith in all of my teammates. Chad was open and took the shot, but it just didn't fall. What can you do?"

In response to LeBron's rhetorical question, some might say: "Finish the job. You brought your team almost all the way back from an 11-point, second-half deficit. You're the best player in America. You guaranteed victory. Get your team over the hump. Take the clutch shot. Make it."

Despite LeBron's many accolades—which include multiple NBA Most Valuable Player awards—the one consistent knock on him throughout his professional career has been that he isn't clutch. Was the final possession against Roger Bacon evidence of that argument even then?

"I was stunned at the time, but now that I see him in the NBA, I realize that's just the type of player he is," Frank said. "When he has the ball for game-winners, he passes if someone's open. I'm not sure if that's a good thing or bad thing. He's a good passer, and he has confidence in his teammates, but I was very shocked when he did that. I was expecting him to make a play."

So, too, was Dave Johnson, who guarded Mraz on the final series.

"I overhelped a little bit because I thought LeBron was going to shoot a three," Dave said. "Mraz was off that game, but I was definitely thinking, 'Oh, shit, I better get out there and get a hand up,' because he was a little too wide open. Luckily I didn't foul him, but it was close. I might've touched his hand—but not enough to call in that situation."

Said Josh, "LeBron always hits the open man. That was one of the biggest things I realized playing against him the second time—that he's not just a scorer. He's a complete player. From my standpoint, I think he just assumed Chad was open. He didn't really think twice. It could be in LeBron's genes that he didn't want to take the big shot, but I'm not so sure that's the case. I think he knew we were going to focus on him."

That said, would Josh have passed in that situation?

"Personally, I wouldn't have, especially on that stage," he said. "I would've wanted to shoot, and unless there were three or four players on me and it would've been ridiculous for me to shoot, I would've made sure I had a chance for an open shot to win the game and the state championship. It's hard to say what he was thinking because he's such a great player. He won two straight state championships, and he can get his shot off at will. Maybe there's more to it, but I don't know. It's hard to say."

The Scrappers, well, they were surprised LeBron passed, too.

"I remember we all had our arms locked," Newt said, "and when LeBron passed, we released a little bit. And then when we saw who he passed it to, we all tensed back up again. Mraz was a shooter. Lights out all year. But it was one of those things in the moment that's like, 'What is LeBron doing?'"

The shock of the pass extended to the stands.

"To this day, that's LeBron's mantra—not a closer," Jerome Harris said. "He's gotta take that shot. He guaranteed victory. At the time, I was totally surprised. But in retrospect, that's LeBron. He's a good kid. He's a good teammate. He really thought in his heart that an open teammate has a better shot than him. And to this day, that's his biggest downfall. He's always proven—even then, as a junior in high school—that he's an unselfish kid. But even as an unselfish kid, you've gotta take clutch shots. Is he clutch? Hell no. But who's more unselfish than him? Who's a more team-oriented player? You can't have 'em both. You can't *ooh* and *ahh* over the triple-doubles—because when you're 6-8 with Karl Malone size, the scoring is easy and the rebounding is easy; the hard part is the 10 assists—and then get mad when he passes the ball. You can't have it both ways. It's like Kobe. People say he's selfish. People say he shoots too much. He's Kobe frickin' Bryant. That's what he does. He always shoots. And he *is* clutch. And people praise him for being clutch. You can't have it both ways. LeBron's a pass-first assassin. He's an assassin, but he's a pass-first assassin."

Monty offered a somewhat different view.

"I think he got scared—not of shooting, but of fouling out," Monty said. "Frank took two or three charges on him. He had four fouls by the end of the third quarter. I don't know if that was in his head or not. He wasn't a great jump shooter yet, and I still don't know if he is. I know he's been criticized for not being clutch, but I think you have to wait and see what he accomplishes. His performance against the Pistons (in the 2007 Eastern Conference Finals), to me, should erase any doubt that he's a complete choke artist. But you gotta win to define yourself."

The Spartans know all about it. In the years following the state final, however, some of Bacon's players haven't been fond of the manner in which SVSM's loss has been rationalized. After the game, for example, much was made of LeBron's quiet start. Many thought that the Irish underestimated Bacon and didn't try their hardest until it was too late. Had LeBron and SVSM taken the game more seriously from the start, the theory goes, then they would have won.

But one fact makes this argument difficult to accept. The Spartans outscored SVSM in three of four quarters in the state final. The only one in which they didn't? The first. SVSM led Bacon 17–15 through eight minutes but was outscored by at least three points in each remaining quarter—16–13, 20–16 and 20–17.

"I just think we were a damn good team," Beckham said. "We only lost three games all year—once to LeBron's team, once to a nationally ranked team (Tabor Academy) and once to CJ. You can talk about not being focused and not being ready to play, but we were a good team. I think we deserve some credit."

As Austin Carr noted throughout the state final, LeBron seemed content to shoot jumpers in the first half, but as the game wore on, he appeared more willing to take the ball into the paint—perhaps because his team was at one point down double digits. But is it possible that his general reluctance to bang in the paint in the first half stemmed, however slightly, from the forearm shiver that knocked him dead in his tracks to start the game? Did he need some time to recover from that mentally? Beckham sent quite a message with that forearm and took a big risk in delivering it. But somehow, none of the officials—Steve Trout, Dennis Morris and Mark Hayman—saw what transpired.

"I didn't see it; none of us did," Trout said. "But that's kind of a gutsy thing to do. If any of us had seen it, it would've been a foul. He (Beckham) had to think, 'If somebody sees me, I'm gonna get called.' He got lucky no one did."

That brings us to the officials, an oft-cited scapegoat for a losing team. After the game, Jerome Harris strolled along the corridors of Value City Arena, celebrating with several Roger Bacon parents. During this time, he overheard numerous SVSM supporters complaining about the refs. Was this just sour grapes, or was the officiating truly unfair? After all, the no-call on the forearm shiver was clearly a break for Bacon. Romeo fouled out. LeBron played the entire fourth quarter with four fouls.

Might there be something to this?

Overall, the three-person crew appointed for that state final had a great deal of experience. Steve Trout had nearly 25 years of service under his belt and was working his twelfth state tournament game; Dennis Morris, who would go on to become OHSAA Director of Officiating and Development—not to mention a Big Ten official—was making his first state tournament appearance; and it was the last game Mark Hayman ever officiated. Thus, the crew offered a mix of veteran savvy and new blood, relatively speaking. In fact, when Morris got his state tournament assignment two months earlier, he was genuinely excited—not only because he'd get to work a state final, but also because there was a great chance that state final would involve LeBron James.

"You always want to be involved in a high-profile game like that," Morris said. "When we knew that we had a shot at that, I was certainly hoping he would get there. It's not a matter of favoring a team; it's a matter of being part of the game."

Morris admitted to being nervous on game day. It was his first state game, and it would be played in front of a record crowd. It was also the first time he or Trout had ever seen LeBron in person, and both were amazed at his physical ability—even in warmups. While both officials relished the responsibility of working such a huge game, there was also a bit of trepidation that came with it.

"One of the things I did not want to do was call something cheap," said Trout, who played four years of prep basketball before graduating in 1969 from Riverdale High School, which is near Upper Sandusky. "You know, there were gonna be 18,000 people in that arena, and they all wanted to see LeBron play. The last thing I wanted to do was call a cheap foul or do something to not allow him to play as well as he could. I wanted him to play as good as he was, and I didn't want to hinder that."

Were there any calls Trout wishes he could have back?

"No, there were not—not in that game," Trout said. "Don't get me wrong. There are sometimes—and we tried to be absolutely 100 percent positive. When you talk about that game and that pressure, you better be 100 percent sure that what you call is correct."

After further deliberation, however, Trout admitted that LeBron's third foul—the one he picked up while trying to block Leonard's shot—might have been clean.

"Just sitting there watching it, it looked like an obvious foul," Trout said. "But looking at the tape, he might not have hit the guy. That was one I may have wanted to take back if I could, but I didn't give him a cheap one."

Of course, even if that foul hadn't been called, one could have been called on the reach-around that was instead ruled a 10-second violation. LeBron's reaction—widening his eyes and taking a deep breath—suggested even he thought he might have gotten away with one. But the 10-second violation was more ambiguous than the blocking foul on Monty that could have—and many say *should* have—been called a charge in the final minutes. In the end, when it comes to fouls, LeBron may have had more good luck than bad.

And then there was the technical foul on Dru Joyce, who was whistled for the violation after chucking the ball toward his own basket in frustration.

"It was an obvious technical foul," said Trout, who made the call. "It was probably frustration on his part, but there was nothing I could have done differently. I had to do that. His father was coaching, and when the technical foul was called, he said something like, 'You can't call a technical foul like that in a close game like this.' Well, sure you can. That was a technical foul (no matter what part of the game it was). But (Coach) Dru Joyce was a gentleman."

Even without the technical, though, Josh was set to go to the foul line with a chance to extend the lead from three to five with 8.9 seconds left. Even if he made only one free throw—he wound up hitting the first and missing the second—it would have been a two-possession game, and odds are Bacon holds on to win. It's likely that the technical foul merely erased whatever slim chance the Irish had at that point of forcing overtime or winning the game outright.

Coach Joyce might agree. After the final buzzer, his son, distraught at the loss, starting wandering to the locker room. Coach Joyce, however, retrieved him and had him return to the court for the medal presentations. When asked about the incident after the game, Coach Joyce told the *Akron Beacon Journal*, "He's believing right now that the technical cost us the game, but it didn't. Our guys just needed to understand that we were going to show class and applaud Roger Bacon and wish them well because they were the better team."

The better team.

Most of Bacon's players have seen *More Than a Game*. Most have at least leafed through *Shooting Stars*—the book LeBron co-authored with Buzz Bissinger—particularly the portion pertaining to the 2002 state final. In both the documentary and the book, LeBron used some curious language when discussing Roger Bacon. In *More Than a Game*, for instance, he explained that the Irish felt confident going into the state final because they had already played Bacon in the regular season and "blew them out." Given that Bacon led that game by 10 points after the first quarter, given that Bacon led by one entering the fourth, given that the game was tied with less than three minutes to go, some might say the phrase "blew them out" is a tad misleading.

"I guess nine points is considered a blowout to him," Josh said. "So I guess in the state final—when we beat them by eight points—you could say we blew them out."

There was also frustration in response to certain parts of *Shooting Stars*. In the book, LeBron discussed how the night before the state final Coach Joyce had the flu, how the players were hanging out with cheerleaders, how the players stayed up well into the night. The next morning, LeBron wrote that he woke up with back spasms—despite feeling perfectly fine the night before—and explained that he wasn't sure if he'd even be able to play in the state final. He said that he could barely walk and attributed the back pain to karma for not taking everything as seriously as he should have.

LeBron eventually said Bacon was a balanced team, a confident team, a more disciplined team. Still, many Spartans felt the praise seemed backhanded. They interpreted LeBron's explanations as saying: well, if Coach Joyce *hadn't* been sick, if we *hadn't* stayed up so late the night before, if I *hadn't* woken up with back spasms, if we *had* taken the game more seriously . . .

"Losers always have an excuse," Newt said. "I could say the same thing if we lost. Well, Josh's ankle wasn't doing too well. We have back problems, too. We have aching bodies, too. Leonard and I just went from playing 80 plays a game during football and having two-a-days, and we're not complaining about it. But that's fine. Your coach can have the flu. Our coach was sick, too. He was sicker than crap all week. He looked terrible. You can go out until 4 a.m. I was up until 4 a.m., too—nervous because I couldn't sleep. We could make excuses, too. That's when discipline comes in. Don't take away somebody else's accomplishment because you think you should have won."

LeBron's back spasms, in particular, were a bit of a mystery for Bacon. Beckham's father, David, recalled LeBron leaping on the scorers' table before the game to get the Irish fans excited. LeBron also jumped on the scorers' table in the first half while chasing a loose ball—even after it was already out of bounds. In the fourth quarter, when LeBron stole a pass from Monty, he raced downcourt for a breakaway jam and took off a step inside the free-throw line. If LeBron was in that much pain, why not just lay the ball in? Or dunk the ball less emphatically? Or conserve energy by not jumping unnecessarily on the scorers' table?

"He didn't seem to be experiencing too many back spasms," David Wyrick said.

Said Frank, "Whenever you lose, you always try to look for an excuse. When we lost to them in the first game, our excuse was we got cheated by the refs. The free-throw discrepancy was terrible. We felt like the refs handed them that game. It's normal to hear (SVSM) not give us much credit, but it doesn't look good from their point of view because they're just excuses."

Said Monty, "They make it sound like they lost the game. That's why we were a better team. We wouldn't have stayed up until 4 a.m. We were more committed to winning. We were more competitive. We were more focused."

Said Josh, "I wish LeBron wouldn't have said some of those things, but being a young person, a lot of people would've done the same. It doesn't really make me mad, though. They can never take away the fact that we won the game. So I just think more about what we did and what we accomplished—and not the fact that they tried to undermine our win. I know what we did."

Despite disliking the manner in which SVSM's loss has been rationalized, Bacon's players credited LeBron for his sportsmanship following the state final. He shook hands with every Spartan—well, all but one of them—and congratulated them on their win both immediately following the final buzzer and also in Bacon's locker room before leaving the arena. The one player who didn't shake LeBron's hand? Monty.

"It's not like I had a problem with him, and I wasn't mad about the guarantee," Monty explained. "But the boxing in the pregame and all that stuff—their show had just worn me out. Their whole show. So I just kind of stayed away. It's not like I would've taken my hand away if he stuck his hand out to shake mine. I was just fine not doing it.

"Besides," Monty continued, smiling, "I was probably still mad about not getting that charge."

The other Spartans, meanwhile, were happy to oblige LeBron.

"I remember shaking his hand after the game," Josh said. "I was at the back of the line, and he looked at me when we shook hands and said, 'Josh, good game. You're a real good player. Keep working.' I just remember looking at him and saying, 'Thanks, same to you.'"

And then there were those who absolutely relished shaking LeBron's hand—particularly Newt.

"I remember after the game, LeBron came over and we're sitting there," Newt recalled. "And I went up to him and shook his hand and said, 'How about that guarantee?' He looks at me with a little smile and says, 'Yeah, that was full of shit, wasn't it?' And he put his head down, smiled and laughed."

The Guarantee. Yes, even at 17, LeBron was an all-world talent. But as sports have shown time and time again, not everyone can be Joe Namath. Winning is hard enough without giving your opponent added incentive. But if LeBron wanted to put himself out there, Cork theorized that perhaps he should have promised the win instead of guaranteeing it.

"You can break a promise," Cork observed. "You can't break a guarantee."

Roger Bacon's win, by any standard, was one of the most impressive wins in prep basketball history—Ohio or otherwise. The fact that it was revenge made it that much sweeter.

The CJ game might have been the turning point of the 2001–02 season—Bacon went 17-0 thereafter—but the Spartans' first encounter with the Irish set the season in orbit. After that night, the Spartans knew they belonged on the same floor with SVSM, and if they belonged on the same floor with SVSM, they belonged on the same floor with anybody.

But what if that game never happened? What if Bill never scheduled it? Would the Spartans have been as confident as they were heading into that state final, or would the aura of LeBron have been too much to overcome?

"It's hard to say yes or no," Beckham said. "I still think we would've played them tough and it would've been a great game—but without that game in December, we wouldn't have been sure. We wouldn't have been sure of how good we were. I left that game thinking, 'We can play with this team any day of the week. We could play with this team 10 times and win seven of them.' And without that, I think the intimidation factor would've still been in play. We had already seen LeBron once, so I think that took some of the hype away and just let us focus on what we needed to do."

Most of the Spartans were in awe of LeBron that December night at Kent State, but they played against him—on a college floor, no less—and kept it close. What if that weren't the case? What if Bacon's first glimpse of LeBron came in the state final under the bright lights of Value City Arena before a record crowd in the wake of the *SI* cover? Would the moment have been too big?

"I honestly feel like if we didn't play them in the regular season, we wouldn't have had a chance in that state game," Tim McCoy said. "That game got us prepared. We got to see the spectacle of what LeBron James was. Just from the first time seeing him, I remember saying, 'Wow, this dude is doing stuff I've never seen before.' And if you throw that in there with the *Sports Illustrated* stuff, I think we would have been way more intimidated."

Marcus Smith agreed.

"There would've been an awe factor, absolutely," he said. "The Chosen One. *Sports Illustrated*. If you don't have a real-life experience to go with that magazine cover, then the hype almost becomes too much. It can cripple you. I don't care how prepared you are or how good you think you are. You need that game. We needed that game. We needed that up-close-and-personal touch to give us that confidence—not that we *can* beat them, but that we *will* beat them. We *will* beat them. Because that's what *we* do. But if you're looking at everything from a faraway distance, you're intimidated. You're fearful. You're scared of things you don't know about. It was huge playing them."

Frank, meanwhile, acknowledged the hype factor but doesn't think it would've decided the game.

"I think it definitely would've been tighter," he said, "but in the end, I still think we would've pulled it out because of our coach."

Coaching. Yes, for all the talk about hype and awe, the game still comes down to matchups, to strategy, to Xs and Os. Bill was damn good at that. So good, in fact, that he made a couple of key adjustments between games—none bigger, perhaps, than starting Frank on Dru Joyce. In the regular-season game, Joyce made five threes; in the state final, he attempted five—and he only made two. That adjustment, suggested by Bobby Holt, paid dividends, but would Bill have given it the green light without that regular-season game? Would Bobby have even suggested it?

"No, there's no way," Newt said. "Nobody can sit here and say that. If we had just done one-guard to one-guard and two-guard to two-guard like we did in the first game, we would've lost. For us to switch like that won the game. I guarantee if we didn't have that regular-season game, we would've lost to them in the state final. After that game, we knew we weren't going to lose to them again. It took that edge away—that aspect of knowing their game versus ours, knowing their mannerisms versus ours, knowing that our offense wouldn't faze them but that our defense would win the game. That state final would have been close, but we never would've gotten over the hump."

Josh and Monty disagreed.

"It would've been different because we wouldn't have been acclimated to such a large crowd and the LeBron theatrics, so you never know if we would've been there mentally," Josh said. "But personally, I feel we were the better team. No doubt we knew who the best player on the court was—LeBron was in another league—but we knew that when you added the sum of their parts versus the sum of our parts, we were better. I don't think we would have had as much confidence going into that game if we hadn't played them in the regular season, but again, that was one of the best decisions Coach Brewer ever made. It was all part of his master plan."

Said Monty, "I think by that point, we were the best team in the state by far. That (regular-season game) helped our approach, but I think we still would've won. We had a great coach, a coach that made us mentally 30 years old when we were 16, 17, 18. Our mental strength, for our age, was through the roof. I've played on college teams that didn't have the mental toughness like we did."

That toughness was on full display just before tip-off.

"When we broke the huddle and our starters walked onto the floor, that's when I knew—we're ready to do this," Tom Thompson said. "You can tell by looking into someone's eyes if they're ready or not. Those five guys, when they broke the huddle, they were ready to go. Those guys were so fearless. There was just absolutely no fear."

Said Josh, "There was a sense of calm. You can call it a quiet confidence. Even before the guarantee, more than any other game I think I've ever played in, we just knew in our hearts that we were going to win. We battled; we worked hard. I never doubted it at all. It's a good feeling to have."

But what if Bacon had won that regular-season game? What if SVSM had been the team out for revenge? Would LeBron still have made The Guarantee? After all, he made it knowing his team had defeated Bacon earlier in the season. Without that, is he bold enough to make the same statement?

"As a coach, I've never said losing a game is a good thing—never, ever, ever have I said that in my life," Thompson said. "But that's the one hindsight I can point to and say it might've given us an edge. If you think about it, what strategically did (SVSM) do differently in the state final? Nothing. Coach Joyce, I'm sure, does great prep work. But they didn't change anything."

Of course, having won the first meeting, perhaps the Irish felt like they didn't have to. That, however, didn't stop SVSM assistant coach Steve Culp from scouting the Spartans four times that season. Before the state final, Culp told the *Akron Beacon Journal* that he left the regular-season game expecting a rematch in March and that the only other Irish opponent that rivaled Bacon's physicality was George Junior Republic, which knocked off the Irish 58–57 in overtime later that season.

But whatever adjustments SVSM made didn't show in the final score. The Spartans scored 71 points in the final—one more than the 70 they scored in the regular-season game. The Irish, meanwhile, scored 63 points in the final—16 fewer than the 79 they scored that night in December.

What does this mean? For starters, it means the aggregate score of both games was as close as it could be—142–141, with SVSM holding a one-point advantage. It also means that Roger Bacon entered the state final playing better defense, which perhaps shouldn't be a surprise. It's no secret that the Spartans and the Irish advanced to the state final playing two different styles of basketball. SVSM, with its explosive offense, played up-tempo and faced its fair share of like-minded nationally ranked teams. Bacon, meanwhile, stayed true to GCL form, slowing the game down and grinding it out. Aside from the regular-season game against SVSM and the holiday tournament in Lewes, Delaware, the Spartans faced teams that didn't garner even a glimmer of national coverage. They faced teams loaded not with future Division I collegiate talent, but rather, solid high school players who relied on good fundamentals and teamwork.

Was Bacon's schedule more advantageous for the state final?

"To beat a team with talent is one thing; to beat a talented team is a whole other story," Jerome Harris said. "That's what Roger Bacon was. St. Vincent–St. Mary, especially in LeBron's senior year, played a lot of AAU-type high schools—and there's a lot in this country. There's none in Cincinnati."

Brian Neal has mixed feelings about AAU. He sees the pros when it comes to exposure and recruiting, but he has seen the cons firsthand. He often spends the first few weeks of each season ridding his players of bad habits they picked up during AAU, particularly on defense (meaning, he reminds his players that they actually have to play it).

Given that several key players for SVSM grew up playing AAU together, given that the Irish played so many nationally ranked teams in 2001–02, is it possible that they fell in love with outscoring people? Is it possible that they didn't commit to defense—or at least not to the degree Bacon did?

The Irish entered the state final averaging 76 points per game—nearly 13 points more than Bacon's 63.1. They were, however, allowing 55.3 points per game—nine points more than Bacon's 46.3.

"That whole year, they never committed to guarding other teams," Brian Neal said of the Irish. "And we were a heck of an offensive team."

Astonishingly, Bacon held opponents below 50 points in 15 of 16 games following the loss at CJ—and below 40 in eight of them. SVSM, by comparison, held just three opponents under 40 *all season*. If defense really does win championships, it seems Bacon had the advantage.

"It doesn't matter how good you are if you can't score," Beckham said.

So, what's the verdict? Upset or not?

"I think if you would've taken a poll of the 18,000 people who sat in the arena that day, 95 percent of them would have said St. Vincent–St. Mary was gonna win," Brian Neal said. "If you would've talked to the 15 or so coaches we played that year, including our league schools, if you would have talked to experts who had seen both teams play, I think there would have been a split jury. Obviously, we didn't have LeBron, arguably the best high school player ever to play. From that standpoint, was it an upset? Yeah, probably, just from the sheer magnitude of who he was and even on to who he's become. But when you look at player-for-player, philosophy-for-philosophy, it's just two great teams. Our motto—and Bill said it after the game—(was) 'We knew they had a great player, but we knew we had a great team.' And our guys, to their credit, believed that through their entire being that we had a chance to win because we were going to stick together and play as a team. We didn't feel it was an upset. We knew we'd have to play really, really well, but playing them earlier in the year gave us confidence to know we could beat them. But when you look at the publicity

(SVSM) got, I think people naturally took it as an upset because we didn't get that publicity. Nobody knew who Roger Bacon was necessarily. We had a lot of great wins that year; we beat a lot of great teams. But because we didn't have LeBron, we didn't have that hype behind us, which makes everybody say greatest upset of all time.

"Was it an upset? Yeah, probably. Biggest upset of all time? No way. Because we were really good. People just didn't know about us."

● ● ● ●

NOT LONG AFTER WINNING state, Josh and Newt—the two St. Clement boys born and raised in St. Bernard—sat next to each other, wondering the same things.

What now? What's next?

And that's when it hit them. There was no now. There was no next. Josh and Newt weren't going to be teammates anymore. Neither were Frank and Dave. Neither were Beckham and Monty. It was over.

What now? What's next?

A few days later, most of Bacon's team went to a local gym to play pickup basketball. They walked in and saw several random guys playing on the other side of the court, guys who wanted to play a full-court game.

So the Spartans gave them one.

But not right away. They got in their layup lines as if it were a Friday night at Fogarty and the opponent were CJ or Alter or St. Xavier. Once loose, they huddled together, they made fun of each other, they high-fived each other—just like they'd always done. When the huddle broke, five players—Josh, Frank, Beckham, Monty and Dave—walked onto the court, while Newt, Tim McCoy and Matt Reed headed for the sideline. There was no bickering over who would start. There was no coach present to tell them their roles, but then again, there didn't have to be; the players just knew them. They did what they had always done. They did what came naturally.

"That pickup game was not a pickup game for us," Newt said. "It was just another game."

The five randoms had no idea what they had gotten themselves into. Somewhat amusingly, they actually thought they had a chance to win. But it wasn't long before they looked at each other in confusion and awe, with heaving breaths and crinkled brows, silently wondering, *Who are these guys?* Of course, if they wanted to know, all they had to do was ask.

These guys are the 2002 Ohio Division II state champions.

The Chosen Ones.

The Team That Beat LeBron.

EPILOGUE

THE HERO'S WELCOME

The rubber match never happened.

The following year, in 2002–03, Roger Bacon—despite graduating six seniors, including Josh, Beckham and Frank—went 15–5 during the regular season and advanced once more to the regional finals. Joining Monty and Dave in the starting lineup were three Scrappers with state rings—Newt, Leonard and Marcus Smith. It was the fifth time in seven years that Bacon would face either Badin or Alter with Columbus on the line; this time it was Alter.

The two rivals split a pair of closely contested defensive struggles during the regular season, and the postseason showdown was no different. With a chance to return to state, Bacon led Alter 14–5 early in the second quarter but saw its lead cut to 18–14 at halftime and eventually trailed 23–22 entering the fourth quarter. Monty, the GCL-North Player of the Year, averaged nearly 20 points per game for the Spartans, but the Knights held him to eight. They zoned; they doubled; they tripled. Monty couldn't move. Bacon lost 34–29. It was the eleventh straight year that a team from the GCL-North advanced to the Division II Final Four—but this time, it wasn't Bacon, which finished 20–6.

"Worst moment of my life," Monty said. "I'm blessed that I haven't had to deal with things worse than that, but that's how hard I took that loss. I felt responsible for that team. I carried our team a lot that year offensively. Talent-wise, we didn't have much. Talent-wise, we should have gone 10–10, but that whole mentality we had (from the year before) carried over. Ten players, eight seniors. Tough as hell team playing defense. It was a team effort. Winning state was so awesome the year before, and I just wanted to do it again. I wanted to play St. Vincent–St. Mary again. Everybody was talking about the rematch. Everybody wanted us to play. Losing to Alter was hard. I still haven't gotten over that."

SVSM, of course, advanced to the state final. The national obsession surrounding LeBron toward the end of his junior year paled in comparison to his senior season. By then, LeBron wasn't just a household name; he was practically part of your family. The Irish played a high-profile schedule jampacked with nationally ranked teams from Philadelphia to Los Angeles. They played undefeated and top-ranked Oak Hill Academy in a game televised on ESPN2 and commentated by Dick Vitale and Bill Walton—and won in blowout fashion, 65–45. Eight games into the season, SVSM was ranked No. 1 in the country by *USA Today*.

As the year wore on, LeBron endured some run-ins with the OHSAA, mainly for accepting two throwback jerseys from a Cleveland-area clothing store as gifts. In January 2003, LeBron, told that he had compromised his amateur status, was ruled ineligible for the rest of the season, and the Irish were forced to retroactively forfeit an 82–71 win over Akron Buchtel. The season-ending suspension, however, was soon rescinded. LeBron was forced to miss two games as punishment, but SVSM won despite his absence.

Had the Spartans defeated Alter in the regional finals, there was a good chance they would have played SVSM once more. Standing in Bacon's way in the state semis would have been—yup, you guessed it—Columbus Beechcroft, which Alter went on to defeat 53–45. For the second straight year, the Irish faced in the state final a team from the GCL, and—just like in 2001–02—it was a team they had beaten during the regular season. SVSM dismantled Alter 73–40 five weeks earlier in Dayton, but the state final was decidedly closer. In fact, Alter, playing at a snail-stuck-in-molasses pace, led SVSM 19–14 at halftime.

"There is no league in the state of Ohio like the GCL," Mitch Perdrix said. "You go through that league, and you ain't afraid to play nobody."

Said Jerome Harris, "Nobody outside of Cincinnati can really appreciate the GCL. Unless you're from the GCL, you don't appreciate the level of competition you get from that. St. X gave us a doghouse of a fight (in 2001–02)—and they had no studs. They shouldn't have even been on our court. But they came to Bacon and almost won. That's what the GCL is all about. It's like the CJ game. We went up there and should have won, but I'm not shocked CJ beat us. The GCL is just so tough."

But LeBron, just as he had done the previous year, took over in the second half, finishing with a game-high 25 points as SVSM won 40–36 for its third state title in four years. The Irish finished the year 25–1—with the retroactive forfeit serving as their only loss—and were named *USA Today* national champions.

Thus, in LeBron's four-year prep career, the Irish went 101–6, including 80–2 against in-state competition. One loss was by forfeit. Two were to Oak Hill Academy. Three were by one point. Disregarding the forfeit to Buchtel, the in-state record becomes 81–1, making Roger Bacon the first, last and only Ohio team to beat LeBron and SVSM between the lines. In fact, the Spartans were the last team to beat LeBron and SVSM between the lines, period.

It remains the most lopsided loss of LeBron's prep career.

• • • •

MONTY ST. CLAIR PLAYED college basketball at Miami of Ohio with Josh and started as a freshman. Bill came to a couple of his games every year, and on those nights, Monty wanted to play his absolute best. During his sophomore season in 2004–05, Miami played at Xavier. Monty looked toward the stands during warmups and spotted Bill and his daughters sitting about 10 rows up from the floor. Monty, who by then had long since let his hair grow out, scored 10 points in the first 12 minutes of the game, and Miami won 66–54. He was so happy to have the game he did in front of his former coach.

Monty, called "Dirk" by his Miami teammates for having a skill set similar to Dirk Nowitzki's, started every game for the Redhawks as a sophomore, but his body wore down as his career went on. He had multiple surgeries, including one on his ankle and another to repair the shoulder tear he sustained during the state final against SVSM in 2002.

"Monty was so skilled, almost to the point where—if he had stayed healthy and could really run and jump—he'd be an NBA-type player," Josh said. "I'll always cherish my time playing with him."

Despite his ailments, Monty, thanks to Bill, gutted his way through his collegiate career, which ended in 2007.

"I went from being soft to essentially getting through college on toughness," Monty said. "When I was a senior (at Miami), other coaches—after facing me for the last time—would say, 'You're one of the toughest players I've ever coached against.' When I got to college, I was ready. I was ready because of Brewer. I had success because I was tough. People say, 'Winning's not everything,' but Brewer taught me winning *is* everything. He never said that, but I took that from him. If you want to accomplish something, work toward that goal. On days when you don't feel like doing anything, you've got to bust your ass. I've played for coaches before him and after him, and none instill it like he did. None instill how hard you have to work. When I was a sophomore in high school, my work ethic and my toughness were my two biggest weaknesses. Now those are my two biggest strengths—and he's a huge reason for that."

In the penultimate game of Monty's career, Miami advanced to the final of the Mid-American Conference Tournament against Akron, with the winner automatically qualifying for the NCAA Tornament. Akron had two players who Monty got to know quite well in college—Dru Joyce and Romeo Travis. Monty started the final, played 10 minutes, took one shot, grabbed one rebound and didn't score. With less than one second left in the game and Miami down 52–50, Redhawks guard Doug Penno, who played for Alter and lost to SVSM in the 2003 state final, banked in a three to win the game, 53–52, and send Miami to The Dance.

Monty had two goals in basketball: to win a state title and play in the NCCA Tournament—and he accomplished both at the expense of Dru and Romeo.

"Dru, Romeo—they were much better players than I was at that point in college," Monty said. "I just had too many injuries—my shoulder, my ankle. I was worn out. And Romeo was a phenomenal college player and a phenomenal pro player overseas. I went over to their bench after the game because they were seniors and they were disappointed. I told Romeo it was a pleasure playing against him all that time."

Miami, seeded No. 14 in the NCAA Tournament, lost to No. 3 Oregon, 58–56, in first-round action. Monty started and played 29 minutes. He finished with zero points and six rebounds. It was the only NCAA Tournament game he ever played in. It was also the last game of his basketball career.

Monty studied business and met his wife, Kim, at Miami. They live in Toledo, where Monty works as a commodities trader. The unrelenting toughness Bill taught him during his years at Bacon sticks with Monty in a completely unrelated field. It affects everything he does and the way he approaches everything. Monty attributes all of that to Bill.

"Some people think I'm insensitive, but to me, there's no excuses," Monty said. "You either do something or you don't. I'm a bottom-line person. With work, I don't care why something was late. It's late or it's on time. It's that mentality (Bill taught)."

Some coaches, Monty said, coach for different reasons. Some take it more seriously than others. Some will have fun, win a few games and use it as an ego booster. Bill never did that. He made the most of every opportunity he was given. Monty loved playing for Bill. Even when he was getting yelled at, he loved playing for him. Bill is one of his idols because he found success as a husband, as a father and as a coach. He found success in everything he did and taught Monty how to do that in his life as well.

"I think I earned his respect," Monty said. "And he definitely earned mine."

Winning state remains a great source of pride for Monty, but while he's happy to say he beat LeBron James, that in itself did not make the 2001–02 team special.

"It's a big deal to win state, but I think the bigger deal is how great of a team we were—not who we beat," Monty said. "I think who we beat helped define to other people how great of a team we were, but I think we knew we were great. Beating LeBron validates that to other people, but I didn't need validation to know that."

• • • •

DAVE JOHNSON PLAYED COLLEGE basketball at Capital University, a Division III school in Columbus. Bill, as he did with a lot of his players, would check in with Dave via email to see how things were going—and not just with basketball.

"He was almost a coach you hated to play for," Dave said. "But looking back, he was your best friend and would do anything for you."

Dave started as a freshman at Capital and played three seasons before walking away from the game. He transferred home to the University of Cincinnati for his senior year.

"I kind of got burned out a bit," Dave said. "I had been playing so much my whole life, and playing D-III is a little different than playing D-I. They don't offer athletic scholarships, kids get filtered in and out all the time—it's definitely different not being on scholarship. All the traveling and practice wears on you after a while."

At Cincinnati, though, Dave found himself missing basketball and playing pickup games all the time.

"Looking back, it's probably something I regret now," Dave said of leaving Capital. "I wish I would've finished, but it is what it is."

Perhaps that regret was what led Dave back to Bacon. Brian Neal called and said there was an opening for an assistant coach, and Dave jumped at the opportunity.

"Playing at Bacon was a special time for all of us, and that's what I want for the kids now," Dave said. "I can't imagine coaching anywhere else."

Although Dave sometimes wishes he had finished his career at Capital, he will carry at least one memory from his college days with him forever. During Dave's sophomore year in 2004–05, the Cleveland Cavaliers held their training camp at Capital. The Cavs were there for close to a week, and Dave, by virtue of playing for Capital, was allowed to sit in the arena and watch LeBron practice. At the end of the week, the Cavs held an on-campus, intrasquad scrimmage that Capital students could attend. The gym was packed. At halftime, Dave was asked to come to center court, where he was recognized for being a member of the only Ohio high school basketball team to ever beat LeBron James.

"It was a complete surprise," Dave said. "I had no idea it was coming."

After the game, Dave and a teammate, Brian Alge, went into the Cavs' locker room, where they spotted LeBron, who was sitting on an exercise bike and talking on his phone. They approached the player who a few months earlier was named NBA Rookie of the Year and asked for his autograph. LeBron obliged. He signed a jersey for Brian, and then Dave presented his—but it wasn't a Cavs jersey, and it wasn't his Capital jersey.

It was his Roger Bacon jersey.

When Dave found out LeBron was coming to Capital, he called home and asked his parents to send it to him, which they did. LeBron went ahead and signed it.

"To be honest, I don't even know if he knew what he was signing," Dave said. "I kind of had a feeling he did because (my team) had been hounding him all week. He'd get off the bus and my teammates were yelling 'Roger Bacon!' and holding up my jersey so he could see it. I don't even know if he was on the floor (when they honored me at halftime). He might have been in the locker room. We never had an actual conversation, but it was neat."

In 2011, Dave married his wife, Laura, also a Roger Bacon grad. He lives in Cincinnati and works in finance. As for his Roger Bacon jersey, it hangs in his basement, signed by LeBron James.

• • • •

LIKE DAVE, MARCUS SMITH played Division III college basketball—first at Transylvania University for one year and then for a year and a half at the College of Mount St. Joseph in Cincinnati. And, like Dave, he eventually gave the game up—not because it became too challenging, but because it wasn't challenging enough. Better yet, it wasn't the game that changed; it was the way the game made Marcus feel.

At Bacon, Marcus felt he was part of something special. Every game was hyped. Every game was sold out. Even when he lost, he felt like a winner. But beyond the glory and accolades that come with playing a major sport at a successful program, the game, when stripped to its core, is a competition, and for Marcus, the competitive fire he acquired at Bacon slowly extinguished in college. He didn't want that to happen, but it did.

"At Bacon, our practices were unreal," he said. "They were so competitive—so competitive. If you weren't performing to the best of your ability, you would get embarrassed. You would get beat. Somebody would beat you in practice."

Marcus remembers one practice in particular during his senior year in 2002–03. When it came to practice, Marcus—thanks to his time as a Scrapper—was almost always ready to go, but one day, he wasn't. He was tired. He wasn't playing all that well. The effort that was almost always there, wasn't. Bacon had a talented freshman class that year, and Bill would occasionally let some of them practice with the varsity. On that day, Marcus got lit up by one of those freshmen—and Bill didn't stop it. In fact, he encouraged it.

"You can tell when someone has checked out mentally," Marcus said. "Brewer didn't care."

Eventually, Marcus picked it up, shut his man down, blocked a shot and scored. As soon as Marcus did that, Bill ended practice.

When Marcus got to college, that practice environment couldn't be replicated. Marcus was thirsting to be yelled at, thirsting to be cursed at, thirsting for a coach to make him run a suicide. But no one did. It was like winning the World Series of Poker and then playing a 10-dollar cash game and begging someone to raise you, to push the action just once. It got so bad that Marcus would intentionally do something wrong just to get disciplined. But the discipline never came.

That wasn't the case in high school. At Bacon, Bill pushed Marcus. If Marcus had checked out mentally, Bill would let him get embarrassed until he un-checked out. If an insult needed to be hurled, Bill hurled it. If a button needed to be pushed, he pushed it. There was nothing he wouldn't do to get the most out of a player. There was no line he wouldn't cross. That, more than anything, is what Marcus missed the most when he got to college. Even though he was starting at Mount St. Joe as a junior, he quit midway through the season.

"Brewer ruined me," Marcus said. "And I mean that in the best way possible."

But in the bigger picture, it's a sacrifice Marcus accepts. Bill didn't have to bring him up to varsity halfway through that 2001–02 season. Bill could have cut ties with him when he became academically ineligible as a sophomore. But he didn't. He stuck with Marcus. He taught him how to win, what it felt like to be a winner and how anything other than winning is unacceptable. And that's not all. He taught him that hard work would be rewarded.

Entering his senior year at Bacon, Marcus assumed he would come off the bench once more, but Bill gave him an important responsibility that summer: he put Marcus in charge of communicating everything to the team. Days and times of summer-league games, changes made to practice schedules or a dawn patrol—Marcus had to let everyone know. Bill and Marcus had a constant line of communication. Two days before the season opener, Bill named Marcus a starter—despite the fact that one of his teammates probably outperformed him in the preseason.

"That's what I loved about Brewer," Marcus said. "He looked beyond what I did on the court. He saw my potential. He was big on chemistry and doing the little things—showing up, being accountable. That's why he made me a starter."

Thus, as a senior, Marcus, one of the last guys added to the freshman team and *the* last guy added to the '01–02 team, was a starter for the defending state champions. Bacon opened the 2002–03 season against Winton Woods, the defending Division I state runner-up, at Xavier's Cintas Center. Marcus still remembers Bill's intensity before the game.

"His face was beet red," Marcus said. "It was like he was in the pressure cooker for that moment in time. It was another season starting, and he was in the zone. I remember looking at him and thinking, 'I don't wanna let this guy down.'"

So Marcus didn't. He made every shot he took that night—5-of-5 from the field, 1-of-1 from the foul line. He finished with 11 points, and Bacon won 64–59.

It was the first varsity start of his career, and Marcus pitched a perfect game.

"Brewer had invested so much in me," Marcus said. "I just didn't want to let him down."

Marcus aspires to be a college basketball coach. He wants to build a program using a system similar to Bill's. He wants to push people just like Bill pushed him and provide in their lives the same structure Bill provided in his. Most important, he wants his influence to extend beyond basketball—because he is proof that a coach can do that.

Marcus, once academically ineligible, has a master's degree in sociology.

"Once you experience that form of winning, once you reach that mountaintop, anything else is just unacceptable," Marcus said. "People say I'm crazy sometimes. No, I'm just really emotional, really competitive. I want to win, and I want to do things the right way. Brewer's the best coach I ever had. Aside from my parents, when it comes to an adult having an influence on my life when I was younger, I don't even know who else I would put (other than him). He's right there. He's like a father figure to me—and I got two fathers. He made me the man I am today. He gave me an opportunity. If I wasn't on that state team, I don't know how different my life would have been. And I don't want to know, either."

• • • •

AS A SENIOR AT Roger Bacon, Jon Newton was named GCL-North Defensive Lineman of the Year and was first-team all-state. He played defensive tackle for the University of Cincinnati from 2003 to 2006 and helped make a game-saving tackle against Eastern Michigan in 2005.

Newt studied criminal justice at Cincinnati and worked for TSA Homeland Security at the Cincinnati/Northern Kentucky International Airport for two years before pursuing his dream of becoming a police officer. He works in Florence, Kentucky.

When reminiscing about the state final, Newt is similar to Monty in that he is more proud of the accomplishment itself (winning state) than what the accomplishment entailed (beating LeBron). Perhaps that is because Newt played against so many great players in college—Ben Roethlisberger and Troy Smith, to name just a couple.

"For me, seeing an athlete like that now, it's just another person," Newt said. "I think we kind of knew what LeBron was going to become. It's rewarding, but it doesn't add or take away anything, I don't think. We won state. We got that ring. Yeah, they have three, but they didn't play us those three years, either."

• • • •

LEONARD BUSH PLAYED LINEBACKER at the University of Indianapolis, where he majored in sports administration. He lives in Indianapolis, works in sales for a manufacturing company and hopes to one day coach.

The 2002 state final still comes up in conversation.

"To see where he is now," Leonard said of LeBron, "I can't believe I played against him. Some people still don't believe it."

While the state title was the pinnacle of Leonard's prep career, he often finds himself reminiscing about the times he and his Bacon teammates shared outside of basketball—before and after practices, on road trips, in places like Delaware and Savannah.

"Those were some of the best times we had," Leonard said. "That really brought us together and made us the team we were."

· · · ·

TIM MCCOY PLAYED BASEBALL at the College of Mount St. Joseph in Cincinnati, serving primarily as a defensive specialist. As a senior, he was team captain and helped his squad to the NCAA Tournament.

Tim, who majored in psychology, is working toward a master's in special education at Xavier University. He is a teacher at St. Joseph Orphanage and has been the varsity head baseball coach at Bacon since 2008. Many of his players have gone on to play collegiate sports.

Like a lot of Spartans on the 2001–02 team, Tim often encounters people who don't believe he beat LeBron James in high school. His students at St. Joseph are among those people, so Tim has to show them certain segments of *More Than A Game*, among other things, to prove it. The reaction is almost always disbelief. Tim, however, has never felt disbelief about what his team accomplished—not now, and certainly not after that state final.

"After we played them that first time, we knew we were gonna see them again; there was no doubt in my mind," Tim said. "And I don't think there was any doubt in anybody's mind that we were gonna win a state championship—no matter who was there. When we started that tournament run, it was done."

· · · ·

NATE WYRICK PLAYED VOLLEYBALL at Findlay for one year, transferred to Cincinnati State for a semester and played basketball for two years at Casper College in Wyoming, where he studied business administration. While Nate enjoyed playing basketball with his friends at Bacon, he does have mixed feelings about certain parts of the experience, particularly not playing in the state final, which was the only game he didn't play in as a senior.

"I have a great memory of that season, but I don't have a great memory of that state-final experience," Nate said. "I just felt like I should have been in there—at least for a little bit. It's like I wasn't a part of it. It still brings back memories and pisses me off. We won a ring, and I was a main part in that. I played in all the other games. I know that. But it just pisses me off I didn't get in the game because I felt like I should have played. Why wait until the last game of the season not to play me?"

Nate said that he and Bill got along well enough after he graduated. They would send emails back and forth. Still, Nate wishes he could've played in that state final—and more throughout his career in general.

"Do I think I underachieved at Bacon? Yeah," Nate said. "But I don't think I had all the opportunities to get to my potential, either. Some guys say I was content. I wasn't content. I didn't have the opportunities to get out there and stay out there. I didn't do it (Bill's) way, and that's how it was. It was his way; we're gonna win his way, or we're gonna lose. He's not gonna change.

"But he taught me a lot about life," Nate continued. "Sometimes you gotta do things you don't wanna do. Even to this day, I still don't think I would've missed those volleyball games to play AAU. I just wouldn't do it. It was a good life lesson, though. There are some people out there—it's their way or the highway. I got the highway. I don't regret it at all. I did what I wanted to do, and I did it well. I could do something for one guy, but then I'd let another 12 down on my volleyball team—and I couldn't do that. I was pissed (about not playing in that state final), but I'm not gonna hold a grudge about it."

Said Brian Neal, "If Nate's the only one (who took issue with his playing time), we're probably pretty lucky. Unfortunately, unless you only keep five players, you're going to have guys on your team who feel like they should play more or have a different role. It's like that on every team. That's why the buy-in is so important."

Nate, who lives in Casper, works for General Electric and has a son named Kade.

• • • •

MATT REED WAS VOTED prom king as a senior at Roger Bacon.

He attended Wright State University in Dayton and majored in organizational leadership. Matt did not play a sport in college but was active in the university's mixed concert choir and men's choral groups. He graduated in 2007 and sells real estate in Estero, Florida. In 2009, he married Beckham's cousin, Stacey, with whom he has a daughter named Reagan.

Whenever Matt sees LeBron on television or in a magazine, he can't help but think back to his days at Bacon with pride and wonder.

"You think of all his accomplishments, and it's still amazing what we did," Matt said. "The guy who has everything really doesn't have everything. The guy who should have four high school state championships only got three."

Even though Matt didn't start many games at Bacon, even though he didn't get much playing time, even though he didn't do a whole lot of scoring, he wouldn't trade the experience of that season for anything. He loved his friends. He loved his teammates. He did anything he could to make them better—and if he had to, he'd do it all again.

"I love being part of great things," Matt said. "And that was a great thing."

• • • •

BECKHAM WYRICK, DESPITE SECOND-GUESSING his decision to play college basketball, remained at UNC-Wilmington. He realized his unhappiness as a freshman had less to do with missing football and more to do with being away from home for the first time and playing for another demanding, Brewer-like coach in Brad Brownell.

As a freshman, Beckham helped UNC-Wilmington win the Colonial League—both the regular-season and conference-tournament titles—and advance to the NCAA Tournament. Before the Seahawks' opening-round game, David Wyrick, as he did before the 2002 state final, told his son to "shock the world." And he almost did. Facing defending national champion Maryland, UNC-Wilmington led 73–72 with five seconds left, but Terrapins guard Drew Nicholas dribbled the length of the court and hit a falling-to-his-right three-pointer as time expired. Beckham played 19 minutes and scored six points in the loss. He played in the NCAA Tournament once more—as a senior in 2005–06—and UNC-Wilmington lost in overtime, 88–85, to ninth-seeded George Washington.

Beckham studied finance at UNC-Wilmington, graduated in the summer of 2006 and has been playing professional basketball in Germany ever since. He has played for Bayern Leverkusen, Brose Baskets Bamberg, FC Bayern Munich and BBC Bayreuth. Despite the initial culture shock, he is now fluent in German and engaged to his fiance, Johanna, who is from Nuremberg.

"I feel almost at home there," Beckham said of Germany. "I don't feel like I'm in a foreign country anymore. My first year was tough, but it's like anything. It's not new forever."

Beckham still has confidence in his game, of course, but he has toned down the trash talk a bit.

"Everyone's good, you know?" Beckham said. "You're one of the best players on your high school team, but take the two best players off your high school team and that's every player on your college team. Take the two best players off your college team, and that's every player on your pro team. When you're an 18-year-old kid, you're cocky. *I'm the best.* That was my attitude then. And I'm still confident in my game, but you learn the game more and learn to appreciate other people's talents a lot more. It's about a respect for your opponent, I would say—and a respect for the game, too."

Beckham still wonders how different his life would be had he pursued football, but he is at peace with his decision. He hopes to play professional basketball into his 30s depending on how his body holds up. Once his playing days are over, he will likely return to the United States and is contemplating a career in business or coaching. Regardless of which path he chooses, Beckham knows that in some circles he will always be remembered best—and perhaps most fondly—for the forearm he delivered to LeBron as a cocky 18-year-old in March 2002.

"When I did that, I had no idea people would be talking about it 10 years later," Beckham said. "The thing that I wonder is, what does LeBron think? He's a worldwide brand, and his name is recognized everywhere. But I think he would recognize us. I think he still thinks about that game. If he saw one of us somewhere, I don't think he'd ignore us. I think he would come over and say hi. Or if I saw him somewhere and said, 'Hey, LeBron, remember me?' I think he has enough respect for me and for that game and for Roger Bacon that he wouldn't blow us off even though he has the right to. He's a worldwide star. But I think we earned that respect from him and those guys."

Beckham may be correct. In December 2011, ESPN reporter Rachel Nichols interviewed LeBron and asked him several questions about his first season with the Miami Heat. Specifically, she asked about his decision to leave Cleveland and what it was like to be perceived as, for the first time in his career, a villain. LeBron explained that several instances in his life have allowed him to learn more about who he is as a person. Included among the experiences he cited: growing up without a father, losing in the NBA Finals, and yes, losing to Roger Bacon in the state final as a junior in high school.

"I think the legend (of what we did) has grown because he's as good as he is," Beckham said. "There's a lot of guys who go to the league out of high school and you never hear about them again. If he became a role player or a bench player, I don't think people would still be calling me for interviews. But because of the success he's had, that game is going to live on forever, I think."

　　　•　•　•　•

Somehow, Frank Phillips, shattered knee and all, managed to play college basketball again. After redshirting the 2004–05 season, Frank returned to action for Findlay and averaged nearly 14 points per game. As a senior in 2006–07, Frank led the Oilers to a 29-2 record and was named a first-team All-American by the National Association of Basketball Coaches. He averaged double figures every year in college and scored more than 1,500 career points.

After college, Frank pursued a professional career overseas, but many teams didn't want to take a chance on him because of his knee. He was considered damaged goods despite the fact that he had played two stellar seasons at Findlay since the injury without any flare-ups. Eventually, he was picked up by Luxembourg Racing, for which he averaged more than 26 points per game during the 2007–08 season. After a one-year stint in Michigan with the Battle Creek Knights—now of the Independent Basketball Association—Frank attended a tryout for the NBA Development League in Painesville, Ohio.

And that's when it happened.

With his team down a point in the closing seconds of a scrimmage, Frank poked the ball away and was about to race downcourt for a game-winning dunk as time expired. But as he turned to grab the ball, his left knee buckled. He heard a pop and lay on the ground once more, crying.

"I knew right away," Frank said. "I knew I was done."

Frank was scared to get an MRI and prayed that it was his MCL—and not his ACL—that he had hurt. But it wasn't just fear that prevented him from getting an MRI; it was money. Because he wasn't officially on a team at that point, Frank didn't have health insurance. Instead of paying out of pocket for an MRI, he put a brace on his knee and played through it. A few weeks later, he tweaked his knee again. This time, he caved and got the MRI, and his worst fears were confirmed. Torn ACL. Frank would have to go through rehab all over again, but this time he would have to do it without the tight-knit family of trainers and medical staff he knew at Findlay.

"I slowly let basketball go," Frank said.

He also didn't have Ashley. They dated for five years, but the relationship ended once Frank went overseas. They do, however, remain in contact.

Frank, who hasn't played competitively since 2009, lives in Cincinnati. In 2010, he went out for a drink with some friends in Newport, one of the main bar districts in Northern Kentucky located along the Ohio River. That was the first time he was in Kentucky since that summer night in 2004.

"I went with like 10 people," Frank said. "They knew I wasn't going unless I had a few people with me. You would've thought I was someone famous. I had an entourage."

Nothing regrettable happened that night. Frank went out with his friends and had fun. He now goes to Kentucky without fear.

Frank's left knee still bothers him. It still gets sore, especially in cold and rainy weather, probably because he only has about one-fourth of his meniscus remaining. Every so often, he wonders what would have happened had that incident in the club not occurred. Would he have led Findlay to a national championship the year he redshirted?

Would he have been picked up by a better team overseas? Would he have tweaked his knee at that D-League tryout? Frank doesn't know. But he does know that his perception of white people hasn't changed. If anyone could develop a dislike or mistrust of an entire race based solely on one experience—as perhaps some people have throughout the course of history—Frank, it could be argued, would be well within his right to do so. But it never happened. And it never will.

"My mom raised me so good that it didn't affect me at all," Frank said. "I didn't look at anyone different the next day."

For all the *what-ifs* surrounding his career, Frank knows he would've loved playing basketball with Josh and Monty at Miami. Charlie Coles would sometimes come to Roger Bacon to scout Josh and Monty, and he'd wind up spending a little time with Frank. It seemed there was a chance Coles would make Frank an official offer, but nothing materialized. Frank understood.

"I felt like I could have played Division I at a mid-major and been successful," Frank said. "But it's not like I was some huge star."

There were no hard feelings, but Frank made sure he was at his best whenever Findlay played Miami, which happened twice in his career. Miami won both games, but Frank held his own. Afterward, Coles told Frank that he was good enough to play at Miami. Those words did more for Frank than any scholarship offer ever could.

"That was enough for me," he said. "That was enough."

Frank, who works at US Bank, is looking for opportunities in coaching. He is unsure of what his future holds, but he does know he would like to one day have a family, one that is close and tight-knit. He wants to talk to his future children every day, even when they become adults. He wants this type of relationship, in part, because he doesn't have it with his own father—and thus, he knows how valuable it can be.

"If I saw my dad right now, I'd give him a hug and ask how he's doing," Frank said. "I still love him with all my heart."

• • • •

JOSH HAUSFELD GOT HIS name on a banner in Fogarty—not for most turnovers in a career, but for winning the 2002 state title. The banner, which includes the names of every player, coach and assistant on that team, hangs behind the basket near the scoreboard. It's not the only banner in Fogarty, but it might be the most special.

"Coach Brewer was the best coach I ever had in any sport," Josh said. "If you had told me that in high school, I would've said, 'There's absolutely no way.' But now that I'm older, now that I have some perspective, I appreciate some of the things that went on. After the state final, the first person I looked for was Coach Brewer. It's that moment when you realize, 'I understand. Thank you.' I'm glad he was hard on me. He got the most out of me, and that's a coach's job. I wouldn't change any of it."

Josh made the MAC all-freshman team at Miami during the 2002–03 season. He battled ankle injuries throughout his collegiate career, particularly as a junior and senior, and didn't always see eye-to-eye with Charlie Coles, who, like Bill, rode Josh harder than anyone else on the team. Josh, however, didn't internalize his battles with Coles as much as he did with Bill at Bacon.

"I was a little older, and I wasn't myself physically," Josh said. "I wanted to be out there, and I wanted to be playing better than I was. I think I probably reacted quicker and spoke up more than I ever did in high school. When Coach Brewer was on me, he might have gotten in my face, cussed me out, challenged me—and I would respond, typically positively. With Coach Coles, he had a different mentality as far as trying to motivate his players. We definitely didn't have the best relationship; we had our battles. But I did respect him. I know there's so much pressure on coaches to win and players to perform. We had a mutual respect for each other. I don't have any hard feelings at all. He was very passionate about the game and taught me a lot over my career."

Josh became a different player at Miami. Once a complete offensive player not exactly known for his defense, Josh—partly because of his ankles, and partly because of Coles—became a three-point specialist and defensive stopper.

"A lot of times, the first hour, hour-and-a-half of practice was dedicated to defense," Josh said. "So I knew early on if I ever wanted to play, I was going to have to become a defensive expert—and that's what I prided myself on."

Although Josh didn't always get along with Coles, who retired in 2012, he never considered transferring.

"I think he reached a point—and maybe it was after all the ankle injuries—where he loved basketball, but he knew there was more to life than that," Mary Beth said. "He loved his teammates."

He also loved his future wife, Kelsey, who played for the women's team at Miami for one year before stepping away from the game to focus on school. Josh and Kelsey met at Miami, but Josh knew who she was well before then.

After beating SVSM in the state final, Josh was selected to play in a local all-star game. He showed up early to watch the girls' all-star game, and at one point, the announcer commented that Kelsey Sullivan, an all-state guard out of Springboro High School near Dayton, would be attending Miami of Ohio.

Kelsey was 5-10 and blonde.

Josh's one-game teammates all looked at him.

"I got my eye on her," he told them.

Josh didn't talk to Kelsey that day, but he saw her that fall at Miami's practice gym during individual workouts and struck up a conversation with her. Nothing major. Days passed. Weeks, even. And then one day, Kelsey approached Josh at Miami's cafeteria and asked him . . .

. . . what his name was.

She had forgotten it. So Josh told her, and—wanting to play it cool—asked her what her name was, too.

"I knew damn well what her name was," Josh said.

Eventually, they started dating and were married in June 2009.

Josh graduated from Miami ranked among the top 10 in school history for career three-pointers made. He considered a career overseas, but after much reflection, decided against it.

"I knew someday I would have to give it up," Josh said. "It was probably more physical than anything. You want to be at your best, but your body's just not letting you."

Said Mary Beth, "I think he knew that eventually it ends. It just does."

After graduation, Josh and Kelsey, in search of warmer weather, took jobs in Atlanta before moving to Tampa. Josh, who works in sales, doesn't regret his decision to forgo a professional career; instead, he looks back on his playing days, especially in high school, with immense pride.

"It almost seems like a day doesn't go by where I don't think about it," he said. "Whenever I see LeBron, I think about that day and that game instantly. Coach Brewer passing. Meg passing. I think about what a great accomplishment it was. I can't help but think LeBron was a great player, but we showed him the power of a team and what a team can accomplish.

"Being in the business world, you're always doing icebreakers," Josh continued. "When you're asked something unique about your life, the first thing that comes to mind is, I played against LeBron in the state final and beat him. Everybody's reaction is the same: 'No, you didn't.' And I always say, 'Yeah, we did. They actually taped the game and I can send you a copy if you don't believe me. Or you can just Google it.'"

Like Dave, Josh has crossed paths with LeBron since the state final. Miami was playing in the MAC Tournament at Gund Arena one year, and a couple of Josh's teammates, Chet Mason and Juby Johnson, who knew LeBron from childhood, noticed he was in attendance. Chet and Juby approached LeBron and then motioned for Josh to come over.

"LeBron said, 'That was a great game. You guys played good,'" Josh recalled. "It was real cordial. It was neat for him to remember me and what we accomplished and how we beat him."

Josh, an avid basketball fan—college and pro—often finds himself pulling for LeBron.

"I root for him," Josh said. "I really do. I think he's a phenomenal player. From what I've seen, he's surrounded himself with pretty decent people, and he's accomplished so much on the court. From my point of view, I'm so glad we beat him. I hated him that day. I wanted to beat his guts. But looking at him these days, I want him to continue to excel. I want him to win multiple championships, and I can't help but think the more successful he is, the more it makes the win we had in 2002 that much better. I think that loss was a turning point in his life because he's referenced it several times. It's always neat to hear because you know you were a part of the game he's talking about."

• • • •

EMILY HOLT AND THE Gutzwillers, among others, continue to miss Meg. Each year since Meg's death, Roger Bacon has hosted the Meg Gutzwiller Alumni Soccer game, which gives former Bacon soccer players—men's and women's—the chance to reunite, play the game they love and reminisce about Meg. The Gutzwiller family works the event each year, and it means a great deal to them that so many alumni, even those living out of state, will return to Bacon each year to help honor Meg. Emily, who lives in Florida, has a tattoo of Meg's jersey number—2—on her foot. She also wears a gold cross similar to one Meg used to wear. She has worn it every day since Meg died.

"She was an important person in our life," Josh said. "We'll always miss her."

Sadly, tragedy struck the Gutzwiller family again in 2007. Mere weeks after Bill Brewer passed away, Mr. and Mrs. Gutzwiller both had heart attacks on the same night and were treated on separate floors of the same hospital. Mr. Gutzwiller survived; Mrs. Gutzwiller didn't. At the funeral, John Jr., who also gave the eulogy for Meg, said that his mother spent her final years missing Meg so much that eventually her heart simply broke. She was 61.

The Gutzwillers, all of whom live in Cincinnati, go out to dinner every year to celebrate the lives of Meg and Mrs. Gutzwiller on the anniversaries of their birthdays and deaths. They wonder what Meg's life would be like and what career path she would have chosen had she lived. While they can't know for sure, they believe it would have involved helping children in some way—perhaps teaching, coaching or counseling. Either way, Meg would've been good at it.

"Everything she did was perfect," Katie said. "She didn't even mean for it to be perfect. It just was."

Many of Meg's friends from high school and college have gotten married. Katie sees the wedding photos on Facebook and can't help but think that her baby sister should be in that wedding, that she should be married, too. But she's not.

Katie wears a heart-shaped locket every day. Inside the heart is a photo of Meg on one side and a photo of her mother on the other.

Katie thinks of them whenever she puts it on. She also thinks of Meg whenever she sees LeBron.

"When I hear his name, I think of Bacon beating him," Katie said. "But I also think of Meg. She was there to help them beat him."

• • • •

THE 2002 DIVISION II state final was the last game Tom Thompson ever coached on a Roger Bacon sideline. Mitch Perdrix stayed on staff as an assistant through the following year, while Mike Cregan and Dave Bidwell followed Bill to Princeton before the 2005–06 season and remained there through 2010–11. All four of them still teach, while Joe Corcoran continues to serve as athletic director at Roger Bacon. Bobby Holt remains on the coaching staff.

Tom stepped down after the 2002 season to spend more time with his family. He found out at the state championship game that his wife, Jill, was pregnant, and the running joke was that they would name their child LeBron. They settled on Jack instead.

Tom still coaches basketball—not to mention cross country and track—at the junior high level. Helping Roger Bacon win state was one of the most rewarding things Tom has ever done, but so too was coaching Maddy Brewer, Bill's youngest daughter. Bill was able to coach Katie and Abby, but not Maddy; he passed away before he got the chance. Tom's daughter, Holly, is the same age as Maddy, and he coached their summer-league team in 2010. Before the season began, Peggy asked Tom to coach Maddy just as Bill would have—tough, firm, unyielding. Tom did his best to meet Peggy's request.

"I'm not sure if I did it justice," Tom said, "but I wanted to give Maddy a flavor of what it was like."

Tom was struck by her personality and how similar it was to Bill's—fiery, competitive, intense. Sometimes too much. There were a lot of times when Maddy—or, "Mad-dog," as Tom calls her—would end up next to him on the bench in foul trouble. "We need the NBA rule in effect for Maddy," Tom joked. "You only get five fouls, but she needs six." Foul trouble or not, there's no denying her talent or knowledge of the sport. Once, at a Bacon game, Maddy signaled for a traveling violation before the referee could even blow his whistle and do the honor himself. Why was this impressive? Maddy was 2 at the time.

So it's fair to say she knows the game as well as—or better—than most girls her age, and while there were several talented girls on that summer-league team, Maddy made it special.

"When we didn't have her, we got beat by a team that we had beaten a couple times," Tom said. "I told Maddy it wasn't because of her, but it probably was."

Tom has four kids. The last was born on November 3, 2007—the day after Bill died. Months earlier, when Tom and Jill found out they were having a boy, they decided almost immediately to name him Adam. Never once did Tom and Jill ever imagine their son would be born in the wake of Bill's death, but when he was, they decided to honor their friend's passing the only way they knew how.

"I remember looking at Jill and saying, 'I know we're not gonna change the name Adam because we had this predetermined, but what do you think about *William* for a middle name?'" Tom recalled. "My wife thinks things through, but she said, without hesitation, 'Absolutely.'

"Now, whenever you name a kid after someone," Tom continued, "they end up taking over some of the traits of that person. And dammit, Bill, some of the stuff he handed down to this kid is just amazing. But that helps me cope at times when I miss him. He does some of the stuff Bill would have done. I'm not saying he's reincarnated in Adam, but I'll tell ya—some of the stuff he does makes Peggy laugh like hell. But it's so true. I do think there's a little bit of Bill in this kid. And to this day, if you ask him what his name is, he'll say, 'Adam William Thompson.'"

• • • •

BRIAN NEAL SUCCEEDED BILL as head basketball coach at Roger Bacon. After Bill accepted the job at Princeton, he walked straight up to Bacon's principal and said, "If you don't hire Brian Neal, you're an idiot." Joe Corcoran agreed. Brian, excited yet nervous, accepted the job.

"You never know if you're really ready (to be the head coach)," Brian said. "Whether you think you are or you're not, you don't really know. It was nice to have Bill there telling me, 'Brian, you're ready.' He didn't have any doubts. But when you put that whistle around your neck for the first time . . ."

It was a rough first year for Brian. After starting 3–0, the Spartans lost five straight and 14 of 15; they sputtered to a 5–16 finish. Some of those struggles were out of Brian's control (his best defender sustained a season-ending injury the first game of the year) and some weren't (a few games into the 2005–06 season, Brian kicked one of his best players off the team for insubordination).

"To this day, I really like him," Brian said of the player. "Good kid, but he's stubborn. He wasn't buying what I was selling. And when you take over a program, Bill taught me one thing: if they aren't buying what you're selling, then you've gotta get rid of them and find someone who will buy what you're selling."

That wasn't the only lesson Brian took from Bill. Once, during a home game in the middle of Bill's tenure at Bacon, Brian committed the cardinal sin of assistant coaches.

"We weren't playing that well, and I don't know what I was thinking," Brian said. "But I'm just sitting there on the bench and observing what's going on—'This guy's not doing this,' 'This guy's not doing that,' 'We're not doing this.' And finally, Bill turns to me and says, 'Will you shut the fuck up? Quit telling me the problems! I can see the problems! Give me some damn answers!'"

Brian sat there, stunned, like a little boy who had just been scolded by his father.

"He kind of put me in my place," Brian said. "But you know what? Isn't that my job? He's a better coach than I. He sees what's going on. Give suggestions. Give solutions to the problems. I tell my guys that all the time. Don't tell me what the problems are. I can see those. Let's figure out what we can do to make this better. At halftime they'll say, 'Coach, we're not rebounding.' Well, no kidding. I can see the stats. How do we fix it?

"It hurt my feelings for a day," Brian said of Bill's outburst. "I didn't like getting yelled at, and I didn't like the message at the time—but it sticks with me to this day."

Like Bill, Brian's early struggles led to success. A 5–16 record became 8–14; 8–14 became 11–13. And just as it did for Bill, the break-out came in year four. In 2008–09, Bacon went 20–4 and won a city title. In fact, during a four-year stretch from '08–09 to 2011–12, Bacon went 76–25, won two city titles and advanced to two regional finals; Brian was named *Cincinnati Enquirer* Coach of the Year three times. Just as it did for Bill, the present looks bright, the future even brighter.

"Bill deserves full credit for where the program is today," Brian said. "He turned it around. I'm just trying to keep it going."

Roger Bacon has advanced to seven regional finals since 1997.

It has not returned to state since 2002.

• • • •

BILL NEVER GOT BACK to Columbus. The man who dedicated nearly 15 years of his life to achieving that goal only got there once—but when he did, he made the most of it.

"He smiled for months," Peggy said. "I'd catch him doing it. I'd just look over and he'd be grinning. 'I know what you're smiling about,' I told him. 'You're not fooling me!' He was just so happy. He had such a beautiful smile. I loved his smile."

A short time before Bill passed away, Peggy asked him how his Princeton team looked heading into the 2007–08 season.

"We'll be all right," Bill said, giving the token response. "But next year we're gonna be darn good."

Peggy was surprised at just how confident Bill was—or better yet, how much confidence he showed. How confident was he? He promised Peggy he'd get back to Columbus—either that year or the following year, in 2008–09. Bill, of course, never got the opportunity to coach either season, but he still made good on his word. Josh Andrews, who coached the junior varsity team at Princeton, was promoted to varsity after Bill's death. In 2007–08, Andrews guided Princeton to an 18–6 record and an appearance in the regional semifinals before bowing out to St. Xavier.

But the following year, it happened, just as Bill said it would. Princeton went 19–1 in the regular season and advanced to state for the second time in school history and the first time since 1972. Once there, Princeton made short work of Toledo St. John's Jesuit in the semis, winning 55–41. But in the final, Princeton ran into Columbus Northland, which possessed perhaps the top big man in the country, a junior named Jared Sullinger, who would become an All-American at Ohio State. Despite trailing by 10 points in the fourth quarter and by six with less than a minute to go, Princeton, buoyed by student-section chants of, "It's for Brewer," came back to tie the game at 58–58 with 14 seconds remaining. Sullinger, however, was fouled with 2.7 seconds left and hit both free throws. Northland won 60–58.

Two points. One possession.

"If Bill had been alive, Princeton would've won the game," Peggy said. "In a two-point game, coaching is the difference. That's not a knock on Josh. I love Josh. But Bill would've done it. Bill would've found a way to pull that one out."

• • • •

IN THE WEEKS AND months after Bill died, Peggy lived in a daze. It wasn't just the big things that hurt—like planning a funeral or coming home to a house without a husband. It was the little things, like sleeping at night or answering a stranger's innocent "How are you?" question.

"When someone asks how you're doing, you're supposed to just say fine and move on," Peggy said. "But I couldn't fake a fine."

Peggy looked to family and friends for support, which they gave, but it wasn't enough. None of Peggy's friends had ever lost a husband. None of them had ever raised kids alone. They could imagine what Peggy was going through, but none of them truly understood. So Peggy took her daughters to group counseling. Peggy would talk with other wives who had lost husbands, while Katie, Abby and Maddy would sit with other girls who had lost daddies. Sometimes it helped. Sometimes it didn't.

Three months after Bill died, Peggy went to a Super Bowl party. At one point in the evening, she looked around the room and took stock of everyone in attendance. She saw people and coaches from Roger Bacon, Princeton and All Saints. Bill was the one common thread that held the group together.

"He had a way of just making great friends," Peggy said. "He would do anything for them, and they would do anything for him."

Peggy still has good days and bad. Milestones are hard. Bill's birthday (May 21), their anniversary (July 23), the day he died (November 2)—sometimes they're unbearable. But so, too, are the days between the raindrops, the days that don't signify or accentuate an important occurrence, but rather the passing of time and the visceral awareness that the man she loved for more than 20 years is gone forever.

Bill was pronounced dead at the hospital in the early hours of November 2, 2007, but in Peggy's eyes, in her heart and in her mind, Bill died at home in his bed. It took Peggy close to two months to sleep in that bed again. She instead slept on an air mattress in Maddy's bedroom. It was just too hard to face. It was too hard to rest in the spot where her husband died alone. And that, perhaps, is the hardest thing of all. Peggy was gone two minutes, and in that tiny window, the most important person in her life lost his own—and she wasn't by his side when he did.

Some days, Peggy still can't forgive herself for that. What if she had gotten the Tums earlier? What if she had made Bill go to the hospital? Would he still be here?

She still asks *why*. She knows she'll never get an answer. She knows she can't change what happened. She tries to focus on how lucky she was to have the years she had with Bill and not dwell on the years she lost. But it's hard. If Peggy has a problem at work, who can she go to for advice? She can go to a friend or family member, but they don't have the same stake in it Bill had. Peggy has three daughters, which means she could have three weddings. Who will walk her girls down the aisle? Bill was a teacher. Teaching the girls to drive was going to be his responsibility. What about college? How many schools should the girls apply to? How many visits should they make? If Peggy has to go somewhere, who's going to watch Maddy?

It's little things. It's big things. Everything's easier with two people. But for Peggy, every decision she makes, small or large, she makes on her own.

It is said that time heals all wounds. Time doesn't heal all wounds. Time might heal some wounds and make others easier to deal with, but it doesn't heal everything. It can't. Time marches on without remorse. Instead of dreaming of her long-awaited retirement with Bill, Peggy longs for memories they never got around to making, sitting by the water and living in a lake house that doesn't exist.

"Twenty years from now, 30 years from now, there will still be a part of my heart missing," Peggy said. "I'll never get over him. And no matter what, it'll always be, in my mind, wrong what happened. He was so young. We had our whole lives ahead of us.

"There isn't a thing I wouldn't do to get him back."

• • • •

IN JUNE 2011, THE Chosen Ones, as they do as often as they can, gathered together to relive that magical season, to relive those eternal 32 minutes when they were better than a legend. "As often as they can" probably doesn't happen as often as The Chosen Ones would like. They live in different cities, different states, different countries. They are no longer boys; they are men. Some have wives; some have children. They have entered the next chapter of their journey. They are scattered leaves wafting in the wind, seeking to make their mark on the world.

Only they already have.

The players and coaches, the wives and children, pile into Joe Corcoran's basement. For some, it's been months; for others, years. And still, there are no handshakes. Only hugs. Peggy and her daughters arrive. The little girls who Bill held after winning state aren't so little anymore. One is almost a teenager. One is in high school. One will go off to college in the fall. They all eat pizza and wings—the Bill staples. The stories are retold, the anecdotes relived. They laugh heartily.

And this, this is where time stands still.

This is where it's clear it hasn't.

Eventually, someone turns on the highlight video. For close to an hour, the standout plays from nearly a decade earlier are shown. The story of that season unfolds with photos, quotes and mobile memories frozen in time. A three from Dave. A block from Beckham. A dunk from Frank. All the top plays are there, along with scores of others.

And then it happens.

Without transition, without notice, Bill's face fills the flatscreen. The up-tempo music ceases, and the sounds of Michael Bolton's "Go the Distance" consume the room. Chatter lulls. Smiles fade. Hearty laughs grow hollow.

Then comes another photo. And another.

The song plays on, as coaches and players, like an empty arena, grow sad and nostalgic.

"Me and Brewer, we didn't always get along," Beckham said. "It's hard to like somebody when you're going through all that; you don't realize how good it is for you until you've gone through it. Maybe I thought I knew better sometimes, but I definitely didn't. Even though he and I had (our disagreements), you don't remember how he yelled at you or how you were pissed off to do this thing or that thing. But you remember the lessons that he taught you—how to be a man, how to be accountable for your own responsibilities, how other people rely on you and want you to live up to those expectations. He really taught me a lot and got me ready for the next stages of my life, and I'll always thank him for that. It was sad to see him go. He was too young, and it's unfortunate he didn't get to see his daughters grow up. The world lost a good one with him."

The legend of Bacon's accomplishment grows with each passing year. SVSM was *the* team with *the* player. And Bacon beat him. The players beat him. They beat him because of Bill.

"It was a coaching masterpiece," Jerome Harris said. "The way Brewer took Newt and Leonard and Marcus and won—because let's face it, you need a bench, especially with Brewer's halfcourt pressure defense—it was unbelievable. The team chemistry, the team defense—it was a masterpiece."

Said Joe Corcoran, "All those kids were special. They were so close-knit—probably the closest-knit group of guys I've ever been around. But without Bill, without him at the helm, maybe we don't get that state championship ring. Those kids bought into his system, and the outcome was something you'll never forget."

After the highlight video, the state final is replayed in its entirety. Peggy still gets nervous watching that game. She knows who wins, of course, but she still gets nervous. Seeing Bill makes her cry. Photos are hard enough, but seeing Bill move, seeing him pace those sidelines—it's too much. Because Peggy knows Bill should still be doing that. After the final buzzer, the camera captures Joe Corcoran wrapping his arms around Bill and jumping up and down all in one motion. It's a great shot, poignant. But for Peggy, it's bittersweet. Cork can't hug his best friend anymore.

Bill is remembered by more than a highlight video. Every year, All Saints, where Bill coached Katie and Abby, held a girls basketball tournament during Labor Day weekend. That tournament is now called the Bill Brewer Labor Day Classic—and has been ever since Bill died. Meanwhile, the Man Cave built by Mike Cregan, Dave Bidwell and Tom Thompson—among others—has become a shrine to Bill. His UD jersey. His Most Valuable Pitcher award. Balls commemorating his 100th and 200th coaching victories. The state championship ball. The yellow tie from Bobby Holt. It's all there, along with every other important artifact from Bill's days as an athlete and coach.

"There's no doubt in my mind that we all lost something when he left," Creegs said. "There aren't many days that go by when I don't think about him. There's isn't a time that I go to Peggy's house and don't go downstairs and bang on the wall where his picture is and say hey to him. He's still missed today."

And he's still affecting lives.

Dan Fleming has coached GCL-South stalwart La Salle for more than 20 years. He's won more than 300 games. In March 2011, following a playoff win at the Cintas Center, Dan felt pain under his armpits. He didn't get much sleep that night. When he woke up the next day, however, the pain was gone, so he drove to Dayton to scout a potential playoff opponent and then returned to Cincinnati to attend his son's grade school game.

That's when his left shoulder started hurting.

In the third quarter, Dan, still tired from tossing and turning the night before, decided to go home and get some rest, but he couldn't get comfortable. The pain persisted through the night. Dan tried sleeping on a chair; he tried sleeping on the floor; he even tried taking a shower, hoping to ease the pain. Nothing worked.

Throughout that night, Dan thought of three people. He thought of his high school basketball coach, who suffered a heart attack when Dan was a junior, and he thought of Skip Prosser, the former men's coach at Xavier who died of a heart attack in 2007 while coaching at Wake Forest.

But mainly, he thought of Bill. Dan always admired and respected Bill. They always got along well. Dan's gameday coaching attire usually included a La Salle polo, but the season after Bill died, Dan coached every game in a dress shirt and tie, just as Bill always did.

"I'm not a tie person," Dan explained. "Other than a wedding or a funeral, you don't catch me in a tie too often."

No matter. It was Dan's tribute to his friend.

As night became morning, Dan, only 48, kept thinking of Bill and what happened to him. He remembered hearing how Bill was having chest pains and how he might have survived had he gotten to the hospital sooner.

I can't wait too long, Dan thought. *I gotta go.*

Dan didn't drink or smoke, and he wasn't overweight. But he knew something wasn't right. Once the pain in his shoulder moved to his sternum, he knew what he had to do. He woke his wife, Melissa, and asked her to call an ambulance.

It was Monday, March 7, not even 6 a.m.

Dan arrived at the hospital, where doctors detected a clog in his left anterior descending artery—also known as "the widow maker." A stent was immediately put in his heart. Doctors told Dan that if he had waited any longer to go to the hospital, he wouldn't be around to tell his story.

Dan wasn't able to attend—much less coach—several of La Salle's ensuing playoff games, but the Lancers, led by Dan's son, Ryan, advanced to the state tournament in his absence. Doctors permitted Dan to return to the sidelines for the final, which La Salle won over Columbus Northland, 59–40. It was the Lancers' second state title in program history and their first since 1996.

And Dan was there to see it.

"When I was leaving the house in the ambulance, I wasn't sure how many more days I was gonna have," Dan said. "So now, whenever I wake up in the morning, I say to myself, 'I got one more day. I got one more day.'"

Every day Dan has, he has because of Bill. This, perhaps, is what Peggy is most proud of. Yes, without Bill, she's become better at teaching her daughters. She's had to. She taught Katie to drive. She's learned how to back a boat down a steep hill and into the water. The things Bill would've taught, Peggy teaches. The things Bill would've done, Peggy does. There's pride in that. It's solemn pride, but it's pride nonetheless.

In August 2011, Peggy moved Katie into her freshman dorm at Dayton. Bill would've loved being there for that—both for love of his daughter and for the wonderful memories moving day would've evoked. Maybe he would've wanted to take a stroll around campus. Maybe he would've wanted to visit the gazebo where he proposed to Peggy decades earlier. Maybe he would've wanted to stop by Flanagan's for a Coors Light.

Maybe.

Instead, Peggy did all of that for him. She did it alone. She even stopped by Milano's and got his favorite sub—a ham grinder. It was a tough day—tougher than Peggy imagined it would be. But even though Bill wasn't there, Peggy and Katie got by. They had to. They, along with Abby and Maddy, have learned to. They still have good days and bad, but these days, the good ones outnumber the bad, especially when they hear from people like Dan Fleming, for they are reminded that even though Bill isn't around, even though they can't see him, he isn't gone.

"He's still helping people," Peggy said. "Even though he's not here, he's still finding ways to help people."

• • • •

SOMEWHERE UNDER THE MOONLIGHT, somewhere on the scarred wastelands between abandoned cornfields and deserted dirt roads, somewhere on the dancing shimmer of asphalt between sequoia skyscrapers and rumbling subways, there's a kid. No one is with him, but he isn't alone. He has his basketball. He has his dream.

The boy's soggy shirt is wet with sweat, his saturated skin glistens, his shoes scuff the earth. Restless dust rises from the dirt for an instant, grows weary and descends to death once more; concrete fades as slowly as the seasons. The boy goes left, goes right and crosses over, eventually shaking the imaginary defender, who lunges for the ball but grasps only shadows.

The boy has a step.

In a few years, when the boy is a little taller, when he can jump a little higher, when he can reach a little farther, perhaps he will drive to the basket and dunk, go up and throw it down just like his hero. But at this moment, life won't allow it. There's no guarantee it'll ever allow it. So the boy waits patiently for a moment that may never come and settles for a midrange jumper. He stops 17 feet from the hoop, squares his body and rises as the ball floats from his fingertips and rotates in the night air.

Something special happens when a ball goes through a net—something perfect, something pure. But just as pure, if not more so, is the brief interlude between release and result, those precious moments when the outcome is unknown and the shooter has nothing to go on but anticipation and hope.

This is when he is most captive.

This is when he is most free.

On this night, at this instant, nothing can stop this boy. Nothing can limit him. Time is endless, opportunity ubiquitous. He sees the present before him and dreams of the future that lies ahead. He envisions not what *could* be, but what *will* be.

Life has not yet taught him the distinction.

Maybe this boy will grow up and one day have a coach like Bill Brewer. Maybe he won't. Maybe he'll grow up and become a Josh Hausfeld, a Beckham Wyrick, a Monty St. Clair, a Dave Johnson, a Frank Phillips, a Scrapper. Maybe he won't make first cut freshman year. But none of that matters now. Now, this boy sees only the thrill of the crowd, the stunned look of the star player, the ecstasy of the game-winning shot. Because somewhere, somewhere deep inside, this boy longs for his chance, his turn, to chase greatness, to not only take his shot but to make it, to prove that he has the courage to be in the arena, to strive to overcome the favored, to seize the day regardless of consequence and to be remembered and revered and considered at long last, once and for all and for all of time, among the chosen.

ACKNOWLEDGMENTS

Deep and sincere gratitude is owed first and foremost to the Spartans of Roger Bacon—for winning a state title, for being so unflinchingly open and honest about what it took to achieve that, and for being so accommodating with me throughout this project.

Thank you, especially, to the players—Josh Hausfeld, Beckham Wyrick, Frank Phillips, Monty St. Clair, Dave Johnson, Tim McCoy, Matt Reed, Nate Wyrick, Jon Newton, Marcus Smith and Leonard Bush—for sharing with me your personal stories of struggle and triumph, the stories that went beyond basketball.

Heartfelt appreciation goes out to Peggy Brewer and her daughters, Katie, Abby and Maddy; as well as Brian Neal, Tom Thompson, Joe Corcoran, Mike Cregan, Dave Bidwell, Jerome Harris, and Bobby Holt. I never met Bill Brewer, but because of you, I feel like I've known him all my life. I consider this a privilege.

Thank you, also, to Emily Holt and the Gutzwillers—John, John Jr., Matt and Katie—for sharing Meg's story. May she never be forgotten.

Several people played pivotal roles throughout the writing and publishing process, including Joseph Tannian, Sue Hartman, Katherine Pickett, Mary Wietmarschen, Evan Thomas and Jessie Ford. My deepest thanks to all of you.

I am indebted to countless others for the creation of this volume.

Thank you, Dr. Avis Meyer, for showing me the way. If there's ever a Mount Rushmore for mentors, you'll be on it.

Thank you, Pat Crowley, for seeing something in me that someone once saw in you.

Thank you, Marc Emral, for giving a desperate kid a chance.

Thank you, Kim Wolterman, for providing the courage and guidance to self-publish.

Thank you, Dan Phillips, for giving and not counting the cost. I aspire to be as good at my craft as you are at yours.

Thank you to my friends and family who have been there for me every day for much of the last decade and beyond. You know who you are.

Thank you to my grandparents and the Eilermans—Rose, Dale, Eric and Scott—for your constant care and encouragement.

Thank you, most especially, to my mother, Mary Ann, and sister, Gina, for giving relentless support, for allowing me to take a chance, for never doubting me even when I doubted myself. Thank you for your patience. Thank you for your love.